Faith and Power

FAITH
and
POWER

The Politics of Islam

Edward Mortimer

Random House New York

Library of Congress Cataloging in Publication Data
Mortimer, Edward.
Faith and power.
Bibliography: p.
Includes index.
1. Islam and politics—Near East.   2. Near
East—Politics and government—1945–
I. Title.
BP63.A4N425   1982   297'.1977   82-40129
ISBN 0-394-51333-9   AACR2
Manufactured in the United States of America
24689753
First Edition

For M.H.M., thanks to whom I am almost a Believer

Contents

9

CONTENTS

Maps and a Diagram

Acknowledgements

ALMOST ALL journalistic activity is in some degree parasitical. An enterprise like this one, which attempts to absorb in a short time, and distil into a short space, an ocean of other people's knowledge, can be presented only with a degree of effrontery, if not mendacity, as the work of a single person. In other words, I could not have done it without an enormous amount of help.

Thanks are due, in the first instance, to the Carnegie Endowment for International Peace, which employed me as a Senior Associate for the year 1980-1, allowed me to spend the greater part of my time on this project, and provided such lavish facilities and services that my return to the humble world of newspaper journalism has been attended by severe withdrawal symptoms. I should like to thank in particular the staff of the Endowment's New York office, especially Larry Fabian, who invited me; my colleagues Selig S. Harrison and Robert Hershman (as well as John Cooley in Washington), who provided guidance, encouragement and intellectual stimulation; Anne Stephan and Barbara Perry, who spent many hours routing out obscure books and periodicals at my request; Anne Chong and Janet Scheldt, who miraculously transformed my much deleted and interlineated typescript into a copy so fair it scarcely needs a printer; Carolina Mancuso, who kindly spared their services for that purpose and in other ways kept the operation running smoothly; my two consecutive research assistants, Jane Stoddard and above all Alan Cantor, whose critical but encouraging and constructive comments on the draft as it emerged

13

were just what any author could wish for; and last but far from least Linda Chittaee, whose interest in and help with the project went far beyond what could normally be expected from a secretary.

Secondly, I thank *The Times* and especially its former editor, William Rees-Mogg, for allowing me a year's leave of absence in which to write the book, after first prompting my interest in the subject.

Friends, colleagues and experts who allowed me to pick their brains or suggested contacts and research materials were legion. I would mention in particular Fouad Ajami, Hasan Akhtar, Ahmad Ali, Tony Alloway, Edward Allworth, Lisa S. Anderson, Said Arjomand, David Barchard, Tahseen Basheer, Alexandre Bennigsen, James Cracraft, Adeed Dawisha, Hamid Enayat, John L. Esposito, Kemal Faruki, Murray Feshbach, Peter Gran, Hasan Hanafi, Eric and Mary Hooglund, Nubar Hovsepian, Kemal Karpat, Nikki Keddie, Robert Mabro, Eden Naby, Sir Anthony Parsons, James P. Piscatori, William L. Richter, Malise Ruthven, Michael Rywkin, Edward W. Said, Majid Tehranian, Hazhir Teimourian, Muhammad Wahby, and Christopher J. Walker.

It goes without saying that none of those mentioned above, in any capacity, is in any way responsible for any of the opinions expressed in the book. Probably every one of them would disagree with at least part of what I have said, even on subjects with which they helped me directly, let alone with the rest. There are others whom I should like to mention but forbear to, lest this point should be misunderstood and cause them embarrassment or worse.

Three people are to be thanked for providing locations that enabled me to isolate myself from my family during the climactic weeks of composition: Lois Wallace, Lana Jokel and Christopher Makins. And thanks, finally, to my family themselves for putting up with this and much else besides: especially to my wife, Elizabeth Mortimer, who became in effect, for a time, the single parent of four children in a foreign country, in very trying circumstances.

E.M.
December 1981

14

constant demand. The idea of writing a book followed almost naturally, and seemed at first a relatively straightforward journalistic enterprise. It was only when I was already committed to the project that I realized what a conceptual minefield I had blundered into.

I had naively thought of Islam as a subject that could be fairly easily identified, defined, described and analysed: an institution, a set of ideas — something more or less comparable to the Roman Catholic Church. I found that Islam is much more protean than that. It is everywhere and nowhere. Islam, we are told, is not a mere religion: it is a way of life, a model of society, a culture, a civilization. If you reduce it to an institution you are both belittling it and condemning yourself to misunderstand it: Islam is not confined to a 'church' whose relations with the state can be codified in a concordat. Islam *is* the state, or should be, if those in charge of the state were true Muslims. Such is the theory, or one theory. (We shall see that it has not gone unchallenged, even within the framework of Islamic argument.) But what of the practice? A phrase frequently found in the works of modern Muslim historians, who attempt to analyse the changing role of Islam in their own societies, is 'the religious institution'. By this they mean the corporate body of *ulamā*, or 'learned men', whose learning qualifies them to expound Islam in general, and Islamic law in particular. In their collective interventions in political and social affairs they do seem to function as an institution. They are not a priesthood; they make no claim to mediate between man and God, they administer no sacraments. But are they not a church, a clergy? What is a church if not a religious institution? What are clerics if not men of religious learning? Yet the moment one uses these words in an Islamic context one incurs the charge of marshalling Islamic reality into Western categories.

In fact one may well be damned as soon as one mentions 'Islam' at all. In the last few years a professor of English literature at Columbia University, who happens to be by birth a Palestinian Arab Christian, has developed a formidable critique of the use of 'Islam', as word and concept, which comes close to asserting that the very notion of Islam is a mischievous invention of Western orientalists—an artificial category that obscures the diversity and even the humanity of non-Western peoples, making them seem mysterious, inscrutable, irrational and, in the last resort, a fair target for imperialist aggression.[1] That is a caricature of his argument, of course. The professor in question, Edward Said, knows perfectly well that 'Islam' is an Arabic word and that Islam had existed, as religion and as culture, for many centuries before Western orientalists got round to writing about it. What he is arguing is that 'Islam', as it figures today in Western discourse (both scholarly and journalistic), has little to do with real Muslims in real Muslim countries. Instead it has a long genealogy in Western thought, reaching back to the fantasies about the lecherous Mahomet and the Terrible Turk entertained by West European Christians of the Middle Ages and the Renaissance.

This may seem unfair to the great tradition of Western orientalism which developed in the nineteenth and twentieth centuries, a tradition which has produced people remarkable not only for their scholarship but also, in many cases, for their sympathetic identification with the Muslim peoples about whom they wrote. Yet the core of Said's argument is not a denial of the qualities or virtues of such people, but rather the assertion that their perspective, whether sympathetic or antipathetic, was distorted by the preconception that 'Islam' was a special category and that Muslims were to be defined first and foremost as Muslims, rather than as Turks or Arabs, men or women, peasants or merchants, radicals or reactionaries.

On the whole I think this point is valid—if not as a criticism of the orientalist tradition itself, then certainly as a criticism of the instant, warmed-up orientalism which we journalists served to the Western public in the excitement of 1979 and 1980. We had our excuses, of course. 'Islamic' events did seem to be bursting out all around us. The glare of the Islamic revolution in Iran was reflected by the Islamic resistance in Afghanistan, the 'Islamization' of Pakistan under Zia ul-Haq, the seizure of the Holy Mosque in Mecca, the guerrilla warfare of the Muslim Brotherhood in

Syria, and reports of Islamic 'revival' with more or less menacing political overtones from almost every Muslim country. We were encouraged, moreover, by groups of earnest Muslims who themselves argue very strongly that Islam is a total way of life, moulding all aspects of thought and behaviour, and that therefore it is right to emphasize the distinction between Muslims and non-Muslims as superseding others, such as those of nation or class. But we were a little too prone to take such claims at face value, and to write about 'Islam' in an anthropomorphic fashion, as though it were an entity with a will of its own, existing independently of the men and women who believe in it and capable of bending them to its own purposes.

That is what I have tried to avoid in writing this book. I have assumed that the actors in politics are not abstract forces but human beings. I do not exclude the possibility that political events are determined by God, but I assume that if so, God acts through human beings. I am not a Muslim, but I believe most Muslims would not object to this assumption. Although belief in miracles is certainly not unknown in Islam, it is not generally encouraged or emphasized by the learned. The 'orthodox' Muslim belief, if I may call it such, is that divine intervention in human history took the form of sending prophets to warn mankind of the right road. What happens after that is a matter of human strength and weakness, obedience and obstinacy. (Whether these qualities are predetermined by divine will, or subject to human free will, is — in Islam as in Christianity — part of an argument about the nature of God Himself, an argument in which there are at least two sides. The idea that all Muslims are fatalists is one of many Western misconceptions about Islam.)

My approach to the subject has therefore been not to ask what Islam is (I have reserved a few reflections on that subject for the Conclusion) but what Muslims think, and say, and do. I have tried to discover in what ways political problems look different to Muslims than to other people, and why. My education (in the school of modern history at Oxford University) predisposes me to answer 'why' questions in historical terms. This may explain

18

why what was planned as a historical introduction has expanded into Part One, comprising four chapters. I think this is justified because what we call 'culture' is essentially collective experience transmitted from one generation to another. Insofar as there is a distinctively Islamic approach to politics, not shared by other cultures, it must derive from the experience of past generations of Muslims.

In the second, and main, part of the book I have tried to isolate the role played by Islam in the twentieth century in the politics of six Muslim societies. But, once again, I use the phrase 'played by Islam' as a conscious metaphor. What I mean is the political interpretations of Islam proposed and acted on by Muslims in these six societies. In particular, I have tried to trace the interaction of Islam and nationalism, which has been the dominant political ideology in most of the Muslim world — as in most of the world in general, and especially those parts of it that were on the receiving end of European imperialism — in this century; and I have tried to highlight the different roles that can be assigned to religion and religious institutions in the life of a Muslim state.

My reasons for choosing these six examples (Turkey, Saudi Arabia, Pakistan, the lands dominated by Arab nationalism, Iran and the Soviet Union) are briefly explained in the Introduction to Part Two. But some sort of apology is owed here to the numerous Muslims — actually the majority — who live in none of these countries. My original synopsis contained an additional chapter entitled 'The Outer Circle: a Briefer Survey of Islam's Spreading Influence in the Far East (Indonesia, Malaysia, Philippines) and in Black Africa'. But as soon as I began serious research for the book I realized that this was an absurdity. The book does not pretend to be a gazetteer of the Muslim world, and if it did it could not possibly relegate such vast, diverse and populous areas to a single chapter. Nor could I get away with treating India and Bangladesh merely as a kind of backdrop for the history of Pakistan, whose Muslim population may well by now be smaller than either of theirs. It is better to be honest. Indonesia at least — the country with the largest Muslim population of all — would have been an excellent subject for a seventh case study. But I have never been there and I know very little about it. I have not as yet had the time or the resources to extend even my journalistic 'expertise' that far. Perhaps I shall have that opportunity in the future. Meanwhile, I offer a book that at least attempts to explore the role of Islam in this century in its historic heartland – the Middle East and Western Asia – which happens also to be the area that has generated our excitement about Islam these last few years.

That should not be taken as implying that people in other areas are any less Muslim. It is not for me, as an outsider, to award diplomas of orthodoxy, or sincerity, or intensity of belief. Nor should it be taken as implying that Islam is the only, or even the most, important factor in the countries that are discussed. On the contrary, my conclusion is to doubt whether Islam can rightly be considered a political factor in its own right, and to see it more as a mode of political expression. In that capacity I think it is important, and I think most of us did underrate its importance before 1978. I think that writing this book has helped me to avoid both that and the opposite mistake, and I hope it may be similarly helpful to the reader.

When writing about other people's beliefs and ideas it is as well to make one's own position clear. I have scattered plenty of clues through the text, but for the record let me define myself as a Christian of the Church of England by upbringing and by emotive affiliation, a sceptic by intellectual training, and a social democrat by political preference.

Glossary

ālim (singular of *ulamā*): learned man.

awqāf (plural of *waqf*): religious endowments.

ayatollah: 'sign of God' — an honorific title given to leading Shi'ite *mujtahids*.

caliph (*khalīfa*): successor to Muhammad as leader of the Muslim community. The four 'orthodox' or 'rightly guided' caliphs, according to the Sunnis, are Abu-Bakr (623–4), Umar (634–44), Uthmān (644–56) and Alī (656–61). For the Shi'a the first three are usurpers, and Ali was Muhammad's directly designated successor.

dhimmī: non-Muslim with 'protected' status in a Muslim state.

faqīh: jurist, expert in divine law.

fatwā: official ruling on a point of Islamic law.

hadīth: the recorded tradition about the words and deeds of the Prophet Muhammad and his Companions, compiled into six authoritative collections in the ninth century AD.

Hanbalī: one of the four recognized schools of law in Sunni Islam, established by Ibn Hanbal (d. AD 855); followed, in particular, by Ibn Abdul-Wahhab in the eighteenth century, and therefore dominant in modern Saudi Arabia.

Hijāz: the western edge of the Arabian peninsula along the Red Sea coast; site of the holy cities of Mecca and Medina.

hijra: migration or withdrawal, particularly that of Muhammad from Mecca to Medina in AD 622.

ijtihād: the use of independent judgement, or original thinking, in interpreting the Koran and the Sunna.

21

Ikhwān: 'brethren'; specifically, the former bedouin, converted to Wahhabi Islam and settled on the land, who formed the shock troops of Abdul-Aziz Al Sa'ud in his conquest of Arabia in the early twentieth century.

imām: spiritual leader. According to context, it can be simply the prayer-leader of a mosque, the appointed leader of Friday prayers in a city (*imam jum'a*), or the holder of supreme religious and political authority, in succession to Muhammad. In Sunni tradition the Imamate in this last sense (or caliphate) is a matter of election and/or consent by the leaders of the community, though the Imam should in principle come from Muhammad's tribe of Quraish. The Shi'ites hold that it passes by specific designation from one Imam to the next, starting with the designation by Muhammad of his son-in-law and cousin Ali.

jahilīya: the state of ignorance prevailing in Arabia before Islam.

jihād: 'struggle in the way of God'. In the Koran, this probably refers to the early Muslim razzias against pagan opponents, particularly the Meccans. Later, any war undertaken in the name of Islam against unbelievers or backsliders. Sometimes used in a non-military, quasi-metaphorical sense. (Cf. 'crusade'.)

Kāfir: pagan, unbeliever.

Khārijism, Khārijites: the first sect to secede from the Islamic community. A group of extreme puritans, who insisted that they alone were the true Muslims, and therefore undertook *jihad* against the mainstream community and its leaders.

khatīb: preacher.

khums: the fifth share of booty taken in the *jihad*, which the Koran reserves for the Prophet. In Shi'a Islam, an income tax levied by the *mujtahids* for the benefit of the community.

Koran (Qur'ān): the Word of God as revealed to, and recited by, Muhammad.

Mahdī: the divinely guided leader who, according to a very old Muslim tradition, will one day come and restore the true Islamic order.

22

majlis: assembly. In traditional Arab society, the regular audience held by a tribal chief. In modern Muslim societies the word is often used for parliaments and other similar bodies.

marja-i taqlīd (plural: *maraji-i taqlid*): 'source of imitation'. Title given to the most learned Shi'ite *mujtahids*.

marja-yi mutlaq: the senior living *marja-i taqlid*, whose authority — if they agree who he is — is recognized by all Shi'ite *mujtahids*.

milla (Turkish: *millet*): 'people' — traditionally a religious community, but later used for 'nation'.

mufti: *alim* appointed by the government to give official rulings on Islamic law.

mujahid (plural: *mujahidīn*): one who fights in the *jihad*.

mujtahid: a person qualified to undertake *ijtihād*.

mulla (from *mawla* — 'lord'): a lesser member of the *ulama* (q.v.).

salaf: ancestors; the Muslims of the first generation(s).

shaikh: 'old man' — a title indicating respect. Most commonly used for learned teachers, but in Arabia also for political rulers, or simply people of importance.

Sharī'a: the Way prescribed for Muslims by God; hence, the divine law.

Shi'a: the family of sects in Islam which regard Muhammad's son-in-law and cousin, Ali, as his rightful successor (see Chapter 2).

Sufism: a religious tradition, not confined to any sect but found virtually throughout the Muslim world, which emphasizes the immanence of God rather than His transcendental aspect. Based originally on mysticism, it later became a vehicle for popular piety and was organized into orders (*turuq*), somewhat similar to the monastic orders of medieval Christendom.

Sunna: the 'beaten path' or tradition of the Muslim community, based on the example of the Prophet and his Companions.

Sunnis: those who consider themselves followers of the authentic Sunna — followers of mainstream or orthodox Islam as opposed to the Shi'a and other sects.

Tanzīmāt: the reforms undertaken in the Ottoman Empire during the mid-nineteenth century, under West European influence.

taqlīd: following or imitating a religious authority. (Can have favourable or unfavourable connotations according to context.)

tarīqa (plural: *turuq*): a particular Sufi 'path' to knowledge of God; hence, an order or brotherhood following a particular *shaikh*.

ulamā: (plural of *alim*): learned men, Islamic scholars.

umma: the community. In Islam, usually the community of believers, but sometimes 'the nation'. (The two are not always clearly distinguished.)

Wahhābīs: followers of Muhammad Ibn Abdul-Wahhab, the eighteenth-century Arabian reformer (see Chapter 3).

watan: nation or fatherland. In modern Arabic, usually the individual Arab state, as opposed to the greater Arab nation (*qaum*).

wilayat al-faqih (Persian: *velayat-e Faqih*): 'guardianship of the jurist', a doctrine elaborated by Ayatollah Khomeini (see Chapter 9).

zakāt: the poor-rate prescribed by the Koran, and levied annually on the believers' capital to support widows and orphans. Opinions differ whether it should be levied compulsorily by the state or left to the believers' conscience, but as an obligation it ranks as one of the five 'pillars of the faith'. (The other four are the *shahada* or affirmation of belief, the regular daily prayers, the fast during daylight in the month of Ramadan, and the pilgrimage to Mecca.)

zāwiya: residence or place of teaching of a Sufi *shaikh*; similar to a monastery.

Note on Transliteration

MUSLIM LANGUAGES (with the exception of Turkish since 1928) are written in Arabic script, but vary quite widely in pronunciation. This makes it impossible, in a work which deals with Muslim countries in which different languages are spoken, to maintain complete consistency in transliteration without being insufferably pedantic. As a general rule I have given proper names and words of Arabic origin in their Arabic form, except where *either* another form is better known in English *or* the Arabic form of a proper name is totally different from the local pronunciation.

As a rough guide to pronunciation, I have indicated long vowels with a horizontal stroke (¯) the first time that a word or name occurs, but I have not repeated this subsequently as that would give the text a tiresomely fussy look. I have used an apostrophe to indicate either a *hamzah* (glottal stop) or an *ayn* (a swallowing noise in the back of the throat) where these occur in the middle of the word, but not at the beginning or end where the sounds are scarcely audible to the unpractised English ear and the apostrophe is easily confused with an inverted comma. The letter 'q' corresponds to Arabic *qaf*, which in Arabic is like a 'k' formed in the back of the throat, but in Persian sounds more like 'gh'.

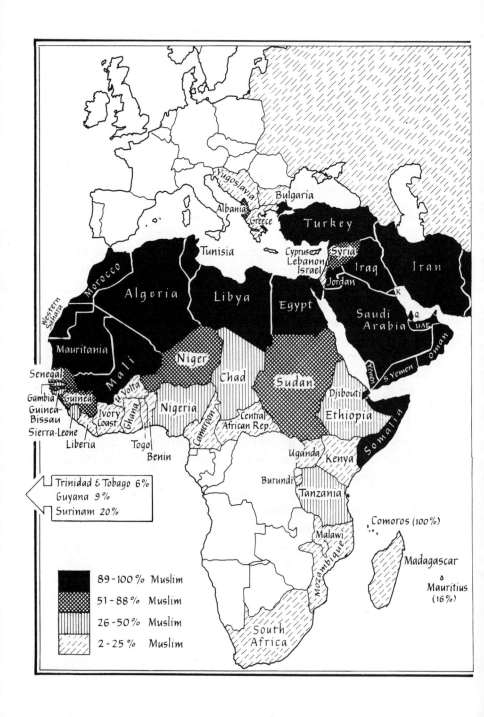

Trinidad & Tobago 6%
Guyana 9%
Surinam 20%

Comoros (100%)

Madagascar

Mauritius
(16%)

■ 89–100 % Muslim

▨ 51–88 % Muslim

▥ 26–50 % Muslim

▨ 2–25 % Muslim

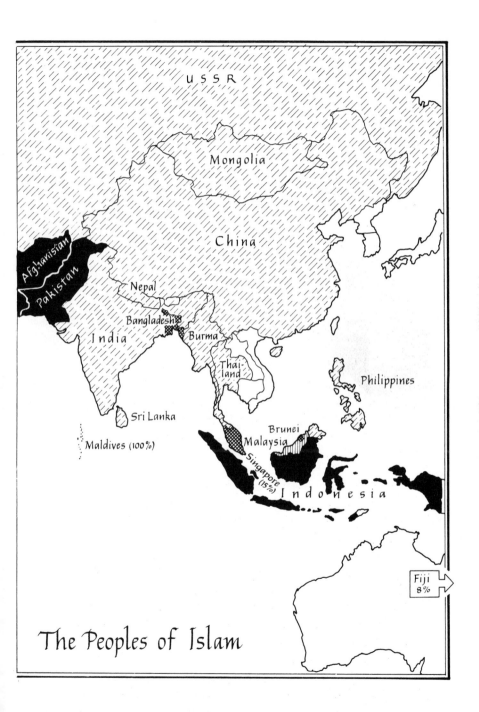

The Peoples of Islam

PART ONE

The Historical Background

CHAPTER ONE

Traditional Muslim Attitudes to Political Power

Render therefore unto Caesar the things which be Caesar's, and unto God the things which be God's.

Luke 20:25

O believers, obey God, and obey the Messenger and those in authority among you.

The Koran, IV, 62[1]

GOD INTERVENED in human history, at a specific time and place, directly and decisively, once and for all, by revealing Himself to mankind. That is the central belief of Islam, as it is of Christianity. Christians believe that God Himself became a human being and redeemed human nature by making it His own. As St John puts it, '. . . the Word was made flesh, and dwelt among us.' To Muslims, as to Jews, that notion seems blasphemous because it detracts from the absolute oneness of God and thus opens the door to idolatry. Muslims believe that the Word of God was communicated *to* a human being. That human being, Muhammad, was chosen to be the messenger of God. Clearly, he was a man of special talents, but no Muslim believes that he was anything other than a man, or that he was the author of the Word of God, which he passed on by reciting it to his fellow human beings. (The word Koran, or *Qur'ān*, means 'recitation'.)

That is why Muslims do not like to be called Muhammadans. They do not regard themselves as followers of Muhammad, but as people who have accepted the Word of God and surrendered themselves to His will. *Islām* means surrender, and a Muslim is one who surrenders. The importance of Muhammad is that he was the human vehicle through which the Word was communicated. The creed in which a Muslim affirms his faith consists of a single sentence: 'There is no God but God, and Muhammad is His Messenger.'

Christians believe that the divine intervention occurred in Palestine, at the time when that country was gradually and painfully being incorporated into the Roman Empire. Muslims believe it happened in the Hijaz (western Arabia), on the fringes of both the later, Greek-speaking Roman Empire (which we now call Byzantine) and its great rival, the Sassanid Empire of Persia, at a time when the two had fought each other to exhaustion and both were on the verge of collapse. These differences of places and time had an important effect on the doctrines of the two faiths with respect to political power.

Jesus of Nazareth was born into a community whose religion was an expression of its national independence, at a time when that national independence was in the process of being crushed. Given the overwhelming power of the Roman Empire, a revival of the Jewish religion in its nationalistic form was bound to lead to disaster — and did so forty years after Jesus's death. Jesus offered a way out of this blind alley by expounding a non-political interpretation of Judaism: 'My kingdom is not of this world.' While claiming to be the national leader (Messiah) whom Jewish prophets had predicted, he offered salvation only in the world to come, and to be achieved by individuals through faith, hope and charity, rather than by the nation through organized revolt. By implication, salvation in this sense was not reserved for Jews only. After Jesus's death, St Paul made this explicit. Christianity became an invitation to all who suffered under the Roman Empire to hope for a better world after death.

Yet the notion of a non-political religion was a novel one, which the Roman Empire itself could not take at face value. The expression of allegiance the Empire expected from its subjects was to acknowledge the divinity of the emperor. Since Christians refused this they were persecuted, with varying degrees of intensity, until the day came (three centuries after Jesus) when the emperor himself became Christian. Once that happened, Christianity was no longer non-political. A Christian ruler was naturally expected to follow Christian precepts, to advance true Christian doctrine, and to suppress heresy. It was more than a thousand years before a school of political thought arose suggesting that religious belief was a matter for individuals, with which the state need not concern itself. Yet all this time Christians kept alive the notion of 'the church' as something distinct from the state. Though church and state might be composed of the same people, they had separate leaderships whose roles were in theory distinct and complementary, even if in practice overlapping and often conflicting. In the last 200 years church and state have moved apart in many Christian societies. Christians have been able to justify this by going back to Christianity's original doctrines.

This has led many people of Christian background to expect something similar to happen in the world of Islam. But that involves a profound misunderstanding, since in most Muslim societies there is not and never has been such a thing as a church. The community of believers founded by Muhammad was, virtually from the beginning, what we should call a state.

Muhammad grew up in the city of Mecca in the late sixth century AD. It was a trading city that had recently grown wealthy and in which the tribal system of the surrounding desert had begun to break down. The rich behaved with arrogance and selfishness while widows and orphans starved. The revelations which Muhammad began to receive in about AD 609 attacked this arrogance and selfishness of the rich and also the gods whose shrines made Mecca a place of pilgrimage and thus increased its wealth. To begin with Muhammad may not have had any political ambitions, but since he was criticizing the ruling class and the bases of its power it treated him as if he had. Life in Mecca was made increasingly uncomfortable for him and his followers until in AD 622 he left the city with a small band of supporters, accepting an invitation to settle in the oasis of Yathrib, afterwards called Medina ('the City'), some 200 miles to the north. It is from this event, the *hijra* or migration, that Muslims date their calendar: a significant choice, since it marked neither the birth of a founder nor the beginning of the revelation, but rather the founding of a state.

In Mecca, Muhammad's followers had been distinguished from other citizens only by their religious beliefs and practices. But he went to Medina to assume a political role — that of arbiter between the clans whose feuds were almost destroying the city — and those Meccans who came with him to Medina were treated as a separate clan under his leadership. From now on, becoming a Muslim meant joining a community whose God-given law overrode tribal loyalties. Muslims were forbidden to attack other Muslims, or to support their own relatives in a blood-feud against other Muslims.

Muhammad soon proved himself a political and military leader of high ability. By the time of his death in AD 632 his community not only ruled Medina and Mecca but had become the dominant power in the Arabian peninsula. Within twenty years after that it had overthrown the Persian Empire and conquered all the Asiatic territories of the Roman Empire except Anatolia (modern Turkey). A hundred years after Muhammad's death a mighty empire stretched from the Punjab to the Pyrenees and from Samarkand to the Sahara.

The ruler of this empire, under God, was the caliph or 'successor to the Messenger of God'. But the caliphs were not successors to Muhammad *as* Messenger of God. In that capacity he could have no successor. The revelation made to him in the Koran completed and superseded those given to all earlier prophets and is valid for all humanity and for all time. Such at least is the belief of the overwhelming majority of Muslims, and those who do not believe it are not accepted as Muslims by those who do. The caliphs were Muhammad's successors not as Messenger but as 'commander of the faithful'. The first of them, Abu Bakr, had been appointed by Muhammad to lead the public prayers in his place during his last illness. But Abu Bakr owed his position as ruler to the decision of the leading members of the Muslim community, taken after Muhammad's death.

The early caliphs, therefore, may be said to have provided both spiritual and temporal leadership, in the sense that a Christian society would understand those terms. But the early Muslims made no distinction between the two. They assumed that only a holy man could provide good government for the community of God's servants, and that the main function of government was to ensure obedience to God's law as laid down in the Koran — though in practice the Koran had to be interpreted and even supplemented by the Tradition (*hadīth*) about what Muhammad himself had said and done. If government was bad, that was not because holy men did not know how to govern, but because the governors were no longer holy. Thus political or social revolts were always justified in religious terms, and what to the modern historian look like dynastic squabbles over political power became deep schisms in religious doctrine.

In time, like other idealistic systems of government based on utopian principles, Islam was adapted by its adherents to take account of human imperfection. After the first few, most of the caliphs were obviously not men with any great spiritual qualifications, and owed their power either to brute force or to heredity. Moreover, in outlying parts of the empire they exercised no real authority. As conscience-keepers of the community they came to be replaced, or at least supplemented, by the *ulamā* or 'learned men' — those who studied deeply in the holy law and provided interpretations of it when difficult cases arose. Gradually, these learned men elaborated the rules derived from the Koran and the Tradition into a science of Muslim law. This law came to be regarded as the essence of the Sharī'a — the way of life ordained by God for mankind. For if the Christian's path to salvation lies through the acceptance and imitation of Christ, that of the Muslim lies through acceptance of and obedience to God's Law. The Law is made by God, not by man. The task of the learned jurists was not to make law, but to ascertain and expound it. It followed that not one of them could claim a monopoly of correct interpretation and, in fact, different schools of jurisprudence were recognized as authoritative in different parts of the Muslim world. But they diverged on points of detail rather than essentials, and where they agreed their verdict was held to be binding. For Muhammad had said: 'My community will not agree on an error.'

As guardians of the Holy Law, the *ulama* came to occupy in the Muslim world a position comparable in some respects to that of the clergy in medieval Europe. Not that they were regarded as having any spiritual power: they could not administer sacraments, pardon sins, pronounce excommunication or in any other way mediate between man and God. But, because they were respected for their learning, and sometimes for their piety and wisdom, their support was needed to legitimize political power; and against a ruler who failed to uphold the Law as they interpreted it they could act as leaders of the opposition and champions of the oppressed. Like the churchmen of the West, they sought to influence political power rather than to assume it themselves.

Gradually, therefore, the political rulers of Islam lost their religious aura. It came to be considered that only the first four caliphs after Muhammad had been truly orthodox. The Umayyad dynasty that succeeded them (AD 661–750) was seen as more or less a reversion to secular kingship. The Abbāsid caliphs, who ruled in Baghdad from AD 750 onwards, enjoyed rather greater prestige. Although in the period of their greatest power their autocratic tendencies and predilection for Persian models of culture and statecraft brought them into conflict with many of the *ulama*,* as their power declined they came to rely more on the *ulama*'s support. Later still, as the empire began to break up and real power was assumed by provincial governors and warlords, the caliphs were retained as symbols of Islamic unity and legitimacy: formal acknowledgement of the Abbasid caliph was the way for a Muslim ruler to indicate that he and his subjects belonged

---

* Persian influence also led them to claim a kind of religious authority which might well have shocked Muhammad and his immediate successors. They called themselves *Khalifat Allāh* — God's deputy — and even 'the shadow of God upon earth'.

to the universal community of Islam and were not heretics or schismatics. That lasted until AD 1258, when Baghdad was sacked by the Mongols. Thereafter, a line of puppet caliphs was maintained in Cairo by the Mamlūk sultans of Egypt, but not recognized anywhere outside their dominions. In 1517 the Mamluk sultanate was, in its turn, conquered by the Ottoman Empire, after which no one seems to have bothered with the title of caliph for more than 200 years.

In a sense, then, all genuine political authority in the mainstream Muslim tradition was secular after the loss of effective power by the Abbasids in the tenth century AD. Virtue and justice were no longer regarded as indispensable qualifications of a ruler. Full enforcement of the Shari'a came to be seen as an ideal rather than a necessity. Political power was no longer the instrument through which the ideal community could be realized, but merely a prosaic necessity for the maintenance of order and security, and thus of the minimum conditions in which the faith could be practised and the Muslim community survive. By the eleventh century AD most of the *ulama* were teaching that obedience was an absolute duty, even to an unjust ruler, since an unjust ruler was better than none at all.

Yet to describe this attitude as legitimizing all *de facto* power, however corrupt, would be going too far. It could equally well be read as smearing all political power with a taint of illegitimacy, since no Muslim state was able to enforce the totality of the Shari'a and all fell short of the high standard supposedly set by Muhammad and his immediate successors. In theory the power of the ruler was strictly limited by the law, which he had no power to make or unmake since it came from God. And if successive generations of the *ulama* set tighter and tighter limits to their own power of interpreting the law, that was partly at least to protect themselves and the community from pressure by the ruler to reinterpret it to suit his interests.

They preached obedience, not in a spirit of servile glorification of the ruler, but rather as a measure of expediency and self-preservation. One must obey unjust princes, wrote Abu Hamid

al-Ghazālī (1058–1111), the great systematizer who has been called
the St Augustine of Islamic thought, but one must not thereby
condone their injustice. The devout Muslim should avoid the
court and company of the unjust ruler, and should rebuke him:
by words if he can safely do so, by silence if words might encourage
rebellion. [2]

The condemnation of rebellion is explicit, but, even in this
thinker who was to be a source-book for Muslim conservatives of
the next eight centuries, there is also an implicit endorsement of
the premises of rebellion: the notion that the political order should
be judged by religious credentials, and that the ruler is failing in
his duty if the Shari'a is not enforced.

We could say, then, that whereas Christianity started as a politically
quietist faith and was drawn by circumstances into activism, Islam
at its beginnings was closely identified with political action but
later accommodated itself to circumstances with a degree of
quietism. But in both cases the adaptation involved a certain
malaise. As the prince of the church was vulnerable to the criticism
of the barefoot friar, so the *alim* (singular of *ulama*) who comfort-
ably rationalized the status quo was never fully armed against
the reformer calling for revolution to restore the supremacy of
the Shari'a and a truly Islamic order. Hence the observation of a
modern scholar that, while the history of Islam tends to be seen
'as an everlasting submission to God's will, in fact it could far
more accurately be characterized as a permanent revolution'. [3]

CHAPTER TWO

The Historic Divisions of Islam

How is it with you, that you do not fight in the way of God, and for the men, women, and children who, being abased, say, 'Our Lord, bring us forth from this city whose people are evildoers, and appoint to us a protector from Thee, and appoint to us from Thee a helper'?

The Koran, IV, 77

THE WORDS 'revolution' and 'revolutionary' have a modern ring to them. Yet they do not seem out of place when applied to Muhammad's achievement in seventh-century Arabia. Muhammad's career was the classic one of a revolutionary leader. He started as a more or less isolated critic of the prevailing social order. Finding his calls for reform unheeded and himself the object of the establishment's wrath, he fled with a small band of dedicated supporters to an area where circumstances assured him a degree of local support. From there he issued a call to arms and began military operations, at first on a small scale which we might today call guerrilla warfare (the harassment of Meccan trading caravans). The conflict gradually escalated through a series of skirmishes, battles, retreats, showdowns with allies or dissident supporters, truces ... with Muhammad all the time expanding his base of support until at last the regime crumbled and he was able to re-enter Mecca as its effective ruler and on his own terms. In the course of the struggle his ideology had been refined and amplified so that finally the old order was replaced by an entirely new system whose internal dynamism, combined with its attractiveness to outsiders, enabled it to impose itself far beyond the particular society to which the original message had been addressed. If that is not a revolution, what is?

Of course, a revolution, once successful, will tend to institutionalize itself and become a point of reference for future generations of conservatives. In the case of Islam we saw part of that process at work in the previous chapter. But we also saw that for such conservatives the revolutionary nature of their theoretical ideal is a kind of Achilles heel. It can always be used against them. The Koran is full of injunctions to the believers to 'struggle in the way of God'. In the context, of course, the struggle (*jihād*) in question was against unbelievers. But was it not logical to suppose that such a struggle would be equally necessary later against those corrupt Muslims who introduced into the Muslim community those very evils of arrogance, selfishness, injustice, etc., which the Koran had denounced in the pagan society of Muhammad's time?

Not surprisingly, it has seemed so to successive generations of Muslim reformers and malcontents. The history of Islam, especially its first few centuries, is full of movements that sought simultaneously to restore what they saw as the true doctrine of Islam and to overthrow the existing political order. Again, it is unlikely that in their own minds the leaders of these movements made any distinction between these two objectives. Many of these movements gave birth to sects that still exist in some form today; and even those Muslims who do not adhere to such sects are indirectly affected by them, since it was in the course of these early conflicts that the Sunna — the Beaten Path or tradition which the majority of Muslims follow — was defined. Some knowledge of them is therefore necessary for an understanding of the contemporary politics of Islam. I shall give here only a most summary and selective account.

Khārijism and Shi'ism, the two great tendencies that split off from the main body of Islam early in its life, both have their origin in events that occurred within a generation after Muhammad's death, as his successors struggled to cope with the unexpected problems of managing an enormous empire. The third caliph, Uthmān, who succeeded in AD 644, came from the Umayya, one of the old ruling families of Mecca. He antagonized many of the soldiers in the conquering Arab armies by appointing his own relatives to provincial governorships and reserving for them a share in the spoils, and also by making the first attempt to impose religious uniformity on the Muslim community: after issuing an authorized version of the Koran he ordered the destruction of all variant copies, thereby imposing his own authority on the provincial preachers. In AD 656 a group of mutinous soldiers returned to Medina and killed him. Muhammad's cousin Alī, who had been passed over when Uthman was elected, was then acclaimed as caliph by the Muslims present in Medina. Ali's failure to take action against those responsible for Uthman's murder, some of whom were his own supporters, led to risings against him and the first civil war between Muslims.

The most serious rising was that of the governor of Syria, Mu'āwīya, a relative of Uthman, who refused to acknowledge Ali as caliph and fought an inconclusive battle against him at Siffin (between Syria and Iraq) in AD 658. After this Ali agreed to let the dispute be judged by two arbitrators 'according to the Koran'. But this compromise was rejected by a group of Ali's more fanatical supporters, who now turned against him, proclaiming 'there is no judgement but God's'. (The implication was that Uthman's murder had been just punishment for his errors as caliph.)

The Khārijites

These people became known as **Khārijites**, from an Arabic word meaning 'to go out' — implying both secession and rebellion. They were the first distinct sect to appear in Islam. As with almost all subsequent sects, their separation was self-imposed. It was they who proclaimed that all who did not follow them were outlaws and unbelievers. By contrast, the mainstream community of **Sunni**

Muslims (those who follow the Sunna) has always been willing to accept a great diversity of opinions, drawing the line only at those which appear to deny either the oneness of God or the finality of the revelation to Muhammad.

The Kharijites maintained that a grave sinner no longer remains a Muslim, and they therefore proclaimed *jihad* against the rest of the community and particularly its leaders, seeking to bring about political change through violence and assassination – of which Ali himself was an early victim in AD 661. They were absolute and uncompromising egalitarians, arguing that all men were equal in the sight of God and equally accountable to Him, and therefore rejecting any notion of privilege, whether for the family of Muhammad, for the Meccan tribe of Quraish from which he sprang, or for the Arabs in general. The only criterion of virtue was of faith. The test of faith was good works, therefore any conspicuous sinner was disqualified. The true believers were instructed by the Koran to 'command good and forbid evil'. This gave them both the right and the duty to overthrow an unjust caliph, and in his place to choose any one of themselves who was morally and religiously irreproachable, 'even if he were a black slave'.

Naturally, this doctrine had a considerable appeal for the underdogs of the Muslim empire, particularly the non-Arab (especially Persian) converts. For the Kharijites carried their egalitarian theology into the social and political sphere as well, favouring an equitable distribution of wealth and a form of primitive democracy. Their continual insurrections disturbed the peace of the eastern part of the empire throughout the Umayyad period (AD 661–750), and continued under the Abbasids. Their forces were repeatedly crushed, and eventually only a more moderate variant of the movement survived – the Ibādiya, which abandoned both the practice of assassination and the excommunication of mainstream Muslims. (It survives today in Oman and in small communities in East and North Africa.)

As far as most Muslims are concerned, the Kharijites put themselves beyond the pale of respectability by their fanaticism and violence against fellow Muslims, and therefore most Muslim movements of today would strongly disclaim any connection with them. Yet in a sense they were the prototype of all subsequent Muslim revival movements, and especially those which are today called 'fundamentalist'.

The Shī'a

Kharijite influence on later Islam has been mainly indirect. But the other great sect, the Shī'a, still has numerous adherents in many parts of the Islamic world, and in Iran it is the official religion of the state. From this tradition came the ideology of the Iranian revolution.

At the time of Ali's death in AD 661 the *Shī'at Alī*, or party of Ali, was probably no more than that: a party or tendency of people supporting Ali's claim to the caliphate. That claim was based on Ali's closeness to Muhammad as a member of his immediate family — his first cousin, in some sense his adoptive brother, the husband of his favourite daughter Fātima and father of his favourite grandsons. (Muhammad had no surviving sons.) Ali was felt to be a more authentic representative of what Muhammad had stood for than the wealthy and worldly Umayyads. His personal piety and virtue may indeed have compared favourably with theirs; but in the minds of his followers this fact was clearly connected with the close blood relationship between the two men.

After Ali's death the leadership of this school of thought passed naturally to his two sons, Hasan and Husain, who were also Muhammad's grandsons. Although they were not strong enough to prevent Mu'awiya from establishing himself as caliph and so founding the Umayyad dynasty, Ali's descendants became an important focus of opposition to that dynasty. The notion spread that rightful leadership of the Muslim community belonged to Muhammad's family, who enjoyed a special sanctity. Only when the rule of Muhammad's rightful heir was established would the tyranny and injustice of the existing order be replaced by good government in accordance with the Koran and the example (Sunna) of the Prophet. This heir would be the Mahdi, a leader directly

43

guided by God. A variety of predictions about this Messianic figure were soon attributed to Muhammad himself.

The Umayyad period was punctuated by frequent revolts based on these ideas. The one that eventually proved successful was led not by Ali's descendants but by those of Muhammad's uncle, Abbās, resulting in the Abbasid caliphate. It was only after this, after the Abbasids had repudiated Shi'ite ideas and made themselves the new establishment, that the Shi'a took on the form of a sect, or rather a family of rival sects, distinct from the mainstream of the Muslim community.

The essential belief of the Shi'a is that the historic caliphs were merely *de facto* rulers, while the rightful leadership of Islam passed through a kind of apostolic succession of Imāms, starting with Ali and carrying on down in the male line. The Imam may or may not be in a position to exercise political power, but his spiritual authority is seen as an essential ingredient of Islam: 'Whosoever dies without knowing the true Imam of his time dies the death of an unbeliever.' The Imam is not equal to the Prophet: the divine revelation in the Koran remains final and complete. But the interpretation of the Koran is not simply a matter of learning. Divine guidance is necessary and this is imparted through the Imam. Thus Shi'ism accepts the notion of spiritual authority in a sense that Sunni Islam does not, and it makes a distinction, even if it is a *de facto* rather than a *de jure* one, between spiritual and temporal authority. The Christian notion of a church, and of relations between church and state, is therefore more closely paralleled in Shi'ism than elsewhere.

Islam in general sanctifies political action. Sunni Islam is the doctrine of power and achievement. Shi'a Islam is the doctrine of opposition. The starting point of Shi'ism is defeat: the defeat of Ali and his house by the Umayyads. Its primary appeal is therefore to the defeated and the oppressed. That is why it has so often been the rallying cry of the underdogs in the Muslim world. Central to Shi'ism's appeal, especially for the poor and dispossessed, is the theme of suffering and martyrdom — a theme reminiscent at times of Christianity. For Shi'ites the Kin of the

Prophet — especially his daughter Fatima, her husband Ali and their two sons Hasan and Husain — are a Holy Family in almost the Christian sense of the phrase; and the passion of Husain, massacred with his family by the armies of Mu'awiya's son, Yazīd, in the hopelessly unequal battle of Karbalā (AD 680), is virtually equivalent to that of Christ, celebrated every year in innumerable passion plays and penitential processions.

'TWELVER' SHI'ISM

The main branch of the Shi'a surviving today is known as that of the 'Twelvers' because it traces the line of Imams from Ali down to the twelfth, after which it comes to a stop. The twelfth Imam is believed to be not dead but hidden, and will one day return as Mahdi to purify the world. This is the Shi'ism that has been the official doctrine of the Persian state since the sixteenth century, and is today followed by about 80 per cent of the population of Iran, by the majority of the Arabs in neighbouring Iraq and by substantial minorities in Turkey, India, Pakistan, Lebanon and the Arab Gulf states, including Saudi Arabia.

In all these countries, except Iran, political power has usually been in the hands of Sunnis. That Twelver Shi'ism has survived so successfully under Sunni rule is mainly due to the fact that historically it was the least politically activist, if not non-political, party within the Shi'a. The nine Imams after Husain were people who escaped repression by the caliphs of their time precisely because they did not put themselves forward as claimants to political power, but were content with providing spiritual guidance to their followers. In time, at least an implicit connection came to be made between the virtue and piety of Ali and his sons and their lack of political success: they were seen as unworldly, even self-effacing men, lacking both the ambition and the deviousness which political success requires. Thus Ali allowed himself to be passed over three times in the choice of caliph, although he knew himself to be the rightful claimant, biding his time until the caliphate was thrust upon him after the death of Uthman. He then proceeded to dismiss all the bad but powerful governors appointed by Uthman, thus uniting them against him instead of manoeuvring to pick them off one by one; and at the battle of Siffin, out of respect for the Koran and reluctance to shed unnecessary blood, he let himself be tricked into accepting arbitration on unfavourable terms. After his death his son Hasan abdicated the caliphate rather than pursue the civil war against Mu'awiya (on whose orders he is, none the less, supposed to have been poisoned); and finally the revolt of Husain, Ali's second son, against Mu'awiya's impious son Yazid, is presented not as a bid for power but as an act of deliberate martyrdom, intended to show up the brutal and sinful character of Umayyad rule and thus inspire a spiritual and moral revival.

According to Twelver doctrine, the Imams did not abandon their claim to leadership of the community. They simply chose not to assert it politically in unfavourable circumstances. Rather than legitimizing the existing government, they authorized their followers to obey it — and even, if necessary, to dissemble their true beliefs — in spite of its illegitimacy. The doctrine of the Hidden Imam made it easier for the faithful to bear the evils of the present, by explaining that the world would be set to rights when — but, by implication, only when — he returned.

OTHER VARIANTS OF THE SHI'A

By no means all Shi'ites accepted the political quietism of the Twelvers. The opposite view was taken by Zaid, a grandson of Husain, who argued that a true Imam must claim the title publicly and strive actively to overthrow the corrupt regime of the usurpers. True to these principles, he led an unsuccessful rising against the Umayyads, in the course of which he was killed. His followers, the **Zaidis**, recognize him as Imam in preference to his quietist brother and nephew, who are the fifth and sixth Imams of the Twelvers, and trace the succession onwards from him. They reject the doctrine of the Hidden Imam and do not insist on an unbroken dynastic succession. For them the Imam may be any adult descendant of Ali who has sufficient learning and military ability, and there may even be 'several imams at one time'. Today they survive only in Yemen, which was ruled by Zaidi imams until 1962. Doctrinally, the Zaidis are closer to the Sunnis than other branches of the Shi'a.

More radical movements, in both social and theological terms, arose among the **Isma'ilis**, followers of Ismā'īl, the eldest son of the Sixth Imam, whom the Twelvers excluded from the succession because he was alleged to have drunk wine. He, and in some cases his son Muhammad, became the focus of a number of movements seeking to overthrow not only the Abbasid caliphate but the whole social order on which it was based, and at the same time to reinterpret Islam, incorporating into it some of the ideas of the Hellenistic Christian culture that had dominated the Near East before its arrival. They held that the Koran contained an 'inner', allegorical meaning, which was secretly transmitted to Ali and by him through the line of Imams. Only through a graded secret teaching, after a careful initiation process, could the faithful gain access to this hidden interpretation. The masses had to be content with the apparent meaning, while the initiate, after ascending through the various grades of instruction, would discover the single divine Truth of which all popular religions are merely inane, garbled versions.

Paradoxically, this ultra-elitist doctrine, by providing the certainty of divine guidance, inspired popular revolts. One of the most interesting was that of the Qarmatians, named after their leader Hamdān Qarmat, who set up a kind of communist people's republic near Kūfa, in Iraq, in the late ninth century AD. They subsequently gained control of Bahrain where their state survived for two hundred years. They upheld the common ownership of all goods of general utility, in the name of the (absent) Imam. But like many revolutionary movements they acquired a reputation for terrorism and atrocities, became objects of widespread hatred, fear and persecution, and eventually disappeared.

A successor movement, better organized, was that of the **Fātimids** — descendants of Fatima and Ali through the line of Isma'il — who in the tenth century AD proclaimed themselves caliphs in North Africa, and ruled Egypt from 969 to 1171. Claiming to be the rightful Imams of all Muslims, they sent emissaries throughout South-West Asia to win converts and foment opposition against the Abbasid caliphs. Once again, subversive religious doctrine appealed to people with political and social grievances, this time particularly in Syria and Persia. While in Egypt the Fatimid caliphate took on the usual characteristics of an establishment, in the east Isma'ilism remained a revolutionary movement.

In 1094 a split occurred when the eastern leader, Hasan Ibn al-Sabbāh, refused to recognize the new caliph, al-Musta'lī, claiming instead to support his brother Nizar, who had disappeared in suspicious circumstances. Ibn al-Sabbah, 'the Old Man of the Mountain', conducted guerrilla warfare against the Abbasids from a remote mountain fortress in Persia called Alamut. The Nizārī sect, which he founded, is better known to history as the Assassins (takers of hashish), a name given to it by its enemies. (Our word 'assassination' derives from the Nizaris' tactic of sending suicide missions to kill the commanders of armies that threatened to overrun their strongholds.) Yet, even this group was tamed by the passage of time. It was revived in more peaceable form in the nineteenth century, and today has a worldwide following, mainly of business people originating from the Indian sub-continent, with well-organized welfare services for its less fortunate members. Its Imam is better known as the Aga Khan. The rival, **Musta'lian**, branch of Isma'ilism is also found mainly in India, as well as in Yemen.

Some offshoots of Isma'ilism took Shi'a doctrine to such an extreme point as to put themselves more or less beyond the pale of Islam. One such group is the Nusairis of Syria, also known as **Alawis** (followers of Ali — a term used in some other countries for the Shi'a in general). There is a good deal of confusion about their beliefs. It is generally said of them that they worship Ali as God (which would certainly make them non-Muslims), but this may be an over-simplification. The point has become a politically sensitive one in Syria because of the dominant position which this hitherto underprivileged community has acquired in the ruling Ba'th party, as a result of its overrepresentation among army

48

officers. The Syrian constitution lays down that the President of the Republic must be a Muslim, and there is some doubt whether President Hafiz al-Asad fulfils this condition. Some say that by pronouncing the *shahada* — 'There is no God but God and Muhammad is His messenger' — Mr Asad in effect renounced the Nusairi creed in which he was brought up and became a Muslim, like Henri IV of France becoming a Catholic. The Alawis themselves, however, claim that they are Muslims, and in the 1970s their claim was endorsed by the leader of the Twelver Shi'ites in Lebanon, 'Imam' Musa Sadr, who was anxious to secure Syrian protection for his community in the Lebanese civil war. (It should be added that Sunni hostility towards Alawis in Syria is not directed at their religious beliefs so much as their alleged corruption and nepotism.)

Similar doubts exist about the **Druzes**, who carried to an extreme the Isma'ili doctrine according to which each of the attributes, or component principles, of God was made manifest to mankind in the personality of a prophet or *imam*. An eleventh-century leader, Darazi, proclaimed that one of the Fatimid caliphs, Hākim (996–1021), was the manifestation of God in His unity. His followers, known as Druzes, address prayers to Hakim and call him 'Our Lord', as well as looking forward to his reappearance. This is generally considered to make them non-Muslims, since the cardinal sin in Islam is to attribute any kind of plurality to God or to place any person or thing on a level with Him. The Druzes do, however, observe some Muslim festivals and some recognizably Islamic laws (though they do not fast during the holy month of Ramadan, nor make the pilgrimage to Mecca). They stopped making new converts soon after their foundation and today remain a closed sect, with members in Lebanon, Syria and Israel. The most famous contemporary Druze was Kamal Jumblatt, leader of the left in the Lebanese civil war, who was assassinated in 1977.

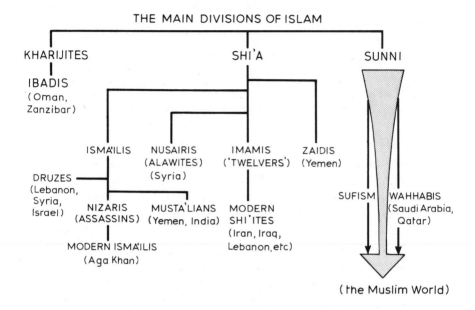

THE MAIN DIVISIONS OF ISLAM

(the Muslim World)

Theology and Politics

By no means all the early disputes within Islam resulted in formal
schisms or the creation of separate sects. More often rival schools
of thought coexisted for a time until one or other of them was
condemned by the consensus of the *ulama* and petered out, but
even then some of its ideas would usually live on, sometimes
synthesized with those of its opponents into a new version of
orthodoxy.

Muslim theology as such lies outside the scope of this book.
But one or two of the early schools of thought need to be mentioned
because their ideas continue to play a part in the struggles of
today. Of particular importance in this respect are the **Mu'tazilites,** or neutralists — so-called probably because they adopted an
intermediate position between the Kharijites, who regarded a grave
sinner as an outright infidel, and the main body of Muslims who

50

considered him a 'sinner-Muslim'. Their importance lies in the fact that they were the first to attempt a justification of Islam in rational and philosophical terms. This led them to argue that reason was an equal source, with divine revelation, of moral truth. They argued that reason was an aspect of the inherent justice of God, and that God could not, by definition, do that which was unreasonable or unjust. Therefore, God could not be held responsible for human acts: human beings enjoy free will and are responsible for their own actions.

The Mu'tazilites' concept of God was a highly abstract one. They explained away all anthropomorphic descriptions of Him in the Koran or the Tradition as mere figures of speech. Rejecting the notion that the Koran was the eternal, 'uncreated' Word of God, they insisted that He had created it in a specific time and place, for a specific purpose.

These ideas have proved very attractive to Islamic modernists of the nineteenth and twentieth centuries, who have found in them a basis for reconciling Islam with some modern Western ideas, including political liberalism. In their time, however, the Mu'tazilites were apologists for political absolutism. The Abbasid caliphs of the early ninth century seized on their doctrine of the createdness of the Koran. For by situating the Koran in a particular place and time the doctrine implicitly allowed for the possibility that in a different place and time God might have something different to say. This in turn implied some discretion for God's representative or deputy on earth at a given time — the caliph or *imam* — to declare 'abrogated' some specific commands of the Koran or to set aside provisions of the Shari'a. By contrast, those *ulama* who struck to a literal interpretation of the Koran and insisted that it was God's uncreated speech, an essential part of His being, were those who sought to limit the power of the caliph, using the Shari'a as the equivalent of a constitution and themselves as the equivalent of a supreme court. (Though, of course, they would not have used that phrase: the only *supreme* court would be the final judgement of God Himself.)

The caliphs and the Mu'tazilites sought for a short time to

impose their doctrine of the createdness of the Koran by force, instituting a kind of inquisition. One of the most famous Islamic jurists, Ahmad ibn Hanbal, the founder of one of the four great schools of law in Sunni Islam, was actually flogged and imprisoned for refusing to accept the doctrine. But after about sixteen years the policy was abandoned and the Mu'tazilites fell from grace. Apparently, the caliphs realized the danger of trying to govern without the *ulama*'s support.

But the Mu'tazilites did not vanish without trace. Their intellectual approach was reflected even in the arguments used to refute them. The great formulator of the orthodox position in the next generation, Abul-Hasan al-Ash'arī, had studied with a Mu'tazilite master. While refuting specific doctrines of the Mu'tazilites, such as their attempt to confine God within the human concept of justice, their assertion that God does not create or produce human actions, that God is pure essence without attributes and that therefore the Koran cannot be His eternal, uncreated speech, al-Ash'ari followed them in seeking to provide Islam with a systematic, internally consistent theology. What is today regarded as 'orthodox' Islamic theology is essentially his system.[1]

The Mu'tazilites were followed by another, more thoroughgoing rationalist movement, that of the **philosophers**, of whom the most important were al-Fārābī (died AD 950), Ibn Sīnā (AD 980–1037), known in the West as Avicenna, and Ibn Rushd (Averroes, AD 1126–98). Their ideas were derived from Greek thought — especially Plato and Aristotle — which they attempted to reconcile with Islam, but did so essentially by reducing the Koran to a kind of brilliant metaphor whose object was to express the rational truth of the universe in terms that were meaningful to the common man. Not surprisingly, this view of religion was unacceptable to the great majority of the *ulama*, and they had relatively little influence on the general development of Islamic thought, except in so far as it was to refute their ideas that al-Ghazali developed his theology. But they were magnificent examples of the freedom and breadth of Islamic culture in its heyday, and did have a notable impact on the thought of medieval Europe. (It was through Averroes that Aristotle was rediscovered by the West.) Consequently, there has been a tendency to rehabilitate them in the last hundred years or so on the part of Muslim modernist intellectuals, who seek to demonstrate the equality or superiority of Islam to the Western intellectual tradition.[2]

Far more important for the future of Islam as a whole was the development of **Sufism**. The original Sūfīs (probably so called in allusion to their simple woollen garments — *sūf* is the Arabic for wool) were essentially mystics: pious Muslims who believed that through meditation and self-discipline they had attained a direct personal experience of God. There is nothing un-Islamic about this; indeed, Muhammad himself was clearly a mystic in this sense, at least in the early part of his career. But Sufism did provide a kind of corrective to the predominant emphasis of the first century of Islam, which was on the expansion and organization of the Muslim community rather than the spiritual development of the individual soul, and on the omnipotence and transcendence of God rather than His immanence and accessibility to direct human knowledge.

As time went on, Sufism itself became gradually institutionalized. Individual mystics attracted groups of followers who learned to imitate their 'path' (*tarīqa*) — a series of mental and sometimes physical exercises leading up to communion with God. In time the word *tariqa* came to mean a group of people following a particular Sufi *shaikh* (old man, teacher), and these groups took on a quasi-monastic organization — sometimes actually living together in a monastery, sometimes travelling, preaching and teaching, rather like the friars of medieval Europe. Thus, one can speak of Sufi 'orders' or 'brotherhoods' (*turuq*), some of which have existed from the twelfth or thirteenth century AD until the present day (usually undergoing many changes and revivals) and can be found in many different countries.

The Sufi preachers developed an approach to Islam based on personal piety, which was often easier for simple people to accept than the somewhat arid, scholastic and legalistic approach of the *ulama*. Through Sufism, Islam was able to absorb many religious beliefs and practices that were non-Islamic in origin but deeply rooted in the culture of the peoples who were converted to Islam. Islam thus adapted itself to widely differing cultures, and after the first generation of Arab military conquest the Sufis became its most effective missionaries. Sufi leaders came to be venerated as local saints and credited with miracles, especially after their deaths, when their tombs often became centres of pilgrimage. They also emerged, at various times and places, as champions of the masses against a corrupt or aristocratic establishment with which the *ulama* had become too closely associated.

Many of the early Sufis were strongly influenced by Shi'ite ideas, at a time when the Shi'a was still more a school of thought than a clearly distinct sect. One such idea, which was to be of great political importance, was that of the Mahdī, the divinely guided leader who would appear at the end of time and restore the supremacy of justice and Islam over ungodly forces. This idea never became a formal doctrine for Sunni Muslims, as it did for the Twelver Shi'ites, but thanks to the Sufi preachers it gained a strong hold on the imagination of many ordinary Muslims who considered themselves orthodox Sunnis, and though not positively endorsed, neither is it condemned by the consensus of Sunni *ulama*.

The *ulama* in general have been suspicious of various aspects of Sufism — essentially those which seemed to encourage superstition — but have been astute enough to try and exercise some control over it rather than condemn it outright. The execution of the ninth-century mystic al-Hallāj, who was accused of identifying himself with God by proclaiming: 'I am the Truth', was a traumatic event, which neither the Sufis nor the *ulama* of later centuries wanted to repeat. A synthesis of the two attitudes, perhaps not fully satisfactory to either side but giving at least a *modus vivendi*, was provided two centuries later by al-Ghazali, whose brother was a leading Sufi and who himself sought to follow the path — though whether he genuinely achieved mystic experience is a .disputed point. His conclusion was that mysticism did not enable one to learn any *facts* about God (or ultimate Reality) that were not already contained in the Koranic revelation; but that it was a meaningful and valuable way of *apprehending* Reality, since true faith should be a thing not only of the mind but of the heart. Properly understood, therefore, Sufism was not a challenge to the Shari'a, but a way of strengthening and deepening one's allegiance to it. The main flock of Sufis thus passed within the fold of Sunni orthodoxy, though there continued to be lost sheep from time to time.[3]

CHAPTER THREE

Decline and Revival

After a while Islam became strangely weak, a piece of whiteness
surrounded by the blackness of its enemies. It was as if God
had absented Himself, leaving it to face the most severe troubles.

Hasan al-Attār (Shaikh al-Azhar, 1831–35)[1]

The Sense of Decay

The conventional view of the history of Islam was that as a civilization it reached its peak under the Abbasid caliphs, two hundred
years after Muhammad, and then began a long decline, which has
gone on almost continuously ever since. The political disintegration
of the Islamic state corresponded to a gradual ossification of Islamic
thought: in Sunni Islam, at least, the jurists declared that the work
of interpreting the Koran and the Sunna as positive law was now
complete, and there was no further need for original thought — 'the
Gate of *ijtihad* is closed' — while in theology and philosophy al-
Ghazali, in the eleventh century AD, provided a complete system
of thought that could thenceforth only be embroidered, not
challenged. Thus, the world of Islam sank gradually into stagnation
and decadence.

That view is no longer fashionable. It has been pointed out
that many of the most dynamic developments in Islam occurred
long after the Abbasid golden age. The Sufi orders developed,
and helped to spread the faith into new regions far beyond the
Abbasid domains, such as Black Africa and South-East Asia. Until

about AD 1500 Muslim thinkers continued to lead the world in astronomy, medicine and other sciences. The sixteenth century saw the rise of new and powerful Muslim states: the Moguls in India, the Safavids in Persia and the Ottomans in West Asia and Eastern Europe. The latter were arguably the world's leading military power until the late seventeenth century, and posed a real threat to the Christian states of Western Europe. Under all three dynasties there was a flowering of art, architecture and literature, with Iran now replacing Iraq as the cultural and intellectual centre of the Muslim world, and Persian replacing Arabic as its literary and diplomatic language. Arabic remained the language of law and theology and here, it is true, a certain conservatism prevailed, at least in form and in theory. But in political and administrative practice a great deal of innovation occurred by quietly ignoring old rules, and political debate could be carried on by using old language to express new ideas.

THE MUSLIM MILLENNIUM

Yet by the eighteenth century AD — ironically the period when West Europeans began to admire and romanticize Muslim civilization — the feeling became general among the Muslims themselves that their world was in decline. Reading history backwards, one is tempted to see this feeling as a response to the growing technical and military superiority of Christian Europe. But in its origins it cannot have been that, for it can be traced back to a period before this superiority was perceptible to Muslims, and some of its most spectacular early manifestations occurred in Muslim communities which had little or no direct contact with Europeans.

Of course, there has never been a time when all Muslims were satisfied that their society was maintaining its standards. In Islam, as in other human societies, reaction to real or imagined regress has been the main stimulant of progress. Any date we assign to the beginning of a more general disillusionment must therefore be somewhat arbitrary. But such disillusionment does seem already to have been fairly widespread around the year 1000 of the Muslim era (AD 1590), when many Muslims expected the end of the world.

What was wrong? The evils initially perceived were moral and spiritual rather than political or economic. They stemmed at least in part from the degeneration or the excesses of Sufism. The Sufi brotherhoods had won enormous mass followings in most parts of the Muslim world, but at the price of adopting a variety of popular superstitions and practices — auto-hypnotic visions, orgiastic rituals, saint-worship — in which the *ulama*, the supposed guardians of orthodoxy, generally did not interfere. The *ulama*, by and large, were content to accept patronage from worldly rulers who paid lip-service to the supremacy of divine law, but who in practice arrogated the legislative power to themselves, particularly in matters of administration, taxation and commerce. In India matters were even worse, as Sufism opened a way for Muslims to absorb Hindu theology. The Mogul emperor Akbar, in the late sixteenth century AD, even developed a heretical court religion of his own, a would-be rational cult based on a synthesis of Islam with other religions.

LAST OF THE GREAT MOGULS

The first reaction in India, around AD 1600, was a reassertion of orthodoxy within Sufism, carried out by the firmly orthodox Naqshbandi order. Its leader, Shaikh Ahmad Sirhindi, became known to his followers as the 'renovator of the second millennium'. It has been said of him that he 'gave to Indian Islam the rigid and conservative stamp it bears today'.[2] On the political level, his ideas were reflected in the policies of the emperor Aurangzeb, the last of the great Mogul emperors, in the late seventeenth century. He dropped the Indian solar calendar in favour of the Islamic lunar one, stopped the celebration of the Persian New Year because of its Zoroastrian origin, appointed censors to control alcoholism and sexual vices, and abolished taxes, such as transit duties, which were not based on Islamic law. He forbade such 'superstitious' practices as building roofs over saints' tombs and making them centres of pilgrimage, and holding processions during the month of Muharram to commemorate the martyrdom of Husain. He also outlawed prostitution, effeminacy in dress and the cultivation of hashish, and discouraged astrology and even music. For Muslims Aurangzeb 'aimed to create something like a welfare state, with free kitchens, inns and subsistence allowances, and the abolition of a number of taxes not authorized by the canon law', while on non-Muslims he imposed the canonical *jizya* (poll-tax) from which his predecessors had spared their Hindu subjects.[3] The Hindus were not necessarily worse off materially, since they benefited from the abolition of many of the uncanonical taxes, but their separate status, outside the Muslim community, was emphasized, in accordance with classical Muslim law and practice.

Aurangzeb's reforms had two aspects. Internally, they were an attempt to purge the Muslim community of corruption and superstition, and to reassert the supremacy of the Shari'a with the state as its instrument. Externally, they were an attempt to reassert the authority of a Muslim state over its non-Muslim subjects. Clearly, the two were connected in the mind of Aurangzeb and the orthodox reformist *ulama* with whom he surrounded himself. The growing inability of the Muslims to dominate the non-Muslims surrounding them reflected the weakening of Islam as the basis of their own society. Islam's external problems were a reflection of its internal decay. That has been the theme of innumerable Muslim reform movements in the three centuries that have passed since Aurangzeb's reign, referring usually to Islam's weakness in face of the Western challenge. But the challenges Islam faced in Aurangzeb's time in India did not yet come from the West: they were, internally, dilution through the infiltration of Hindu customs and beliefs, and, externally, the rising religious and political militancy of the Hindu Marathas and the Sikhs.

OTTOMAN MALAISE

The Ottoman Empire, of course, had much more direct contact with Christian Europe. (I use this term, rather than 'Western Europe' or 'the West', because one of the most important challenges to Muslim, and especially Ottoman, power was to come from the rise of Tsarist Russia.) Although some of the political and social problems which Ottoman society experienced in the seventeenth century were the effect of economic changes occurring in the Christian world, it was not until the end of that century or the beginning of the eighteenth that Christian powers began to demonstrate their military superiority. Yet from the beginning of the seventeenth century numerous Ottoman writers expressed the feeling that their social order was in decay, and a reaction developed in the form of preachers condemning the corruption and worldliness of both the *ulama* and the temporal rulers, and calling for a restoration of law based exclusively on the Koran and the Sunna of the Prophet.

The Arabian Reformation: Āl Wahhāb and Āl Sa'ūd

It is true that it was not until the eighteenth century that these ideas generated a political movement, but when they did so it was on the fringes of the Empire — not its borders with Christendom but the area most remote from Christian influence or impact of any kind: the Arabian desert.

Muhammad Ibn Abdul-Wahhāb was born in the obscure desert town of Uyaina in AD 1703, into a family of learned lawyer–theologians. He was shocked, it seems, by the laxity of the society in which he grew up — its neglect of the prescribed rites and prayers, its promiscuity, its tolerance of superstition — and was much influenced by the doctrines of Ibn Taimiya, a rigorously orthodox theologian who had argued against the excesses of Sufism some four hundred years earlier. After visiting Mecca and Medina, and also studying at Basra in Iraq, he returned to his native Najd (central Arabia) and began to preach moral and spiritual regeneration. He attacked belief in the power of saints and pious men and all the associated practices, such as worship of saints' tombs and reliance upon the intercession of the Prophet or the saints. Further, seeing that the *ulama* had long connived at such practices, he also attacked blind acceptance of authority in religious matters, calling on Muslims to apply their own minds and consciences to the Koran and the Sunna, rather than rely on traditional interpretations. Not unlike Martin Luther, he sought to strip away all the medieval superstitions which had attached themselves to Islam (mainly through the medium of Sufism) and restore it to the purity of the first generations; and in order to do so he had to challenge the established religious authorities.

Although through Ibn Taimiya he was a follower of Ibn Hanbal, founder of one of the four classical schools of Sunni jurisprudence, Ibn Abdul-Wahhab was opposed to any of the schools being taken as an absolute and unquestionable authority.* He thus reopened the 'gate of *ijtihad*' (independent thinking) — which earlier generations of *ulama* had declared closed — and condemned *taqlīd* (servile imitation). The precedent was comparable to Luther's in importance, and aroused comparable fears among the religious and political establishments of the time.

Like Luther, too, Ibn Abdul-Wahhab sought protection and support from a local prince, who tied his political fortunes to the new doctrine. This was Muhammad Ibn Sa'ūd, ruler of the small neighbouring principality of Dir'īya, who in 1744 gave asylum to Ibn Abdul-Wahhab when the latter's attacks on local shrines (tombs and sacred trees) had provoked his expulsion from his native city. The two men then formed an alliance. Ibn Sa'ud promised to accept the responsibilities of an Islamic ruler as defined by Ibn Abdul-Wahhab, while Ibn Abdul-Wahhab promised him that if he did so, 'perchance Almighty God will conquer you conquests, and recompense you with spoils of war far more ample than your present revenues.'⁴ And so it proved. The early history of the Wahhābīya — as the movement came to be known — was in several respects an authentic repetition of the early history of Islam. The same evils were denounced: injustice, corruption, tribalism, adultery, indifference to the plight of widows and orphans and above all — the root of all the others — idolatry, or 'association' of others with God. Once again, emphasis on the

* Actually this position had been taken by earlier followers of Ibn Hanbal, including Ibn Taimiya, but this had been generally forgotten.

61

unity of God was combined with emphasis on the brotherhood of all Muslims, irrespective of social rank or tribal affiliation, and the aggressive energies of the community were turned outward, against the enemies of Islam, in a *jihad* or holy struggle. Once again the result was a political entity both more cohesive and more dynamic than its neighbours, which was thus able to expand and to unify, at least temporarily, the greater part of the Arabian peninsula.

But there were two significant differences. First, this time the *jihad* was undertaken against people who believed they were already Muslims, but who were accused, on the evidence of their behaviour, of backsliding into unbelief. Like the Kharijites of old, the Wahhabis were led by the logic of their position to regard themselves as the only true believers and the rest of the Muslim world as apostates. Secondly, this time the spiritual leader did not himself assume political power. He was content to see the business of conquest and government carried on by the dynasty of Sa'ud, while he himself provided religious guidance. There was thus an implicit division between temporal and spiritual authority—a distinction which, as we have seen, did not exist in the early days of Islam.

It is unlikely that either Muhammad Ibn Abdul-Wahhab or Muhammad Ibn Sa'ud was clearly aware of this. The former certainly did not regard his religious responsibilities as excluding war or politics. The latter, who had hitherto styled himself *shaikh* or *amir* — titles with no religious significance — now took the title of Imam, which clearly implied religious as well as political leadership. He did so, of course, with the support and encouragement of Ibn Abdul-Wahhab, who thus in theory recognized his authority in religious as well as political matters. Yet at the same time it was clear that Ibn Abdul-Wahhab was superior to him in religious learning and the prime mover in the religious revival. Ibn Sa'ud's qualifications for the Imamate were political rather than spiritual. This became clearer as it passed on in his family from generation to generation, with each Imam choosing his own successor, while the descendants of Ibn Abdul-Wahhab, who became known as the family of Āl Shaikh,* supplied the leading *ulama* of the new state, right down to the present day. The Imamate of the Saudi rulers came gradually to resemble the position of the kings of England as head of the church: it implied that their political authority extended also to matters of religion. Under that authority, a specific religious competence was vested in the Al Shaikh, who were, so to speak, their archbishops of Canterbury.

Outside Arabia, the impact of the Wahhabiya was felt on various levels. It was a challenge to the authority of the Ottoman government. That did not matter much so long as it was confined to the interior of the peninsula, over which the Ottomans had little control anyway, but became more serious when it spread westwards to the Hijaz — the region of Mecca and Medina — and eastwards to the shores of the Persian Gulf. It was a source of outrage to many pious but traditionally-minded Muslims when shrines that were regarded as sacred by the whole of the Muslim world were attacked and destroyed. This happened in 1802 when Sa'ud ibn Abdul-Aziz, the grandson of Muhammad ibn Sa'ud, invaded Iraq and destroyed the town of Karbala, massacring the population and demolishing the tomb of the martyr Husain, the Prophet's grandson. This of course was especially horrifying to the Shi'a, for whom 'Wahhabite' remains a term of abuse to this day, but shocking to Muslims in general. There were similar scenes the following year in Mecca, where the invading Wahhabis destroyed all the domes built over the tombs of heroes and heroines of early Islam, and other sites connected with Islamic legend. In 1805 it was the turn of Medina, whose people submitted after a long siege, agreeing to the destruction of all their domed tombs.

These provocations, both political and religious, brought a reaction in due course in the shape of an invasion of Arabia carried

---

* The word *Āl*, not to be confused with the definite article *al-*, denotes a family or tribe. *Shaikh*, originally 'old man', is a very general way of expressing respect. Perhaps the nearest English equivalent would be 'Master'. Thus, it is used most commonly to refer to learned teachers, but in Arabia also for political rulers or simply people of importance, and in modern Saudi Arabia it is virtually equivalent to 'Mr'.

out by the ruler of Egypt, Muhammad Ali Pasha, in the name of the Ottoman government. By 1819 Muhammad Ali's forces had reconquered not only the Hijaz but Najd itself. The Saudi capital, Dir'iya, was destroyed, the Imam Abdullah ibn Sa'ud sent as a prisoner to Istanbul and executed, and Wahhabism temporarily suppressed.

But Wahhabism had another impact that was even more widespread, through its power of inspiration and example. Its doctrines, more or less accurately understood, had an appeal to thoughtful Muslims in lands where the question of allegiance to the new Saudi state did not arise as such. In the nineteenth century we find movements referred to as Wahhabiya cropping up in places as far apart as India and West Africa. How far these were directly influenced by the ideas of Ibn Abdul-Wahhab is not always clear. In fact 'Wahhabi' was not a term used by his followers to describe themselves. Its implied sanctification of their founding father was contrary to their philosophy. (They preferred to call themselves Unitarians.) By their opponents the term 'Wahhabi' came to be used widely and loosely to describe movements which seemed dangerously subversive or fanatical, rather as 'communist' has been used in some circles in this century. Some of the movements so described were not strictly Wahhabi at all. But by and large they had something in common with Wahhabism, namely the desire to purge Islam of its medieval accretions, to break with the corrupt establishment of their time, and to restore what they believed to be the authentic beliefs and practices of the Prophet and his immediate successors. It is from the Wahhabi movement that we can date the revival of Islam as an activist and revolutionary force.

The Indian Reformation: Shah Waliullah and his Disciples

When Ibn Abdul-Wahhab was studying in Mecca and Medina in 1730–32 he may have met a young Indian scholar of exactly his own age who was also studying there and who, like him, was deeply distressed by the decadence of contemporary Islam and convinced of the need for reform. This was Shah Waliullah of Delhi (1703–64), who has been described as 'the greatest intellectual Muslim India produced' and as the first Indian Muslim 'who felt the urge of the new spirit in him'.[5]

Shah Waliullah lived at a time when the Muslim empire in India was rapidly disintegrating after the death of Aurangzeb in 1707. Aurangzeb's attempt to recreate an orthodox Islamic state which could reassert its authority proved to have been a failure. It had provoked strong hostility and resistance among the Hindus without inspiring a real revival of piety or self-confidence among the Muslims. After his death Muslim princes feuded with one another and much of the empire was overrun by the Sikhs and Marathas. The power of Britain and France was also beginning to be felt. After being for centuries the only full citizens of the state, Muslims discovered that they were an unpopular and vulnerable minority.

Shah Waliullah realized that if Islam was to be revived, in India and elsewhere, a far more profound and sweeping reform than Aurangzeb's was necessary. Like Ibn Abdul-Wahhab, he denounced the decadent scholasticism of the traditional *ulama*, based on servile copying of precedent, and called for the application of *ijtihad* (independent reasoning) to religious problems. Rather than adhering to any one of the four traditional schools of learning, he urged the use of *ijtihad* to sift the conclusions of all four by comparing them with the text of the Koran and the *hadith* — the accepted tradition of Muhammad's sayings and actions, as collected and authenticated by scholars some two hundred years after his death.

But Shah Waliullah's approach was considerably more sophisticated than that of Ibn Abdul-Wahhab. For the latter, it was simply a matter of stripping away the later accretions and getting back to the letter and the spirit of Islam as preached and practised by the Prophet. On one side was true Islam, clear and unchanging, on the other falsehood and corruption: one had only to choose between the two. Shah Waliullah, by contrast, saw that there was a constant need for new *ijtihad* as the Muslim community progressed and expanded and new generations had to cope with new problems. Thus, the rulings and interpretations given by earlier generations of scholars might have been perfectly right for their time and place, but yet have to be discarded or improved in the circumstances of today. The essence of Islam, contained in the Koran and the *hadith*, was indeed unchanging, but the detailed practice was not. In seeing that religious thought was affected by changing social needs and conditions, Shah Waliullah was ahead of his time, whether in the Muslim world or in Christian Europe.

One aspect of Islamic decadence of which Shah Waliullah, because of his geographical origin, was even more acutely aware than Ibn Abdul-Wahhab, was the extent to which Islam was becoming fragmented, not only politically (that had happened long before) but in terms of belief and practice, into separate geographical areas. It was in an attempt to overcome this that he wrote his main theological work in Arabic rather than Persian, which was the dominant literary language of Muslim India in his time. Writing in Arabic, he made his ideas accessible to fellow scholars in every Muslim country. But he also wanted to bring the ordinary educated Muslims of India into direct contact with universal Islam and to free them from dependence on their petty-minded local theologians. For that purpose he made a translation of the Koran into Persian, and his sons later translated it into Urdu — the Persianized form of Hindi that most Indian Muslims spoke, which gradually displaced Persian as a literary language during the eighteenth century.

This enterprise was bitterly attacked by conservative *ulama*. The Koran itself insists repeatedly on its Arabic character, and it was generally felt that to translate it into any other language amounted to tampering with the Word of God. From today's perspective the argument is not a very strong one, since the importance of the Koran's being in Arabic is in the text itself clearly bound up with the need for clarity and accessibility to the reader or hearer: 'This is speech Arabic, manifest'; 'An Arabic Koran, wherein there is no crookedness'; 'Behold, we have made it an Arabic Koran: haply you will understand.' Even so, it seemed

66

to many *ulama* that translation amounted to rewriting, and thus to human usurpation of a divine function. Translations were in fact made, but in the guise of a vernacular commentary or exegesis on the Arabic text. Shah Waliullah was the first Muslim who claimed openly to make the text itself available in a language other than Arabic, and this was an innovation far more radical than the move to translate the Bible into European vernaculars during the Reformation. (The Latin Vulgate then in use was itself, after all, a translation from Hebrew and Greek.)

But Shah Waliullah's radicalism was not confined to the sphere that we should call religious. He called also for a reform of the social order, so sweeping that it may fairly be called a revolution. He saw the root cause of Islam's decay, in India and elsewhere, as being the manifest injustice and exploitation on which the power and luxury of the feudal ruling class was based. He denounced especially the system of taxation, which fell heavily on the hard-working poor and benefited the idle rich. Anticipating Marx, he held that the basis of wealth was labour, and that no one had the right to live off the fruits of others' labour without contributing his own. Anticipating Adam Smith, he warned that the welfare of a society was dependent on that of all workers who produced its wealth: the collective prosperity of society depended on the individual prosperity of its industrious citizens. Consequently, labour should be fairly remunerated and not unfairly taxed — and the criterion of fairness could not be simply what a starving labourer was forced to accept. Hours of work should be fixed. Workers should be allowed leisure for social and spiritual better-ment, for cultivating their minds and thinking of the future.

Like Adam Smith again, Shah Waliullah insisted on the importance of commerce: this should be regulated by government to prevent dishonest or monopolistic practice, but not impeded by the imposition of heavy taxes.

Anticipating Henry George, he argued that land was given by God for the use, not the ownership, of human beings. Its use should therefore be regulated by the community in the general interest and its exploitation by idle landlords outlawed. No one, he wrote, has the right to consider himself the master either of land or of his fellow men; and those in authority should not be encouraged to consider themselves in that way by flattery.

Like John Locke, finally (whom he cannot have read), Shah Waliullah held that the position of a ruler was equivalent to that of a trustee. Moreover he was entitled, in Shah Waliullah's view, only to such remuneration as would enable him to live like an ordinary citizen.

Shah Waliullah also developed what seems to us a very advanced theory of natural rights: every man was entitled to food, clothing, housing and such sustenance as would enable him to marry and to raise and educate his children; from the state he was entitled to expect equal treatment, without distinction of creed, caste or race, as well as protection of life and property and 'guarantee of honour'. Separate communities also had a right to the preservation of their language and culture, to be assured through a confederal political structure under a restored universal caliphate.[6]

Shah Waliullah had no opportunity to put these ideas into practice. In practical politics his efforts were limited to attempts to rouse Muslim rulers to a *jihad* against the Indian enemies of Islam (Marathas and Jats). In this he had some temporary success towards the end of his life when the ruler of Afghanistan, to whom he had addressed an eloquent appeal, inflicted a crushing defeat on the Marathas at the battle of Panipat (AD 1761). But meanwhile the power of the British East India Company was growing rapidly in Bengal. The decline of Muslim power could be briefly checked, but not reversed.

SAYYID AHMAD BARELVI

There was indeed something of a contradiction between Shah Waliullah's condemnation of the feudal princes and his appeal to rulers of essentially that type to undertake the *jihad*. After his death it became obvious that these rulers were in any case unable to restore Muslim power, and in the nineteenth century his followers organized themselves into an independent *jihad* movement under the leadership of Sayyid Ahmad Barelvi, a disciple of Shah

68

Waliullah's son and successor, Shah Abdul-Aziz. This movement was to become a thorn in the side of India's British rulers, who labelled it 'Wahhabi', though in fact it does not appear to have been influenced by the Arabian Wahhabiya. (Sayyid Ahmad made a pilgrimage to Mecca in 1822–23 — ten years after Muhammad Ali had reconquered it from the Wahhabis and suppressed their ideas.) The movement was based on Shah Waliullah's ideas, but with a greater emphasis on the 'purification' of Islam from un-Islamic beliefs and practices, especially those borrowed from the Hindus.

Once again it seems not to have been, in its origins, a response to the 'challenge of the West'. It was directed more against the Sikhs, who were persecuting Muslims in North-Western India, than against the British, who refrained from interfering with Muslim freedom of worship or personal life in the territories under their control.* Like Shah Waliullah, Sayyid Ahmad appealed to external Muslim rulers — those of Bukhara, in Central Asia, and of Afghanistan — to undertake *jihad* against the Sikhs and re-establish Islamic rule in India. But he also organized military action on his own account without waiting for them to act, setting up his own little state, in which his own interpretation of Islamic law was strictly enforced, in the frontier hills. But unhappily, his followers were mainly Pakhtun tribesmen whose superstitions and factions he was unable to overcome. Finally, he was defeated and killed by the Sikhs in 1831.

It was only later that some of his followers found themselves fighting British power, when the British had replaced the Sikhs in the Punjab and were beginning to interfere in Afghanistan. From 1840 onwards the movement was increasingly active in resisting the British, until in 1857 it allied itself with the Indian Mutiny. The Mutiny was in part an expression of Muslim discontent and many of the *ulama* not only supported it but actually fought in it. 'In that part of British India where Muslims were influential

---

* But Shah Abdul-Aziz, in 1803, did declare that territory under British rule was no longer within the 'house of Islam', and encouraged Muslims to emigrate from it to other Muslim lands.

and also where their religion and culture had become strongly rooted ... the Mutiny took on the definite character of a *jihad*.'[7] After it, the British took firm action against the remnants of Sayyid Ahmad Barelvi's movement and persecuted it all over India. But it continued to give the British trouble on the North-West Frontier right up to the time of the First World War.

The overriding objective of the *jihad* movement was to establish an independent Muslim state in which true Islam, purged of semi-pagan practices, could be practised. The *jihad* itself, which was to achieve this, was seen, as it had been by the first Muslims, as an activity of spiritual as well as military significance, the culmination of a life of dedication, after prayers and fasting and pilgrimage to Mecca.

After the failure of the Indian Mutiny some of Shah Waliullah's followers turned to more peaceful methods of preserving the Islamic heritage under non-Muslim rule. One group in 1876 founded a school of law and theology at Deoband, which became the main centre of conservative Muslim thought in India, while a different aspect of Shah Waliullah's legacy was represented by the Muhammadan Anglo-Oriental College at Aligarh, founded in 1877 by the modernist and pro-Western reformer Sir Sayyid Ahmad Khan.

The African Reformation: Sufism Revived

By around AD 1800 the impulse for reform seems to have been felt in almost every part of the Muslim world, but perhaps most strongly in the peripheral areas, where compromise with indigenous local beliefs and practices had produced nominally Muslim communities far removed from the classical model as it was understood in the Middle Eastern heartlands of Islam. In these peripheral areas, from Indonesia to West Africa, we find in the early nineteenth century movements striving to inculcate greater orthodoxy and uniformity — that is, urging a stricter adherence to the Koran and the Sunna and attacking practices of non-Muslim origin.

Such movements were generally led by people who had made the pilgrimage to Mecca, and one explanation given for them is simply that better communications made the pilgrimage easier to undertake for Muslims from faraway places, and generally made Muslims in different parts of the world more aware of what one another were doing and saying. That may indeed have become an important factor in the late nineteenth century, when Western technology did improve communications in many parts of the Muslim world, but it hardly can have been as early as 1800. The world then was becoming a smaller place for Europeans, who were rapidly expanding their contacts with Asia and Africa by the sea routes, but not necessarily for Muslims, who had for centuries been travelling and trading across both continents, mainly by land. To some extent, indeed, the internal communications of the Muslim world were beginning to suffer from the development of new trade routes, which were largely in European hands. This was particularly the case in Africa, where trade across the Sahara was declining while trade through the coastal ports, especially in slaves, was growing.

Such alterations in patterns of trade helped to disrupt Muslim and partly Muslim societies, and this may in turn account for the rapid spread of the reform movements. Some of these appear to have been inspired by the Wahhabiya, such as the *jihad* of Uthman dan-Fodio in central West Africa (which led to the founding of Sokoto and the other Muslim emirates of northern Nigeria) or the rising of the 'Padris' in Sumatra.

Other movements, especially in Africa, took the form of a reform of Sufism, leading to the foundation of new orders or brotherhoods which came to play an important political role. The difference between these movements and the others was less clear-cut than might be supposed, for what was involved was not a revival of the original mystical content of Sufism, but rather the use of Sufi organization to propagate a renewed spiritual zeal, generally combined with a firm insistence on orthodoxy.

71

TIJANIYA

In North and West Africa the most important of the reformist Sufi orders was the Tijaniya, founded by the Algerian Ahmad al-Tijani (1737–1815) at Fez, then the centre of government of the Moroccan Sultan. Al-Tijani had emigrated from Algeria after clashing with the Ottoman Turkish authorities there, against whom his animosity was so strong that he prayed 'that God would make the Turks lose Algeria in the same way that he allowed the Muslims to lose Spain to the Christians.'[8] He was well received by the Sultan, Moulay Sulaiman, although the latter was influenced by Wahhabi ideas and hostile to the Sufi orders in general. Probably he was impressed by al-Tijani's reformism and his denunciation of the older Sufi orders and their corrupt practices. By the time of his death al-Tijani had a considerable following both in Morocco and in Algeria, and thereafter the order continued to expand, particularly south of the Sahara where it was taken up in the mid-nineteenth century by the great Fulani leader Al-Hajj Umar, who built a powerful Muslim state in the valleys of the upper Senegal and upper Niger. He too proclaimed *jihad*, but directed his energies as much against local pagans — and non-Tijani Muslims who allied with them — as against the expanding power of the French. He was killed in battle, by fellow Muslims, in 1864. The state continued under his son Ahmadu, who signed a treaty with the French and maintained good relations with them until, in the 1880s and 1890s, they gradually overran his territory.

AHMAD IBN IDRĪS

The revival of Sufism in North Africa also had repercussions further east. Like al-Tijani (and perhaps influenced by him), the Moroccan Sufi Ahmad ibn Idrīs wished to purge Sufism from what he regarded as the degeneration of mysticism into mumbo jumbo and saint-worship. He accepted the value of genuine spiritual exercises for the religious development of the individual, but considered they were 'not suitable for the higher purpose which he was aiming at, that is, the unity of the endeavour of Muslims united in the bond of Islam.'[9] He left North Africa to go on the pilgrimage in 1799, lived in Egypt for a time and went again to Mecca, this time to settle and teach, in 1818. He attracted a large number of pupils but fell foul of the *ulama*, whom he accused of corrupting the faith. Although he was a Sufi, his ideas sounded altogether too similar to those of the Wahhabis who had recently been expelled from the holy city. He was charged with heresy and had to flee to the southern Arabian province of Asīr, where the Wahhabis were still in control. He was left in peace there until his death in 1837.

Two major new orders were founded by disciples of Ahmad ibn Idris — the Mīrghanīya (or Khatmīya), which became dominant in eastern Sudan, and the Sanūsīya, which was to be the foundation of modern Libya. Both were dominated by the families of their respective founders, both of whom came from outside the area where they acquired their following. Muhammad Uthmān al-Mīrghanī was a Meccan whose family came from Central Asia, while Muhammad ibn Ali al-Sanūsī was an Algerian. Both also claimed to be descendants of the Prophet.

SANUSIYA

The 'Grand Sanusi', as he was later known, was born in 1787. He is another example of a leader who early in life became pre-occupied with the state of the Muslim world as a whole: 'He was struck by the fact that although there were a number of rulers, chiefs and learned men in the world of Islam, yet this world was torn asunder by rivalries and strifes. He thought that the scholars and shaikhs lost religious zeal and no longer cared for the spread of knowledge and education.'[10] He travelled to Cairo and studied at the great university of al-Azhar, but was disappointed to find that the *ulama* there were little more than hangers-on of Muhammad Ali Pasha and the other great Ottoman officials in the city. They in their turn denounced him, and the Muftī — the *alim* appointed by the government to give authoritative rulings on Islamic law — issued a long *fatwā*, or ruling, refuting his alleged errors and 'innovations'. Among these was the abandonment of the four recognized schools of law and 'the acceptance without intermediaries of the commandments of the Book and the Sunna.'

The *fatwa* is interesting as a statement of the traditional *ulama*'s case against all the new reform movements, from Ibn Abdul-Wahhab onwards, which insisted on going back to the raw texts of the Koran and the *hadith*. It acknowledges that al-Sanusi's own interpretation of these texts is perfectly orthodox and makes it clear that his heresy lies not in any specific interpretation but in the very fact of asserting the validity of the text 'without intermediaries'. It points out that the *hadith* is not a single, authoritative text, but is itself a collection of reports which have to be carefully sifted and interpreted. This work of sifting and interpretation was precisely what the four classical schools had accomplished, and could not now be brashly jettisoned.

Even the Koran itself could not simply be taken as it stood. Some passages in it were abrogated or modified by other, later passages. 'Some texts are absolute in their meaning in one chapter, while in others they are defined with greater reservation.' Others required very careful interpretation, which only the 'four Imams' — i.e. the founders of the four schools — had the authority to provide. 'The four orthodox schools are the best results, the finest extraction, of all schools, because they count among their partisans many men dedicated to the search for truth and blessed with vast knowledge. Deviation from these four schools shows the desire to live in error.' It was therefore obligatory to follow one of the four schools; to recommend the Sufi path as an alternative was 'to transgress, to deviate from the general, legal path.' Equally unacceptable was the claim to exercise *ijtihad* — independent reasoning — in interpreting the sacred texts. 'For no one denies the fact that the dignity of *ijtihad* has long disappeared and that at the present time no man has attained this degree of learning. He who believed himself to be a *mujtahid* would be under the influence of his hallucinations and of the devil.'[11]

Undaunted by this solemn rebuke, al-Sanusi proceeded to Mecca where he became a disciple of Ahmad ibn Idris. After the latter's death he founded a *zāwiya* (monastery) in Mecca, but in 1840 he was forced to leave. After travelling back and forth across

North Africa he settled on Cyrenaica (eastern Libya) as the most promising field for his reformist work, and founded a new *zawiya*, called al-Baidā, in the hills of the interior. Though this was a relatively fertile region he found most of his converts among the nomads of the surrounding desert, and his missionary outlook made him look southwards to the semi-pagan tribes of the Sahara and the black peoples beyond, in what is now the republic of Chad. In 1856 he moved his base to Jaghbūb, deep in the Libyan desert — partly to avoid interference by the Ottoman government and partly to strengthen his influence in the central Sahara. He died there in 1859.

Under his son and successor, Sayyid al-Mahdi, the Sanusiya spread over a vast area of north, west and equatorial Africa, from Lake Chad to the river Senegal and from the Wadai (eastern Chad) to the Mediterranean. Many of the masses in these regions were convinced that Sayyid al-Mahdi, who was to come of age in the year 1300 of the *hijra* (AD 1882–83), was *the* Mahdi — the divinely guided leader who would at last set Islam to rights and whose appearance was supposed to have been foretold by the Prophet himself. But Sayyid al-Mahdi himself denied this categorically and emphatically, as he also rejected the position of *khalīfa* (deputy and successor) offered to him by his Sudanese contemporary Muhammad Ahmad, who did claim to be the Mahdi (and of whom more below). His call, Sayyid al-Mahdi explained, was 'to reform Islam through peaceful means and not through bloodshed.' Similarly, he refused to help Urabi Pasha's revolt against British and French influence in Egypt in 1882, and expressed anxiety about the repercussions for Egypt (rightly, since the outcome was British occupation of the whole country). He respected the nominal authority of the Ottoman Sultan, and insisted on his followers abiding by the laws and rules of the Ottoman administration, using the Egyptian example to warn that the consequence of rising against the Ottoman authorities could be to bring about occupation by Christian foreigners. Yet in 1876 he had also refused to help the Ottoman government in its war with Russia. In 1890 he politely refused an invitation to visit

Istanbul, and when the Ottoman governor of Cyrenaica visited him at Jaghbub he was careful to conceal his stocks of arms. His policy, in short, was to avoid political entanglement and interference as far as possible.

Even so, the spread of the Sanusiya was seen by the French as a threat to their expanding influence in Central Africa. In 1902, the year of Sayyid al-Mahdi's death, France began to wage war on the Sanusis, gradually occupying and destroying their centres south of the Sahara. Then, in 1911, the Italians attacked Libya from the Mediterranean. The Ottoman Empire made only a brief attempt to defend its province before signing a treaty with Italy in 1912 under which it nominally proclaimed Libya's independence, but in fact left the Italians a free hand. The burden of resisting the Italian invasion fell on the Sanusiya, which was thus almost in spite of itself transformed into a state. The Ottoman general Enver Bey informed the Sanusi leader, Sayyid Ahmad al-Sharīf, that the Sultan had entrusted the affairs of the Libyan people to him, whereupon Sayyid Ahmad formed a 'Sanusi Government'. Under his leadership, and later under that of Sayyid Muhammad Idris, the grandson of the Grand Sanusi, the Sanusiya was the backbone of resistance to Italian colonial rule. The Italians did succeed in conquering and occupying the whole country, destroying the Sanusi *zawiyas*, but when they were driven out by the British in 1943, Sayyid Idris was able to return to Cyrenaica as the recognized political leader of the people, and in due course to become King Idris I of Libya.

THE MAHDI

Finally, this survey of the so-called 'pre-modernist' reform movements in Islam would not be complete without some account of the Sudanese 'Mahdīya'. Muhammad Ahmad, who proclaimed himself as the Mahdi in the Sudan in 1881, is probably the only claimant to that title of whom the European or American high school student ever hears. This is principally because of the dramatic fate of Charles George Gordon, the British general who perished in Khartoum in 1885 at the hands of the Mahdi's forces after a siege lasting nearly a year. We therefore tend to think of the Mahdi as a leader of fanatical Muslim resistance to the imperialism of Christian European powers.

But things are not so simple. When the Mahdi launched his movement the Sudan was under Egyptian rule, and Egypt had not yet been occupied by the British. It was, in name at least, a province of the Ottoman Empire, ruled in the Sultan's name by the dynasty that Muhammad Ali had founded. Many of the senior officials originated, like Muhammad Ali himself, from the northern parts of the Empire. The language of the court and high administration was Turkish, and the Sudanese referred to their rulers as Turks. It was against 'the Turks' that the Mahdi aroused his countrymen's feelings. These 'Turks' were, of course, mainly Muslims, even if lax ones by his standards, and their appointment of Christian Europeans like Gordon to high administrative posts was, in his eyes, only one among their many vices. Moreover the British, when they occupied Egypt in 1882, were not at all anxious to get involved in the Sudan and their purpose in sending Gordon back there in 1884 (he had previously been governor-general in 1877–80, appointed by the Egyptian government) was actually to arrange the withdrawal of the Egyptian troops and administration.

The Mahdiya was not, therefore, a revolt of Muslims against Christian rule, nor primarily a movement of resistance against European penetration, though it later became that by a mixture of accident and necessity. It was yet another revolt of Muslims against a Muslim government which was held to be failing to uphold true Islam, with the additional grievance in this case that it was a government controlled by foreigners. (Like the Kharijites and the Wahhabis, the Mahdi accused his opponents of backsliding into unbelief and therefore proclaimed a *jihad* against them.) It can also be seen as the revolt of a specifically Sudanese Islam, in which the Sufi orders were predominant, against the dry, scholastic Islam of Egyptian officialdom, the tone of which was set by the *ulama* of al-Azhar.

Muhammad Ahmad himself was a Sufi by training; indeed, it

was his reputation and following as a Sufi *shaikh* that gave his claim to be the Mahdi — which he announced just as the thirteenth Muslim century was drawing to a close — its initial credibility. The claim, however, put him outside and above the Sufi orders, which he intended to supersede and abolish. He drew a parallel between his own career and that of the Prophet — calling at first on his followers to undertake the *hijra* (migration), by leaving the territory controlled by infidels and joining him. Only when the Egyptian administration, after consulting the *ulama*, attempted to arrest him for spreading false doctrine, did he resort to *jihad*, proclaiming: 'I am the Mahdi, the Successor of the Prophet of God. Cease to pay taxes to the infidel Turks and let everyone who finds a Turk kill him, for the Turks are infidels.'[12] He said that the obligation to lead the *jihad* against unbelievers had been laid on him by the Prophet in a vision. He also claimed direct descent from the Prophet on both sides of his family, and defended his claim to the Mahdiship against the scepticism of the *ulama* by asserting that the knowledge and power of God were not to be limited by the rules of men. Subsequently, his military victories were adduced as further proofs of his divine mission. He even claimed that the Prophet had appointed him four *khalifas* or successors, corresponding to the first four 'orthodox' caliphs — one of them being Sayyid al-Mahdi al-Sanusi, who prudently declined the honour.

Unlike earlier reformers, the Mahdi did not advocate the application of *ijtihad* (independent judgement) to the Koran and the Sunna, although he was in effect applying it. He simply by-passed this problem by claiming direct inspiration from God, so that his own proclamations superseded traditional jurisprudence. He thus came perilously close to usurping the Prophet's position as bearer of the final revelation, but avoided it — to the satisfaction of his followers, at least — by making the Prophet himself the intermediary, or at least the guarantor of the validity, of his own inspiration:

Information came from the Apostle of God that the angel of inspiration is with me from God to direct me and He has appointed him. So from this prophetic information I learnt that that with which God inspires me by means of the angel of inspiration, the Apostle of God would do, were he present.[13]

Such a claim would certainly have horrified Ibn Abdul-Wahhab. Yet the Mahdi's divine inspiration led him to a puritanical interpretation and rigorous enforcement of the law very much in the manner of the Wahhabis. He sought to stamp out Sudanese customs which appeared un-Islamic, such as the relative freedom of women. He ordained that women must be veiled, and any going about bare-headed were to be beaten. The same penalty was extended to parents of unveiled girls of five years of age. Women were forbidden to go into the market-places or public streets under penalty of 100 lashes. Anyone speaking to a strange woman, even to give or answer a greeting, was to fast for two months and to receive 100 lashes. Like the Wahhabis again, the Mahdi strictly forbade smoking as well as drinking. Indeed, he is said to have claimed that the Prophet had told him: 'The sin of the smoker of tobacco is heavier than that of the drinker of wine, for the drinker of wine is beaten with eighty lashes and the smoker of tobacco is beaten with 100 lashes.'[14]

The Mahdi died in 1885, at the height of his success. The state which he had founded survived for another thirteen years, but was finally crushed by the British under Kitchener. Like so many other movements whose initial preoccupation was with the internal condition of Islam, the Mahdiya found itself at the end in unequal confrontation with the expanding power of 'the West'. By 1900 it was this inequality itself that preoccupied most thinking Muslims, and the attempt to confront it was producing new kinds of political movement throughout the Muslim world.

CHAPTER FOUR

Western Impact and Muslim Responses

West's typhoon turned a Muslim into a true Muslim
The way waves of the ocean nourish a pearl
in the oyster ...

Muhammad Iqbal[1]

The Triumph of Christian Power

Conflict between Christian and Muslim powers was a more or
less permanent feature of the Middle Ages. Within a hundred
years of Muhammad's death Islam had conquered most of the
Christian lands in the Near East, the whole of North Africa, Spain,
and had penetrated into France. The defeat of the Arabs by Charles
Martel at Tours in AD 732 and his grandson Charlemagne's advance
into northern Spain marked the limit of Islam's expansion into
Western Europe, but two hundred years later the Arabs conquered
Sicily and (briefly) parts of Southern Italy. In the eleventh century
AD a Christian counter-attack began, with advances in Spain, Sicily
and most spectacularly in Syria and Palestine where the Crusader
Kingdom of Jerusalem lasted a hundred years. Thereafter, the
pattern was one of Muslim retreat in the west (where the last
foothold in Spain was lost in 1492) but renewed advance in the
east. Not only were the Crusaders from Western Europe expelled
from the Levant, but Muslim Turks gradually overran what was
left of the Byzantine Empire: Asia Minor, the Balkans and Greece.
In 1453 Constantinople fell and became Istanbul, the capital of

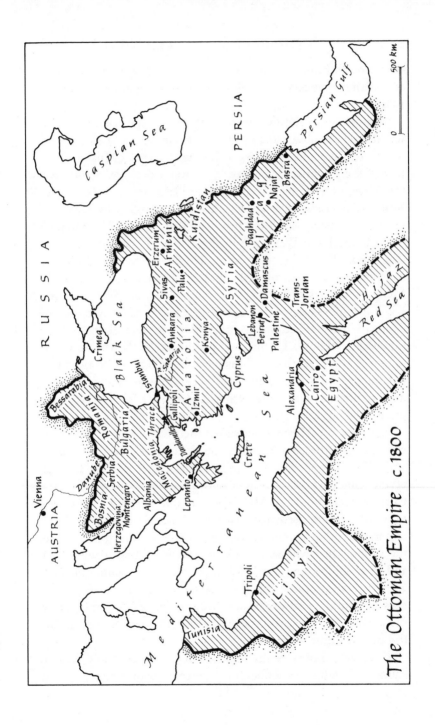

The Ottoman Empire c.1800

the Ottoman Empire. The Turks then pressed on north and west, conquering Hungary and halting only at the gates of Vienna in 1529.

Meanwhile, in the thirteenth century AD, the eastern Muslim world had been devastated by the Mongol invasions. (Christendom was saved from a like fate largely by the valour of a Muslim army, that of the Egyptian Mamluks, who won a decisive victory over the Mongols at Goliath's Well, near Gaza, in AD 1260.) Some Muslim historians have argued that Islam never fully recovered from this disaster, which 'destroyed all that the Muslims had built up in Central and West Asia in the course of six centuries', and that it was thus ultimately responsible for the relative decline of Muslim civilization compared with that of Christian Europe. 'The Mongols had destroyed irrigation works laboriously built in arid areas; they devastated schools, colleges, and libraries. On the one hand, the basis of economic prosperity had been destroyed; on the other, intellectual effort was paralysed. In the course of the following two centuries the Muslims did build up powerful states, but intellectually their effort had necessarily to be concentrated upon rediscovery and conservation of what was left, thus restricting originality and upsurge.'[2]

However, the Muslims converted their Mongol and Tatar conquerors, and thereby extended the domain of Islam to Russia, which lived for more than two centuries under the 'Tatar yoke' of the Golden Horde. It was only in 1480 that Ivan III, the Christian grand duke of Muscovy, was able to throw off Mongol overlordship and cease payment of tribute. Seventy years later, under the ruthlessly centralized leadership of Ivan the Terrible, the young Muscovite state took the offensive, first driving back and then subjugating the Muslim peoples to its south and east. In 1552 Ivan captured the Tatar capital of Kazan, on the Volga, thus inaugurating an expansionary drive that was to end only in the late nineteenth century when the Russian armies reached the frontiers of India and China.

The balance was beginning to shift in favour of Christian Europe, though in ways not always perceptible to contemporaries.

The discovery of America offered Christendom an area of vast resources in which to expand. The arrival of American treasure in Europe helped to stimulate the rise of capitalism and hence the organization of large-scale industry and technical innovation. And while Columbus sailed west in search of the Indies, Vasco da Gama actually reached India by sailing round Africa. The Portuguese became the first Christian power to challenge Muslim maritime supremacy in the Arabian Sea and the Indian Ocean. In 1509 they inflicted a crushing defeat on an alliance of Muslim fleets, including that of Egypt, near Diu on the west coast of India. According to a modern Muslim author, 'this was more serious a matter than even the Mongol holocaust, because it led to the economic strangulation of the Muslim East', and so ultimately 'to the enslavement of the entire Muslim world either directly or indirectly.' But, the same author adds, the contemporary Muslim world 'tragically seems never to have realized this. The vast and rich empires of the Ottomans, the Persians, the Uzbeks and the Mughuls took no remedial measures to save the situation.'[3] In fact, Portuguese supremacy did not last long, and the seventeenth century saw the rise of a new Muslim maritime empire in the Indian Ocean, that of Oman.

In the sixteenth century the Ottoman Sultans were less worried by Portuguese power than by Christian Spain's defeat of their Mediterranean sea power at Lepanto in 1572. On land they remained the masters of the entire Near East and the Balkans, and were taken seriously as a threat to central Europe until their second unsuccessful siege of Vienna, in 1683.

From then on we may say that the Muslim world was strategically on the defensive wherever it came into contact with Christian power. Vast as it was, stretching from the Atlantic to the Pacific and from the upper Nile to the Volga and the Danube, it found itself virtually encircled by the expanding powers of Christian Europe. From the north the Russians pushed steadily towards Central Asia, the Caucasus and the Black Sea, taking the Crimea from the Ottoman Empire in 1774 — the first mainly Muslim region it had lost. In the south and east the Portuguese were followed by Dutch, French and British whose presence, at first essentially maritime and commercial, began to assume a territorial aspect with the conquest of Bengal by the British East India Company in 1756–57. In the north-west the Habsburg Empire reconquered Hungary and part of what is now Yugoslavia.

A new era, in which European powers took for granted the availability of Muslim lands as both theatre and prize of intra-European rivalries, may be said to have opened with Napoleon Bonaparte's invasion of Egypt in 1798. Although this French occupation lasted only three years, it was defeated by British sea power, not by Muslim resistance. It revealed the helplessness both of the nominal ruler of Egypt – the Ottoman Sultan – and of the actual rulers, the Mamluk aristocracy (originally a military slave caste imported from distant lands). It also provided, for Arabic-speaking Muslims at least, the first opportunity of direct contact with post-Enlightenment European culture.

During the nineteenth century, the British completed the conquest of India, Burma and Malaysia, the Dutch of Indonesia, the Russians of the Caucasus and Turkestan. British power, expanding from India, established itself at Aden and in the Persian Gulf. Three times British troops invaded Afghanistan, while Russian troops on several occasions occupied parts of northern Iran. If these two countries remained independent, at least in name, it was only as a buffer zone between Russian and British expansion. In 1907 a secret agreement marked out British and Russian 'spheres of influence' in Iran and recognized British 'interests' in Afghanistan.

In Africa, France seized Algeria in 1830. Expanding from there and from former slave-trading settlements dotted along the Atlantic coast, she proceeded to subdue all the central Sahara and most of the Muslim-populated territory in West and Equatorial Africa – the main exception being the emirates of northern Nigeria, which fell under British 'protection'. France occupied Tunisia in 1881. Britain occupied Egypt in 1882, and in the 1890s moved up the Nile into the Sudan, crushing the state founded by the Mahdi. Spain expanded some historic footholds in Morocco and the Western Sahara, but the main part of Morocco came under French influence, culminating in a protectorate in 1912. On the southern fringes of the Muslim world, Germany took the Cameroons and Tanganyika, King Leopold of the Belgians carved out a personal empire in the Congo, and Britain helped herself to Zanzibar (which had become the centre of the Omani empire), Kenya and Uganda. Italy took Eritrea and divided Somaliland with Britain, while France got the strategically placed port of Djibouti, at the mouth of the Red Sea. Even the local Christian empire of Ethiopia joined in the scramble, subduing various neighbouring Muslim peoples, though it was itself to fall victim to a belated act of Italian imperialism in 1936. Before that, Italy had begun her conquest of Libya in 1911.

Algeria, Egypt, Tunisia, Sudan, Libya: all these Muslim countries were, at least in name, parts of the Ottoman Empire. During the same period the mainly Christian territories of the Ottoman Empire in Europe were one by one wrenched away from it: Montenegro, Bessarabia, Serbia, Greece, Rumania, Bosnia, Bulgaria, Macedonia; even predominantly Muslim Albania and Western Thrace. Within the Asiatic part of the Empire, demands for special status emanating from Christian minorities, such as Armenians and Lebanese Maronites, were supported by European powers. Crippled with debt and ever more arrogantly bullied by the great powers of the day, the Empire would probably not have survived so long had not Britain been anxious to keep the Russians away from the Mediterranean. To try and get away from this uncomfortable dependence on Britain, the Ottoman rulers cultivated an alliance with the rising power of Germany, which was to prove their undoing. In 1914, lured by visions of a historic revenge on Russia and a heroic liberation of the Turkish-speaking Muslim peoples from Russian domination, they entered a major European war on what turned out to be the wrong side. Russia was indeed defeated, but her allies, France and Britain, joined by Italy, Rumania, Greece and the United States, survived to win the war and to complete the dismemberment of the Ottoman Empire.

Those Muslim Arabs who rose in revolt against the Empire,

believing in British promises of an independent Arab state, were cruelly disillusioned: they found that Britain and France had secretly agreed to divide the Arab Middle East into spheres of influence. Britain occupied Iraq, Palestine and Transjordan, while France took Lebanon and Syria; and these arrangements were institutionalized under 'mandates' issued by the newly formed League of Nations, in which Christian states were the majority. A French general, arriving in Damascus, rode to the tomb of Saladin, the Muslim leader who had defeated the Crusaders 700 years before, and, knocking on the gates, proclaimed: 'Saladin, we have returned!'

In Turkey proper, Istanbul and the Straits were under Allied military and naval occupation. Greek troops occupied Eastern Thrace and Smyrna (Izmir) and marched towards the interior, while French and Italian forces occupied parts of the south. By 1920, when the moribund Ottoman government signed a treaty with the Allies, only the Anatolian hinterland was not under the direct control of a Christian power. Neighbouring Iran, whose neutrality had been violated by British, Russian and Ottoman forces, was in chaos, with Britain now the dominant presence since both the Russian and the Ottoman empires had collapsed. British influence was likewise paramount, though less directly applied, in Afghanistan and most of Arabia. There was scarcely such a thing left as a Muslim state not dominated by the Christian West.

The Muslim Dilemma

It is hard to see how a thinking Muslim of the early twentieth century could have looked at the events of the past 200 years as less than a historic catastrophe for the religion and the civilization to which he belonged. Islam was supposed to be the highest and final form of religion, comprehending and transcending all others. It was supposed to regulate not only relations between man and God but also those between man and man, thereby providing an ideal social system and the basis of a unique civilization. Of course it had never, after the first few decades, been perfect: the practice had always fallen short of the ideal. Injustice and warfare within the community of believers, the 'house of Islam', had never been completely abolished. Yet for many centuries the house of Islam had housed the most splendid and advanced of human civilizations, and it had been a house in any part of which any Muslim could feel at home. It had provided a fixed framework for his life and a kind of security, which contrasted with the insecurity of the 'house of war' — the outside world where unbelievers ruled and uncouth customs prevailed. Now, it seemed, the house of Islam had fallen, and the demons of the house of war were let loose throughout the Muslim world.

How could this happen? Only two answers were possible. Either the claims of Islam were false and the Christian or post-Christian West had finally come up with another system that was superior, or Islam had failed through not being true to itself. In the latter case, once the true Islam had been rediscovered and practised it could not fail to reassert its superiority, in the political domain as in others.

It is a remarkable testimony to the strength of Islam, to the hold that it maintained over the minds and emotions of its adherents even in the most adverse circumstances, that the first of these two answers has very seldom been openly propounded by any figure of note in any Muslim country. Many Muslims have been fascinated by modern Western civilization, and not a few have privately ceased believing in God or in the Koran as Word of God. But such people, when they sought to influence the ideas and behaviour of others in the Muslim world, have seldom if ever ventured to attack Islam as such. They have always preferred to claim that their ideas correspond to the true spirit of Islam, and that their opponents, while clinging to the letter, are ignoring or falsifying the spirit. In other words, even those who, privately or subconsciously, were persuaded by the first answer sought to convince others, and often themselves, that it was really a form of the second. If they found an aspect of Islam which seemed to have contributed to the political and military failures of Muslim peoples, they denounced it as not truly Islamic; if they found it desirable for Muslims to imitate some aspect of modern Western civilization, they proclaimed that aspect not only compatible with Islam but, if possible, fundamentally Islamic. The scientific method, human rights, democracy, socialism – these and many other apparently Western phenomena were found on investigation to have Islamic origins. If something worth having was not found in contemporary Muslim society, that was either because Muslims had misguidedly abandoned it or, at worst, because Islam, having somehow lost its natural qualities of 'originality and upsurge', had allowed another, inferior civilization to get in first with something it should have been able to think of for itself.

The most obvious effect on Islam of the rise of Western power was therefore to strengthen the reformist zeal, which, as we saw in the last chapter, was already sweeping through many Muslim societies in the eighteenth and nineteenth centuries. The inability of the Muslim world to mount effective resistance against Western expansion confirmed the thesis of the reformers, that Islam was decadent and needed to be restored to its pristine vigour and purity. But it also widened the range of opinion among reformers about the precise content of the reform to be undertaken. Which were the key aspects of Islam that had fallen into neglect and needed to be restored? The reformers of Islam, like those of Christianity in the sixteenth century, had had to justify their dissent from established tradition by claiming the right of original interpretation (*ijtihad*), and in so doing they opened the gate to diversity of interpretation. In Islam, however, the main emphasis was not on theology or spiritual authority, but on issues of public policy and political authority. So the result was the appearance, not of a multiplicity of religious sects but of schools of thought advocating different courses of action.

How should Islam respond to the challenge of the West? By being more truly itself. That answer was more or less unanimously given, but meant very little since there was no consensus on what Islam's true self consisted of. Beyond this, the responses given revolved around two key ideas:

1 Muslims must discover the sources of Western strength and tap them in order to strengthen their own society;
2 Muslims must unite in resistance to Western domination.

Some thinkers developed only one of these ideas while rejecting or ignoring the other. Others combined the two in various forms and various proportions. In practice, the idea of learning from the West proved easier to implement than that of unity and resistance. Yet the results generally fell short of what had been hoped. The Muslim world today is still far from having caught up with the Industrial North — the Christian or ex-Christian powers — in political, military or economic strength, and there is no consensus about the value of what it has learned from those powers, or about what, if anything, it still needs to learn. Also, the fact that some Muslims have learned more than others has introduced new and uncomfortable divisions into most Muslim societies.

Learning from the West: The Reform of the Ottoman Empire

The notion of the house of Islam as a single community of believers, whose members owed solidarity to one another in any conflict with outsiders, was of course far from new. It was indeed an essential element of Islam as preached by Muhammad. The Muslim masses of each succeeding age have felt an instinctive sympathy whenever they hear of fellow Muslims being attacked or oppressed by non-Muslims. But in practice, Muslim rulers had felt justified in ignoring such sentiments whenever there was tactical advantage to be gained from an alliance with non-Muslims in an inter-Muslim conflict. Even the great Abbasid caliph Harun al-Rashid, whose reign is remembered as a golden age of Islamic achievement, carried on a friendly correspondence with his Christian contemporary Charlemagne, at a time when the latter was engaged in hostilities against the Umayyad rulers of Spain.

(Later, in medieval Spain, alliances of Muslim princes with Christians, such as El Cid, against other Muslims, became quite commonplace.) Until at least the late eighteenth century the main Muslim states were more preoccupied by their conflicts with each other than by any general threat to Islam from outside. Even in the nineteenth century, expressions of solidarity were generally a matter of lip-service rather than statements of serious intent to take risks or make sacrifices where one's own interests were not directly threatened.

By contrast, curiosity about the secret of Western success and anxiety to profit from it were quite genuine. At first, the problem was assumed to be purely technical and military. From the 1730s the Ottoman government made a number of attempts to create a new army on European lines. A school of military engineering was briefly set up, with a Frenchman as director, and later a school of mathematics for naval officers. In 1798 a new Sultan, Selīm III, came to the throne and embarked on a wholesale and far-reaching reform of the army. Training schools were opened, in which the instructors were mainly French and in which the Italian and French languages were studied. Some of these schools had libraries of French books, 'mainly but not wholly technical.' Meanwhile, books on mathematics, navigation, geography and history were being translated into Turkish and printed on the first Turkish press, established under government patronage in the 1720s.[4]

Such reforms can be looked at in two ways: as an attempt to strengthen the community as a whole, or as an attempt to increase the power of the Sultan by bringing in foreigners and foreign ideas at the expense of the traditional elites — in this case particularly the Janissaries, who were the traditional military caste, and the *ulama*, who were the traditional intellectual elite and looked with deep suspicion on any ideas originating outside their own field of knowledge. These two groups had become closely connected over the centuries and together exercised an effective ideological hegemony over rest of Ottoman society. They were able to mobilize considerable popular support for their opposition to Selim's reforms, exploiting the discontent created by the Empire's economic decline. In 1807 Selim was deposed.

Meanwhile, in Egypt a strong ruler, governing in the Ottoman Sultan's name, had emerged from the chaos left behind by Bonaparte's invasion: Muhammad Ali Pasha. Egypt had tasted not only French military power but also the methodical efficiency of French administration. Muhammad Ali saw that Western techniques could help an ambitious ruler increase and consolidate his power. He massacred the Mamluks — the Egyptian equivalent of the Janissaries — and confiscated their lands. He created a modern army and navy, trained by French officers, and a relatively efficient, centralized system of administration and taxation, as well as the first newspaper in the Islamic world. He abolished the traditional tax-farming arrangements and regulated the system of *awqaf*, or religious endowments — thereby, whether intentionally or not, undermining both the system of Islamic schools and the social position of the *ulama*. Socially, economically and politically the *ulama* lost ground to a new elite, in which foreigners, including Europeans, were prominent, and knowledge of European languages and European affairs was highly valued.[5]

Neither Selim III nor Muhammad Ali was seeking to imitate the political institutions of Western Europe, or to import European philosophical principles or social and moral values. To an Egyptian student who told him he had studied civil administration in Paris, Muhammad Ali replied sternly: 'It is I who govern. Go to Cairo and translate military works.'[6] Yet this anecdote is double-edged: it illustrates what has become the perennial dilemma of the Muslim Westernizer. The student whose Western education has been arranged with a view to his translating military works, or managing an oil well, acquires an interest in Western civil administration, or Marxist theory, or sexual freedom and equality. To import Western techniques without being contaminated by Western 'values' has proved a persistently elusive goal.

The area of the Islamic world in which it was possible to ignore Western techniques was shrinking steadily. Certainly it was not possible in a place like Istanbul, which was the capital of a European empire and a focal point of European strategies. Selim III's successor, Mahmud II, shared his conviction that reform was essential, but waited patiently until pressure had built up to the point where the *ulama* and Janissaries were unable to cope with it. Their opposition taught him, moreover, that something more than a mere modernization of the army was needed. Only a much more far-reaching reform of government and society would enable the Empire to hold its own among the new European powers.

Beneath the surface the effects of Selim's reforms continued to work, as a new generation of Ottoman soldiers and diplomats grew up who spoke European languages and understood European ideas. At the same time, the Empire was confronted with the revolt of its Greek subjects (supported by Russia and Britain), which the Janissaries were unable to suppress, whereas Muhammad Ali's success in suppressing the Wahhabi revolt in Arabia was evidence of the value of reform. The community of believers was no longer strong enough in itself to maintain its hold over non-Muslim peoples; reform was essential if the Empire was to retain their loyalty. In this realization lay the germ of secularism: implicitly, in the minds of the reformers, the Ottoman state ceased to be identified with the community of believers and began to exist for the benefit of all its inhabitants equally, without distinction of creed. But they were never able to express this view unambiguously, for it involved too radical a break with traditional Islamic thought. Nor, it is fair to say, was there much of a response from the non-Muslim peoples of the Empire, who were caught between their own religious traditionalism on one side and the glittering vision of national independence on the other. It was to be a hundred years before a 'secular' state came into existence, and it did so on the ruins of an empire which had forfeited the loyalty not only of non-Muslims but also of non-Turks.

None the less, the scope of the Westernizing reforms introduced in the nineteenth century should not be underestimated. In 1826, choosing his moment carefully, Mahmud II 'destroyed an institution of five centuries' standing in a few hours of cannonfire.'[7] The Janissaries were disbanded and the *ulama* did not dare to protest. There followed half a century of reforms, known collectively as the Tanzīmāt (Reorganizations). A new army was created, whose officers had little or no contact with the *ulama*, and was used to impose the authority of the central government at least on the Asiatic parts of the Empire. (The African provinces remained largely autonomous, while the European ones became more and more so as a result of pressure from the Christian powers.) Schools were also established to train officers, doctors and civil servants. Educational missions were sent to Europe. An official newspaper was founded. Feudal land tenure was abolished, and the system of religious endowments reformed.

Besides opening a Military Academy, and sending military students to England, France, Prussia and Austria, Mahmud founded a School of Medicine, in which modern — i.e. Western — medical science was taught. The language of instruction was French. (Mahmud explained that the old Muslim books on medicine were written in Arabic and had not yet been translated into Turkish, whereas they had been translated into European languages, and 'the Europeans have been busy improving upon them for more than a hundred years.'[8]) At first, because of opposition from the *ulama*, dissection and autopsy were not allowed (they were said to be against Islam) and wax models were used instead. But later, at the request of the school's academic director (an Austrian), Mahmud's successor Abdul-Majīd authorized the use of human corpses. In 1847 an American visitor found the students carrying out autopsies in a routine manner and asked one of them if this was not contrary to his religion. The reply he received (in French) was: 'Well, sir, this is not the place to come looking for religion!'[9]

This anecdote shows that something was happening to Islam which was certainly not part of the reformers' intentions, but resulted from the misconceived opposition of the *ulama* to innovation of any sort. Instead of encompassing the totality of Ottoman state and society as it had formerly done, religion was coming to be seen as a particular aspect of life identified with a particular group of people who were losing the respect of the more dynamic

93

and adventurous elements in society by their unrealistic and petty conservatism.

The process had started more than a hundred years before, at the time of the introduction of the printing press: the *ulama* had at first been opposed to this, but were persuaded to authorize it *except for books on religious subjects*, thus implicitly setting religion apart from life in general and especially from anything modern. This became a more serious matter in the nineteenth century as the new intelligentsia began to absorb the European idea of progress. For the military, intellectual and administrative elites modernity and novelty came to seem positive values, whereas in Islam, as expounded by the *ulama*, they were negative ones. Thus, the advocates of progress were made to seem, and even to feel, 'bad Muslims'.

In fact the *ulama*, like most conservatives, were much more pragmatic than they made themselves out to be. Once any given change became irresistible they accommodated themselves to it and even made use of it; for instance, by Mahmud's time the ban on printed books on religious subjects had been quietly dropped. But they were always a step or two behind, and since they cast themselves as defenders of Islam they made Islam appear to be so, too.

Another example was their reaction to the rapidly spreading fashion for Western-style dress in Ottoman urban society — a fashion which Mahmud strongly encouraged. By sticking to their traditional costume the *ulama* emphasized the distinction between themselves and other social groups with whom they had previously been closely identified: army officers, state officials and intellectuals. They took on, for the first time, the appearance of a clergy.*

---

* The *ulama* did make one striking contribution to the general appearance of the Ottoman middle and upper classes in the nineteenth and early twentieth centuries. They dissuaded Mahmud from fitting out the army with peaked caps, on the ground that the peak would prevent the soldiers from touching the ground with their foreheads during prayer. He therefore had to fall back on the rimless fez, which became the characteristic Ottoman headgear.

Correspondingly, the Shari'a was no longer understood to mean the entire way of life of Muslim society, as regulated by the divine law in which the *ulama* were expert. It came instead to be thought of as a particular area of law — religious law — dealing mainly with family matters (marriage, divorce, inheritance), while other areas of life were regulated by secular laws. To some extent this had always been the case in practice, for the Sultan had regulated many matters by decree; this was held not to involve setting aside the Shari'a, but to be simply an exercise of judicial discretion within the limits set by it. Mahmud, however, went much further. He abolished the office of Sadrazam (Grand Vizier), through which his predecessors had exercised both spiritual and temporal authority, and set up two separate systems of courts. The 'Shari'a courts' came under the authority of the Shaikh-al-Islam, the official head of the *ulama*, who until then had been something like a Minister of Justice or Attorney-General. Now he began to seem more like the spiritual head of the Muslims, on a level with the Jewish Grand Rabbi and the Greek Orthodox Patriarch. Mahmud set up a separate council to deal with legal and judicial matters that fell *outside* the realm of the Shari'a, and promulgated what amounted to secular penal codes, defining the responsibilities of government officials and judges, and prescribing penalties for corruption.[10]

The reform process became more systematic under Mahmud's successor Abdul-Majid, who in 1839 issued a kind of charter. In the preamble to this it was made clear that the purpose of reform was not to destroy the Shari'a but to restore it. The Empire's decline was attributed to 'a disregard for the sacred code of laws and the regulations flowing therefrom.' The proposed remedy, however, was 'to seek by *new* [italics mine — E.M.] institutions to give to the provinces composing the Ottoman Empire the benefit of a good administration.' These new institutions would come under three headings:

1 The guarantees insuring to our subjects perfect security for life, honour, and fortune.

2 A regular system of assessing and levying taxes.

3 An equally regular system for the levying of troops and the duration of their service.[11]

The measures involved would apply equally to all the Sultan's subjects, whatever religion or sect, and their implementation would be guaranteed by a solemn compact of the Sultan, the *ulama* and the great men of the Empire. By implication (though how far this implication had been clearly thought out is doubtful) the Empire was going to be transformed into a secular nation, to which members of all religions would feel the same patriotic loyalty, without ever ceasing formally to be the embodiment of the *umma* — the community of Muslim believers.

In the next twenty or thirty years many practical steps were taken in this direction: central and local government were re-organized, conscription introduced, civil, criminal and commercial courts set up, new penal and commercial codes promulgated. In theory all these benefited Muslims and non-Muslims alike. But the benefit to the non-Muslims was much more direct and obvious. From the Muslim point of view the reforms were decidedly double-edged. By making government and taxation more efficient they increased the Sultan's power over his subjects, while by down-grading the Shari'a they removed the theoretical restraints on his authority. Moreover, the reforms were enacted under pressure from Christian powers who seemed intent either on breaking up the Empire, or on completely dominating its economy, or both, and for both purposes they were using the Christian minorities as a kind of Trojan horse. If the European powers wanted a reformed administration, it was apparently in order to use that administration more effectively for their own purposes, at the expense of the Muslim population.

For all their enthusiasm for West European ideas and institutions, the authors of the Tanzimat were not democrats. They were believers in enlightened despotism. At this time, after all, democracy was still far from being generally accepted in Western Europe itself. The demand for democracy and a constitution in the

96

Ottoman Empire was first formulated, not by the westernizing reformers of the Tanzimat but by their opponents. In 1859 a secret political organization was formed to advocate a 'genuine' application of the Shari'a — meaning, this time, the formation of an assembly representative of the people and a government directly responsible to the *umma*.[12] This current of thought later became known as the Young Ottoman movement, and in 1876 it succeeded in obtaining a constitution. European contemporaries were at first unsure whether to label it progressive or reactionary, since on the one hand it was opposing some of the measures of Westernization, which they believed essential if the Empire was to progress, while on the other it was appealing to principles of democracy and constitutional government which were generally recognized as progressive in a European context.

In fact, the contradictions were on both sides. Western liberals, then as now, had difficulty in realizing that their own principles were being violated when a pro-Western autocratic government imposed reforms on a Muslim country without considering or consulting the views of the people. At the same time, the Young Ottomans, while no doubt sincere Muslims and defenders of Islam, were presenting in Islamic terms some ideas which they themselves had derived from contact with the West. For instance, their leading thinker, Namık Kemal, laid great emphasis on the ideas of natural rights and popular sovereignty. He was the first in a long line of Muslim apologists who argued that these ideas are entirely compatible with Islam, are inherent in it, or even are superior in their Islamic form to the version expounded by Western writers. Whatever one thinks of the validity of these arguments, they cannot disguise the fact that in their modern form the ideas in question entered the Muslim world from the West.

Constitutional government, Kemal argued, was not an innovation or heresy for Muslims. It was an expression of the age-old Islamic principle of consensus, embodied in the saying attributed to Muhammad that 'my community will not agree upon an error.' Traditionally this had been taken to mean that a consensus among the *ulama* was the ultimate arbiter of any question about the correct interpretation of the Shari'a. But since the *ulama* themselves derive their authority, not from any divine nomination but simply from the respect of the community as a whole for their learning, it can be argued that in the last resort it is the consensus of that wider community, i.e. of the people, that is required. (An example often given is the spread of coffee-drinking in the Islamic world in the seventeenth century: the *ulama* 'almost unanimously took the view that coffee-drinking was unlawful and punishable with the same penalties as wine-drinking, and a number of persons were actually executed for indulging in this vicious practice.'[13] In spite of this, the prohibition was so generally ignored that in the end the *ulama* gave up the struggle, and today coffee is freely consumed by even the most die-hard conservative and the most rigorous 'fundamentalist'.)

The next step in the argument is that if the interpretation of the law ultimately depends on popular consensus, correct interpretation and good government are best obtained by consulting the people. A precedent for this was found in the ceremony of *bay'a*, in which each new caliph had been acclaimed, or acknowledged, by the people, or their representatives. Although in practice this had been very much a rubber-stamp procedure, its existence could be taken to imply that without popular recognition the caliphate was not valid. (In arguing thus, Islamic constitutionalists were unconsciously aping their Christian predecessors, who, in order to challenge the divine right of kings, had grafted a theory of popular sovereignty on to various half-remembered and ill-understood feudal traditions.) The Ottoman Sultans, according to Kemal, had inherited the political authority of the caliphs only by popular consent. In order to retain that consent they had to set up constitutional machinery for ascertaining the popular will. The decisions reached through this machinery, being decisions of the whole community, would not be tampering with the Shari'a but implementing it. As the equivalent Christian argument has it: *vox populi vox Dei* (the voice of the people is the voice of God).

Learning from the West: Muslims under Western Rule

While the leaders of the Ottoman Empire were struggling to avert its collapse by learning the secret of its rivals' strength, other Muslims were already living under the rule of those rivals and learning, willy-nilly, a great deal about their mentalities and methods. In few places did Muslims accept the imposition of Christian rule without a fight, but, as the nineteenth century wore on, it became increasingly clear that there was little prospect of successful military resistance. New generations grew up for whom foreign rule was an unchanging fact of life, whether they liked it or not. Many Muslims learned the languages of their new rulers, travelled to their home countries and took an interest in their internal debates. This experience generally sharpened the educated Muslim's awareness of the backwardness of his own society and the oppression under which his countrymen lived. He saw that this oppression was not simply a matter of non-Muslim rule: it was also internal to Muslim societies. Their traditional leaders had been incapable of defending them against the foreigner; now for the most part they were subservient to foreign rule, being anxious to preserve their own privileges. Often, indeed, the only aspects of foreign rule which they did oppose were those from which their people might have benefited. By discouraging their countrymen from pursuing Western education, they helped to maintain the society as a whole in a state of backwardness and subjection.

In almost every such territory, therefore, Muslim reformers arose who advocated the adoption — though always selective — of Western ideas and practices. I shall here give a very brief account of two such movements: one in British India, the other in the Muslim lands conquered by Russia.

SAYYID AHMAD KHAN AND THE REHABILITATION OF INDIAN MUSLIMS

In India the failure of the great revolt of 1857 — the Indian Mutiny — marked the beginning of a new historical phase. It was clear that British rule would continue for the foreseeable future. The Muslims, as the former ruling group, stood to lose more from this than the Hindus, to many of whom British rule offered new opportunities of employment and relative emancipation. The British held the Muslims mainly responsible for the revolt and consequently discriminated against them in various ways. But the Muslims also discriminated against themselves, at least in parts of India, by keeping their children away from British schools and so preventing them from qualifying for jobs in the administration.

Sayyid Ahmad Khan, descended on his father's side from generals and high officials of the Mogul court and on his mother's from merchants who prospered in the service of the British East India Company, set out, at first almost single-handedly, to rescue his fellow-Muslims from the blind alley to which continued British rule seemed to condemn them. He set himself a dual task: to convince the British that the Muslims were loyal subjects who could make a valuable contribution to the success of British India, and to convince the Muslims that they would gain much more by co-operating with the British and learning from them than they would by carrying on futile resistance or withdrawing into a sulk.

Sayyid Ahmad Khan was well aware of the Tanzimat in the Ottoman Empire and was influenced by some of his Ottoman contemporaries, particularly the Tunisian Khair al-Dīn Pasha who occupied a kind of middle position between the Tanzimat reformers and the Young Ottoman constitutionalists, arguing that freedom of expression, which had come in the wake of Western influences, should be used for revolutionizing the ideas and minds of Muslim peoples, but not going so far as to assert the sovereignty of the people. (He approved in principle of the Young Ottoman demand for an elected assembly, but thought it dangerous in fact.) Khair al-Din wanted the *ulama* to acquaint themselves with 'the facts' about the modern world, so that they could co-operate constructively with 'the men of State' in working out laws and policies that suited the times but were in agreement with the principles of the Shari'a.

But Sayyid Ahmad Khan despaired of the capacity of the *ulama* to do this, at any rate in India, and therefore took upon himself the burden of reinterpreting Islam to suit the conditions of his own day. He was one of the few modern Muslim reformers who were prepared, not merely to assert that a given set of policies was founded on a correct understanding of Islam, but to attempt to justify this by a wholesale and deliberate revision of traditional Islamic theology. He re-read the Koran in the light of nineteenth-century Western science, and concluded that there was no contradiction between the two. Revelation and natural law were identical: 'Islam is Nature, and Nature is Islam.' (This affirmation earned him and his followers the derisive sobriquet of *neicheriya*, or naturists.) He thus defended himself against the accusation that by promoting Western education he was undermining the bases of religious belief. On the contrary, he said, scientific discoveries only served to illuminate the Law of Nature, of which God was the author, and there could be no contradiction between His Word (the Koran) and His Work (the universe and its laws). Sayyid Ahmad thus aligned himself with the Mu'tazilites of early Islam (see Chapter 2, pp. 50–3), whom he also followed in challenging the orthodox view that the Koran is 'the eternal and uncreated Word of God'. This was one of a number of traditions that he attacked as being unsound, even though they were included in one or more of the six generally accepted collections of *hadith*. Relying heavily on the examples of Shah Waliullah and his son Shah Abdul-Aziz (he had known the latter in his youth), Sayyid Ahmad worked out principles of exegesis for interpreting the Koran, and principles of historical and textual criticism for judging the authenticity of the *hadith*.

It was perhaps unfortunate that such a bold modernizer of Islamic doctrine should also have been an advocate of unswerving political loyalty to Western (British) rule. This gave some Muslims the impression that religious modernism was a device for making the Muslim permanently subordinate to the West both politically and mentally, although in reality the object was to enable him to catch up with the West intellectually and so be in a better position to defend and advance his own culture. From a historical perspective, one can say that Sayyid Ahmad's modernism — his view that Islam has nothing to fear from scientific inquiry, that it can and must be adapted to new circumstances while remaining true to itself — was something of permanent value, which has since been very widely accepted, whereas his pro-British policies were related only to the specific political context of his time and place. Already by the time of his death in 1898 these policies were becoming anachronistic. There was no longer any real danger of a repetition of the events of 1857. The British were no longer discriminating against the Muslims, but if anything in favour of them because of 'Sir' Sayyid's success in holding them aloof from the incipient nationalism of the Indian National Congress. (His acceptance of a knighthood from Queen Victoria was an eloquent symbol of the role he played.) The effect was to deepen the isolation of the Muslims from their Hindu compatriots, who tended to see them as toadies of the British.

That perhaps did not worry Sir Sayyid unduly, since he considered that for a Muslim, membership of the community of believers was a nationality in itself, superseding 'all territorial and ancestral conventions'.* But there was an apparent inconsistency between this belief and his support for Britain when Britain was in conflict with a Muslim power such as the Ottoman Empire. By the end of his life this attitude had come close to isolating him even with the Indian Muslim middle-class intelligentsia.

THE 'JADID' MOVEMENT IN THE RUSSIAN EMPIRE[15]

The Muslims of the Volga basin, the Crimea, the Caucasus, the Kazakh steppes and Central Asia found themselves living, in the late nineteenth century, under the colonial rule of a power that had itself gone through the experience of 'Westernizing' reform. Russia, a weak and backward country on the eastern fringes of Europe, can be considered the first 'oriental' society to have felt the impact and the challenge of 'the West'; and Peter the Great, its ruler from 1682 to 1725, was surely the prototype of all the

---

* Though he also believed that the Hindu and Muslim 'nationalities' together composed 'the nation that lives in India'.[14]

Westernizing autocrats who were to mark the history of Asia and the Islamic world over the next three centuries. Even before his time Russia had been an expanding power, moving southwards down the Volga and the Don and eastwards across Siberia. But its success in becoming and remaining a great imperial power was clearly bound up with its absorption of Western techniques, institutions and culture.

In the nineteenth century, Muslims under Russian rule observed this example and sought to apply it to their own case. They sought to inculcate in their own societies the 'Western' virtues which Russian reformers had cultivated in the eighteenth century: 'enlightenment', the scientific method, positivism and faith in progress. Seeing Russia's success in undermining the Ottoman Empire through the cultivation of pan-Slavism they responded, as speakers of Turkish languages, by inventing pan-Turkism. At the same time Muslims under Russian rule were influenced by the Tanzimat and other events in the Ottoman Empire. Lacking opportunities of modern education in their own country, the Muslim intellectuals sent their children to study in Istanbul and Beirut, and even in Cairo and Medina. Turkish textbooks and, from 1873 onwards, newspapers, were brought into Russia in ever-increasing quantities and helped to develop a 'national' awareness among the Muslims.

The reform movement had religious, cultural, educational, and political objectives. On the religious level, it followed in the footsteps of so many other Islamic revival movements by condemning the servile copying of traditional authorities (*taqlid*) and claiming the right to free interpretation (*ijtihad*) of the Koran and the *hadith*. The first to voice this call in the Russian territories, around 1855, was a Tatar *alim* from Kazan, Shihab al-Din Marjani. Like many others, he called for a return to the pristine purity of Islam, but urged his fellow Muslims to study modern Western sources and to attend Russian schools, even though he himself knew no European language. (Sayyid Ahmad Khan similarly devoted his life to promoting English education without ever becoming fluent in English himself.) He succeeded in founding a school of reformist theologians, which became influential on both sides of the Russo-Ottoman frontier. They were known as advocates of *usūl-i jadīd* (new foundations or principles), or simply as *jadīds* (modernists). By 1905 their school of thought had become dominant among the Tatars, although in Turkestan (Central Asia) — parts of which were still ruled by Muslim emirs under Russian tutelage — the establishment remained rigidly conservative.

On the cultural front, the striking feature was the emergence of a new Muslim literature, modern both in its style and in its subject-matter, written by and for the emerging bourgeoisie. Its authors were openly partisan, arguing first for religious and educational reform and women's emancipation, then for equal rights with the Russians and finally in defence of the cultural and political autonomy of the Muslim peoples. Among them, the leading figure was Isma'il Bey Gasprinski, a Crimean Tatar, whose newspaper *Terjuman* ('Interpreter'), published from 1883 onwards in the Crimea, was for many years the most widely read and influential Muslim paper in the entire world. He called for the unity of the Turkish peoples of Russia under the spiritual leadership of Ottoman Turkey, and for a renewal of Muslim culture by contact with the West through both Russian and Turkish channels. For this purpose he developed and used in his paper a kind of Turkish lingua franca — a simplified form of Ottoman Turkish, purged of Arabic and Persian loan-words and supplemented with some words taken from Crimean Tatar. This was adopted in turn by other Muslim newspapers both in the Crimea and on the Volga, and even in Turkestan.

Gasprinski was also active on the education front, setting up model schools in which secular subjects were taught as well as the Koran. By 1916 there were more than 5,000 of these *jadīd* schools throughout Russia and the model had been copied also in Turkey, Iran, and even India. The general educational level of the Tatars developed very rapidly, and by the early twentieth century Kazan was rivalling Istanbul, Cairo and Beirut as one of the intellectual capitals of the Islamic world (though in Central Asia the overall literacy rate was still only 4 per cent in 1917).

All these reforms helped to revive the self-confidence of the Muslims and encouraged them to react politically against Russian rule. Until 1905, however, there were few who thought in terms of a direct and open struggle against Russia, as this seemed a hopeless and disastrous course. Like Sayyid Ahmad Khan again, and for many of the same reasons, Gasprinski argued that Islam had more to gain from peaceful coexistence and lasting co-operation between Russia and the Muslim world, than from a futile revanchist war. But Russia's defeat in 1905 by Japan—a non-Christian, Asiatic power—and the ensuing revolution, which shook the foundations of the Tsarist regime, gave some of the Muslims greater confidence. An extremist wing of the *jadids*, the Islahists (from Arabic *al-islah*, meaning reform), developed rapidly into a violently anti-Russian movement, imitating the strikes, the mass demonstrations and even the individual terrorism of the Russian revolutionaries. Soon Muslim socialist groups also made their appearance; they and the nationalists joined hands in a common struggle against both the Tsarist regime and the Muslim conservatives who preferred the status quo to any reform.

Muslims of the World, Unite!

THE OTTOMAN CALIPHATE

Belatedly, perhaps, in the second half of the nineteenth century, Muslims began to take seriously the idea that they should unite to resist the spread of European domination. Beleaguered Muslims, in India and Central Asia, looked about desperately for a Muslim power to which they could appeal for help. They fixed their hopes, somewhat pathetically it seems in retrospect, on the Sick Man of Europe—the Ottoman Empire. This was, in terms of territory and population, much the largest independent Muslim state still in existence, and its territories included the historic heartlands of Islam: the holy cities of Mecca, Medina and Jerusalem, and the successive centres of power and learning in the age of classical Islam—Damascus, Baghdad and Cairo.

The Ottoman Sultans, if anyone, could claim to have inherited the authority of the ancient caliphs. In fact they had begun to make this claim in the late eighteenth century, at the time of the loss of the Crimea. Their object was to present themselves as legitimate 'protectors' of Muslims under Russian rule at a time when Russia was demanding recognition as protector of Christians under Ottoman rule. But they did not take it up seriously until the 1860s and 1870s, when Sultan Abdul-Azīz was receiving appeals for help from Central Asian Muslim rulers whose lands were being conquered by the Russians. In 1876 the claim was enshrined in the new Ottoman constitution: 'His Majesty the Sultan is, in his capacity of Supreme Caliph, the protector of the Muslim religion.'

The promulgation of the constitution was followed immediately by a series of disasters for the Empire. In 1877 Russian armies overran the Balkans, reached Istanbul, and forced Sultan Abdul-Hamīd II to accept a humiliating treaty, which amounted to a virtual abandonment of the remaining Ottoman territories in Europe as well as concessions at the eastern end of the Black Sea. This treaty was then revoked because it was seen as a threat to British and other Western European interests (!) and in 1878 a scarcely less humiliating settlement was dictated by a congress of European powers meeting in Berlin. Britain took Cyprus from the Ottoman Empire by way of compensation for Russian gains elswhere; France was given a free hand in Tunisia, which she proceeded to occupy in 1881; and in 1882 Britain occupied Egypt.

For the first time Muslims in most parts of the Empire felt themselves directly endangered by European power. The very survival of the *umma* — the community of believers — now seemed threatened. So, as Islam celebrated its thirteenth centennial (in AD 1882), Muslims both inside and outside the Empire were looking to the Sultan-Caliph for leadership. Clearly half a century of reforms had failed either to secure the loyalty of his non-Muslim subjects or to appease the European powers. Even Britain, which had for so long shored up the Empire as a bulwark against Russia, seemed now to have acquiesced in its dissolution and to be joining in the scramble for the pickings.

Sultan Abdul-Hamid, who reigned from 1876 to 1909, has conventionally been depicted variously as a reactionary despot, cynically manipulating religious feelings in pursuit of an imperial fantasy, or as 'a terrified animal, fighting back blindly and ferociously against forces that he could not understand',[16] and/or an unwitting tool of German imperial expansion. But while it is certainly true that atrocities were committed against non-Muslims during his reign (the worst being the massacres of Armenians in 1894–95), and also that his policies ultimately failed, it is only fair to say that in basing those policies on Islam, or at least on an appeal to pan-Islamic solidarity, he was responding to a genuine, widespread and largely spontaneous current of Muslim feeling among the lower classes, with whom he communicated through Sufi orders, as well as more conventional channels. His reign was later dubbed 'the Hamidian despotism' by the Arab nationalist historian George Antonius, but contemporary sources yield very little evidence of Arab opposition whereas there is substantial evidence of both Arab and Turkish support, especially in the earlier years of the reign.

It is also wrong to say that Abdul-Hamid 'threw away the constitution'.[17] Although he prorogued the National Assembly for more than thirty years and persecuted the Young Ottoman leaders, he did so by virtue of powers that the constitution gave him. In effect, he exploited the defence-of-Islam element in Young Ottoman thought to suppress the liberal-democratic element. Nor was he a systematic opponent of all forms of Westernization. Indeed, he carried on the Tanzimat tradition of importing innovations from the West, which increased the efficiency of the state and so his own power over his subjects. In his time, for instance, more than 30,000 kilometres of telegraph lines were constructed, 'extending even to remote corners of the Hejaz and Yemen.'[18] But in the realm of ideas he did encourage a return to traditional interpretations of Islam and a refutation of modernism in all its forms. He also encouraged and patronized some of the Sufi orders. One very old Islamic idea was revived and tirelessly propagated: the idea that the caliph was the actual or potential ruler of Muslims everywhere. 'The caliphate was not merely a spiritual power; it was a state. Islam was not merely a religion; it was a nationality, a political community, a civilization. The cause of decline was not only the loss of unity but also the penetration of secular ideas from the outside world.'[19]

In a sense Abdul-Hamid was simply reverting to the reformism of the earlier part of the century: that of Selim III, or of Muhammad Ali in Egypt. Like them, but perhaps with a clearer idea of what was at stake, he was trying to import Western techniques and material goods while sticking to traditional Islamic values. Even the *ulama* in his time admitted the desirability of taking over 'the material aspect' of European civilization — 'those things ranging from sewing machines to railroads and battleships' — and issued *fatwas* (legal rulings) to allow such goods into the country, while arguing that on the 'spiritual' side Muslim society had nothing to learn from the West.[20] The period was, in fact, one when Western material civilization in all its forms was pouring into the Ottoman Empire, and many ideas and customs were coming with it. Only the overtly political ideas were seriously repressed by the regime, and the effect of this was if anything to increase interest in them among the intelligentsia.

Abdul-Hamid's pan-Islamic ideas touched an emotional chord, but achieved at best only a brief postponement of the Empire's dissolution. This was because they had little substance to them. In reality he had neither the ability nor the will to lead the Muslim *umma* in a *jihad* against Western domination. Behind the rhetoric, he was himself as much dependent on European powers as his predecessors, the main difference being that British advice, influence and capital were partly replaced by German. Foreign control of the Empire's economy increased during his reign through the establishment of the international financial corporation known as the Administration of the Ottoman Public Debt, which administered the state finances for the benefit of the state's creditors, and through the increased flow of foreign capital into public works projects, particularly railways, of which the Berlin-to-Baghdad (via Istanbul) was the most famous while the Hijaz (designed to make the Mecca pilgrimage more widely accessible) was the most 'Islamic'. (Both, in fact, helped to open up remote districts, hitherto beyond the reach of Westernizing change.) 'Everything of economic importance (banking, large-scale trade, the construction of railways, harbours, irrigation works, bridges, mines, etc.) was financed and carried on by foreigners.'[21]

THE 'SAGE OF THE EAST'

One of those who propagated Abdul-Hamid's claim to the caliphate and the leadership of all Muslims, with rather too much zeal for the Sultan's own comfort, was Sayyid Jamāl al-Dīn 'al-Afghānī', known in Arabic literature as the Sage of the East. He was probably the first Muslim to realize clearly that 'the entire Islamic world, not just this or that part of it, was threatened; and by the West as a powerful, dynamic entity'; and the first 'to use the concepts "Islam" and "the West" as connoting correlative — and of course antagonistic — historical phenomena.'[22] He is one of the most genuinely pan-Islamic figures in modern history, both in his life and in his ideas; and his influence on subsequent political movements in the Muslim world — both those of Islamic revival and those of nationalism — has been considerable. Yet he is a complex and enigmatic figure, who does not lend himself to simple categorization. He can be seen as a last, forlorn defender of the old house of Islam, trying desperately to organize resistance against the inrush of Western civilization, but ignored or betrayed by Muslim rulers who were themselves under the spell of the enemy. Or he can be seen as one of the great modernizers, seeking to discover the sources of Western strength and urging his fellow-Muslims to strengthen their own civilization by learning from the West's example. Or again it has been argued that he was not really a Muslim in the traditional sense at all, but a man imbued with secular concepts learnt from the West, for whom Islam was an instrument rather than an end in itself.

Although Jamal al-Din always described himself in later life as an Afghan, it has now been established beyond doubt that he was in fact born in Iran, in 1838–39, and brought up there as a Shi'ite.

Shi'a Islam too had been shaken by revival movements in the late eighteenth and early nineteenth century, and one of these, that of the 'Shaikhis' — followers of Shaikh Ahmad Ahsa'i (1753–1826) — appears to have had a definite influence on Jamal al-Din's thought. The Shaikhis stressed the philosophical and mystical aspects of Shi'ism and argued that the Koran encompassed many different levels of meaning. They also maintained that, in the absence of the Twelfth Imam (see p. 45), there is always in the world a perfect Shi'i who can guide men in right ideas and action: the ideal guide of the age. Both these ideas were later used by Jamal al-Din to argue for a renovation of Islam.

He may also have been influenced by 'Babism', a Messianic movement which swept through Iran in the 1840s and 1850s. Its leader, Ali Muhammad of Shiraz, declared himself to be the *Bāb*, or gate, to the Twelfth Imam himself, bringing a new religious dispensation that superseded the law and teachings of the Koran. Babism was 'somewhat equalitarian regarding social classes and the sexes, favorable to economic enterprise, and in general more in tune with the demands of modern society than the traditional religion.' Probably its popularity was 'tied to the economic and social dislocations brought by the early Western impact in Iran.'[23] (The Baha'i religion, which is non-Muslim, developed out of Babism in the 1860s. It has been the object of intense hostility from the *ulama* because it claims to be a new revelation, coming after and superseding the Koran, and because its founders were Muslims who thereby apostasized from Islam — a capital offence in traditional Islamic law.) Jamal al-Din himself was certainly not a Babi, but he may have been influenced by the political activism of the Babis and their bold reassertion of the link between the state of Muslim society and the quality of Islam as a religion.

As an adolescent Jamal al-Din studied at the Shi'ite holy city of Najaf, in Iraq. He then spent some years in India. After a further series of ill-documented wanderings, including a trip to Mecca and possibly also to Istanbul, he somehow established himself in the mid-1860s as a senior adviser to the ruler of Afghanistan whom he encouraged to oppose British influence and rely on Russian support. In 1868 he was expelled from Afghanistan after the victory of the pro-British claimant to the throne. He then went to Istanbul, where he impressed the reformers of the late Tanzimat period as a man of traditional Islamic learning who was nonetheless enthusiastic about the need for educational reform and scientific thought. In 1870 he made a speech at the opening of a new university in Istanbul urging the Islamic *milla* (people or nation) to study all branches of science and follow the example of 'the civilized nations', i.e. the West. But later in the same year he went too far, giving a lecture in which he compared prophecy with philosophy as 'the noblest crafts'. Even though he concluded that prophecy was superior this was considered akin to blasphemy and was seized on by the *ulama*, who were conducting a campaign against the university and its director.

Jamal al-Din was expelled from Istanbul and went to Egypt, where he lived throughout the 1870s, attracting a circle of fervent disciples and involving himself in nationalist agitation against European influence. Expelled from there too in 1879, he returned for three years to India, where he attracted attention principally by his vigorous polemical attacks on the 'naturism' of Sayyid Ahmad Khan. He then moved to Europe and edited an Arabic newspaper in Paris, which called for Muslim unity and was widely distributed in the Muslim world. Cultivated by the British Arabophile, Wilfrid Scawen Blunt, in the mid-1880s he entertained hopes of persuading Britain to evacuate Egypt and adopt a conciliatory policy towards Islam in general. Despairing of this, he returned to his native Iran and then went on to Russia. For several years he busied himself with trying to promote good relations between Iran and Russia, in order to resist the growth of British influence in Iran.

Iran's history in the nineteenth century had been in some ways similar to that of the Ottoman Empire on a smaller scale. Like Turkey, Iran found herself caught between Russia and Britain. Russia's interest was primarily in southward territorial expansion, Britain's in staving off the Russian threat to India while cornering the Iranian market for British trade. In 1828, by the treaty of

Turkomanchai, Russia imposed a fine of twenty million roubles on Iran for attempting to reconquer what had been her own territory in Azerbaijan (west of the Caspian Sea). Russia was by then already in possession of northern Azerbaijan and was trying to extend her empire further south. Tabriz, the capital of southern Azerbaijan, was occupied as a security for payment of reparations. To pay the Russians, Iran had to borrow elsewhere.

As in the Ottoman Empire, borrowing money from the West went along with attempts to strengthen the Iranian state through Westernizing reforms and technical innovations. During the long reign of Nāsir al-Dīn Shah (1848–96) these policies were pursued somewhat inconsistently, mainly under two of his chief ministers: Amīr-i Kabīr (1848–51) and Mirza Husain Khan Sipahsalar (1870–73). The former established a Polytechnic College in Tehran, with departments of medicine, mining, engineering and military sciences. The latter established the cabinet system, reorganized the army and provincial administration, and persuaded the Shah to undertake the first of three journeys to Europe 'for the purpose of observing the European way of life in order that His Majesty may introduce more benefits for the people of Persia.' After each of these visits a number of Western innovations appeared in Iran.[24]

But the reforms were less far-reaching than in Turkey, whereas the mortgaging of Iran's economy to foreign capitalists, through the granting of concessions and monopolies, went even further. Iranians repeatedly demonstrated their hostility to this foreign control, and in these protests the Shi'ite *ulama* often played a leading part—in contrast to their Sunni counterparts in the Ottoman Empire, who after 1826 were wholly subservient to the government in political matters and spoke up only to oppose certain social and educational reforms.

By the late 1880s the ageing Shah Nasir al-Din had become hostile to any kind of reform or Westernization, but his need for cash made him willing to grant larger and larger concessions to British businessmen. By 1890 Jamal al-Din had lost hope of reversing this policy and began actively fomenting opposition to the

Shah and his government. This activity earned him yet another expulsion, a particularly unceremonious one. In January 1891 he was seized from a shrine where he had taken sanctuary, roughed up and forced to ride in chains through the mountain snows to the Ottoman border. But from Iraq (then part of the Ottoman Empire) he continued his agitation, and helped to forge the alliance of radical reformers and Shi'ite *ulama* which led the great tobacco protest of 1891–92. This movement was directed against all the Shah's many economic concessions to foreigners, but focused especially on the granting to a British subject of a monopoly on the purchase, sale and export of all Iranian tobacco. Jamal al-Din apparently played a part in persuading the most respected leader of the Shi'ite *ulama*, Hājji Mirzā Hasan Shīrāzī, who was living in Iraq, to involve himself in the movement. After unsuccessfully urging the Shah to change his policies, Shirazi, in December 1891, issued a *fatwa* that read: 'In the name of God, the Merciful, the Forgiving, Today the use of *tonbaku* and tobacco in any form is reckoned as war against the Imam of the Age (may God hasten his Glad Advent!).' The success of the boycott that followed 'amazed outside observers, and the British Foreign Office finally began to see that it was hopeless to try to save the concession.'[25] The tobacco concession was finally cancelled in 1892, but organized opposition to the government continued, culminating in the Iranian Constitutional Revolution of 1905–11. The alliance of the *ulama* with nationalists and radicals against a monarchy associated with foreign powers has been a recurrent theme of Iranian history ever since.

Jamal al-Din's last years, from 1892 to 1897, were spent in Istanbul, to which he was invited by Abdul-Hamid II. It appears, however, that the invitation was aimed more at keeping him under control than at making use of his services or listening to his advice. He was not allowed to publish anything during the whole of his stay, though he was encouraged to write letters to the Shi'ite *ulama* urging them to support the Sultan's claims to the caliphate. (There was little or no response, which is not surprising since these claims were clearly incompatible with Shi'ite beliefs.) His last achievement, as inspirer if not conspirator, was the assassination of Nasir al-Din Shah in 1896 by one of Jamal al-Din's devoted followers. After unsuccessful attempts by the Iranian government to obtain his extradition, Jamal al-Din died of cancer in Istanbul in 1897.

How, then, should one describe Jamal al-Din? In later life he liked to pose as a champion of orthodoxy, a reputation that was strengthened posthumously by the fact that his best-known written work was an attack on 'materialism', which lumped together under that name Western rationalists from Democritus to Darwin and various well-known deviations in Islam. It was written in Persian and first published in India in 1881 as *The Truth about the Neicheri sect and an Explanation of the Neicheris*, but later more widely distributed in Arabic translation under the title *Refutation of the Materialists*. Its main target, though it does not mention him by name, was clearly Sayyid Ahmad Khan, whose followers were known to their opponents as 'Neicheris', and whom Jamal al-Din attacked more directly in a series of articles published during the same stay in India. He poured scorn on Ahmad Khan both for his attempt at rationalist interpretation of the Koran and for his promotion of British education among Indian Muslims.

Yet it is clear from his other writings that Jamal al-Din was very far from being a traditionalist. Though he presented himself as an *alim* — a man learned in the law — and couched his arguments in traditional religious phraseology, the burden of them was often precisely the need for Islam to learn from the West in order to compete with it. He devoted a lot of time and energy to proving that scientific study, which had been such a crucial element in Western progress, was in no way contrary to Islam, and indeed that it was an essential feature of Islamic civilization, whose loss was the main cause of Islam's latter-day decadence. In fact, he seems at times so thoroughgoing a modernist that the venom of his attack on Sayyid Ahmad Khan is hard to understand. The explanation of it is probably political; he was so determined to discredit Sayyid Ahmad's pro-British views that he deemed it essential to attack their philosophical base as well and to make out that Sayyid Ahmad was undermining the foundations of Islam itself.

Actually a case can easily be made for thinking that Jamal al-Din was the more secular-minded of the two. Even his arguments in defence of religion have a secular ring to them: he seeks to prove its social utility rather than to affirm his own faith. Moreover, in some of his articles written in India we find him appealing to Indian unity rather than to pan-Islamic sentiment and even asserting that unity of language is a more durable basis for a nation than unity of religion. And in an exchange with the French philosopher Ernest Renan he readily concedes that Islam, like other religions, has been an impediment to scientific progress, seeking only to rebut the charge that Islam is worse than other religions or that the Arabs as a race are especially to blame!

Jamal al-Din al-Afghani is thus an example of three types of Muslim response to the West: the defensive call to arms, the eager attempt to learn the secret of Western strength, and the internalization of Western secular modes of thought. No doubt this explains the great prestige he has continued to enjoy in the twentieth century in many parts of the Arab and Muslim worlds, among people of widely divergent political opinions — a prestige going well beyond his influence during his lifetime. He was a man of traditional learning, appealing in traditional terms to believers and urging them to resist the onslaught of unbelievers. He was a would-be reformer who wanted Islam to meet the challenge of the West by learning from its example. And yet Islam as such seems not to have been his main interest. It has even been questioned whether in his heart he was a believer at all. Certainly he was quite prepared to dissemble aspects of his life and ideas for political purposes. For instance, he succeeded in convincing the world that he came from Afghanistan and had been educated as a Sunni, which enabled him to be taken seriously as an *alim* by other Sunnis throughout the Muslim world.

The significance of this is worth stressing. Afghani was not *converted* to Sunnism. He did not repudiate or denounce the Shi'a. On the contrary, as we have seen, he actively supported and encouraged the Shi'ite *ulama* of Iran in their opposition to Nasir al-Din's foreign concessions. Nor did he bother himself with seeking a doctrinal reconciliation between Sunnis and Shi'ites. He simply ignored the distinction, which was to him of no interest, but took pains to ensure that he was associated with the mainstream branch of Islam so that he could reach a wider audience.

The consistent thread in all Afghani's activities and writings is not Islam as such but anti-imperialism. He was a champion of Asian and African peoples confronted by European imperialism in its most dynamic age. Islam was what these peoples had in common: a sense of shared destiny, and also a means of communication, enabling Afghani to migrate from one to the other preaching his message and making himself understood — or being accepted, at least, as a member of the community with a right to be heard.

It is difficult to describe Afghani as a nationalist, since he disguised his own national origin and took little account of national frontiers. Certainly he was not a socialist — he had little to say on economic or social questions. Yet his outlook resembled that of many socialists in setting movements of national liberation in an internationalist perspective. Afghani is the intellectual ancestor of many of the 'progressive' nationalist leaders of what came in the mid-twentieth century to be known as the Third World: Sukarno, Nasser, Ben Bella, etc. He is a hero for the nationalists of the Muslim world, and a villain for those who regard nationalism as a poison of European origin which has done the Muslim world only harm. The leader of this latter school of thought, Professor Elie Kedourie (himself by origin an Iraqi Jew), has in fact devoted a short book to arguing that neither Afghani nor his most prominent disciple, the Egyptian Muhammad Abduh, can be regarded as orthodox Muslims.* Yet while it is clear that Afghani's personal beliefs were different from those he publicly affected, it seems arbitrary to assert that whatever was new in his outlook derived from Western or European models. That Afghani was interested in and influenced by some Western ideas is undeniable. But there is no evidence that he was inspired by any European ideology in his reaction to imperialism.

* *Afghani and 'Abduh* (London, 1966).

It is probable that he acquired his strong and consistent anti-British feelings as a result of living in India during and immediately after the Mutiny of 1857, in which Muslims played a primary role and after which they suffered discrimination from the British authorities. Sayyid Ahmad Khan reacted to this by trying to prove that British suspicions of Muslim loyalties were unjustified. Afghani reacted in the opposite way, by seeking to broaden the base of anti-British resistance — both in India itself, where he sought to encourage a nationalism cutting across religious divisions, and elsewhere, where he advocated a pan-Islamic response to expanding British power. (Another way in which he resembled later nationalist leaders was his willingness to play off rival imperial powers which posed a less immediate threat, such as France and Russia, against the one which he saw as the primary threat, namely Great Britain.)

The very fact that Afghani chose to concentrate mainly on the Islamic rather than the national dimension makes it unlikely that European nationalism was the primary influence on his thinking. This suggests that, although later nationalists in Muslim countries came to adopt a much more extensive vocabulary of Western origin, together with some Western notions about what exactly a nation is, the development of nationalism in those countries was not a purely artificial import, but a natural reaction to foreign penetration. It also suggests that Islam provided a ready-made conceptual framework for such a reaction. Afghani, whatever his precise metaphysical beliefs, was an authentic Muslim in the sense of being a product and an exponent of Muslim culture. Being a man of exceptional intelligence and breadth of outlook (from which his vanity and mendacity should not distract us) he was ahead of his time. But his example showed that Muslim culture was capable of reacting to Western penetration in its own way. It could not ignore the impact of the West, but nor would it simply be effaced by Western culture. The history of Islam would develop. It would not come to an end.

PART TWO

Islam, State and Nation in the Twentieth Century: Six Case Studies

In the twentieth century this question has been explicitly at the head of the Islamic political agenda. The Islamic world, like the rest of the 'Third World', has been struggling to free itself from Western political and economic domination, to redefine its own identity and to formulate its own response to Western ideas. In the process a great number of new Muslim states have come into being, and the few old ones that survived have mostly been transformed almost beyond recognition. Nearly all the founders and developers of these states have been inspired by some form of nationalism. In some cases it has been an explicitly secular nationalism, which separates religion from the state. More often — indeed, so long as the primary objective was a *united* national movement against Western domination, always — it has been a nationalism including a call for the defence of Islam against non-Muslim aggression. Many of the followers of such movements have understood this call as a pledge to restore the traditional Islamic order, but that has usually not been what the nationalist leaders meant. In the first place, it is questionable whether nationalism, once it becomes an articulate political doctrine rather than a simple gut reaction to foreign interference, is compatible with Islam as traditionally understood. The Arabic words used in most Islamic languages for nation — *milla* and *umma* — have historically meant 'people' or 'community', and in most cases the community in question has been defined by religious criteria. The community to which Muslims belong is the *umma* founded by Muhammad, and although there have been many different, often rival, Muslim states, each of them presented itself within its jurisdiction as the embodiment of this community of believers. The idea of a nation-state based on ethnic, linguistic or geographical criteria cuts across that notion, especially of course when it includes non-Muslims. Almost all the new Muslim nation-states, therefore, have had some difficulty in defining themselves, both in relation to the worldwide *umma* of Muslims and in relation to their own non-Muslim citizens.

Secondly, a Muslim state is understood by most Muslims to mean a state governed, at least in theory, by the Islamic law, the Shari'a. In practice, as we have seen, Muslim rulers had allowed themselves a very wide discretion in enforcing the Shari'a and in legislating for areas of public life where it did not seem to apply, and the *ulama*, by and large, had sanctioned this. But that was precisely what many of the Islamic reformers felt had been wrong with traditional Muslim society and the root cause of its political decline. The Islamic order they wanted to restore was not, strictly speaking, the traditional one, but an 'authentic' one, which they believed to have been that of the Prophet and his Companions.

In most Muslim countries, by the time national independence was achieved, the traditional way of life had already been thoroughly disrupted. It was not possible simply to go back to the day before Western domination arrived (even if such a day could be precisely identified) and carry on. Whatever happened was going to be a new stage in Islamic history. Many people, particularly among the elites who had received some Western education, believed that some of the Westernizing changes that had occurred were beneficial and could be incorporated into the new Islamic order. Others believed that all Western influence should be rooted out, along with other sources of corruption; that the new society should follow the law as laid down in the Koran and the Sunna much more rigorously than the old.

The question then arose: what *is* Islam? To that question there are many answers, so that the really crucial question is: whose answer is authoritative? Is it the ruler, who holds power by God's grace? But rulers also fall from power and are replaced by others with different opinions. Does Islam change with every coup d'état? Surely not. Then is it the *ulama* — those who have devoted their lives to studying Islam and its law? Many believe so, particularly among ... the *ulama* themselves. But are the *ulama* infallible, even when they all say the same thing? The example of the ban on coffee (see p. 98) suggests that they are not; and anyway infallibility is an attribute of God. To attribute it to a group of human beings, even the wisest, may involve the cardinal sin of *shirk* — associating others with God. True, the Prophet is supposed to have said that 'my community will not agree upon an error.' But was that not a way of saying that every Muslim must use his own intelligence and follow his own conscience, since God's guidance is available equally to all, and that in the last resort the authority of the *ulama* depends on the approval of the people? Is it then for the people to decide what is Islam? But the people are uneducated and ignorant. They may include non-Muslims. Even if formal adherents of other faiths are excluded, how can we know, in these corrupt days, that nominal Muslims have not, in fact, been seduced by communism or some other atheist philosophy? Would Islam really be safe in the hands of the people, without some guidance and control? But then, who should choose the guides and controllers? So the argument goes on, and it is never likely to be resolved to everyone's satisfaction.

Every Muslim state has somehow to define the role that Islam plays in it, and a modern Muslim state has either to choose between Islam and nationalism or to find some synthesis of the two. The 'politics of Islam' in the twentieth century is essentially a quest for solutions to these two problems. I have not attempted in this book to follow the argument in every part of the Muslim world. Instead I have chosen six areas, which together make up most of Islam's historic heartland, and in each of which the problems have been posed in a different form. The first is Turkey, which took the radical and surprising decision in the 1920s to be a pure nation-state and not an Islamic state at all. I shall try to show how this decision came to be taken, what it was supposed to mean, and what it has meant for the Turkish people in practice.

Secondly, I shall describe the formation and development of Saudi Arabia, which constitutes the opposite end of the spectrum: a state founded on purely Islamic principles, in an area where contact with the West had been minimal and therefore the need for a nationalist doctrine was not felt. But it is now so heavily involved with the West, economically and culturally, that the definition of its Islamic identity has become a problem almost comparable to that of the Ottoman Empire in the nineteenth century. Then I shall turn to Pakistan, a new nation founded by and for the Muslims of India, a nation whose problems in defining Islam are also problems in defining itself. Next will come the Arab states of the Levant and the Nile valley, where the dominant political doctrine has been Arab nationalism, which claims Islam as the national religion of the Arabs. Then Iran, where a national revolution, carried out in the name of Islam, has had profound implications for the rest of the Muslim world. Finally, I shall look at an area that remains under 'Western' rule, and try to disentangle the strands of national and religious feeling which keep alive a separate 'Muslim' identity within the Soviet Union.

First Turkey, then; but before we can properly speak of 'Turkey' as such we must complete the story of the decline and fall of the Ottoman Empire. We left it in Chapter 4 under the somewhat spuriously 'Islamic' rule of Sultan Abdul-Hamid, experiencing more and more rapid economic penetration by West European powers. The scene is set at the bedside of the Sick Man of Europe.

CHAPTER FIVE

Turkey — Muslim Nation, 'Secular' State

> You are aware that by the terms of the Constitution equality of
> Mussulman and Ghiaur was affirmed but you one and all know
> and feel that this is an unrealizable ideal.
>
> *Talât Bey, speech to a 'secret conclave'*
> *of the Salonika Committee of Union*
> *and Progress, August 1910*[1]

Ottomanism, Turkism and Islam (1908–21)

In 1908 the personal rule of Sultan Abdul-Hamid came to an end
when army officers in the remaining European provinces of the
Empire rebelled and forced him to reactivate the constitution. This
was no mere coup d'état. Its nearest parallel in recent history might
be the Portuguese revolution of 1974: a popular revolt led by
officers whose losing battle to hold together a collapsing Empire
had convinced them the political system under which they served
was indefensible. The civilian population — not only the Christian
minorities but the by now considerable number of Muslims who
had some contact with Western ideas and who resented both the
illiberalism of the regime and its inability to resist foreign encroachment — greeted the revolution with tremendous enthusiasm. It
inaugurated, as revolutions do, a period of genuine freedom of
expression combined with great political confusion. Yet there was
also something about it of the coup in Algiers in 1958, carried

out by French officers against the French Fourth Republic. For the 'Young Turk' officers of 1908 were not resigned to the break-up of the Empire. They intended to strengthen it by making all its citizens free and equal, and integrating them into a single Ottoman nation. They still thought of themselves as Ottomans, not Turks. The name 'Jeunes Turcs' was coined in French, for European consumption, to describe the original Young Ottoman movement of the 1860s. By 1908 it was used very loosely to describe the opponents of Abdul-Hamid's regime, who were not united, either in organization or in ideology.

The faction which emerged as dominant after 1908 was the Committee of Union and Progress (Ittihad ve Terakki Cemiyeti*), whose members and supporters are generally referred to as Unionists or Ittihadists. As the name implies, their first preoccupation was with maintaining the unity of the Empire. They made explicit what had been only implicit in the statements of the Tanzimat reformers: that from now on there would be equal citizenship for all Ottoman subjects irrespective of religion. They opposed any association or movement which tended to divide the Empire's inhabitants on religious, racial, or national lines. This meant the abolition of the traditional *millet* system, under which religious minorities had been organized as separate, 'protected' communities, governed according to their own law by their own religious leaders, who were responsible to the Sultan for their loyalty and good behaviour. In theory it meant a step up for these minorities, who had hitherto been in a subordinate position, formally excluded from the state (since the latter was identified with the Muslim *umma*). In practice it was much too late. The Christian *millets*, reacting against their subordination and encouraged by European powers, had developed into nationalities (the word *millet* means 'nation' in modern Turkish) which aspired to full self-government and even national independence. The Unionists were, in effect, proposing to suppress the national institutions and nationalist movements of emerging nations.

* In modern Turkish, c corresponds to the English j, ç to the English ch, ş to the English sh, and ı to -er in English 'father'.

127

Once this was apparent, it was inevitable that the Unionist regime would be no less fiercely opposed by non-Muslims than the pan-Islamic regime of Abdul-Hamid. Indeed, the Christian nationalities of the Balkans, who were already far advanced towards independence, did not wait to see what the new regime would be like. Immediately after the revolution Bulgaria declared her independence, Crete announced its union with Greece, and Austria proclaimed the annexation of Bosnia and Herzegovina, forestalling their union with Serbia. This was followed, in April 1909, by an attempted Muslim counter-revolution in Istanbul, whose supporters claimed to be defending the Shari'a.

The Unionists suppressed the revolt and deposed Sultan Abdul-Hamid, whom they naturally assumed to be involved in it. But they denied that it was any part of their intention to undermine either the Shari'a or the caliphate. They thus reaffirmed the Islamic character of the state and enclosed themselves in the same contradiction that had beset every Ottoman reform movement from the Tanzimat onwards. They prohibited the formation of political associations based on or bearing the name of ethnic or national groups, closed down the existing Greek, Bulgarian and other minority clubs, and for the first time took steps to conscript non-Muslims into the armed forces. The unity of the Empire, it was now clear, would have to be maintained not by consent but by force.

That applied also to Muslims, and particularly to non-Turkish Muslims. Many of these had responded favourably to Abdul-Hamid's policies, which by reasserting the Islamic character of the Empire had enabled them to identify with it and see it as less foreign. (Arabic-speaking Muslims, especially, had been well represented in the Sultan's entourage.) Many more reacted unfavourably to the centralizing and increasingly authoritarian policies of the Unionists, with their emphasis on the Ottoman character of the Empire and particularly on the use of the Ottoman — i.e. Turkish — language. The soldiers who took part in the abortive counter-revolution of 1909 were mainly Albanian Muslims. Thereafter disaffection spread rapidly among Arabs,

Albanians and other non-Turkish Muslims. The Muslim parts of the Empire were beginning to be infected with the nationalist disease that had carried off their Christian neighbours.

Soon the Turks were infected too. To them the germ was brought across the Black Sea from the Russian Empire, where (as mentioned in Chapter 4) Muslims had developed pan-Turkism in response to Russian pan-Slavism. These Muslims soon realized that the Ottoman Sultan-Caliph, Commander of the Faithful, was in no position to give them effective support or protection against their Russian conquerors. But they still found Istanbul a natural place of refuge and cultural centre, a place from which they could import books and ideas in their own language. As they felt their way towards a national consciousness, based on language and history, they were well aware that both language and history connected them to the Ottoman Turks, and they sought to make the Ottomans — in whose language even the word 'Turk' carried contemptuous overtones — aware of it as well.

The Ottoman Turks might have remained indifferent to this pan-Turkish appeal if their existing Empire had not been so visibly dissolving under the impact of other people's nationalisms. Neither the old vision of the community of believers under a strong and righteous Muslim ruler, nor the new-fangled, half-baked notion of an Ottoman *patrie* to which peoples of different race and creed could feel equal loyalty, was capable of holding the Empire together and thereby restoring the self-respect of its ruling group. By 1914 it was difficult for an educated man to feel inordinately proud of being either a Muslim or an Ottoman. Perhaps there was something to be said for being a Turk.

The Unionists themselves, between 1908 and 1914, drifted towards this point of view. After the disastrous war of 1912, in which the Empire lost almost all its remaining European territory (as well as Libya), the Committee of Union and Progress strengthened its hold on the government. From then until 1918 the Empire was ruled by a dictatorial triumvirate of three men: Enver, Jemal and Talât. To describe these men as Turkish nationalists would be misleading. They had identified themselves with what was left of the Ottoman Empire and they were determined to restore its prestige. They certainly had no intention of voluntarily relinquishing any of its non-Turkish territory. But in their effort to restore Ottoman greatness they were prepared to play both the Islamic and the Turkish card. Encouraged by their German allies they dreamed, not of recovering the lost territory in Africa and the Balkans but of liberating their Turkish fellow-Muslims from the Russian yoke and building a new Turco-Muslim Empire that would stretch into Central Asia. With such hopes they entered the First World War on the German side in October 1914. At their instigation the Sultan-Caliph called on all Muslims to rise up in a *jihad* against their colonial masters — Russian, French and British. Humiliatingly, the call went largely unheeded. Tatar Muslims fought in the Russian army, Indian Muslims (admittedly with some misgivings and desertions) in the British, Algerian and Senegalese Muslims in the French (though there were some risings in North Africa). Even Arab Muslims joined the British, rebelling against Turkish rule.

The only semblance of an effective step taken towards the realization of the Unionists' pan-Turkish dreams was the deportation and massacre of the Armenians, whose presence in eastern Anatolia and the Caucasus was an obstacle to the creation of a homogeneous Turco-Muslim state. The Armenians in the Empire before the First World War numbered between one and a half and two million. Of these about one million were killed, half of whom were women and children, about two hundred thousand forcibly converted to Islam, and the remainder driven from their homes and left to starve.[2]

The Caliph's call for a Muslim uprising in the Russian Empire evoked a response only after Russia had collapsed and withdrawn from the War in the spring of 1918, when the (Shi'ite) Muslim Turks of Azerbaijan asserted their independence and linked up with Ottoman troops, who advanced through the Caucasus and reached Baku on the Caspian Sea in September. This invasion was marked by a further massacre of some fifty to one hundred thousand Armenians (partly in revenge for a massacre of Muslims by Armenians and Russians earlier in the year). On the other fronts, however, the Ottoman Empire was now finally disintegrating. As early as March 1917 the British had captured Baghdad, and in December Jerusalem. In September 1918 they inflicted a major defeat on the Ottoman forces in northern Palestine and, with Arab help, entered Damascus in early October. In the Balkans, another Allied force opened the road to Istanbul. The Unionist ministers resigned and the Sultan appointed a new government, which signed an armistice with the victorious Allies on 30 October, just twelve days before the German surrender on the Western front. On 13 November an Allied fleet anchored in the port of Istanbul, and within a month an Allied military administration was set up. On 8 February 1919, the French general Franchet d'Esperey, deliberately imitating the gesture of Sultan Mehmet the Conquerer in 1453, rode into Istanbul on a white horse given by local Greeks. Strategic points in various parts of Anatolia were occupied by different Allied armies. In May a Greek army landed at Izmir and began to advance eastwards, making it clear that it had come not for a temporary occupation, but to annex western Anatolia permanently to a greater Greece.

Against this prospect, exhausted and demoralized though they were, the Muslims of Anatolia rose in revolt. They did so under the leadership of Mustafa Kemal, who later took the name of Atatürk — father of the Turks — and who is rightly considered the founder of the modern Turkish nation. He was already a national hero in 1919 because of his role in the defence of the Dardanelles and the Gallipoli peninsula against British attack during the First World War. The struggle on which he now embarked was to culminate in the founding of the Turkish Republic. Yet the idea of a Turkish nation, living in a country called Turkey, was probably not clear in the minds of most of his supporters when they began the struggle, and perhaps not even in Mustafa Kemal's own. It was an idea that crystallized in the course of the struggle.

The slide from Ottoman nationalism to Turkish nationalism was almost imperceptible, and perhaps would never have gone so far if the Ottoman Sultan and his government had not decided to oppose the nationalists and collaborate with the occupying Allied forces. And the nationalist struggle was also a struggle to defend Islam — the last remaining stronghold of the House of Islam — against the overweening Christian invaders. The nationalists proclaimed as their goal the defence of the 'Islamic lands' and the 'Islamic population' and the preservation of the 'Islamic Caliphate and Ottoman Sultanate'. Their manifesto, later known as the National Pact, did not refer to Turkey or the Turks as such, but to areas 'inhabited by an Ottoman Muslim majority, united in religion, in race and in aim.' It was originally adopted, in August 1919, at a congress in Erzerum of delegates from the eastern provinces of Anatolia, in many of which Kurds outnumbered Turks.* Later, in a slightly modified form, the Pact was accepted by the last Ottoman parliament, meeting in Istanbul. It demanded self-determination for the Arab parts of the Empire now under Allied occupation, but insisted that all other parts inhabited by a Muslim majority should remain an undivided whole.

Parliament adopted the Pact in February 1920. On 16 March British forces entered the Turkish quarters of Istanbul and arrested 150 nationalist sympathizers, including some members of parliament. The Sultan acquiesced in this, and two and a half years later the victorious nationalists decreed, on Kemal's insistence, that the Sultanate had ceased to exist from that date. Meanwhile, however, they continued to fight in the name of the Sultan-Caliph, even while defying his authority.

On 18 March parliament voted a protest against the arrest of its members and prorogued itself indefinitely. The next day Kemal called for elections to a new emergency assembly which would meet in Ankara, a small Anatolian hill town where the nationalists had set up their headquarters. On 11 April the Sultan dissolved parliament and the Shaikh al-Islam issued a *fatwa* (legal ruling) denouncing the nationalists as a gang of common rebels whom

---

* The nine-man representative committee elected by the congress included three Kurds, one of whom was a *shaikh* of the influential Naqshbandi order, as well as two Turkish religious leaders.

132

it was the imperative duty of any loyal Muslim to kill on the orders of the Caliph. An 'army of the Caliphate' was recruited for this purpose.

Ignoring this, Kemal's 'Grand National Assembly' met in Ankara, began its proceedings with a solemn prayer at the Haji Bayram mosque, and affirmed its unswerving loyalty to 'the holy and inviolable person' of the Sultan. In spite of the Shaikh al-Islam's anathema, the nationalists did not lack support from the *ulama*. They took the line that the Sultan-Caliph was not a free agent, and obtained a *fatwa* of their own from the Mufti of Ankara, endorsed by 152 other *muftis* throughout Anatolia, calling on the Muslim population 'to do all to liberate the Caliph from captivity.' Fully one-fifth of the members of the Grand National Assembly itself were either *ulama* or leading members of Sufi orders. They played an important role in the executive as well as joining eagerly in the debates. And Mustafa Kemal himself, in the summer of 1920, spent considerable time studying the early history of Islam. When touring the countryside, 'he often went directly to the mosque, participated in the Friday prayers, and even mounted the *minbar* [pulpit] to deliver impromptu *khutbas* [sermons]', discussing the religious reforms he had in mind for after the victory.[3] After his great victory over the Greeks at the Sakarya river, in August 1921, the Assembly voted him the title of 'Gazi' — victor in the holy war.

The nationalist struggle thus took on the character of a *jihad*, and it was seen as such by Muslims outside Turkey. The Arabs of Syria and Palestine, shattered by British and French betrayal of their nationalist hopes, followed with excitement the news of Mustafa Kemal's success in upsetting the Allies' plans for Turkey. The Muslims of India sent money for what they understood as a struggle to secure the independence of the caliphate. To encourage such support, the nationalists organized a pan-Islamic conference at Sivas (another Anatolian hill town) in February 1921.

Even the Turkish national anthem, adopted by the Grand National Assembly in March 1921, was taken from an intensely religious poem by 'our religious poet' (as the Minister of Education called him), Mehmet Âkif. The poem contained such lines as: 'Though the West gird itself with a wall of steel, my bosom filled with faith is my fortress. Fear not; how can this faith of a people be smothered by that monster called "Civilization" which has but one tooth left in its jaw?'*

Inevitably, a struggle so imbued with religious feeling had also to be seen as a struggle to restore and purify Islam, and the members of the Grand National Assembly saw this in fairly traditional terms. In its first year the Assembly passed a prohibition law forbidding not only drinking and gambling but also cardplaying and backgammon. It also set up a Shari'a committee, to check all Bills for conformity with the divine law.

The Creation of the Turkish Republic (1922–24)

Once victory was assured, Kemal soon revealed that he had quite other ideas about the direction reform should take. The first step, in November 1922, was the abolition of the Sultanate, while the caliphate was retained as a purely religious office without political powers. Kemal justified this with a lengthy disquisition on the history of the caliphate, citing particularly the later Abbasid period when the caliphs had lost all real power but had acted as symbols of Islamic unity and legitimacy. He encountered strong opposition from members of the Shari'a committee (mainly *ulama*), but cut off the discussion by explaining that the Turkish nation had already 'effectively taken sovereignty and sultanate into its own hands'. This was 'already an accomplished fact', and even if the Assembly did not agree with it, 'the truth will still find expression, but some heads may roll in the process.' The implied threat, combined with Kemal's now immense prestige and the extraordinary force of his personality, secured the passage of his proposal with only one dissenting voice, which was drowned by cries of 'Silence!' The resolution declared that 'the Turkish people consider that the

* These lines do not figure in the official national anthem, which is only the first two stanzas of the poem.

134

form of government in Istanbul resting on the sovereignty of an individual had ceased to exist on 16 March 1920 and passed for ever into history.' It then laid down that the caliphate, though belonging to the Ottoman house, rested on the Turkish state, and that the Assembly would choose as caliph 'that member of the Ottoman house who was in learning and character most worthy and fitting.'[4]

The Sultan who had collaborated with the Allies against the nationalists, Mehmet VI, then went into exile, and another member of his family was chosen as caliph. It remained unclear, however, what the exact constitutional position of the caliph was — what, indeed, was the constitutional nature of the new regime. Kemal's contention that the caliphate was a purely religious office, without any temporal powers, had not been written explicitly into the resolution, and its legal and theological soundness continued to be strongly contested by *ulama* both inside and outside Turkey. Although he could no longer claim sovereignty as such, it could still be, and was, argued that the caliph was legal head of state with responsibility for enforcing the Shari'a. The government included a Minister of Shari'a, in effect the successor of the Shaikh al-Islam, who claimed wide powers in virtue of the fact that the state was still an 'Islamic caliphate'. The next step, therefore, after the election of a new Grand National Assembly, was the proclamation of the Republic. The Constitution, which had been adopted in 1921, already stated that: 'Sovereignty belongs unconditionally to the nation. The government is based on the principle of the people's direct rule over their own destiny'; and that the Grand National Assembly was 'the only real representative of the people . . . the holder of both legislative and executive power.' An amendment, adopted in October 1923, removed all ambiguity by stating: 'The form of government of the state of Turkey is a Republic . . . the President of Turkey is elected by the Grand National Assembly in plenary session from among its own members. . . . The President of Turkey is the head of the state . . . and appoints the Prime Minister.' But it also specified that 'the religion of the Turkish state is Islam.' Fifteen minutes after the adoption of the amendment, Mustafa Kemal was elected president of the world's first Islamic republic.*

The caliphate was thus divorced from the Turkish state and became a kind of papacy, with something of the same relationship to Turkey that the papacy had to Italy. That is, in theory it was an international institution, which just happened to have its head-quarters in Turkey, but in practice its history, including a long history of temporal power, gave it considerable weight and influence in Turkish society and politics. In Italy Mussolini was to solve this problem in 1929 by a Concordat between the Italian state and the Vatican. Had Mustafa Kemal chosen to take that road in Turkey he could have bargained from a position of much greater strength. He could have argued that his own credentials as a Muslim leader were as good as those of any member of the Ottoman dynasty and had himself acclaimed as caliph. Alter-natively, he could have acted on the precedents he himself had cited from the Abbasid and Mamluk periods and kept on the caliph as a powerless figurehead and an instrument of Turkish influence elsewhere in the Muslim world.

But Mustafa Kemal's intentions were more radical. He wanted Turkey to be a completely sovereign and independent nation, and he believed that this was possible only if there were a complete break with the old Islamic legitimacy, not only in practice but in theory. He was impervious to any temptation to try and rebuild the Ottoman Empire — refusing even to attempt the reconquest of his birthplace, Salonika. He believed that such ambitions and entanglements had been disastrous for Turkey in the past and must at all costs be avoided in the future. (For the same reason he rejected pan-Turkism.) He resolved to use the surge of Turkish national-ism, while it was still strong, to destroy the caliphate while it was still weak.

The nationalist movement's very success in defeating the

---

* At least in modern times. The phrase 'Islamic Republic' is now sometimes used to describe the original Muslim state as it existed under Muhammad and his four 'orthodox' successors. A 'Tripoli Republic' was established by nationalists in Libya in 1918, but failed to achieve international recognition.

Armenians and Greeks and defying the European powers had raised the prestige of Turkey, and so aroused greater interest in and enthusiasm for the caliphate in other Muslim countries. These non-Turkish Muslims were worried by the proclamation of the Republic and other indications that Turkey was now embarking on a secular, westernizing path. Was the new-found leader of the Muslim world about to desert them? What was going to happen to the caliphate? In India even Shi'ites, for whom the Ottoman claim to the caliphate was in theory untenable, had become interested in the Ottoman caliphate as a political focus of Muslim unity. In November 1923 two of their leaders, the Aga Khan and Amir Ali, wrote to the Turkish government stressing the importance of the caliphate and claiming that uncertainty about its future was having 'very disturbing effects' among their Sunni compatriots. They urged 'the imminent necessity for maintaining the religious and moral solidarity of Islam by placing the Caliph-Imamate on a basis which would command the confidence and esteem of the Muslim nations and thus impart to the Turkish state unique strength and dignity.' They sent copies of their letter to several Turkish newspapers.

Kemal seized the occasion, pointing out scathingly that Indian Muslims had fought *against* the caliphate in the First World War and that the signatories of the letter had themselves publicly rejected the caliph's declaration of *jihad*. His supporters adroitly presented the letter as part of a British plot to use the caliphate as an instrument for meddling in Turkey's internal affairs. Then, on 1 March 1924, Kemal opened a new session of the Assembly with a speech which emphasized the safeguarding and stabilization of the Republic, the creation of a unified national system of education, and the need to 'cleanse and elevate the Islamic faith, by rescuing it from the position of a political instrument, to which it has been accustomed for centuries.' On 3 March his proposals were passed by the Assembly: the caliph was deposed, the caliphate abolished, and all members of the Ottoman house banished from Turkish territory.

Henry VIII without Cranmer (1924–38)

Although the Ottoman claim to the caliphate had only been seriously pressed for the last sixty years or so, it had by now acquired such significance, as a symbol of beleaguered Muslims' aspiration to unity, that Kemal's abolition of it amounted to a radical break between Turkey and the house of Islam, comparable to Henry VIII of England's breach with the Church of Rome. Indeed, Kemal's objectives during this period seem to have been quite similar to those of the English Reformation: he did not want to disestablish Islam but to reform it, to free it from the grip of the obscurantist *ulama* and make it something that the ordinary Turkish citizen could understand and feel his own. He wanted to make sure that religious institutions in Turkey were controlled by the Turkish people, through their newly founded national state, rather than the other way round.

Just as in England the break with Rome was followed by the dissolution of the monasteries, so in Turkey the abolition of the caliphate was followed by a wholesale assault on the country's religious institutions. The office of Shaikh al-Islam and the Ministry of Shari'a, the religious schools and colleges, the Shari'a courts: all were abolished within two months.

As in England, too, the response was a rising in defence of the old order in the remoter and more backward parts of the country — in this case, Kurdistan.* The Kurds had fought on the nationalist side on the understanding that they were defending Islam against Christian invaders (and, in particular, defending their homeland against the proposal to incorporate much of it into an Armenian state, which figured in the Treaty of Sèvres, imposed by the Allies on the Sultan's government in 1920). They had, by and large, been loyal subjects of the Ottoman Empire so long as the central government did not interfere too much in their local affairs. In 1919 Mustafa Kemal had promised that Kurds and Turks would have equal rights in independent Turkey. But the Kurds now found

---

* Kurdistan — the country of the Kurds — comprises south-eastern Turkey and parts of Iran, Iraq and Syria.

themselves co-opted into a 'Turkish nation' which they had scarcely heard of before. Kurdish is in fact an Indo-European language, related to Persian and subdivided into several dialects, but wholly distinct from Turkish. Yet the new nationalist regime denied the existence of any separate cultures within Turkey and made the Kurds into Turks by decree. Historians were ordered to produce 'scientific proof' of the identity of the two nations. Also, as part of a drive against 'feudalism' a law was passed giving the government authority to expropriate large land-holdings in the eastern provinces. This was directed against Kurdish tribal leaders and the *shaikhs* of Sufi orders, many of whom had become owners of large tracts of land. Respected local leaders were thus removed from the area, and their lands were given, not to local landless Kurds but to Turkish or Turkicized settlers, mainly Muslims who migrated to Turkey from what had been the European provinces of the Empire.[5]

The Kurds feared that the government planned to disperse them over western Turkey and settle Turks in their place. They complained that the use of the Kurdish language in schools and law courts was restricted and Kurdish education as such forbidden, that all senior officials in Kurdistan were Turks, that they were getting no benefit from the taxes they paid, that the government had rigged the 1923 elections in the Kurdish provinces, that it was deliberately setting Kurdish tribes against each other, that Turkish soldiers raided Kurdish villages taking away animals and foodstuff, that Kurdish soldiers were victimized and discriminated against in the armed forces, and that the government was trying to exploit Kurdish mineral wealth for the Turks' benefit. In this atmosphere the abolition of the caliphate seemed to sever the last moral bond between the two peoples.

In 1925 a major revolt broke out in Kurdistan, which was both nationalist and religious. Its leader, Shaikh Sa'īd of Palu, was a *shaikh* of the Naqshbandi order with great local influence. He called on the Kurdish tribes to join in a *jihad* against the Ankara government. Not all of them did, as the government was able to exploit inter-tribal rivalries, but a large area of Turkish Kurdistan did rise in revolt. A number of district capitals were taken and the Turkish officials expelled or taken prisoner. The military forces in the eastern part of the country were inadequate for dealing with the revolt and there were doubts about their loyalty – partly because many of the rank and file were Kurdish, partly because some of the Turkish commanders were personally opposed to Mustafa Kemal's new policies. For a moment there seemed to be a serious threat to the new regime. Mustafa Kemal dismissed his liberal prime minister, Fethi, and rushed through a Bill 'for the Maintenance of Order' giving the government virtually dictatorial powers for two years. Special 'independence tribunals' were set up, and those in the east were given summary powers of execution. The main opposition party, to which the senior commander in the east, Kâzım Karabekir, belonged, was outlawed. Large numbers of fresh troops were sent to the east, using the Baghdad railway through Syrian territory. Altogether at least 35,000 well-armed Turkish troops were deployed against the rebels, as well as continuous bombing by the airforce. Within two months the main rebellion had been crushed and Shaikh Sa'id captured, although limited guerrilla warfare continued for years. There were extremely brutal reprisals: hundreds of villages were destroyed and thousands of innocent men, women and children killed. The population of entire districts (several hundred thousand people) was deported to the west.

On 29 June 1925, the 'independent tribunal' in Diyarbekir, the centre of the area where the rebellion had occurred, condemned Shaikh Sa'id and forty-seven other leading Kurds to death. At the same time it ordered the closing of all the Sufi *tekkes* (convents) in Kurdistan. This marked the beginning of a second wave of attacks on religious institutions and traditions which were regarded as Islamic. In August Mustafa Kemal made a series of speeches in northern Anatolia on the theme of Turkey's need to put aside the symbols of the past and align itself with 'civilization', by which he clearly meant modern Western civilization. He attacked in particular the traditional costume, which he denounced as being neither 'national' nor 'civilized and international'. 'A civilized, international dress is worthy and appropriate for our nation,' he said, 'and we will wear it. Boots or shoes on our feet, trousers on our legs, shirt and tie, jacket and waistcoat — and, of course, to complete these, a cover with a brim on our heads. I want to make this clear. This headcovering is called "hat".'[6] This was a declaration of war on the fez, which although adopted only a century earlier (see p. 94, fn.) had now become a kind of badge of Muslim identity, in Turkey and in many other countries.

Kemal also attacked the Sufi *turuq*, blaming them for the superstitious mentality which, he said, was holding Turkey back from modernity and civilization. He declared:

I flatly refuse to believe that today, in the luminous presence of science, knowledge, and civilization in all its aspects, there exist, in the civilized community of Turkey, men so primitive as to seek their material and moral well-being from the guidance of one or another *shaikh*. Gentlemen, you and the whole nation must know, and know well, that the Republic of Turkey cannot be the land of *shaikhs*, dervishes, disciples and lay brothers. The straightest, truest Way (*tariqa*) is the way of civilization. To be a man, it is enough to do what civilization requires. The heads of the brotherhoods will understand this truth that I have uttered in all its clarity, and will of their own accord at once close their convents, and accept the fact that their disciples have at last come of age.[7]

In fact, Kemal did not wait for the brotherhoods to dissolve themselves of their own accord. He returned to Ankara and promulgated a series of decrees. The brotherhoods were dissolved and banned, their assets impounded, their convents and sanctuaries closed, their prayer meetings and ceremonies prohibited. Persons not holding a recognized religious office were forbidden to wear religious vestments or insignia, and all civil servants were ordered to wear the costume 'common to the civilized nations of the world' — i.e. the suit and hat. The laws confirming the decrees, passed in November 1925, went even further: all men were now required to wear hats by law, and the wearing of the fez or turban became a criminal offence.* A month later the Western calendar was officially adopted: from now on events in Turkey would be dated not from Muhammad's *hijra*, but from the birth of Christ.

This second wave of reforms affected the lives of ordinary people more immediately and directly than the first, and consequently aroused much more widespread resistance. The powers of the 'independence tribunals' had to be twice renewed, and the law for the Maintenance of Order was kept in force until 1929. But Kemal pressed on. In 1926 European codes of civil and criminal law, of contract and commerce were adopted. This implied the abolition of polygamy, of unilateral divorce and of the traditional Muslim rules of inheritance. There was no longer any part of Turkish law which could be said to be derived from the Shari'a. It even became legally possible for a Muslim woman to marry a non-Muslim man, and for any adult to change his or her religion at will.

All this happened in a state of which Islam was still the constitutional religion, and whose population was far more homogeneously Muslim than that of the Ottoman Empire had ever been. The Turks had eschewed pan-Islamic ambitions, but they still thought of themselves as by definition Muslim. Anyone who was not a Muslim was not a Turk, and on these grounds a number of Turkish-speaking Greek Orthodox Christians were identified as Greeks and sent to Greece in the exchange of populations that followed the end of the Greco-Turkish war in 1923 (while many of the 'Turks' who came to Turkey were in fact Greek-speaking Muslims). There were non-Muslim citizens of the Turkish republic, but they were not considered members of the Turkish nation, and in some respects their participation in public life decreased; although called up for military service they did not bear arms and were not commissioned, while their numbers in the civil service dwindled rapidly.

Since Islam was so central to the idea of Turkish nationality,

---

* Contrary to a widespread myth, women in Turkey have never been forbidden by law to wear the veil. But Kemal did denounce it as an 'object of ridicule', and there were municipal orders against it in some places.

it was natural for Turkish nationalists to proclaim Islam as their national religion and to seek to develop a national version of it. As one of them was later to put it: 'We want to construct a Turkish Islam, which will be ours, relevant to and integrated with our society, just as Anglicanism is Christianity in a thoroughly English fashion. Anglicanism is not Italian, not Russian. Yet no one accuses it of not being Christian. Why should we not have an Islam of our own?'[8] Why, in other words, should Mustafa Kemal not repeat the achievement of Henry VIII?

The question is an intriguing one, and requires an answer, for it is now fairly clear that that has not happened. At its simplest, the answer must be that nationalism is not enough. Anglicanism is not simply the result of Henry VIII's break with Rome, even though that is its starting-point. Anglicanism as a distinctive religious tradition results from the adoption and encouragement, by Henry VIII and his successors, of Protestantism, or at least of certain aspects of it. It was a marriage of English nationalism with a religious reform movement, which may be wholly or partly explained by reference to social factors, but which was certainly a genuine and important movement of religious thought. Secondly, this reform movement was, among other things, a drive to translate the scriptures and liturgy of the Christian church into vernacular languages. In England this movement drew strength from, and in turn stimulated, the emergence of modern English as a literary language of remarkable vigour. Anglicanism was thus lucky enough to acquire a liturgy, that of Archbishop Thomas Cranmer, and later an Authorized Version of the Bible, which rank among the formative classics of English literature.

It was not unreasonable for Mustafa Kemal to hope for a similar combination of factors working in favour of Turkish Islam. We have seen that since the eighteenth century Islam had been shaken by a series of reform movements, which had something in common with the Reformation of Western Christianity and some of which (in India notably) included a drive to translate the Koran into the vernacular. Turkey, like England in the sixteenth century, was just emerging as a self-conscious nation-state, and the Turkish language was undergoing a major transformation as Persian and Arabic loan-words were discarded and the mannerisms of Ottoman prose and verse were replaced by a more natural and popular style. Could not the modernizing reform movements of universal Islam espouse Turkish nationalism, and produce a distinctive Turkish variant of Islam?

Mustafa Kemal was interested in that possibility. In 1923 he announced preparations for the establishment of a board of Islamic studies, 'to study Islamic philosophy in relation to Western philosophy, to study the ritual, rational, economic, and demographic conditions of the Muslim peoples', and to educate modern scholars of *ijtihad* (creative interpretation of the Koran and the Sunna) and *tafsīr* (Koranic commentary). In 1924, when the religious schools and colleges were abolished, they were replaced by a Faculty of Divinity in the University of Istanbul and new schools to train modern-minded *imams* (prayer-leaders) and *khatībs* (preachers), under the direction of the Ministry of Education. Kemal himself set the example with his sermons in Turkish, and urged the *imams* and *khatibs* to do likewise. Above all, he wanted a Turkish translation of the Koran that would command general respect, and he was convinced that the man to do this was the author of the national anthem, the 'religious poet' Mehmet Âkif. In 1926 the National Assembly voted funds for the project, and Âkif was formally invited to undertake it, even though he had settled in Egypt in protest against Kemal's reforms.

Âkif at first accepted the commission. He was both flattered and tempted by the opportunity to become the Cranmer, or the Coverdale,* of the Turkish reformation. But in the end his option was that of Thomas More. He was determined to remain part of the universal Islamic community, and he could not accept that the Turkish state had the right to overrule the worldwide consensus of the *ulama*. He found that that consensus, represented not only by the *shaikhs* of al-Azhar but also by Rashīd Ridā, the leading Arab modernist of the day, was still opposed to the idea of trans-

* Miles Coverdale, sixteenth-century English translator of the Bible.

lating the Koran. On reflection, Âkif refused the commission, and never completed the translation even though the money was kept in trust in case he should change his mind.*

The fact is that the various revival movements of the Islamic world were not prepared to identify themselves with the kind of reform that Kemal had undertaken. Essentially this was because he was not just rejecting the authority of a corrupt and obscurantist religious institution, but deliberately importing into a part of the Muslim world a model of 'civilization' from outside; and not just from outside but from those very European powers which had conquered and were exploiting so many Muslim countries. It was as though Henry VIII, after rejecting the authority of the Pope, had gone on to reshape English society with ideas and institutions borrowed from the Ottoman Empire. One can imagine that in those circumstances Luther, Zwingli, and their English followers would have been reluctant to recognize the new English regime as a variant of Protestantism.

There was another contradiction involved. The Europe which Mustafa Kemal took as his model was one in which the notion of state church or national religion was no longer generally accepted. In England the Church was still officially established, but Richard Hooker's notion of church and commonwealth as perfectly coextensive, two different aspects of the same community, had long since been abandoned. In France and the other advanced nations of Western Europe, state and church had been legally separated. Gradually Kemal seems to have realized that he was being inconsistent with his own modernism in seeking to bring about a reform of religion through the agency of the state. The logical conclusion of the path he had been pursuing was to disentangle the state from religion altogether. Accordingly, in 1928, the clause specifying that 'the religion of the Turkish state is Islam' was deleted from the constitution. This was followed in the same year by the introduction of the Roman alphabet in place of Arabic

---

*Kemal renewed the invitation as late as 1936, but Âkif remained obdurate. Unlike Sir Thomas More he did not incur martyrdom, but ended his days in comfortable exile.

script — a measure that in time would greatly widen the mental gulf between Turkey and the rest of the Muslim world.

Consistency, however, is seldom achieved in politics. Although the Turkish state had renounced its connection with Islam, in practice it considered religion far too important and dangerous a force to be left in the hands of the religious-minded. While non-Muslim communities retained their autonomy in religious matters, the mosques, the Islamic endowments (*awqāf*), the education, appointment and payment of *imams* and *khatibs* all remained firmly under government control. Religious education, instead of being freed from state control, was almost entirely phased out. Attendance at secular elementary schools was made compulsory in 1930. The last two professional schools for training *imams* and *khatibs* were closed in 1932, and the following year the Faculty of Divinity was reduced to an Institute for Islamic Research within the Faculty of Letters. The only Islamic education still available at any level was provided by a number of Koran courses, which for some reason were left under the Directorate of Religious Affairs rather than the Ministry of Education. The government's point of view apparently was that since Islam was a people's religion without clergy, no special education was needed to understand it.

The government did not succeed in banning the use of Arabic inside the mosques, but in 1932 the public call to prayer was given in Turkish for the first time from the mosque of Santa Sophia, in Istanbul, and a few months later this practice became general, on instructions from the Directorate of Religious Affairs. 'It seems that this one act of government interference in the ritual caused more widespread popular resentment than any of the other secularist measures.'[9]

Outside the mosque, Turkey continued to move further away from Islamic tradition. The wearing of religious dress of any kind, other than at places of worship or at religious ceremonies, was forbidden. Women were given the right to vote and to be elected to parliament. All Turks were obliged by law to adopt surnames, and Sunday replaced Friday (the day of public worship in Islam) as the weekly day of rest in government and public offices. The

Santa Sophia mosque (originally built as a Byzantine cathedral) was withdrawn from worship and turned into a museum. Finally, in 1937, secularism or 'laicism' was written into the constitution as one of the fundamental principles of the state. By the time of his death in 1938, Kemal Atatürk seems to have lost interest in Islam as such. 'I admit,' he said, 'that man cannot do without faith, but I believe that ... throughout history the Turk has respected all beliefs cherished as sacred, and that his religion is neither this nor that particular religion. All faiths are worthy of reverence to him.'[10]

Secular State, Muslim People (1938–81)

THE RETREAT FROM EXTREME KEMALISM

The paradoxical situation had now been achieved of a secular state in which the religion followed by 90 per cent of the people* was tightly controlled by the government, yet virtually forbidden to show its face in public. But the attachment of the people to Islam remained very strong, and was probably strengthened by the growing unpopularity of the government, mainly for economic reasons which were aggravated during the Second World War. Kemal's revolution brought into existence a nationalist elite, larger and more thoroughly Westernized than its counterpart in most other Muslim countries, but did little either for the peasants or for the traditional middle class. Among these classes nostalgia for the old 'Islamic' order grew stronger as the excitement and hopes of the revolution faded. A modern Turkish authority on the subject, Dr Şerif Mardin, attributes 'the continuing intensity of religious belief' among large groups of Turks after a quarter of a century of secular policy 'to the real impoverishment of Turkish culture that resulted from Republican reform and to the unchanged starkness of human relations in Turkish society from 1923 onwards and from the village upwards. Republican symbolism,' he con-

* Today the figure is 98 per cent, owing to the emigration of most remaining Christians.

147

tinues, 'was too shallow and lacking in aesthetic richness to "take":
it did so only in the most superficial sense of generating expecta-
tions among the young school-age population the realization of
which it denied them as adults. On the other hand, in Turkish
society, at the village level, human relations were, and are, un-
deniably nasty and brutish.'[11]

In 1945, after twenty-two years of one-party rule, President
Ismet Inönü announced that he would welcome the formation of
one or more opposition parties. The leaders of the Democratic
Party, which was formed in response to this invitation, were all
former members of the ruling People's Party and committed to
preserving the achievements of Kemalism. Their main policy plank
was a demand for less state interference in the economy. But their
programme included, among its eighty-eight points, the statement
that 'our party . . . rejects the erroneous interpretation of secularism
in terms of enmity towards religion; it recognizes religious freedom
like the other freedoms as a sacred human right', and went on to
demand the appointment of a committee of experts to report on
the question of religious education including the re-establishment
of the Faculty of Divinity. It soon found that this item was one
of the most popular in its programme and, as political life became
freer, increasing pressure for greater religious freedom was felt.

The government, becoming aware of its unpopularity, began
to make concessions. In 1947 the Ministry of Education accepted
new guidelines for the teaching of religion outside schools. In
1948 foreign exchange was allowed for the first time to persons
who wanted to make the pilgrimage to Mecca. In 1949 the tombs
of Muslim 'saints' were reopened for visitors, and an optional
two-hour course in modernized Islam was offered in primary
schools on Saturday afternoons: an overwhelming majority of
parents rushed to enrol their children. At the same time, fifteen
training courses for *imams* and *khatibs* were opened, and later the
same year the Faculty of Divinity was reopened, though now in
the University of Ankara rather than that of Istanbul.

Islam and Islamic functionaries became more visible again.
Religious dress as such was still forbidden, but

soon old gentlemen with beards and berets were to be seen in many places, voicing their views and demands with growing vigour.... Mosque attendance rose considerably. Many of the mosques were now equipped with amplifiers; inscribed Arabic texts appeared on the walls in cafés, shops, taxis, and in the markets, and were offered for sale in the streets. Religious books and pamphlets were written and published on an ever-increasing scale.[12]

In May 1950 the Democratic Party won a landslide victory in 'the first free and honest election under the Republic',[13] and came to power. Its first act was to abolish the penalty for giving the prayer call in Arabic. (The Turkish prayer call has not been heard since.) Soon afterwards religious education was made a regular part of the curriculum for the fourth and fifth grades in primary schools (though parents were allowed to opt out if they so wished). Later the *imam-khatib* courses became special middle and secondary schools.

The Democratic Party remained in power for ten years. At first it retained and even increased its popularity, as Turkey benefited from the economic recovery in Western Europe and the Korean War boom. The prime minister, Adnan Menderes, therefore had little need to make further concessions to demands for the restoration of Islam. It was later, when things began to go wrong economically, that he tried to arrest his party's decline by courting the 'religious vote'. Religious education was permitted in secondary schools, the *imam-khatib* schools were given official recognition, Menderes made a personal donation of a 100,000 Turkish lira for a new mosque and claimed that between 1950 and 1957 1,500 mosques had been built and 86 old ones (including the great Süleymaniye mosque in Istanbul) repaired. Koran recitations and sermons were introduced on the state broadcasting network, and pilgrims to Mecca were given government help. In spite of all this, the Democrats lost ground in the 1957 elections, but they avoided outright defeat.

By 1960 the Democratic regime had succeeded in identifying itself in the public mind with the revival of Islam, while at the

149

same time its mismanagement of the economy had provoked widespread unrest and it was resorting increasingly to repression. The armed forces carried out a coup against it in order to safeguard 'Kemalist values'. This turned out to mean a return, not to militant secularism, but to Kemal's earlier Islamic reformism. The new head of state, General Cemal Gürsel, declared:

> Those who blame religion for our backwardness are wrong. No, the cause of our backwardness is not religion but those who have misrepresented our religion to us. Islam is the most sacred, most constructive, most dynamic and powerful religion in the world. It demands of those who believe in this faith always to achieve progress and higher wisdom. But for centuries Islam has been explained to us negatively and incorrectly. That is why we are lagging behind the nations of the world.

The government, he said, would not oblige the muezzins to go back to giving the call to prayer in Turkish.

> The path we are following is such that the day will come when, for the enlightenment of our people, the demand for the recitation in Turkish of the call for prayer and of the Koran will come from below, from the people themselves. In our efforts we are following such a path. We are preparing the relevant organizations and training the necessary elements in such a way as to ensure that our people are trained and prepared in this way.[14]

To ensure that Islam would remain under state control, the inclusion of the Directorate of Religious Affairs in the administration was written into the new constitution.

However, the military junta remained in power only eighteen months, and the civilian politicians who succeeded it were well aware that there were no votes in reforming Islam. The main legacies of the junta were a more liberal constitution and a proportional electoral system, which for the first time allowed leftist parties to surface in Turkey during the 1960s. (This also reflected the expansion of higher education and of the industrial working class.) The right-wing parties responded by promoting Islam as an 'antidote to communism'.

The principal party of the right, succeeding the now-banned Democrats and supported by much the same social groups, was the Justice Party (JP) led by Süleyman Demirel, who became prime minister in 1965. His government made further concessions to religious conservatives, for instance by establishing higher Islamic institutes in Istanbul and Konya, which catered for the graduates of the *imam–khatib* schools. The latter were thus able to bypass the Faculty of Divinity in Ankara, which the conservatives regarded as secular and modernist. The Turkish state had now provided (with financial help from groups of private citizens) an educational structure through which a new generation of traditionally-minded *ulama* could be produced. At the same time religious instruction was extended from the lower to the upper secondary schools (*lycées*).

ISLAM IN TURKEY TODAY

While these changes were being made in the official position of Turkish Islam, a number of unofficial Islamic organizations had surfaced or resurfaced, taking advantage of the freer religious climate of the 1950s. Among them were some of the old Sufi *turuq*, and at least one which had not been well known in Turkey before: the Tijaniya, which we met in North and West Africa in Chapter 3. In other words, this was the reformist and activist neo-Sufism of the nineteenth century, rather than the colourful mystic folklore (whirling dervishes and the like) which Turkey had known in the past. The new Turkish Tijanis attracted attention in the early Fifties chiefly by smashing busts of Atatürk — something which the Democratic government swiftly showed it was not prepared to tolerate.

The tendency away from mysticism towards a more legalistic, orthodox conception of Islam was also apparent in the Naqshbandi order, which has been more active (or at least more visible) in Turkey since the 1950s. Several Naqshbandi *shaikhs* became involved in the movement known as Nurculuk ('followers of the light'). This was founded by a man who called himself Sa'īdī Kurdī (Kurdish Sa'id), but is known to the Turks as Saīd-ī Nursī after his birthplace, the village of Nurs in Kurdistan. Born in 1873, he had appealed to Sultan Abdul-Hamid to open schools where education was in Kurdish because Turkish schools were useless for most Kurdish children. He was in touch with Kurdish nationalists in Istanbul, and played a leading role in the attempted Islamic counter-revolution of 1909 (see p. 128) In the First World War he commanded militia troops and distinguished himself by his bravery and (it is said) by saving the lives of 1,500 Armenians whom he was ordered to kill, but sent across the Russian lines into safety. In the War of Independence he sided with Mustafa Kemal, but went into opposition when he discovered Kemal's plans for secularization and Westernization. After Kemal's suppression of the Kurdish revolts and elimination of all references to a separate Kurdish identity, Sa'id continued to call himself Sa'idi Kurdi, 'the only public person who dared to bear such a name.'[15]

Exiled and many times imprisoned, Sa'id wrote a huge series of pamphlets, which were published after 1950 under the title *Risale-i Nur* ('Treatise on the Light'), hence the name Nurcu applied to his followers. These pamphlets, written in Turkish, call for the re-establishment of a truly Islamic state, based on the Koran and the Shari'a and ruled by a council of *ulama*. Polygamy should be permitted again and the religious colleges reopened.[16] But they also argue that scientific knowledge is God's bounty to man and that modern technology should be used rather than passively suffered.[17] Sa'id-i Nursi was also passionately anti-communist. After his death in 1961 his movement remained influential, and in recent years it has played a significant role on the right wing of Turkish politics.

Another comparable group, though not directly connected to any of the Sufi orders, is that of the Süleymancis, founded by an *alim* who objected to the control and censorship of Koran courses by officials of the Directorate of Religious Affairs. Some of its local representatives are described as 'aiming to establish the army of Islam instead of the Republic and restore the Caliphate.'[18] This group is particularly well organized among the 2.5 million Turkish emigrant workers in Germany, where it is said to have branches in no less than 211 cities, with a headquarters in Cologne.[19]

Besides these overtly militant religious groups, there was a growth in the Fifties and Sixties of trade and artisan associations with a religious bias. Among the shopkeepers, artisans and merchants of Anatolia, nostalgia for an Islamic order grew stronger as they found themselves unable to compete with the rapid expansion of large-scale capitalist industry and commerce, and at the same time felt threatened by the growing militancy and improving organization of trade unions and left-wing parties. (One of the latter, the Workers' Party of Turkey, began in the 1960s to recruit significant numbers of workers outside the big cities.)

These petty bourgeois classes had supported the Democratic Party and at first supported its successor, the JP. But the JP leader, prime minister Süleyman Demirel, was firmly committed to free enterprise and refused to take measures to protect small business from competition. Moreover, he was committed to financing Turkey's development with loans from the West, which meant a gradual opening of the Turkish market to Western goods and Western capital, and he supported Turkey's association agreement with the European Economic Community (EEC), signed in 1963, which provided for a gradual lowering of tariff barriers and eventually for full Turkish membership of the Community. During the 1960s the traditional business sector became increasingly alarmed about the effects of these policies. Its spokesman, Professor Necmettin Erbakan, the secretary-general of the Union of Chambers of Commerce and Industry, came into conflict with Demirel, whom he accused of being pro-American and the backer of big business interests in Istanbul, Izmir and the large industrial centres, at the expense of the small traders of Anatolia.

Demirel responded by getting Erbakan sacked from his job at the Chambers of Commerce and preventing him from standing as a JP candidate in the 1969 election. Erbakan ran as an independent and was elected in Konya (a traditional centre of Islamic piety and site of the tomb of Jalal al-Din Rumi, a great medieval Sufi poet who had founded the order of Mevlevis or 'whirling dervishes'). Once in parliament, he formed a new political organization, the National Order party, which he said would fill the place on the right vacated by the JP's alleged 'drift to the left'. His programme was a transparent appeal to Islamic puritanism, including promises to close ballet schools and other such sources of moral corruption, and he won the active support of the clandestine revivalist Nurcu movement, as well as the Naqshbandi order with which he was himself connected.

In 1971 the armed forces, alarmed by Demirel's inability to control the spread of leftist radicalism and violence in the working class, again seized power. As part of a general political clamp-down they opened proceedings against Erbakan's new party for violating the constitution by using religion for political purposes, and obtained its proscription by the Constitutional Court. Undaunted, Erbakan founded the National Salvation Party (NSP), which was clearly a continuation of the previous one, and astonished political commentators by winning 11.8 per cent of the vote and forty-nine seats in the general election of 1973. He found himself holding the balance in the new parliament and was able to obtain an important place for himself and his party in coalition governments, first with the centre-left Republican People's Party (RPP) under Bülent Ecevit in 1974 and then with the JP under Demirel in 1975–77.

Even in the government, however, Erbakan had to be discreet about the religious aspect of his policies. There was always the risk that the armed forces would intervene again if the constitution were openly flouted. He chose, therefore, to be Minister of Industry, and concentrated on attempts to stimulate Turkey's industrial growth through a series of very expensive — and according to his critics uneconomic — state-financed projects. In foreign affairs he took a strongly nationalistic line (opposing, for instance, any concessions to the Greeks on Cyprus), did his best to paralyse Turkey's relations with the EEC, and argued instead for the creation of an 'Islamic common market' with Turkey's Arab neighbours, whose new-found oil wealth made this idea seem at least superficially attractive. He also managed to reduce the level of Turkey's relations with Israel, though without achieving a complete break.

Erbakan did obtain some concessions on the strictly religious front — most notably the acceptance of graduates from *imam–khatib* schools as teachers of general subjects in primary schools. But he lost the support of the Nurcus, who transferred to the Justice Party, and in the 1977 elections the NSP's vote dropped to 8.6 per cent. At the end of that year Erbakan lost his place in the government when Demirel resigned and Ecevit was able to put together a new coalition with defectors from the JP. In late 1979 this government in turn fell, after a series of JP victories in by-elections, and Demirel returned to office. This time he did not bring Erbakan into the government, but relied on the NSP's support in parliament. The price was some further small concessions, including the authorization of religious services in an annex of the Santa Sophia mosque, which occurred in early 1980.

In the late 1970s Turkey's political and social fabric was visibly unravelling. Rising oil prices and reckless expansionist policies had rendered the country's foreign debts virtually unmanageable. The economic slowdown in Europe resulted in a decline both of employment opportunities and of foreign currency earnings. Teenagers who had grown up in the shanty towns of Turkey's major cities, or who migrated into them from rual areas in a usually vain search for work, were often recruited by groups of the extreme left or extreme right, both of which advocated and practised the use of violence for political ends. By 1980 terrorism was claiming more than 100 lives each week.

The Islamic revolution in neighbouring Iran has led many Western commentators to wonder whether Turkey might not be heading for an experience of the same sort. Certainly a militant, revivalist Islam is one of the ideologies competing to rescue Turkey's young people from nihilism and despair. Erbakan's NSP is a rather tame reflection of this but has given it some cover. In 1976, in order to compete with the fascistic 'Idealist Youth' groups run by a rival right-wing party, the Nationalist Action Party, the NSP formed a militant youth movement of its own, whose members carried out frequent armed attacks on leftist students and teachers, and also on Shi'ites, known in Turkey as Alevis.

The Alevis were a downtrodden and intermittently persecuted community in the strongly orthodox Ottoman Empire, suffering from their identification with the hostile power of Iran. Consequently, they espoused Mustafa Kemal's secularism with some enthusiasm, seeing in it a chance to get equality and full civil rights at last, and have generally been associated with the left in republican Turkish politics. For this reason right-wing forces, particularly the Nationalist Action Party, have sought in the last few years to drum up support by playing on Sunni prejudice against the Alevis, and have been helped in this by the Nurcus, who regard the Alevis as worse than unbelievers. The worst sectarian incident of this type occurred at the end of 1978 in the town of Kahramanmaraş, in south-eastern Turkey, when more than 100 people were killed.

Fears that Kemalist secularism was in danger may have been one of the factors that provoked the armed forces to take power yet again on 12 September 1980. The generals are said to have been outraged by an Islamic rally held in Konya on 6 September, with strong NSP support, ostensibly to demand the 'liberation of Jerusalem'. The meeting was officially organized by the World Assembly of Islamic Youth and attended by delegates from twenty Arab countries. Arabic banners were displayed, children sold turbans and young people wore prayer beads. After the coup, the martial law command in Konya charged four NSP leaders with organizing a demonstration 'against the secular laws of the country'. In Ankara, Erbakan and other NSP leaders were arrested and charged with trying to alter the fundamental principles of the state.[20]

It is worth noting that under the military regime there has been no return to militant secularism. Though professing, once again, to restore authentic Kemalism, the generals composing the new junta are well aware of the importance attached by the people to their Islamic identity and of the futility of trying to impose alien values. They have also continued the policy, which emerged during the 1970s, of seeking to strengthen Turkey's links with the rest of the Islamic world in the hope of getting economic and political support. At the Islamic summit in Ta'if, Saudi Arabia, in January 1981, Turkey was represented for the first time by her prime minister. (Initially she had sent only non-political officials to such gatherings, and latterly the foreign minister.) Following the summit the junta further reduced its relations with Israel (already at only consular level), though it has so far (April 1982) avoided a complete break. Close co-operation between Turkey and the Arab world has been inhibited partly by divisions within the Arab world itself. Turkey has not been prepared to sacrifice its Western ties to a non-aligned 'Islamic' foreign policy, as radical Arab states such as Libya would like, whereas conservative ones like Saudi Arabia and Kuwait have given substantial aid to Turkey only as part of a Western package. Turkey's other Muslim neighbour and historic rival, Iran, has so far offered little more than verbal promises of support, being too much preoccupied with its own domestic interests and conflicts.

Most of those who know Turkey best agree that anything like an Islamic revolution there is a very remote possibility. Atatürk's reforms went too far and too deep to be reversible after sixty years. But what is true is that, on the one hand, Turkey is still far from finding a solution to her political and social problems, and, on the other hand, the Kemalist state has not succeeded in producing a convincing national version of Islam to legitimize its power. Even though many loyal servants of the state are also sincere and believing Muslims, the state as such is not supported by any lively or organized religious tradition. Any kind of Muslim activism implies a degree of disloyalty to, or at least ambivalence about, the state. Between the secularism of the state and the religion of the people there is an unbridged gap. The 'real impoverishment of Turkish culture', resulting from the uncom-

CHAPTER SIX

Saudi Arabia — the Koran as Constitution

A constitution? What for? The Koran is the oldest and most efficient constitution in the world.

King Faisal, 1966

From Wahhabi Imamate to Saudi Kingdom

Mustafa Kemal's abolition of the Ottoman Caliphate in 1924 left a vacancy in the leadership of the Muslim world. In many places outside Turkey there were protests and expressions of dismay, but no one seems seriously to have entertained the idea of contesting or reversing the *fait accompli*. No one invited the exiled caliph to set up his headquarters elsewhere; since he had been elected, little more than a year before, by the Turkish National Assembly, his argument for contesting the right of the Turkish National Assembly to depose him would have been weak. Nor was there any attempt to bestow the caliphate on another member of the Ottoman house. It was generally recognized that the Ottoman Caliphate was a Turkish institution, an expression of Turkish overlordship of, and responsibility for, the historic heartlands of Islam, and a symbol of Turkish claims to leadership in the Muslim world as a whole. For better or worse, the Turks had lost their empire, waived their claims and abdicated their responsibilities. If Muslims wanted leadership they would now have to look for it elsewhere.

Not all Muslims had accepted the validity of the Ottoman claim to the caliphate in any case. The Shi'ites of various persuasions continued to believe in their Imams, whether hidden or visible (though, as we have seen, some Indian Shi'ites had come to attach moral and political importance to the Ottoman Caliphate without accepting its spiritual validity). But even among the Sunnis there were many who pointed out that, according to tradition, 'the imamate belongs to the Quraish' — that is, the Meccan tribe into which Muhammad was born. Clearly the Turkish Ottoman dynasty, originating from Central Asia, did not fulfil this qualification. If anyone in modern times could rightfully claim the caliphate, he must at least be an Arab, and preferably a descendant of the Prophet.

' The notion of an Arab caliphate might perhaps have gained wider support in the late nineteenth century if its most enthusiastic propagator had not happened to be an Englishman, Wilfrid Scawen Blunt. Blunt, a friend of Jamal al-Din al-Afghani, was in fact a genuine if somewhat romantic Arabophile, and even Islamophile, who bitterly opposed the British occupation of Egypt. But he also had close contacts with senior British politicians, whom he tried (generally without success) to influence in a pro-Muslim direction. In the circumstances it was hardly surprising that many Muslims viewed him and his ideas with suspicion, and regarded the proposal for an Arab caliphate as a British subterfuge to break up the Ottoman Empire, weaken Muslim unity, and get the holy places of Islam under indirect British control.

Yet naturally some Arabs were attracted by the idea, as also were some of the Khedives (Viceroys) of Egypt. The Khedives, descendants of Muhammad Ali, thought that assuming or controlling an Arab caliphate would give them a good pretext for declaring independence from the Ottoman Empire (of which Egypt remained officially part until 1914, even though occupied by the British) and becoming a major Middle Eastern power in their own right. The most directly interested party, however, was the Arabian Hashimite dynasty, which not only claimed descent from the Prophet but had actually been ruling over Mecca and Medina for the best part of a thousand years. During the First World War

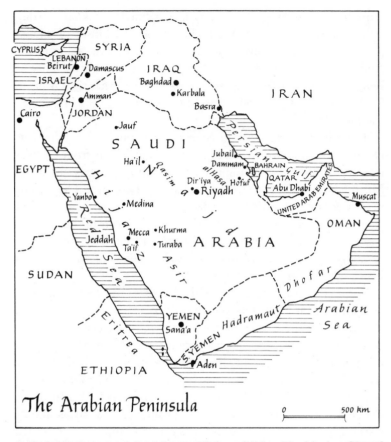

The Arabian Peninsula

0   500 km

the British, by promising to reward the reigning Hashimite, Sharīf Husain,* with an Arab kingdom embracing the entire Fertile Crescent — what are now Jordan, Syria and Iraq — persuaded him to revolt against the Ottoman Empire. The Hashimite contribution to the British war effort was, in fact, well rewarded. Although the Sharif's son Faisal, who had ridden into Damascus with T. E. Lawrence, was thwarted by the French in his attempt to install

* The Hashimites used the title Sharif (noble), which is customarily accorded to the Prophet's descendants in the Arab world. In Iran and the Indian subcontinent Muhammad's descendants are more commonly called Sayyid — an Arabic word, meaning 'lord' or 'prince', which is now so loosely used in Arab countries that it often serves to translate 'Mr'.

himself there as king, the British later named him king of Iraq, and installed his brother Abdullah in Amman as Emir of Transjordan. The Sharif himself, who had taken the title 'King of the Arabs' in 1916, remained in Mecca and was recognized only as King of the Hijaz. In 1924, as soon as he heard that the Ottoman Caliphate had been abolished, the Sharif proclaimed himself Caliph.

The weekly newspaper in Mecca began publishing telegrams of congratulation which allegedly were pouring in from all over the world, but most of these were probably spurious. In many Muslim countries there were expressions of outrage. The Hashimites were by now widely regarded as British stooges, and pilgrims from all over the world had experienced the effects of the Sharif's corrupt and inefficient administration of the holy places. He certainly lacked the prestige to decide unilaterally a matter in which all Muslims were concerned.

Within the Arabian peninsula, the Sharif's power was declining. He had a much more able and forceful rival: the Sultan of Najd, Abdul-Aziz ibn Abdul-Rahman Al Sa'ud,* a descendant of that Sa'ud ibn Abdul-Aziz who had conquered and 'purified' Mecca in 1803 and a believer in the same Wahhabi doctrine. In Najd (central Arabia) Wahhabism had survived and the Sa'ud dynasty had recovered from its overthrow by Muhammad Ali's forces in 1819† and from a later eclipse at the hands of local rivals, the Al Rashīd. In 1902, in a daring raid, the young Abdul-Aziz succeeded in retaking the capital, Riyadh. From there, in a series of campaigns, he gradually established his control over Najd and won acceptance as the authentic Imam — religious and political leader† of the Wahhabis. In 1913 he also won control of the neighbouring Hasa region, on the coast of the Persian Gulf, driving out the forces of the Ottoman government. Under his leadership, Wahhabism was once again combining militant reform with military expansion.

Abdul-Aziz developed a new kind of fighting force. The essence

---

* Often referred to in the West as 'Ibn Saud'.
† See p. 64.

of Islam, since Muhammad first preached it, had always been the rejection of the primitive beliefs and morals of the nomadic bedouin and the inculcation of rational, civilized religion — seen as appropriate for a sedentary and especially an urban population. Ibn Abdul-Wahhab's movement in the eighteenth century had been, at least in part, a protest against the fact that bedouin customs had again become prevalent among the inhabitants of the towns and villages of Najd, and a call to them to renounce the desert and undertake the *hijra* (migration) back to true Islam and settled civilization.

This call was repeated in the early twentieth century, when bedouin tribesmen themselves answered it in large number. The converted tribesmen were known as *Ikhwan* or Brethren. They undertook the *hijra* away from their nomadic, tribal existence and settled in co-operative, agriculturally orientated colonies, which thus became known as *hijras*. They knew that as nomads they would not be able to live up to the demands of the faith. '*Al-din hadari*', they said: faith is sedentary.

The atmosphere of the *hijras* was one of fervent monasticism* — the monasticism of the great crusading orders. The Ikhwan were determined to spread their new-found faith, and to spread it by force of arms. They also needed to do so, for they were inexperienced farmers, and agriculture in the arid plateau of central Arabia is far from easy. Legitimate plunder, taken from unbelievers and idolaters in the course of the *jihad*, was their best hope of avoiding starvation. They were therefore ready and eager to fight, in order to extend the domain of true Islam ruled by their Imam, Abdul-Aziz Al Sa'ud. In 1920 they conquered for him the mountainous and fertile region of Asir, immediately south of the Hijaz. In 1921 they finally defeated his rivals, the Al Rashid, taking their stronghold of Ha'il in northern Najd. In 1922 they went on to conquer Jauf in the far north. Thus, by the time Sharif Husain proclaimed his caliphate in 1924, his kingdom was surrounded on three sides by the territory of Abdul-Aziz.

* But not in the sense of celibacy. The Ikhwan took their women and children along with them.

There was a long-standing enmity between the two families, which had been revived during the First World War. Though he himself had been glad to accept a British subsidy, Abdul-Aziz disapproved of the Hashimite–British alliance and the Sharif's pretensions to be 'King of the Arabs'. In 1916 he wrote to the Emir of Mecca appointed by the Ottoman government, referring to the Sultan as 'His Majesty, the Caliph' and declaring himself 'under the orders of the Turkish Government and prepared to do anything you desire', if only supplies of ammunition were made available, against Husain and his sons 'who have transgressed the Law of the Holy Prophet.' He particularly criticized the Sharif for allowing Christians to enter the holy places. In 1918 there was actual fighting at the oases of Khurma and Turaba, between Hijaz and Najd, in which the Ikhwan first demonstrated their effectiveness as a fighting force, to the discomfiture of the Hashimites and the surprise of their British backers.

In 1923 the British government cut off the subsidies it was paying to both Abdul-Aziz and the Sharif. This tilted the power balance in Abdul-Aziz's favour: it weakened the Sharif, removed any incentive for Abdul-Aziz to avoid incurring British displeasure and at the same time gave him a strong incentive to gain control of the Hijaz and its lucrative pilgrim traffic. The Sharif's assumption of the caliphate, preposterous from a Wahhabi point of view, provided a good pretext. Once again the Wahhabis were ready to 'purify' the holy places, but this time they could do it in such a way as to earn the gratitude and respect, rather than the outraged disapproval, of the rest of the Muslim world. In the process they would bring into being a new Muslim state: the Kingdom of Saudi Arabia.

Abdul-Aziz was no doubt a sincere follower of Ibn Abdul-Wahhab's teachings, but he did not share the simple fanaticism of the Ikhwan. His concern to make a good impression on non-Wahhabi Muslims outside Arabia is an example of this. He was very careful not to appear to be acting simply in his own name or for his own self-aggrandizement, as the Sharif had done. He called a meeting of *ulama* and other leading people, at which his aged father presided, which sent a message, by Abdul-Aziz's son Faisal (then aged 19) to the Muslims of every country. It proposed that as soon as the current pilgrim season was over the Wahhabis, acting on behalf of the *umma*, should march into the Hijaz and depose the pseudo-caliph. There were not many answers, but a positive one from Indian Muslim leaders gave the British government an excuse for leaving the Sharif to his fate.[1]

A band of Ikhwan, sent on reconnaissance into the Sharif's territory, attacked the summer resort of Ta'if, in the hills above Mecca, without waiting for Abdul-Aziz himself to arrive, cutting the throats of all the men and boys they could find (some three or four hundred people) and murdering the local *ulama* in the mosque which, because of its domed tombs, they regarded as a place of idolatry. It looked as though the excesses of the 1803 conquest of the Hijaz were about to be repeated blow for blow. This was not what Abdul-Aziz wanted, and he is said to have wept with dismay and disgust. He was able to prevent the atrocities from being repeated when Mecca itself surrendered (the Sharif having been persuaded to abdicate by the merchants and *ulama*) a few weeks later. On 13 October 1924 Abdul-Aziz entered Mecca as a pilgrim, and proclaimed himself Guardian of the Holy Places. The following year Medina, too, fell to him, and he reassured foreign Muslim opinion by preventing the Ikhwan from destroying the Prophet's tomb.

Abdul-Aziz made no attempt to claim the title of caliph. His Imamate was more or less equivalent to a caliphate as far as the Wahhabis were concerned, and it carried with it effective political power. A symbolic, supranational caliphate was not recognizable to him as an Islamic institution and meant very little. Thus he had been prepared to pay lip-service to the Ottoman Caliphate when he thought it might supply him with ammunition, and apparently had even agreed in principle, after the conquest of Ta'if, to a suggestion that he should recognize the Sharif's caliphate if the Sharif in return would recognize him as political leader of Arabia. Political power was what interested him. When later he was asked whether he would accept the authority of another Arab leader if the Arabian peninsula could be united under a pan-Islamic movement, he replied: 'We know ourselves, and we cannot accept the leadership of others.'[2]

His concern for non-Wahhabi Muslim opinion arose from an awareness that, whereas political power in Najd, and even in Hasa, depended mainly on local factors and only marginally on external ones, political power in the Hijaz was a matter of direct concern to other Muslim powers — as his ancestors had found out when their conquest of the Hijaz had provoked the wrath of the Ottoman Empire and the invasion of Muhammad Ali. He was determined not to repeat that experience. Accordingly in October 1925 he wrote, somewhat disingenuously, to the governments of the main Islamic states of the day (Egypt, Iraq, Turkey, Persia and Afghanistan): 'I have no wish to be master of the Hijaz. It is a mandate which has been entrusted to me until the Hijazis have chosen a governor who can consider himself the servant of the Muslim world and who will work under the watchful eye of the Muslim peoples.' Three months later it was clear that he himself was after all the governor in question, but he took the title of King of the Hijaz, rather than simply incorporating the Hijaz into his existing Imamate or Sultanate.* He was under a good deal of pressure. The Iranian government, reflecting the profound mistrust of Wahhabism felt by all Shi'ites since the destruction of Karbala in 1802, sent a commission of inquiry to look into the damage done to tombs in the holy cities during the Ikhwan's onslaught, while Indian Muslims called for the formation of an international organization representing all Muslim states to administer the holy cities.

If only for financial reasons, Abdul-Aziz had to reassure prospective pilgrims that their safety would be guaranteed and their traditions respected. He announced that he would continue to rule the Hijaz not only according to the laws of Islam, but in the interests of the entire Islamic community. Indeed he wanted to show that pilgrims would benefit from his stricter administration.

* Abdul-Aziz had begun to use the secular title of Sultan after defeating the Al Rashid in 1921.

In March 1926 he ordered the Hijazi tribes, on pain of death, to desist from exploiting the pilgrims, whether by exacting tolls, escort fees and protection money, or by selling holy water, amulets and other superstitious artefacts. Later in the year he even endowed the kingdom of Hijaz with a constitution. The courts there continued to apply the Ottoman regulations, derived from the Hanafi school of legal thought, in spite of protests from the Wahhabi *ulama* who followed the Hanbali school.*

Gradually Abdul-Aziz did impose unity, and a degree of uniformity, on his wide domains. In 1927 he began to use the title of King in relation to Najd and his other possessions, as well as the Hijaz, and in 1932 the whole became a single Kingdom of Saudi Arabia. Similarly, a series of edicts were issued requiring magistrates to rely mainly on six Hanbali legal textbooks. But Abdul-Aziz — true in this to the spirit of Ibn Abdul-Wahhab — made it clear that they could use texts from other schools in cases where Hanbali law was silent or unclear on the point at issue.[3]

The years between 1924 and 1932 saw another, more substantive change in the nature of the Saudi state. Abdul-Aziz had broken decisively with the Ikhwan. Besides curbing their iconoclastic zeal in the Hijaz, he incurred their censure by adopting such 'un-Islamic' inventions as motor-cars, telephones and radio, and by levying 'un-Islamic' taxes, particularly on tobacco. The Wahhabi *ulama* strictly forbade the use of tobacco, in the same terms as that of alcohol, and anyone found smoking it in Najd was publicly whipped or otherwise punished. But in the Hijaz large quantities were consumed, and Abdul-Aziz saw the trade as a valuable source of revenue. Under pressure from the Ikhwan he agreed (temporarily) to stop taxing it, but also stopped the gifts or salaries which he had regularly paid to the Ikhwan, explaining that as a result of their puritanism 'straitened means have fallen on me and you'. This of course only exacerbated their discontent.

Moreover their usefulness to him had really ended with the conquest of the Hijaz, since the practical limits of crusading

* See pp. 172–3.

expansion had been reached. The new kingdom was surrounded by states whose borders were defined and protected by British power. The only exception was the Imamate of Yemen in the south-west, where a border war did continue intermittently until 1934. But Yemen, a mountainous country, much more densely populated than the rest of Arabia, did not lend itself to easy conquest by converted bedouin on racing camels. The Ikhwan preferred to raid northwards, across the new and arbitrarily drawn frontier of Iraq. Abdul-Aziz forbade this because Iraq was under British mandate and he did not want a confrontation with the British. The Ikhwan ignored his orders, and he turned a blind eye to their continued raids until, in 1929, deterred by British forces from crossing the border, they turned their destructive energies against tribes and merchants on his side of the frontier who were under his protection. This provoked a revulsion even of Najdi public opinion against the Ikhwan, enabling Abdul-Aziz to raise an army and to obtain the approval of the *ulama* for a campaign against them which, with some help from the infidel inventions they objected to, soon proved decisive. By 1930 the Ikhwan had ceased to exist as a military force. The Saudi state could no longer be identified with a militant reform movement determined to impose its own version of Islam on the rest of the world. It had become one Islamic state among others, with defined borders and a government prepared to temper religious zeal with worldly pragmatism.

Probably Abdul-Aziz had seen it that way all along. Though by all accounts a devout man, he was not averse to worldly pleasures, and seems to have regarded the Ikhwan as a useful if primitive instrument rather than a movement to which he was ideologically committed. He did not share, for instance, their antipathy to music, at least when it was vocal and of the traditional Arab type. There is a charming story of him on a journey in the desert with some twenty companions, looking round and saying: 'There are no Ikhwan with us. He who has a good voice will now let us hear it.' Whereupon, 'We started to sing, *wallah!* and Abd'ul Aziz was most pleased.'[4]

Neither Abdul-Aziz in his later years nor any of his successors ever referred to themselves publicly as Imam. And in 1955, two years after Abdul-Aziz's death, his friend Harry St John Philby could write: 'the dreaded words, *Ikhwan* and *Wahhabi*, have scarce been heard in the land for twenty years, and are only remembered now with something like a blush.'[5]

Islam and Change: the Modern Saudi State

Philby also drew a striking picture of some other changes that had overcome the Kingdom by the end of its founder's life:

In the name of military efficiency the once forbidden charms of music were openly paraded on the palace square, or blared in the face of a monarch, who sickened at the sound. The forbidden cinema reared its ogling screens in scores of princely palaces and wealthy mansions to flaunt the less respectable products of Hollywood before audiences which would have blushed or shuddered at the sight but ten or fifteen years ago. Liquor and drugs have penetrated, more or less discreetly, into quarters where, in the old days, people had been slain at sight for the crime of smoking tobacco, which has now become a substantial source of State revenue. Even the seclusion of women has been tempered to the prevailing breeze of modernism; and the motor-car provides facilities for visits to some beach or desert pleasaunce, where they dance or frolic to the tunes of a gramophone (another prohibited article) in the latest summer frocks from Paris, or dine *alfresco* in strapless bodices.[6]

What had happened? Had Abdul-Aziz, having broken with the Ikhwan, decided, like Mustafa Kemal, to wrench his country away from the past and build a modern 'civilized' nation? Certainly not. He resembled Kemal, perhaps, in being a hard-headed politician who preferred to build a solid power-base within geographical limits than to pursue a pan-Islamic vision, but hardly in anything else. He could see the usefulness of motor-cars, telephones and the radio — and convinced the *ulama* that the last of these was not contrary to Islam by demonstrating that it could faithfully transmit the text of the Koran. He was aware of Britain as a great power that had to be treated carefully, and he could rationalize his friendship with her by saying that the British were Christians, People of the Book, and therefore preferable to idolaters and backsliding Muslims such as Sharif Husain and his supporters. But he certainly did not think of the British or other Europeans as more civilized than himself, or that their way of living and thinking was one for Arabians to follow. When he saw his people and his relatives beginning to do so it profoundly saddened and disturbed him.

What brought Western goods and customs flooding into his country in the last years of his life was something which at first had seemed the answer to all his problems: the discovery of oil, which happened on Saudi territory only in 1938. Production began in 1939, but did not take off on a large scale until the end of the Second World War, when it rose from 20,000 barrels per day in 1943 to more than half a million by 1949. At first the Saudi government received a royalty of only 21 cents per barrel, but in 1950 a deal was made under which the Arabian American Oil Company (Aramco) paid tax on its profits to the Saudi government instead of to the US government. Payments to Abdul-Aziz jumped from $39.2 million in 1949 to $110 million in 1951. Over the period 1948–60 he and his successor received nearly $2.9 billion from this source.

Abdul-Aziz had no budget and never controlled his expenditure systematically. He belonged to a tradition in which generosity was one of the principal qualities expected of a leader and the principal means by which he secured the loyalty of his followers; and in which extended families were expected to stick together in good fortune and bad. He distributed his new-found wealth more or less haphazardly, especially among his very numerous sons. Many of them saw no reason to spend it on anything but their own pleasure, and the only way they could do that was by travelling abroad and by importing Western luxuries. This in turn, combined with the needs of the oil industry itself, resulted in a rapid increase in the number of foreigners living in the country.

The process continued under Abdul-Aziz's son Sa'ud, who succeeded him in 1953. Sa'ud did not inherit his father's political flair, and had even less sense of financial organization. He spent lavishly on new palaces for himself as well as on gifts for tribal leaders to ensure their support. The Kingdom staggered from financial crisis to political crisis until, in October 1962, Sa'ud was obliged by a council of senior princes to hand over effective power to his brother Faisal, who at last endowed the country with a set of more or less regularly functioning institutions. In 1964 Sa'ud was formally deposed and Faisal became king in his place. Faisal remained in full control until his assassination in 1975. The structure, style and even policies of government in Saudi Arabia today remain very much as he established them.

What is the nature of that government, and what role does Islam play in the state? In the first place, it is not a theocracy, if by that term is understood government by a priestly caste claiming a divine mandate to govern. The *ulama* themselves utterly reject such a notion: they assert that the Kingdom is not theocratic 'since it derives its authority from the people.'[7] The *ulama* do not claim any special inspiration from God, either direct or indirect. Such a claim would be entirely contrary to the Wahhabi interpretation of Islam. They are respected and consulted only on account of their learning.

Nor do they, in fact, govern the country. We saw in Chapter 3 that Ibn Abdul-Wahhab did not put himself forward as a ruler, but recognized and promoted the Imamate of the Al Sa'ud. His descendants and the other leading *ulama* of Saudi Arabia today continue to uphold the political authority of the Sa'ud dynasty even though the heads of the latter no longer use the title 'Imam' but the purely secular one of 'King'. The King continues to consult the *ulama* and clearly their support is very important in legitimizing his rule, but there are signs that the monarchy's control over them has been growing rather than the other way round. A very significant step was taken in this direction in 1970 with the creation of the Ministry of Justice, to replace the former office of Chief Mufti. The Minister of Justice is a senior *alim* and a member of the Al Shaikh family (i.e. a descendant of Ibn Abdul-Wahhab), but he is also a member of the council of ministers and the head of a government department, carrying out the King's instructions. In other words the administration and enforcement of the Shari'a has become merely one aspect of government among others, rather than the definition of what government is. The Saudi Kingdom is becoming less like the original *umma* of Muhammad and more like, say, the Ottoman Empire.

Secondly, while in theory the law in Saudi Arabia is simply the eternal, God-given Shari'a, that does not mean that in practice legislation to meet the particular needs of the time is impossible. Since the 1950s a number of codes have been issued by royal decree regulating different areas of life which for one reason or another did not receive detailed attention in traditional Islamic jurisprudence, or in which the twentieth century brought radically new conditions: for instance, Commerce (1954), Nationality (1954), Forgery (1961), Bribery (1962), Mining (1963), Labour and Workmen (1970), Social Insurance (1970) and the Civil Service (1971). All this is not seen as adding to or modifying the Shari'a, but simply as implementing it by appropriate administrative action. Legislation in that sense has been part of Islamic tradition since at least the eleventh century AD. In the Ottoman Empire such man-made laws were called *qānūn*, a word which, like our 'canon', is derived from the Greek *kanōn*, used for laws issued by the Byzantine emperors. The Saudis prefer the word *nizām* — order or regulation — to make it quite clear that they are not usurping the role of law-maker, which belongs to God.

Of course such legislation must not run counter to the Shari'a, where there is a consensus on what the relevant provisions of the Shari'a are — and the Saudi *ulama* still hold that the consensus needed is *their* consensus, the consensus of those qualified by their education to express an opinion, rather than the consensus of the community as a whole. But they have shown a certain flexibility in interpreting the Shari'a, and in this they are faithful to the tradition of Ibn Hanbal, Ibn Taimiya, and Ibn Abdul-Wahhab. Because this tradition is associated with crusading puritanism it has a reputation in the Islamic world for being very restrictive and inflexible. But this is a misunderstanding. A key principle of Hanbali thought is that 'things are assumed to be allowable unless there is proof of their prohibition', and the Hanbalis had never accepted the view of other Sunni schools of thought that the 'gate of *ijtihad*' was closed. Only the consensus of the Prophet's own time was permanently valid, in their view; whatever had not been settled then was always open to reinterpretation through independent reasoning in the light of new circumstances. The scholar had a responsibility to use his own judgement.*

The result is that Hanbali legal rulings can in fact be more 'progressive' than those of other schools. For instance, while polygamy (up to four wives) is clearly allowed by the Koran it is not positively prescribed. The Hanbalis therefore argue that a contract between husband and wife, binding the husband not to take other wives (or not to do so without the first wife's consent), is valid and binding because it contains nothing contrary to the Shari'a, whereas other schools of thought hold that such a contract is invalid and not binding. The Young Turks used this Hanbali ruling when they reformed Ottoman family law in 1917, and it was subsequently incorporated into the modernized family laws of Jordan, Syria, Morocco and Iraq.

In a number of instances the Saudi *ulama* have shown themselves amenable to royal pressure. As already mentioned, they accepted King Abdul-Aziz's argument that the radio was acceptable because it could be used to transmit the Koran. Similarly, he was able to persuade them that photography was permissible, even though pictorial art is not, on the grounds that photography does not involve human usurpation of the creative function, but simply brings together light and shadow created by God. In 1944 the *ulama* supported him against accusations (from a veteran of the Ikhwan) that his oil concession to the Americans was illegal because it involved selling Muslim land to unbelievers. Likewise they

* In practice, Wahhabi scholars have often come up with very rigorous interpretations of the law. But they do so by reasoning from first principles, rather than by slavishly following precedent.

accepted, after initially opposing, a number of innovations introduced by Faisal when he was Crown Prince: the introduction of
television (1958), and of education for women (1960), and the
abolition of slavery in 1962. In 1964 they ratified the result of
Faisal's power struggle with his brother Sa'ud, by declaring the
latter's deposition 'in the public interest', but only after a consensus
on this point had already been reached by the senior princes of
the royal house. To deal with cases where the more conservative
among them feel unable to give positive support to change, the
ulama now endorse the idea that there can be a consensus even
when some of them remain silent.[8]

Saudi Arabia, then, is not a theocracy but an Islamic monarchy,
in which the king claims to derive his authority from the people
and to rule them with their consent in accordance with the holy
law. In principle he accepts the authority of the *ulama* as interpreters of the law, but in practice he exercises wide discretion,
including what amounts to legislative power in many areas of life,
and by a combination of patience and pressure he can usually
obtain from the *ulama* the ruling that he wants. What makes Saudi
Arabia interesting is not that the Islamic order there is frozen and
immutable, but that it has developed organically, applying its own
principles. Saudi Arabia has experienced neither direct colonial
rule nor the rule of an elite which believed that the West had
reached a higher stage of civilization and that the world of Islam
must follow it. Her rulers, as far as one can tell, remain sincerely
convinced of Islam's superiority, not only as a moral but also as
a social system. 'We believe neither in socialism nor in communism,
nor in any doctrine outside Islam,' King Faisal (himself a descen-
dent of Ibn Abdul-Wahhab, through his mother) once declared.
'We only believe in Islam.' There may be some changes that some
of them would like to introduce sooner or faster, but are held
back from by respect for the *ulama*'s opinion. If so, that is not
because the *ulama* as such have the power to stop them, but
because they still have a role, rather like that of the Press in
Western democracies, as both formers of and spokesmen for public
opinion.

No doubt it would be possible for a radical government to create a different kind of public opinion by appealing directly to the people and bullying the *ulama* into supporting it, just as Western governments can sometimes mobilize a 'silent majority' beyond the Press. That has been done in other Muslim countries. But just as a democratic government knows that if it systematically ignores or dragoons the Press it is destroying the system which produced it, and from which it derives its legitimacy, so the Saudi royal family know that their rule is legitimized by an Islamic system of which respect for the *ulama* is a key part. Paraphrasing King James I of England, they could say: no *alim*, no king.

The result is that many features of traditional Islamic law are still enforced today in Saudi Arabia, and because the tradition is a Wahhabi tradition the interpretation of the law is often puritanical and the enforcement of it very strict. The sale and public consumption of alcohol are forbidden (though that of tobacco no longer). Women are not allowed to drive cars, or to travel unaccompanied by a male relative, or to do any work that involves dealing with men to whom they are not related. Commerce and labour must stop during the five daily hours of prayer. No church or temple of any religion other than Islam is permitted on Saudi soil. The charging of interest on loans is illegal, though in practice banks apply 'service charges' which have much the same effect (and the government, of course, receives interest on its substantial holdings in foreign banks). Thieves are still punished by amputation of the hand, drinkers and a wide range of other offenders by flogging, adulterers on occasion (as in the famous *Death of a Princess**) by execution. The law is enforced by a corps of *muttawwiun* ('those who obey or volunteer'), sometimes called religious police, under the supervision of Public Morality Committees which keep alive the spirit of the Ikhwan.

---

* In 1980 a British television 'docudrama' caused a short but serious crisis in Anglo–Saudi relations. It was based on the execution for adultery of a princess of the house of Sa'ud on the orders of her grandfather, the King's elder brother.

An 'Islamic' Foreign Policy

We may sum up Faisal's achievements by saying that he created a state in Saudi Arabia, which until then had been nothing more than the personal dominion accumulated by his father. This state, like the principal individuals composing it, is phenomenally wealthy. The export of oil has brought it a foreign currency income far in excess of its needs. This was relatively true even in the 1960s, when the price of oil was much lower than it is now. It was during that decade that Saudi Arabia emerged as an important regional power, starting with its intervention in the Yemen civil war at the end of 1962 to support the royalists against the Egyptian-backed republic. Since 1973 it has also emerged as something of a world power, partly because of the multi-billion dollar currency reserves it has accumulated and partly because its oil production policy has become a matter of crucial importance to Western industrialized nations.

It is, therefore, a country with a foreign policy of some consequence. How has the Islamic character of the state affected that policy? Here, too, the main lines of policy were established by Faisal, whose view of the world derived essentially from his understanding of Islam. One may say that Saudi foreign policy is traditionally Islamic in that it takes much more account of religion – and, by extension, of ideology – than it does of nationalism. There is not really such a thing as Saudi nationalism, or a Saudi nation. (There is, of course, a Saudi nationality, but this is a purely legal and administrative thing, with little or no emotive significance.) The only nationalism which affects, or might affect, Saudi Arabians is Arab nationalism, and that is something the Saudi rulers in general, and Faisal in particular, have strongly distrusted from the moment they first came across it – which was probably the moment in 1916 when Sharif Husain of Mecca proclaimed himself 'King of the Arabs'.

In Faisal's time Arab nationalism was associated above all with Gamal Abdul Nasser who tried to use it to overthrow what he saw as corrupt and reactionary Arab monarchies and to make

Egypt the leader of a 'progressive' (later 'socialist') and non-aligned Arab world. In the chaotic conditions of Sa'ud's reign (1953–64) Saudi Arabia seemed an easy target. Even some members of the royal family — the so-called 'Free Princes' — were infected with the nationalist virus in a mild form, and at one point (in 1960) Sa'ud tried to use them to reduce Faisal's influence.* When Faisal returned to power in 1962 their leader, Prince Talal, went into exile in Cairo and founded a Front for the Liberation of Arabia. Later in the year, when the civil war broke out in Yemen, some pilots from the Saudi airforce defected to Egypt and one of them claimed that: 'There is an organization in Saudi Arabia which includes free officers and civilians. All of them are waiting an opportunity, which we hope will come very soon.'[9] Later still, after his dethronement in 1964, Sa'ud himself went to Cairo and fulminated against his brother on Nasser's 'Voice of the Arabs' radio station.

Faisal therefore had ample reason to distrust Arab nationalism, which he regarded as a spurious doctrine invented for the purpose of smuggling foreign ideas, such as socialism, into the minds of Muslim Arabs. That is not to say that he attached no importance to the fact of being an Arab. To be an authentic Arab of Arabia, a member of the race to which the Koran was sent and a speaker of the language in which it was revealed, was to him a very important privilege, about which he felt no need for lessons from Egyptians. 'We do not need to import foreign traditions,' he said. 'We have a history and a glorious past. We led the Arabs and the World.... With what did we lead them? The Word of the One God and the Shari'a of His Prophet.'[10] Being Arab for him was thus a special way of being Muslim and gave you a special responsibility towards Islam. But to cultivate an 'Arab nation', distinct from the Muslim *umma*, was unacceptable — a form of idolatry.

It was therefore not just as a diplomatic ploy but as a matter of principle that, during the 1960s, Faisal sought to trump Nasser's pan-Arabism by founding a pan-Islamic movement, the Muslim

---

* Sa'ud himself took over the prime ministership, which Faisal had held since 1958, and gave other ministries to 'progressives', including Prince Talal.

World League, using the annual pilgrimage as an occasion to confer with other Muslim leaders and to make major speeches setting out his ideas. His success was limited so long as Nasser was in the ascendant, but after Nasser's disastrous defeat by the Israelis in 1967 things began to change. Nasser had to drop his ideas of pan-Arab revolution and concentrate on building solidarity between the existing Arab regimes. There was a series of Arab summit conferences at which the oil-producing Arab states, with Saudi Arabia foremost among them, were given a place of honour and influence. Egypt, Syria and Jordan, the states which had lost territory to Israel, accepted Saudi subsidies to rebuild their economies and armed forces. Throughout the Arab world there was a questioning of the value of nationalism, and it was widely asserted that the defeat was a punishment of the Arabs for straying from the path of true Islam. In 1969 an Australian Christian fanatic set fire to the Aqsa mosque in Israeli-occupied Jerusalem. The outrage which this caused throughout the Muslim world enabled Faisal to convene an Islamic summit conference at Rabat in Morocco, at which it was agreed to set up a permanent organization.

In the 1970s Saudi influence grew with Saudi wealth, although since Faisal's death in 1975 that influence has perhaps been less firmly and consistently exercised. Saudi Arabia has become one of the major sources of foreign aid for developing countries. By far the greater part of this aid has gone to Muslim countries, with a clear preference for governments that pursue what the Saudis consider authentically Islamic policies. This means, first and foremost, opposition to communism and Soviet influence, and to any other radical ideologies which might act as their stalking-horses; and secondly, willingness to move towards at least an approximation of enforcement of the Shari'a as it is understood in Saudi Arabia. A third element is solidarity with the Arab consensus on how to handle the conflict with Israel. Faisal's own conviction that Zionism was actually part of a communist world conspiracy may have died with him, but his successors remain extremely sensitive to the danger that the Israel issue may be exploited against them by nationalist and pro-Soviet forces in the Arab world. They have made it clear (as Faisal never did) that they are prepared to accept peace with Israel in principle, but they know that their close association with the United States, Israel's main backer, renders them vulnerable to the accusation that they are betraying the Arab and Islamic cause, and they are therefore acutely concerned to cover their flank on this issue by maintaining a common Arab position with the broadest possible support. That is why President Sadat of Egypt, who scored very highly on anti-communism and opposition to Soviet influence and rated at least a B+ for emphasis on Islam in his domestic policies, forfeited Saudi support after his desertion of the Arab united front on the Israeli issue in 1977.

As well as giving support to Muslim governments which share their aims, the Saudis naturally look with favour on groups within Muslim countries which seek to move them in that direction, such as the Muslim Brotherhood in Egypt and the Jamaat-i-Islami in Pakistan.* Both these movements are widely assumed in their respective countries to enjoy Saudi financial support, though whether this comes directly from the Saudi state or from sympathetic individuals within the royal family is not clear. In 1980, when I interviewed Saudi Justice Minister Ibrahim al-Shaikh in Riyadh, I was mildly surprised to be given a copy in French (but printed in England) of *Towards Understanding Islam* by Abul A'la al-Maududi, the founder and late leader of Jamaat-i-Islami. This kind of support can be both ideological and financial (just as the Soviet Union supports foreign communist parties partly by purchasing their publications in large quantities).

Of a less directly political nature, though still in the general perspective of strengthening Islam against rival, radical ideologies, is the aid given to promote the teaching of Arabic in non-Arab Muslim countries, for the construction of mosques, cultural centres, Islamic schools and universities, for the financing of radio programmes on Islam, and in the form of scholarships for foreign Muslims to study in Saudi universities.

* See Chapters 7 and 8.

Non-Arab Muslim governments which have benefited from Saudi aid, based on the above principles, include those of Pakistan, Bangladesh, Malaysia and Indonesia in Asia and Nigeria, Uganda, Mali, Niger, Cameroon, Gabon and (until 1980) Chad in Africa. Support has also been given, of course, to the Afghan *mujahidin* who are waging *jihad* against the atheist Soviet invaders of their country. A cheque for $25 million was somewhat flamboyantly handed over to a group of 'Islamic' Afghan leaders at the Islamic foreign ministers' conference in Islamabad, Pakistan, in May 1980.[11] Equally obviously, the use of Islam to justify radical policies and/or criticisms of the Saudi regime itself, as in Colonel Qadhafi's Libya or Ayatollah Khomeini's Iran, meets with strong Saudi hostility and condemnation. And even though, at the Ta'if Islamic summit of January 1981, the regime associated itself with a call for independence from *both* superpowers, there seems no likelihood, as long as the present rulers remain in power, that it will adopt a genuinely non-aligned policy. King Khalid, Crown Prince Fahad, and foreign minister Sa'ud al-Faisal (son of the late king) are all genuinely and deeply embarrassed by United States support for Israel. Of that there can be no reasonable doubt. But this embarrassment stems from their view, inherited from King Faisal, that the interests of Islam are in the last resort identified with those of the 'free world' — which Faisal saw as the Christian world, ruled by 'people of the book' — against those of atheistic communism, and there is no reason to think that will change. The contradiction they see is in American support for Zionism, which they believe is clearly contrary to American interests in the Middle East, rather than in their own support for the United States. The Ta'if resolution shows, however, the extent of the strain to which this aspect of US policy subjects them.

Mecca and After: the System Under Stress

Although the Saudi regime appears much stronger and more influential today than it did in the 1960s, its foreign policy remains strikingly defensive in style and tone. There is more of a preoccupation with 'threats', and especially with the real or supposed Soviet threat, than with opportunities for positive achievement. (This probably makes the Reagan administration more congenial to the Saudis than its predecessor, in spite of Reagan's ostensibly less sympathetic approach to the Palestinian question.) The fall of the Shah in Iran and his replacement by an Islamic revolutionary regime undoubtedly increased that feeling of insecurity. So too, in spite of many official and semi-official statements belittling its importance, did the incident at Mecca in November 1979. Coinciding (though not directly connected) with disturbances among the Shi'ite population of the Hasa province, where the oilfields are, this incident was the most serious breach of public order in the Kingdom since the suppression of the Ikhwan in 1930 — much more serious than the assassination of King Faisal, which was the work of a single, probably deranged, member of the royal family. These events demonstrated that the regime faces challenges to its legitimacy based not only on 'foreign' ideologies such as nationalism, liberalism or Marxism but also, potentially much more dangerous, within the framework of Islam itself.

At 5.30 a.m. on the first day of the year 1400 of the Muslim calendar (20 November 1979) the dawn prayers in the Holy Mosque at Mecca (the place towards which Muslims all over the world face when they pray) were interrupted by a group of armed men who proclaimed one of their number as the Mahdi and proceeded to barricade themselves in the mosque, trapping many of the worshippers (mostly Pakistanis) inside. They held out against government troops in the mosque itself for five days, and in the cellars and retreats underneath for a further ten. By the time the rebels surrendered, 127 people on the government side had been killed or wounded. The Holy Mosque had been profaned by bloodshed and the prestige of the Al Sa'ud as its guardians badly damaged.

The rebels called themselves 'Ikhwān', and their leader, Juhaiman al-Utaiba, was a relative of one of the tribal leaders involved in the Ikhwan revolt of 1928–30. Juhaiman had been educated at Medina University, which was founded in 1960 by members of the Egyptian Muslim Brotherhood (Ikhwān al-Muslimūn) driven into exile by Nasser. In the early Seventies he attended lectures there given by Shaikh Abdul-Aziz ibn Baz, a blind scholar of exceptional learning and thoroughly obscurantist views,* who is now head of the Council of Ulama (and who in that capacity was to sign Juhaiman's death warrant in January 1980). In 1974 Juhaiman left the university with a group of ten followers and started preaching in his tribal homeland of Qasim (west-central Arabia). The group also bought a house in Riyadh and 'engaged in strident addresses in downtown mosques.'[12] In 1978 they started publishing pamphlets written by Juhaiman, arguing that the royal family was wicked and corrupt ('they worship the riyal' — the Saudi currency) and should be opposed. Juhaiman and ninety-eight followers were arrested, but released after six weeks at ibn Baz's request, promising that they would hold no further public assemblies. It was apparently only after this that Juhaiman broke with ibn Baz, alleging that he had been 'bought' by the corrupt rulers, and also developed the idea that one of his companions, Muhammad Abdullah al-Qahtani, was the Mahdi. A new pamphlet, expounding the doctrine that the Mahdi would be named in the Holy Mosque amid violent opposition from existing powers, was published in 1979.

This marriage of the chiliastic, visionary doctrine of the Mahdi with the puritanism of the Wahhabi Ikhwan shows that the movement was nothing if not eclectic. The group that carried out the occupation of the mosque contained not only people of Arabian tribal background but members of Islamic activist groups in Kuwait, Egypt, the Indian subcontinent (even, according to one report, Black Muslims from the United States), all of whom had come to study Islamic law and theology in Saudi universities — an unforeseen result of the government's foreign aid policies. In other

---

* In 1966 he wrote an essay condemning the Copernican 'heresy' and asserting that the sun orbits around a fixed earth. King Faisal suppressed the essay, but it was quoted with delight by Nasser's press. See David Holden and Richard Johns, *The House of Saud* (London 1981), p. 262.

words, the movement had both a local and a pan-Islamic dimension. To say that it had wide support in Saudi society would certainly be misleading. Most Saudis, like most Muslims everywhere, were profoundly shocked by the use of armed force to seize Islam's holiest shrine. Yet it is striking that this choice of target was the *only* aspect of the revolt which many Saudis criticized in private conversation. Many of them echoed, in milder form, the graffito that appeared in the toilets of Riyadh University in spring 1981: 'Juhaiman, our martyr, why didn't you storm the palaces? The struggle is only beginning.'[13]

There is no doubt that the extent of corruption, particularly within the royal family, has become a major source of resentment and irritation to much of the Saudi population. Although most Saudis have benefited in some degree from the oil bonanza (they are better off, at least, than the immigrant workers whose manual labour is covering the country with new cities, factories, ports and airports, and who lack the most elementary trade union rights) the benefits are far from equally distributed. A poll carried out by the newspaper *Okaz* revealed that 11 per cent of heads of families on the outskirts of Jeddah, when asked their 'dearest wish', replied: to have enough to buy meat once a week.[14] Eighty per cent of Saudis are still illiterate and lack marketable skills. But, for the present at least, resentment of the royal family's behaviour is probably sharper among the prosperous and now usually Western-educated middle classes: the most frequent subject of complaint being not the commissions taken on government contracts, but the practice of granting large areas of development land, which are then either bought back by the government for vast sums or developed by the owner at a huge profit. Billboards along the highways advertising the princely ownership of these soon-to-be-filled spaces are felt to add insult to injury.[15]

The manner in which the princes spend their wealth is no less resented because it jars so obviously with the public enforcement of an 'Islamic' moral code. The innovations which shocked Philby in 1955 are a hundred times more widespread today, and the reaction of the government to criticism on this score has been simply to enforce the law with greater severity *in public*.* 'Business and household life (and even road safety) are almost completely unregulated while the Press, hotels, swimming pools and attendance at the mosque are closely watched by both the authorities and responsible citizenry.'[16] The behaviour of the ruling class inside their palaces — let alone on their numerous trips to Europe and the United States — remains notoriously a constant violation of the Shari'a as officially interpreted in Saudi courts.

A gap between private and public morality exists in many countries, and the Saudi royal family may well get away with it for some time yet. But the government's tendency to issue vague promises of reform and then not follow them up suggests a certain uneasiness and infirmity of purpose. In particular, there is the question of the constitution. One was reportedly agreed upon as long ago as December 1960, when King Sa'ud brought the 'Free Princes' into his government. But it was never officially proclaimed. In 1962 Faisal in his turn promised a 'Basic Law', which

---

* An aspect of this is the increasingly strict enforcement of Islamic law on the public behaviour of non-Muslim foreigners. In Abdul-Aziz's time the few Westerners in the country had to do without most of the advantages of modern technology, but were allowed to live more or less as they pleased. For instance, they could import alcohol (and paid tax on it to the King's treasury), and Western women were allowed to drive cars. But restrictions have multiplied as the number of foreigners has increased (it is now 2.5 million out of a total of about 7 million) and as Saudi society itself has begun to be contaminated by Western habits. Significantly it was the murder of a British diplomat by one of Abdul-Aziz's sons, in a drunken rage, that led the old king to ban alcohol in the last year of his life. Philby remarked in 1957 on the paradox that 'while in the days of extreme religious and national fanaticism not so long ago, the despised stranger within the gate was accorded a wide measure of latitude in the enjoyment of his own way of life undisturbed, the general acceptance by the Arabs themselves of foreign ways and standards has been accompanied by a series of pin-prick restrictions on the amenities and privileges of the foreign benefactor.' This is still more true today when 'almost everyone has — or has had — a friend in jail, many awaiting a hearing years after the alleged offence: young Americans imprisoned without trial for drug smuggling; Britons for selling hooch; Europeans for giving a party at which drink was served and women danced with men other than their husbands.' (*Financial Times*, 28 April 1980.) The authorities seem to feel a need to prove to Saudi public opinion that unbelievers are not being let off lightly.

would 'set forth explicitly the fundamental principles of government and the relationship between the governor and the governed, organize the various powers of the State and the relationship among these powers, and provide for the basic rights of the citizen, including the right to freely express his opinion within the limit of Islamic belief and public policy.' But four years later the Law had not been published, and Faisal replied to questions about it with the remark about the all-sufficiency of the Koran given at the head of this chapter. Again after Faisal's assassination in 1975 Prince Fahad announced that a consultative assembly and a constitution would be set up. And in January 1980, after the Mecca incident, he promised that the consultative assembly (Majlis al-Shura) would be formed within two months.

Two months later a nine-man committee was formed, chaired by the Minister of the Interior, Prince Nayif ibn Abdul-Aziz, to draw up the statute of the Assembly and make recommendations on its final form. This was taken by many qualified observers to mean that something was really going to happen, and that the royal family was at last taking the need for reform seriously. But more than a year later, in April 1981, the best that Prince Nayif could announce was that the King would 'soon start consideration' of the Committee's suggestions.*

Whether such an assembly, composed of appointed members, would make any great difference in practice is doubtful. But the inability of the government even to follow up its own declared intentions on such a point (or to make any serious attack on corruption within the royal family) gives a disquieting impression of drift. Behind this lies a growing tension between the interpretation of Islam officially expressed by the state and the economic and social realities of the country. If not resolved, it seems this tension is bound sooner or later to prove explosive.

* In March 1982 Prince Fahad said that a system of 'consultation and collective responsibility in decision-making, through a select group of learned men' would be announced in June (Associated Press, 29 March 1982).

CHAPTER SEVEN

Pakistan — Islam as Nationality

Self: How would you describe the 'vital principles' of Pakistan?
Jinnah: In five words: 'the Muslims are a Nation.'

Beverley Nichols, The Verdict on India
(*Bombay, 1944*)

Introduction

In Turkey a deliberate choice was made to build a 'secular' republic in a Muslim country, on the ruins of an Islamic empire. In Saudi Arabia an Islamic kingdom was coming into existence at the same time, but its Islamic nature was not so much a matter of deliberate choice as a spontaneous expression of the society that gave birth to it — a society to which the concept of secularism was simply unintelligible.

A generation later, in 1947, a new Muslim state came into being in the Indian subcontinent, in territory part of which had been under British rule for 100, and part for nearly 200 years. It was a new state and it took a new name: Pakistan, 'land of the pure'. It defined itself as a state 'wherein the Muslims shall be enabled to order their lives in the individual and collective spheres in accord with the teachings and requirements of Islam as set out in the Holy Quran and the Sunna.' It declared that 'sovereignty over the entire universe belongs to God Almighty alone' and that therefore authority would be exercised by the people of Pakistan only 'within the limits prescribed by Him.'[1] Later it proclaimed itself an 'Islamic Republic', and built itself a capital city called Islamabad.

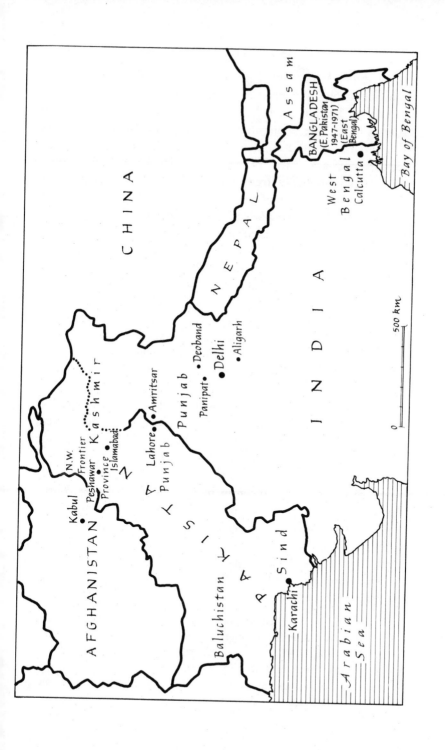

All this was very much a matter of deliberate, indeed self-conscious choice. Whereas the Saudi state continued and developed an existing Islamic order, Pakistan was an attempt to recreate an Islamic order after a long period of Western colonial rule; it was also a rejection of the independent, united, multi-confessional, secular India advocated by the Indian National Congress. Both these things implied a tremendous effort of will. Pakistan was therefore an experiment of great significance for Muslims wherever (which was almost everywhere) the incursion of the West had broken the continuity of their political tradition. Saudi Arabia was an interesting example of a traditional Islamic state surviving, and to some extent adapting, held together by Wahhabi reformism. But Pakistan was setting out to be a model of much wider applicability and greater attractive force: a modern Islamic state.

But what was Pakistan? What did its founder, Muhammad Ali Jinnah, mean when he declared that 'the Muslims are a nation'? Was he reviving the idea of the universal *umma*, the single community of believers overriding all other divisions and loyalties, whether tribal, regional or linguistic? Was Pakistan to be the nucleus of a pan-Islamic state which would gradually spread as successive groups of Muslims threw off the yoke of other powers or ideologies and joined themselves to it, until the worldwide 'Muslim' nation was at last united?

In fact Jinnah did not mean that. He was referring specifically to the Muslims of the subcontinent and arguing that they constituted a nation in their own right. But there was great ambiguity about the relationship between nationality and religion as he expressed it in the interview conducted in 1943, part of which is quoted at the head of this chapter. The interviewer, Beverley Nichols, went on to ask him: 'When you say the Muslims are a Nation, are you thinking in terms of religion?' Jinnah replied:

Partly, but by no means exclusively. You must remember that Islam is not merely a religious doctrine but a realistic and practical code of Conduct. I am thinking in terms of life, of everything important in life. I am thinking in terms of our history, our heroes, our art, our architecture, our music, our

188

laws, our jurisprudence.... In all these things our outlook is
not only fundamentally different but often radically antagonistic
to the Hindus. We are different beings. There is nothing in life
which links us together. Our names, our clothes, our foods — they
are all different; our economic life, our educational ideas, our
treatment of women, our attitude to animals ... we challenge
each other at every point of the compass.

This passage has since been quoted in Pakistan both by people
wishing to argue that Jinnah's view of the differences between
Muslims and Hindus was an essentially secular one (and therefore
that Pakistan as he envisaged it was to be a secular state) and by
people who point out that he viewed Islam as relevant to all aspects
of life, and who argue from that that he envisaged Pakistan as a fully
Islamic state in which life would be regulated entirely by the Koran
and the Sunna.

To some extent this ambiguity is inherent in the very nature
of Islam. Islam can be described as 'a secular religion' or, if that
is felt to be a contradiction in terms, as 'much more than a religion'.
From there it is argued, either that an Islamic state is in fact a
secular state, or that a secular state is in full accordance with the
principles of Islam. That may sound like two ways of saying the
same thing, but in practice the two statements have radically
different implications. The first means that secularist arguments
can be disregarded because the Koran and the Sunna provide for
this world as much as for the next and everyone, including non-
Muslims, has their place and their rights assured in an Islamic
state. The second means that there is no need to base the state
directly on the Koran and the Sunna because if the state embodies
the ideals of secularism, equality and justice it will *ipso facto*
embody the central values of Islam.

This ambiguity has been the source of constant debate in
Pakistan throughout its existence. But bound up with it is an
ambiguity about the nature, and even the existence of, the Pakistani
nation. We have seen that even in Turkey this ambiguity occurs
in an attenuated form, since even though Turkey is a 'secular'
state a Turk is assumed to be by definition a Muslim. But at least

there was a Turkish language on which a Turkish national identity could be founded, since it bound Turks together and differentiated them from other Muslims. In the case of Pakistan, Islam itself was taken as the identifying and differentiating factor. That worked quite well until the state actually came into being. Muslims in India were indeed strongly conscious of their Muslim identity as something that radically distinguished them from Hindus. But they were not grouped together geographically, nor did they all speak the same language. If they were not part of an Indian nation there was no obvious reason why they should consider themselves a single nation at all, *unless* Islam itself were to be reasserted as a worldwide nation (*umma*).

If one accepted, as most people did, that the reunification of the worldwide *umma* as a single nation was not practical politics, and that therefore, for the foreseeable future, the world was going to contain a variety of distinct Muslim nations, then there was no self-evident reason why the Muslims of the Indian subcontinent should only form one of these nations rather than two or more.

These two interrelated problems — the meaning of an Islamic state and the relation between Islam and national identity — have dogged Pakistan throughout its history. From the beginning there was a problem in that more than one-third of the Muslims in the subcontinent remained on the Indian side of the partition lines, while a smaller but still substantial number of Hindus found themselves in Pakistan. If Jinnah's statement that 'the Muslims are a Nation' were taken as a definition of Pakistan, this would have meant that 40 million Pakistanis were living in India, while a quarter of the population of East Pakistan were foreigners. This would have been unworkable. In practice, therefore, Pakistan had to be defined territorially, which meant that non-Muslims in Pakistan received Pakistan citizenship while Muslims in other parts of the subcontinent did not.* But geography proved a very

* There is a close parallel with another state, which came into being the following year, on the basis of a religious community redefined as a 'nation', namely Israel. Israel is supposed to be a Jewish national state, but it has a large minority of non-Jewish citizens, while the majority of Jews are neither residents nor

unsatisfactory basis for national identity in Pakistan, because its territory consisted of two quite distinct areas with more than a thousand miles of India in between. They differed in language, culture and economic interests, and eventually, after twenty-four years of uneasy cohabitation, they fell apart in circumstances that were traumatic for both. Islam had not proved a strong enough bond to hold them together. East Pakistan, which had been the junior partner although it had the larger population, secured its independence thanks to an Indian invasion and became Bangladesh; the name implied that Bengali nationalism, rather than Islam, would be the dominant ideology of the new state. West Pakistan was left alone to carry on the name and the ideal with which Jinnah had endowed it, though ironically it now has only the third largest concentration of Muslims in the subcontinent: Bangladesh comes first and India second.

The Origins of Pakistan

Pakistan was thus an idea before it was a country, and whether it is a nation remains doubtful even today. It is probably the only country in the world which describes itself, in official literature published by the government for distribution to the foreign Press, as 'an ideological state'.[2] According to this official literature, the idea of Pakistan represents 'a synthesis of parallel streams of Muslim thought in the subcontinent' — one being the *jihad* of Sayyid Ahmad Barelvi, presented somewhat misleadingly as a movement of resistance to British colonial rule, from which 'the

---

citizens (though under the 'Law of Return' they can become citizens automatically if they take up residence, whereas further settlement of Indian Muslims in Pakistan was barred by the Pakistan Citizenship Act of 1951). As a result, several of Israel's problems have paralleled those of Pakistan, e.g. the problem of the non-Jewish minority, which cannot identify fully with the state and feels itself the victim of discrimination; conflicts between groups of different geographical and cultural origins thrown together by immigration; disputes over criteria for deciding who is and who is not a Jew; influence of religious authorities and religious activist groups seeking to enforce conformity on their fellow citizens, disproportionate to their actual support among the population.

large body of his Hindu compatriots stood aside';* the other being Sayyid Ahmad Khan's movement to strengthen the Muslim community through modern education. The movement of Sayyid Ahmad Barelvi is described as 'essentially religious', that of Sayyid Ahmad Khan as 'essentially political' — presumably because Sayyid Ahmad Khan's religious ideas are not popular with those now in power in Pakistan. His political ideas must also be a source of some embarrassment, since it is claimed that he 'wanted the Muslims to use the very tools of the colonialist to oust him', whereas, in fact, Sir Sayyid strongly discouraged any notion of ousting the British and said it was important that they stay in India for a long time.

SAYYID AHMAD KHAN

It is right, however, that Sir Sayyid should be given credit as one of the originators of Pakistan, for two reasons. First, he undoubtedly did encourage the Muslims to be more aware of the heritage, culture and interests which set them apart from the Hindus. Secondly, by promoting Western education he helped to create the class of Westernized Muslim intellectuals of whom Jinnah was the supreme example — the class which led the struggle for Pakistan and which has provided it with most of its leaders and virtually all its administrators since the state's establishment.

But it was not until long after Sir Sayyid's death in 1898 that the idea emerged that the Muslims were a nation, which could or should be separated politically from the rest of India. He himself referred to Muslims as a 'nationality', but none the less believed that the peoples of India, Hindu and Muslim, made up a single nation. He thought that continued British rule was necessary in order to hold this nation together and to ensure that the Muslims, being a minority, got fair treatment. It is a reasonable inference that if he had been confronted with the fact of British withdrawal he might have demanded a separate Muslim state. But he was not so confronted in his lifetime; it was a choice that he not only did

---

* Since his movement was in fact directed mainly against the Sikhs, this is not entirely surprising. (See Chapter 3, pp. 68–9.)

not make but actively sought to spare his fellow Muslims from having to make.

The All-India Muslim League was formed eight years after Sir Sayyid's death. It was based on his ideas (the first of its three stated objectives was to foster a sense of loyalty to the British government among the Muslims of India) but intended to give them more effective political expression as a counterweight to the growing influence of the Indian National Congress. It was, however, a gathering of notables rather than a mass movement. The main thrust of political activity among Indian Muslims became increasingly anti-British, especially after 1911 when the British gave in to Hindu pressure and rescinded the partition of Bengal. (The Muslims had been promised that East Bengal, where they were in a clear majority, would be kept as a separate province.)

THE KHILĀFAT MOVEMENT

Muslim hostility to the British also focused on the question of the Caliphate and British policy towards the Ottoman Empire. This was an issue on which many Muslims were in disagreement with Sir Sayyid during his lifetime. 'We are devoted and loyal subjects of the British government,' he had said. 'We are not the subjects of Sultan Abdul-Hamid II; ... He neither had, nor can have any spiritual jurisdiction over us as *Khalifa*. His title of *Khalifa* is effective only in his own land and only over the Muslims under his sway.' These views were resented by his contemporaries, and later bitterly repudiated.[3] As Britain's relations with the Ottoman Empire grew more strained, support for the Caliphate became a way of expressing Muslim hostility to Britain and aspirations for a revival of Islam's political fortunes.

This point of view was expressed by religious scholars, more orthodox or traditional in doctrine than Sayyid Ahmad Khan yet politically bolder, since they felt that support for the Caliphate was quite consistent with a political alliance with Hindus. The most important were Maulana Muhammad Ali (1878–1931) and Maulana Abul Kalām Azād (1888–1958), both of whom in 1911–12 started newspapers which sought to awaken indignation at the way Western powers were trampling the rights and interests of Muslims throughout the world. Clearly influenced by the ideas of Jamal al-Din al-Afghani (although he saw himself as more of a religious and less of a political reformer), Azad attacked Sayyid Ahmad Khan and other Westernized modernists as 'those heretics and hypocrites who, during the last forty years, had co-operated with the Satans of Europe to weaken the influence of Islamic Caliphate and Pan-Islam.' He urged the Muslims to get rid of their fear of the Hindu majority, which, he said, had been deliberately planted in their minds by the British. He enlarged the concept of *jihad*, equating it with the struggle for independence in which Hindus too could take part:

> Remember that patriotism demands from Hindus that they should struggle for their country's independence. But for Muslims, this is a religious duty, a *jihad*. You are fighters for God's battle and *jihad* includes every endeavour which is made in the name of truth and freedom. Today those people [Hindus] who are engaged in a struggle for their country's progress and independence are also waging a *jihad*. You should have been in the forefront of this *jihad*.[4]

Not surprisingly, when the Ottoman Empire joined in the First World War on the German side and the Sultan-Caliph issued his own call to all Muslims to join in the *jihad*, the British government promptly interned both Azad and Muhammad Ali and suppressed their newspapers. While there was no Muslim revolt in India in response to the Sultan's call, there was undoubtedly bitterness that Britain was making Muslim soldiers in the Indian army fight against their fellow Muslim Turks. At the front in Mesopotamia (Iraq) there were frequent desertions and executions. Even the cautious and Westernized leaders of the Muslim League were infected with concern for the future of Turkey and bitterness towards the British. In 1916, under the influence of Muhammad Ali Jinnah, the League signed a pact with the Indian National Congress, demanding steps towards self-government for India in recognition of Indian participation in the war effort.

After the war matters were exacerbated by British occupation of Muslim lands in the Middle East and by repression in India itself, including the famous Amritsar massacre of April 1919 in which 379 people were killed and at least 1,200 wounded. It was in this atmosphere that the Khilāfat movement developed — a movement aimed simultaneously at saving the pan-Islamic caliphate (*khilafat*) and at driving the British out of India. Again, this movement was not at all a Muslim separatist movement. Initially at least it enjoyed Hindu as well as Muslim support. Mahatma Gandhi attended the first Khilafat Conference, held at Delhi in November 1919 and urged the Muslims to launch a non-co-operation movement to force the British to maintain the caliphate in Turkey and respect its rights. Gandhi strongly advocated Hindu support for the Khilafat, arguing that, by showing respect for the religion of the Muslims, Hindus would obtain respect for their religion (and specifically an end to cow-slaughter) from Muslims in return. Thus for a time there was an alliance of Muslim and Hindu religious activists with a radical anti-British programme, enjoying considerable mass support in both communities, while Westernized moderates in both communities (including Jinnah) were urging caution and pragmatism.

Among the Muslims, the idea was revived that India under British rule was no longer part of the 'house of Islam' but had become part of the 'house of war', from which good Muslims should emigrate. Thousands of Muslims did so, selling their land and property and flocking into Muslim Afghanistan from the neighbouring Indian provinces of Sind and North-West Frontier. The Afghan government, unable to cope with the influx, was obliged to turn them back.

In July 1921 a second Khilafat conference was held in Karachi, and solemnly declared 'allegiance of the Muslim population to His Majesty the Sultan of Turkey, the Commander of the Faithful.' Paradoxically it also sent its congratulations to 'Ghazi Mustafa Kemal Pasha and the Angora [Ankara] Government' which were then engaged in a desperate struggle against the 'army of the caliphate'. But of course the conference understood Kemal's cause (as did many of his supporters in Turkey at the time) as a struggle to free the universal caliph from foreign control. (For similar reasons the Indian Khilafatists felt nothing but contempt for Sharif Husain of Mecca and his family. In 1920 Muhammad Ali had led a deputation to press the British government to restore the pre-war frontiers of the Ottoman Empire, and especially to restore to the caliph the custody of the holy places in the Hijaz and Palestine.) If the British government were to take any military measures against Mustafa Kemal's government, the conference threatened that Indian Muslims would resort to civil disobedience, 'with the concurrence of the Congress', would proclaim 'the complete independence of India and the Indians' and would establish a republic.* Meanwhile, it urged local Khilafat committees 'to devise measures to absolutely stop drinking within their districts.'

The unity of Muslim and Hindu religious enthusiasm was too good to last. In August 1921 there was a rising of Muslim peasants against Hindu landlords in Malabar (south-western India) and a Khilafat kingdom was declared. Hindu houses were sacked, temples desecrated and thousands of Hindus forcibly converted to Islam. Inevitably this led to a cooling of Hindu enthusiasm for the Khilafat movement, especially when one of the Muslim nationalist leaders attempted to defend what had happened on the grounds that as the country was in the 'house of war', the Muslim rebels were justified in suspecting the Hindus of collusion with the British government, and 'if the Hindus became Mussalmans to save themselves from death, it was a voluntary change of faith and not forcible conversion'![5]

The Khilafat movement inevitably petered out once it transpired that the Turks themselves were prepared to hand over the Arab lands to Britain and France, and especially after Mustafa Kemal had abolished the caliphate in 1924. (Yet the British Viceroy had at one point taken the movement seriously enough to send a telegram to the Secretary of State for India recommending that

---

* This implied, however, that if the British abstained from military measures against Kemal (as in fact they did), Indian Muslims would *not* take part in the struggle for Indian independence.

suzerainty over the holy places be restored to the Ottoman Sultan, and to ask permission for this recommendation to be published.) It was 'the first and the only movement in which both Hindus and Muslims had played a joint role on a mass scale.'[6] Its leading ideologue, Abul Kalam Azad, who had appeared something of a religious fanatic, remained a prominent figure in the Indian National Congress and became an ardent advocate of a united, secular India and a bitter opponent of Muslim separatism;* during his last years he was Minister of Education in the government of India. The Muslim separatist movement was to be led not by religious scholars but by the Westernized and to all appearances highly secular figure of Muhammad ali Jinnah.

IQBAL, JINNAH AND THE MUSLIM LEAGUE

Credit for first formulating the idea of Pakistan, in the sense of a separate state for the Muslims, is generally given to Sir Muhammad Iqbāl (1875–1938), 'poet, philosopher, political thinker, and altogether the most eminent figure in Indian Islam of the twentieth century.'[7] In his presidential address at the annual session of the Muslim League in 1930 he said: 'I would like to see the Punjab, North-West Frontier Province, Sind and Baluchistan amalgamated into a single state. Self-government within the British Empire or without the British Empire, the formation of a consolidated North-West Indian Muslim state appears to me to be the final destiny of the Muslims at least of North-West India.' This statement certainly foreshadows rather strikingly the Pakistan of today (as opposed to the Pakistan of 1947–71, which included what is now Bangladesh). But an examination of the context reveals that Iqbal in 1930 was not actually proposing a Muslim state completely separate from India. He spoke of 'a Muslim India within India', arguing, as against the Hindu nationalist demand for a unitary government, that 'the life of Islam as a cultural force *in this country* [italics mine — E.M.] very largely depends on its centralization in a specified territory.' This would

---

* Azad was not alone in this. Many Muslim intellectuals remained Indian nationalists — and therefore anti-separatist — up to 1947 and even beyond.

give the North-West Indian Muslims 'full opportunity of development *within the body-politic of India*' [italics mine — E.M.] and
would enable them to be 'the best defenders of India against a
foreign invasion, be that invasion one of ideas or of bayonets.' It
would also, by enabling the Muslims to govern themselves rather
than other people (as in the past), give Islam 'an opportunity to
rid itself of the stamp that Arabian Imperialism was forced to
give it, to mobilize its law, its education, its culture, and to bring
them into closer contact with its own original spirit and with the
spirit of modern times.'

Iqbal's state would have been part of an Indian Federation, in
which residuary powers were left to the self-governing states rather
than to the central government; and he emphasized that the Hindus
should not 'fear that the creation of autonomous Muslim states
will mean the introduction of a kind of religious rule in such states.'

The Muslim League to which Iqbal made his remarks was a
small and unrepresentative organization, and it did not adopt his
speech as a political platform. From 1931 to 1934 Jinnah, who
had been a leading light of the League, was away in London and
the League all but ceased to exist. After that he did his best to
infuse new life and vigour into it, but even in the provincial
elections of 1937 it won only 4.6 per cent of the total Muslim
votes. It did not fight these elections on a separatist programme
in the territorial sense, but only on the demand that the Muslims
be recognized as a separate community within the country and
given proportional representation at all levels. Jinnah claimed that
there was 'no difference between the ideals of the Moslem League
and of the Congress, the idea being complete freedom for India.'
He only wanted Congress to recognize 'there is a third party in
this country and that is the Moslems. We are not going to be
dictated to by anybody.'

It was only after 1937 that the League moved to a separatist
position, and only then that it began to win mass support. Whether
there is a causal relationship between these two facts is very hard
to say. Some Pakistani historians believe that 'the demand for
Pakistan reminded Muslims of their past glory and opened before

them vast and fascinating vistas of future greatness.'[8] Others suggest that Indian Muslims were not much interested in Islam as a political slogan until the particular circumstances of the decade 1937–47 arose. That, on the whole, seems to me the more plausible view. If the idea of a Muslim state in which Islam could 'mobilize its law, its education, its culture' had had the same appeal for ordinary Muslims as it had for Iqbal, surely politicians would have taken it up and built a mass movement upon it at a much earlier stage. But the positive attraction of such an idea was not sufficient.

That is not to say that the idea had *no* appeal. But an idea by itself is seldom if ever enough to mobilize large numbers of people for political action, especially if it is an idea that involves radical change. Generally speaking, people only became enthusiastic for one kind of change when they feel threatened by another kind, or at least when it is clear that the status quo is unlikely to continue. What happened in India in 1937 was that for the first time, under the Government of India Act of 1935, elected provincial assemblies, with governments responsible to them, were set up. Most of these governments were dominated by the predominantly Hindu Indian National Congress. What had until then been an abstract notion — a self-governing India under majority (that is Hindu) rule — suddenly became quite concrete, and most Muslims realized that they did not want it. The symbol of Hindu rule was the adoption of 'Bande Mataram' — a song from a strongly anti-Muslim Hindu revivalist novel — as an Indian national anthem.

The name 'Pakistan' is believed to have been invented in Cambridge, England, by an Indian Muslim student, Choudhry Rahmat Ali, who was one of four signatories of a leaflet in which the word first appeared in January 1933. Apparently he envisaged an Indo-Persian Muslim nation whose 'original Fatherland' embraced Iran and Afghanistan as well as north-west India. 'It means,' he later wrote, 'the lands of the Paks — the spiritually pure and clean. It symbolizes the religious beliefs and the ethnical stock of our people; and it stands for all the territorial constituents of our original Fatherland.'*⁹ Unlike Iqbal, he invisaged his state as a completely independent federation, allied with two other Muslim states — one in north-east India (Bengal and Assam) and the other in the south (Hyderabad). This idea was partially reflected in the famous Lahore Resolution (sometimes called the Pakistan Resolution although the name 'Pakistan' does not appear in it), adopted by the Muslim League in March 1940. This said that 'the north-western and eastern zones of India should be grouped to constitute "Independent States", in which the constituent units shall be autonomous and sovereign.' A great deal of misery and bloodshed might have been avoided if this programme had been adhered to. It was only in 1946, and for reasons that have never been clarified, that the demand became for the Muslim majority areas to be constituted into 'a sovereign state'. The word 'Pakistan' was apparently used pejoratively by the Muslim League's opponents to attack the Lahore Resolution, and was only adopted officially by Jinnah in 1943.

Blueprint for an Islamic State

The Muslim had demanded a state where undominated by the Hindu he could improve his lot and enjoy a position of economic independence. The present argument that Pakistan was demanded in order to enable or compel the Muslims to lead their lives in accordance with the injunctions of Islam was then [in 1947] in nobody's mind. The transcendental had not yet been lowered into a commonplace and the Holy Book and Tradition had not been converted into a potent weapon of the politician, though implicit in the demand had been the hope that Pakistan would provide a favourable ground for experimentation in Muslim social and political doctrines.

*PAKISTAN, according to Rahmat Ali, is an acronym standing for *P*unjab, *A*fghania (North-West Frontier Province), *K*ashmir, *I*ran, *S*ind, '*T*ukharistan', *A*fghanistan and Baluchista*N*. I have not succeeded in identifying Tukharistan.

So wrote Muhammad Munir, former chief justice of Pakistan, in the *Pakistan Times* of 23 June 1964. His memory served him only partly right. The hope that he mentions in the last sentence was to some extent already explicit by 1947, as indeed it had been in Iqbal's presidential address of 1930. It was in 1947, for instance, very shortly after independence, that Jinnah said: 'The idea was that we should have a state in which we could live and breathe as free men and which we could develop according to our own light and culture *and where the principles of Islamic social justice could find free play.*' (Italics mine — E.M.) In another speech he said: 'Pakistan not only means freedom and independence but a Muslim ideology which has to be preserved.'[10] It seems clear, therefore, that the idea that Pakistan was demanded in order *to enable* the Muslims to lead their lives in accordance with Islam, in the sense that that was at least part of the motive for demanding it, was indeed present in Jinnah's mind. To enable, but not to compel. That really has been the crux of the argument which has raged in Pakistan ever since about the Islamic nature of the state. It was inevitable that some Muslims, when offered 'a favourable ground for experimentation in Muslim social and political doctrines', would see it as a chance, and therefore a duty, to recreate a truly Islamic community in which the divine law would be properly enforced. In other words, it was inevitable that public life in Pakistan would be dominated, or at least profoundly affected, by arguments about the Shari'a and its correct interpretation.

At least one of the Indian Muslims who migrated (yet another *hijra*) to Pakistan in 1947 believed he had a clear idea of what the Shari'a was and what an Islamic state should be. This was Maulana Abul A'la Maududi, who has been described as 'much the most systematic thinker of modern Islam.'[11] Paradoxically, he and his group, the Jama'at-i-Islami (Islamic Society), had until then been among the most vociferous opponents of the creation of Pakistan. Maududi, born in 1903, had started his political life as a fervent Indian nationalist. Then, in the mid-1920s, disillusioned by the failure of the Khilafat and non-co-operation movements, and the widening split between Muslims and Hindus, he began to think in a more specifically Islamic way and to urge his fellow Muslims to work towards a genuinely Islamic society based on the Koran. He came to see the influence of Western ideas and customs as a greater danger than the mere political domination of the British, and he identified nationalism as one of the most insidious of these un-Islamic ideas. In this he included not only Indian nationalism but also the essentially secular Muslim nationalism of Jinnah and the Muslim League, who spoke of Islam as a cultural heritage and a source of national identity rather than as a living ideal that ought to be put into practice. But once Pakistan was set up, Maududi argued that since it had been fought for and won in the name of Muslims and their Islamic aspirations it was logically obliged to justify its existence by becoming a truly Islamic state. Needless to say, his opponents never failed to point out that he had been against setting up the state in the first place, to which he would reply:

> The real thing for us is that even if we can get a yard of land where Allah's will can prevail, that will be sacred over all others. We'd wanted the entire India to be a land of Islam. So how could we be opposed to the attainment of a country in the name of Islam? But those in the forefront of the Pakistan Movement did not appear to us to be true Muslims. That is why we had our doubts.[12]

For Maududi, the essence of Islam was a summons to give exclusive obedience to God. Sovereignty, in his view, belongs only to God, and to accept any other source of authority, for instance the will of the people, is equivalent to idolatry. Secondly, he argued that Islam was a completely rational 'system'. Everything in the universe, he explained, obeys laws ordained by the Creator, with the exception of human beings who are endowed with free will. But human beings know perfectly well how they *should* behave, because the law of human conduct ordained by God is also revealed to them by God, first through the Holy Book of God (of which the Koran, revealed to Muhammad, is so to speak the final and definitive edition) and secondly through the guidance derived from the lives of the messengers who came with the book. All life that observes the plain commandments of the law is Islam or submission to God, and all that does not is *Jahiliya* — the word traditionally used for the state of ignorance in which the Arabs lived before Islam.

Maududi criticized not only the modernists, whom he accused of smuggling un-Islamic Western ideas into the minds of Muslims under the guise of reforming Islam, but also the conservatives. Like so many Islamic reformers, from Ibn Abdul-Wahhab onwards, he accused the traditional *ulama* of diluting Islam by adding rules of their own devising to the clear commands of the Koran and the Sunna. They were so confused, he believed, by their own scholasticism that they were no longer able to distinguish the fundamentals of Islam from the details of its application, and therefore identified Islam with the elaborate structure of the medieval legal schools. The remedy, as always, was to go back to the original sources. The valid Sunna, for Maududi, was only that which could be shown to have been already accepted in the time of the Prophet and his four 'orthodox' successors. Anything later than the death of Ali in AD 661 was, in Maududi's eyes, not Islamic and had no normative value for modern Muslims. In this he showed himself close to the method and spirit of the modernists, even though his understanding of the norms to be derived from the period before 661 was radically different from theirs.

Maududi is perhaps the first Muslim thinker we have come across who may fairly be called 'fundamentalist', since he argued that the Koran and the Sunna were quite clear as they stood and that the Muslim has only to accept what he finds there. But even he was quite well aware that in reality there are many points on which the Koran and the Sunna are silent, that many of the commands which are found there do require interpretation, and that even the clear commands have to be understood in the light of one's own historical circumstances. In short Maududi, like his predecessors, had to resort to *ijtihad* (personal judgement), and invoke the help of reason. But he insisted that *ijtihad* must be carried out according to the spirit of the clear commands and not against them. The sin of the modernists, in his view, was that they twisted the Koran and the Sunna to bring them into line with prejudices derived from outside Islam — principally from modern Western liberalism. He agreed with them in holding that Islam requires the exercise of reason by the community to understand God's decrees, in believing, therefore, that Islam contains nothing contrary to reason, and in being convinced that Islam as revealed in the Book and the Sunna is superior in purely rational terms to all other systems. But he thought they had gone wrong in allowing themselves to judge the Book and the Sunna by the standard of reason. They had busied themselves trying to demonstrate that 'Islam is truly reasonable' instead of starting, as he did, from the proposition that 'true reason is Islamic'. Therefore they were not sincerely accepting the Book and the Sunna as the final authority, because implicitly they were setting up human reason as a higher authority (the old error of the Mu'tazilites). In Maududi's view, once one has become a Muslim, reason no longer has any function of judgement. From then on its legitimate task is simply to spell out the implications of Islam's clear commands, the rationality of which requires no demonstration.

The political doctrine which he based on this view was highly simplistic. Islam had to be enforced, and all that was needed for that purpose was to ensure that the right people, holding the right ideas, should occupy the posts of governors. He held, for instance, that Pakistan would suffer no more devastation from the overflow of the river Indus once he had succeeded in establishing people in government who cared enough to do something about it. He put implicit faith in the party which he had founded, the Jama'at-i-Islami, as a tool for achieving the Islamic revolution that would put such people into power; and he cited the Fascists in Italy and Germany, and the Communists in Russia, as examples of groups which, though tiny minorities in a total population, were able to exercise effective control. His programme for the future of Pakistan was the expansion of the Jama'at-i-Islami until it had absorbed the state and had, to all intents and purposes, become the state. Such a totalitarian approach might justifiably cause alarm in the case of communism or fascism, but in the service of Islam, he thought, it need alarm no one, since God's commands working in the life of the state would be just and benevolent to all.[13]

As for the form of the state, Maududi of course took the government of Muhammad and the first four caliphs as his model, but gave it as far as possible a democratic interpretation. The head of state should be the supreme head of legislature, executive and judiciary alike, but under him these three organs should function 'separately and independently of one another'. He should be elected and must enjoy the nation's confidence and regard, otherwise there is no limit on his tenure of office. The legislature or Consultative Assembly 'should consist of a body of such learned men who have the ability and the capacity to interpret Qur'ānic injunctions and who in giving decisions, would not take liberties with the spirit or the letter of the *Shari'ah*.' They too must be 'persons who enjoy the confidence of the masses' and may be chosen by 'the modern system of elections' or by other methods which may be found appropriate to 'the circumstances and needs of modern times'. They can, of course, legislate only within the limits set by the Koran and the Sunna. On matters of policy they should ideally be able to tell whether the head of state is right or wrong, and in the event of irreconcilable difference of opinion between them and him there should be a referendum, 'after which the one whose opinion is rejected by the people should resign.... But so long as it is not possible in our country to create a consultative body of that calibre and to foster that spirit and that mentality, there is no other alternative but to restrict and to subordinate the executive to the majority decisions of the legislature.'[14]

Maududi continued: 'The formation of parties and cliques within the Legislative Assemblies should be constitutionally prohibited. Various parties in the country may take part in the election as parties for sending to the Assemblies the most suitable members in their opinion but after the election the members of the Assembly should owe allegiance solely to the State, its Constitution, and the entire Nation, and should vote and act according to the dictates of their own conscience.'[15] Non-Muslims would be eligible 'for all kinds of employment except for keyposts.'[16] They would not have the right to vote in presidential elections. They might elect their own representatives to parliament, voting as separate electorates, but should not be in a position to influence the choice of Muslim representatives. This is to ensure that 'the basic policy of this ideological state remains in conformity with the fundamentals of Islam.'[17] Women should not be eligible either as head of state or as legislators, since 'according to Islam, active politics and administration are not the field of activity of the womenfolk.' Their right to vote 'should be qualified, at least for the present [this was written in 1952], by a certain standard of education.' But there should be a separate Assembly composed of women and elected by women only, which the legislature should consult on all matters concerning women's welfare, and which would also have 'the full right to criticize matters relating to the general welfare of the country.'[18]

The main lines of this vision of an Islamic state were already clear in Maududi's mind when he arrived in Pakistan in 1947. This gave him a great advantage because many people there, having gone through such an enormous effort to get a separate Muslim state, shared the feeling that it ought to be an Islamic state, but few if any of them had a clear idea of what that meant. Maududi's totalitarian vision was tailor-made to fill that vacuum.

From Jinnah to Zia (1948–77)

Jinnah died in September 1948, barely a year after the state came into existence. Deprived of the authority and charisma which he enjoyed as 'Quaid i-Azam' (supreme leader), the Western-educated and modernist-inclined leaders of the Muslim League began to feel vulnerable to the agitation for an Islamic order, which seemed to have aroused considerable mass support. The immediate issue was Kashmir, a Muslim-majority province which had been taken into union with India by its Hindu dynastic ruler. The Pakistan government claimed it as rightfully part of Pakistan and encouraged local Muslims to resist Indian rule, referring to their struggle as *jihad*. At the same time, not wishing to risk a general war with India, it denied any direct involvement in the fighting. Maududi pointed out that the government could not have it both ways. If there was *jihad* it was the duty of all Muslims, and *a fortiori* for the Muslim government which claimed to be the rightful protector of those concerned, to take part. But since the government said that Pakistan was not fighting in Kashmir, logically there could be no *jihad*. Maududi's aim in saying this was 'to expose the duplicity of the government and force it to take a direct part in the war of liberation.'[19] But the government accused him of disavowing the heroic Kashmiri *mujahidin* and, by denying their struggle was a true *jihad*, condemning them to an infidel's death if they were killed. On this pretext, in October 1948, Maududi suffered the first of many arrests for 'activities prejudicial to the security of the state'.

In March 1949, while Maududi was still in prison, the prime minister, Liyāqat Alī Khān, introduced in the Constituent Assembly a resolution defining the 'Objectives' of the new state, which eventually became, with some verbal changes, the Preamble to the Constitution. Maududi's group claimed this resolution as the fruit of their efforts, and certainly it did represent a concession to demands for an Islamic state. It was this resolution which affirmed that 'sovereignty over the entire universe belongs to God Almighty alone', that therefore the people of Pakistan were to exercise power only 'within the limits prescribed by Him', and that Muslims would be 'enabled to order their lives in the individual and collective spheres in accord with the teachings and requirements of Islam as set out in the Holy Quran and the Sunna.' It did also say that 'the state shall exercise its power and authority through the chosen representatives of the people' and that 'the principles of democracy, freedom, equality, tolerance and social justice, as enunciated by Islam, shall be fully observed.' Moreover, it promised provision for minorities freely to profess and practise their religion, and to enjoy the same fundamental rights 'including equality of status, of opportunity, and before law' as Muslims. But

this was seen as a significant retreat from Jinnah's inaugural speech
to the same Assembly in August 1947, when he had said:

> You may belong to any religion or caste or creed—that has
> nothing to do with the business of the State (Hear, hear)....
> We are starting in the days when there is no discrimination,
> no distinction between one community and another, no discrimi-
> nation between one caste or creed or another. We are starting
> with this fundamental principle that we are all citizens and equal
> citizens of one State (Loud Applause).... Now I think you
> should keep that in front of us as our ideal, and you will find
> that in course of time Hindus would cease to be Hindus and
> Muslims would cease to be Muslims, not in the religious sense,
> because that is the personal faith of each individual but in the
> political sense as citizens of the State.[20]

Ominously, Hindu members boycotted the session of the Assembly at which the Objectives Resolution was passed unanimously
by the Muslim members; and one of the influential *ulama* who
spoke in support of it explained that, since an Islamic state was
an ideological state, 'people who do not subscribe to those ideas
may have a place in the administrative machinery of the state but
they cannot be entrusted with the responsibility of framing the
general policy of the state or dealing with matters vital to its safety
and integrity.'[21] The personal views of Liyaqat Ali Khan and his
cabinet were no doubt very different. A year later they negotiated
a pact with the Indian government which guaranteed to the
minorities in both countries equal opportunity with the majority
to participate in public life, hold political or other offices and serve
in their countries' civil and armed forces, and Liyaqat pointed to
the Objectives Resolution as guaranteeing these rights. But others,
including Maududi, read the Resolution as pointing to an exclusively Islamic state. Their objection was 'that this was a mere
resolution: there was no change in the government's attitude. Our
assessment was right—that our leaders can get a State but cannot
enforce Islam.'[22]

WHO IS A MUSLIM?

The contradiction was brought out into the open in 1953 when a theological dispute on the issue 'who is a Muslim?' led to serious violence and temporarily paralysed the government. The dispute concerned a sect variously known as Ahmadis or Qadianis, founded in the nineteenth century by one Mirza Ghulam Ahmad of Qadian who claimed to have received revelation direct from God, thereby denying the finality of the revelation to Muhammad. Soon after the establishment of Pakistan a campaign began to have the Ahmadis declared a non-Muslim minority and to dismiss those who held prominent public offices, including especially the foreign minister, Sir Muhammad Zafrullah Khan. Religious leaders publicly denounced Zafrullah as an apostate and some even declared that, as apostates, the Ahmadis should be put to death. Maududi served as spokesman for the *ulama* in this movement, although he did not advocate actual violence against the Ahmadis, and tried unsuccessfully to restrain his own followers from becoming involved in it. The leading part, according to Chief Justice Muhammad Munir who conducted the official inquiry, was a group called the Ahrar, which before partition had sided with the Indian National Congress and had denounced Jinnah and the Muslim League in even more violent terms than had Maududi.

The meetings to denounce the Ahmadis became so emotional that in some cases people would leave the meetings to search out Ahmadis and kill them. Yet the authorities were very reluctant to take action against the violence. Apparently the Muslim League leaders both in the federal government and in the provincial government of the Punjab, where the disturbances occurred, felt that by appearing to protect the Ahmadis they would incur too much unpopularity. The federal prime minister, Khwaja Nazim-ud-Din, is thought also to have had genuine religious scruples about going against the opinion of the *ulama*. But at the same time he was unwilling to give in to their demands because of the effect that this would have had (especially the dismissal of the foreign minister) on Pakistan's international reputation. After long hesitation he rejected the demands and ordered the arrest of the agitating *ulama*.

Complete mayhem then broke out in Lahore, the capital of the Punjab, with widespread 'loot, arson and murders'. Even then,

> in the meeting of citizens at the Government House on the afternoon of 5th March no leader, politician or citizen was willing to incur the risk of becoming unpopular or marked by signing an appeal to the good sense of the citizen.... The machinery of Government showed signs of a total collapse on the morning of 6th March when the [provincial] Government publicly announced its surrender to anarchy.... The situation went completely out of control and the citizen realized the imminence of the danger to his life and property. The military could wait no longer and took over.

Martial law was proclaimed, with the approval of the federal government, and the chief minister of the Punjab was replaced.

A court of inquiry was set up under Justice Muhammad Munir to investigate the cause of the disturbances. It inquired not only into the facts but also into the ideas behind the agitation and their implications. Interrogating a series of religious leaders, including Maududi, it found that while all agreed that the Ahmadis were not Muslims no two of them gave the same answer when asked how a Muslim could be defined, and it concluded that their agitation for an Islamic state was highly dangerous since there was no clear consensus on what an Islamic state implied. It found that the *ulama*'s outlook was 'narrow because they are specialists in one branch of life. ... You cannot do without specialists, but you need a "general practitioner", a person well grounded in all subjects which are the particular province of the specialist, to co-ordinate their activities.'[23]

Clearly this role was assigned to political leaders, but they had signally failed to fulfil it. Physically the government was able to suppress the riots. But ideologically it was disarmed. The political leaders were essentially men of liberal, modernist views, who in discussion with Europeans would have eagerly refuted any suggestion that Islam was an intolerant or obscurantist religion. But when faced with intolerance and obscurantism in practice they lacked the self-confidence to tell the people that the *ulama* were misrepresenting Islam. No doubt they suspected that the *ulama* were closer to the people than they were themselves.

AYUB KHAN

Islamic modernism in the Indian subcontinent might be said to have been unlucky in its political associations. In nineteenth-century India its leading exponent was Sir Sayyid Ahmad Khan, who politically was something of a British stooge. In twentieth-century Pakistan the first ruler who tried seriously to put a modernist interpretation of Islam into practice, and the only one to do so at all consistently, was not a democratically elected leader but a general who came to power by a military coup and ruled by mainly authoritarian methods. This was Muhammad Ayub Khan, who came to power in 1958 and set out to 'liberate the spirit of religion from the cobwebs of superstition and stagnation which surround it and move forward under the forces of modern science and knowledge.'[24]

Ayub explained his Islamic philosophy in a speech in May 1959:

When the link between life and religion is snapped, life goes on in one direction or another but religion is reduced to a lifeless object incapable of resilience or progression, and it is continued in the precincts of mosques and mausoleums. Islam seems to have suffered this fate. While mankind has made great advances in science and philosophy, religion has remained static for centuries.

The miracle of Islam was that it destroyed idolatry, and the tragedy of Muslims has been that they rendered religion into the form of an idol.[25]

This modernist outlook was reflected in the new Constitution of 1962, in the establishment of an Advisory Council on Islamic Ideology and an Islamic Research Institute, and in the Muslim Family Laws Ordinance of 1961. But Ayub made no serious attempt to mobilize a mass movement in support of his reforms, and once he began to allow open opposition he found that he had to bow on several points to the protests of the *ulama*. For instance, the Constitution was amended to restore the name 'Islamic Republic', which had been dropped, and to reassert that God would allow the people to exercise authority only 'within the limits prescribed by Him'. Dr Fazlur Rahman, appointed by Ayub as Director of the Central Institute of Islamic Research (whose task was 'to assist in the reconstruction of Muslim society on a truly Islamic basis'), had to resign after mass demonstrations directed by *ulama* and *mullah*s (local religious leaders) who objected to his modernist views. The *ulama* were incensed that Ayub did not acknowledge their status as advisers to the government, preferring to staff the Ideology Council, Islamic Research Institute and Commission for the Reform of Muslim Family Laws with people who had studied in Western universities.

The *ulama* particularly objected to the liberal, and in their view unorthodox, *ijtihad* applied to Muslim family law by the Commission on Marriage and Family Laws, and they succeeded in weakening the Muslim Family Laws Ordinance with omissions and qualifications. But the Ordinance did embody the main recommendations of the Commission which were:

1 That a son whose father died before his grandfather should no longer be disinherited from the grandfather's property in favour of his uncles.
2 That a divorced wife could remarry her husband without first marrying a third person and consummating the marriage with him.
3 That a husband could be fined for taking a second wife without first obtaining permission from an Arbitration Council.
4 That the age of marriage for women be raised from 14 to 16.

The Ordinance was vigorously opposed by the *ulama*, but on this point Ayub did get mass support — from women's groups — and the Ordinance remained on the statute book.

Ironically, when Ayub submitted himself to a presidential election in 1964 his opponent was a woman — Fatima Jinnah, sister of the state's founder — and he won with the aid of a *fatwa* from the pro-government *ulama* who ruled that a woman could not be head of state under Islamic law. A further irony was that Maududi, who in 1952 had firmly laid down that the head of state should be a male and quoted both Koran and *hadith* to prove it, dissented from the *fatwa* and aligned himself with Miss Jinnah's supporters. Apparently he felt that at least she would make a more Islamic and less tyrannical president than Ayub.

'ISLAMIC SOCIALISM'

The later years of Ayub's rule were marked, in West Pakistan, by the rise of the Pakistan People's Party (PPP), led by Zulfikar Ali Bhutto, who, after being eased out of his post as foreign minister in 1967, began to campaign against Ayub's government on a socialist platform, criticizing the gross social and economic inequalities in the country. He encountered opposition from most of the *ulama* and especially from Maududi's Jamaat-i-Islami, for whom socialism was merely yet another foreign and un-Islamic ideology, if anything more poisonous than Ayub's modernism. Bhutto tried to meet this criticism by claiming that his was a specifically 'Islamic socialism', based on Islamic rather than Western models. One of his supporters, Haneef Ramay, argued that the Islam of the Prophet and the four orthodox caliphs was based on solidarity and equality (*musawat*) and was therefore in essence socialist.

In East Pakistan discontent with Ayub's rule took the form of Bengali nationalism and resentment of Punjabi dominance in the state. Faced with mounting unrest in both halves of the country, Ayub stepped down in March 1969, handing over power to the army commander, General Muhammad Yahya Khan. He called elections for a new national assembly in which East Pakistan would have a majority of seats, reflecting its larger population. The elections were held in December 1970. The PPP campaigned on a manifesto proclaiming that Islam was its faith, socialism its economy and equality the basis of its social organization. The *ulama* opposed this vigorously; 113 of them issued a *fatwa* condemning socialism as *kufr* (unbelief) and ruling that anyone who advocated, supported or voted for it put himself outside the pale of Islam. Maududi attacked 'Islamic socialism' as a piece of transparent dishonesty: 'They found out that their socialism cannot dance naked.... After realizing this they started calling socialism "Islamic".... If it is really based on the Quran and the Sunnah then what is the need for calling it socialism? ... Now when they see that this too does not work they have started calling it Islamic equality (*musawat*) and *Muhammadi musawat*. The object is the same — pure socialism.'[26]

In spite of all this, Bhutto and his PPP scored an impressive victory in West Pakistan, winning 58.7 per cent of the seats, against 2.9 per cent for the Jamaat-i-Islami (JI), while two more traditional *ulama*-based parties — Jamiyati-i-Ulama-i-Islam (JUI) and Jamiyat-i-Ulama-i-Pakistan (JUP) obtained 5.1 per cent each.

This was the last election in Pakistan which is generally conceded to have been fair, and the only one in which traditional and fundamentalist programmes for an Islamic state were pitted directly against a proposal for 'Islamic socialism', put forward by a party that the *ulama* had almost unanimously condemned as anti-Islamic. The results suggest that Pakistani voters are quite capable of disregarding the *ulama*'s opinion when presented with an alternative which seems directly relevant to their own lives. This fact makes it all the more curious that Bhutto, when he in his turn was faced with mass opposition and violence in 1977, believed he could save his regime by making concessions to the *ulama*.

THINGS FALL APART

But that is to anticipate. The immediate aftermath of the 1970 election was dominated not by rival interpretations of Islam, but by the crisis between East and West Pakistan caused by the landslide victory in East Pakistan of the Bengali nationalist National Awami Party, led by Shaikh Mujib-ur-Rahman. This crisis was so mishandled by Yahya Khan's government (with some encouragement from Bhutto) that by the end of 1971 Pakistan had suffered a humiliating defeat at the hands of Indian forces, and East Pakistan proclaimed its independence as Bangladesh.

This national disaster provoked extensive soul-searching in West Pakistan. People asked

questions which are no longer academic inquiries or theoretical concepts but questions of national continuity and survival. What are the links that bind the people of Pakistan? What is the soul and personality of Pakistan? What is our national identity and our peculiar oneness which makes us a nation apart from other nations?[27]

Islam, as Chief Justice Munir has since pointed out,[28] had 'proved to be too tenuous a bond to keep the two wings together.' He implied by this that Islam was an inadequate basis for national identity, and that West Pakistan by itself had better prospects. He and other writers pointed out that Bengal had not been included in the original blueprints for Pakistan and argued that the country had only 'eventually found its real identity' after the 1971 war. Geological, geographical, ethnic and historical grounds were put forward for regarding the Indus valley and the mountains to the north and west of it as a distinct national unity separate from the rest of South Asia.[29]

Yet even the inhabitants of this area — which does not correspond to that of any historic state — do not constitute a nation by any conventional ethnic or linguistic criteria. West Pakistan is in fact an amalgam of four provinces — Punjab, Sind, North-West Frontier and Baluchistan — each of which has its own language, traditions and culture. Urdu, the Indo-Persian lingua franca of the Mogul empire, is generally spoken and understood in the towns and among the educated classes (though the latter for many purposes prefer English) and has been adopted as a national language, but many of the rural masses remain beyond its reach. A further problem is that the Punjab is much more heavily populated than the other three provinces, and that Punjabis are overwhelmingly dominant in the administration and the armed forces. Resentment of this had been the main factor leading to the breakaway of Bangladesh, but it was also widely felt in the three non-Punjabi provinces of West Pakistan. Zulfikar Ali Bhutto, to whom Yahya Khan handed over power immediately after the disaster, had the exceptional advantage from this point of view of being himself a Sindi, so that in Sind, at least, the issue was muted during his years in power. But unfortunately he carried on the high-handed tradition of his predecessors in dealing with autonomist movements in Baluchistan and the North-West Frontier. In 1973 he dismissed the elected provincial government of Baluchistan and placed the province under military rule, thereby provoking the armed rebellion that he was ostensibly trying to prevent.[30] He also imprisoned the Pushtun autonomist leader in the North-West Frontier, Abdul Wali Khan, who in his defence gave a neat summary of Pakistan's identity problem:

> I had a very interesting question asked once in this connection. The question was obviously intended to put my loyalty and patriotism to test — What are you, Wali Khan. A Musalman — A Pakistani or a Pushtoon first. My reply was simple — I said I am a six thousand years old Pushtoon — a thousand year old Musalman, and a twenty seven years old Pakistani —
>   After all what makes us think that a Pushtoon cannot become a Musalman — or a Musalman a Pakistani — These are historical facts and we just cannot shut our eyes to them.[31]

There was also the problem of the *muhajirun* — those who had migrated from other parts of India in 1947 and for whom, therefore, the geographical area of West Pakistan had no special historical significance. Their only reason for being in Pakistan was that they were Muslims. It seemed to most people, therefore, that Islam was still an essential element in Pakistani identity; and many went further, arguing that if it had not been strong enough to hold East and West Pakistan together, that was because Pakistanis had not taken it seriously enough. They pointed out that

> the wish to see the kingdom of God established in a Muslim territory ... was the moving idea behind the demand for Pakistan, the corner-stone of the movement, the ideology of the people, and the *raison d'être* of the new nation-state.... If we let go the ideology of Islam, we cannot hold together as a nation by any other means.... If the Arabs, the Turks, the Iranians,

God forbid, give up Islam, the Arabs yet remain Arabs, the Turks remain Turks, the Iranians remain Iranians, but what do we remain if we give up Islam?[32]

PAKISTAN LOOKS WEST

In one other respect the severance of Bangladesh helped to strengthen West Pakistan's sense of Islamic identity. As Bhutto himself explained in 1972:

The severance of our eastern wing by force has significantly altered our geographic focus. This will naturally affect our geopolitical perspective. The geographical distance between us and the nations of South-East Asia has grown ... at the moment, as we stand, it is within the ambit of South and Western Asia. It is here that our primary concern must henceforth lie.[33]

In fact Pakistan's relations with South-East Asia had not been all that close in the first place. But what has happened since 1971 is that the emphasis of Pakistan's foreign policy has been less on competition with India within the South Asian subcontinent (a competition that had proved frustrating and unrewarding for Pakistan) and more on developing closer relations with the Muslim states of West or South-West Asia, alias the Middle East. Pakistan can now think of itself, not as a part of northern India, but as the eastern extremity of a continuous belt of Muslim territory which stretches to the Atlantic ocean and includes the historic heartlands of Islam.

Like Turkey, Pakistan in the 1970s could hope to derive material as well as psychological satisfaction from a foreign policy emphasizing Islamic solidarity, as the Muslim oil-producing states of the Middle East become important markets (especially for manpower) and important sources of economic aid. And after 1971 Pakistan needed, even more than Turkey, both a psychological and an economic boost. Bhutto was well aware of this, and therefore made great efforts to develop an 'Islamic' foreign policy, eagerly responding to the Saudi quest for a wider Islamic community in which the heady drug of Arab nationalism could be diluted to a harmless stimulant. While Saudi Arabia and other Gulf states provided the cash, Pakistan has provided much of the manpower, and much of the zeal, for the network of supranational 'Islamic' institutions that has developed during the last decade under the umbrella of the Organization of the Islamic Conference.

Bhutto made numerous trips to the oil-producing states and emphasized the theme of Islamic brotherhood in his speeches. In February 1974 he was host to an Islamic summit conference in Lahore, at which he accepted Egyptian President Anwar Sadat's appeal for reconciliation between Pakistan and Bangladesh in the name of Islam, thus adroitly using the theme of Islamic brotherhood to mask a concession which might otherwise have involved loss of face, but which was necessary in order to obtain the release of 90,000 Pakistani soldiers who had been prisoners of war in India since 1971. He also, it seems, used the argument of Islamic solidarity to obtain Libyan help in developing Pakistan's nuclear energy programme. This in turn led to Western fears that the two countries were co-operating to produce an 'Islamic bomb'.

DECLINE AND FALL OF BHUTTO

Although 'Islamic' parties played a prominent part in the agitation that led to his downfall in 1977, there is not much evidence to suggest that the growing unpopularity of Bhutto's regime had anything to do with religion as such.* The main factor was disappointment at his failure to fulfil the promises of the PPP platform, either in political or in economic affairs. Politically, Bhutto in power proved much less democratic and liberal than he had sounded in opposition. His treatment of autonomists in Baluchistan and the North-West Frontier has already been mentioned. This was part of a general pattern of authoritarian behaviour. Political opponents were beaten up, journalists thrown into prison, elections rigged and so on. Economically, the social

---

* As early as 1975 Bhutto had shown himself sensitive to pressure from the *ulama*, when he agreed to declare the Ahmadis a non-Muslim minority and to re-word the oath of office for the President and prime ministers so as to require explicit belief in the finality of Muhammad's prophethood.

reforms which Bhutto attempted made little difference to the grinding poverty of the peasant farmers and their quasi-feudal subjection, especially in the Punjab, to big landlords. Increasingly these landlords themselves occupied influential positions within the PPP, while most of the left-wingers who had helped Bhutto to found it either resigned or were expelled as the leadership drifted to the right.

At the same time some of the 'Islamic' parties, and Jamaat-i-Islami in particular, increased the emphasis on egalitarianism and social justice as elements of Islam, while remaining hostile to the 'foreign' doctrine of socialism. The fact that Bhutto's 'socialism' produced such meagre results gave greater credibility to this Islamic propaganda. The Pushtun peasants felt that at least the *mullahs* who supported the JUI were closer to them and their problems than the PPP apparatchiks, while among the urban lower middle class the militants of JI were respected for their dedication and honesty, and admired for their work to solve social problems on the local level. (This might perhaps be compared with the gratitude and sympathy which Communists have won from oppressed groups in certain West European countries through dedication and hard work — or Catholic priests in parts of Latin America. A strong ideological commitment can produce good social results, at any rate at a local level.)

Bhutto's own exploitation of Islam for political propaganda may also have helped, ironically, to strengthen the credibility of Islamic opposition groups, since it made him more vulnerable to their charges of hypocrisy. There was a feeling that politicians and big shots had merely talked of Islam while continuing to exploit the poor, and that it was time to try the real thing — the literal reconstruction of the 'Order of the Prophet' (*Nizam-i-Mustafa*) proposed by Jamaat-i-Islami and other groups. 'All of us should pray for the early implementation of Nizam-i-Mustafa as the poor have nothing to lose but their chains,' said a reader's letter in the *Pakistan Times* shortly after Bhutto's fall. Everything else, it seemed, had been tried. An Islamic order was the last hope. 'We don't know how it will work, or even if it will work. We don't know whether banks can be run without interest or whether strong punishment will stop crime. But we'll try.'[34]

In January 1977 Bhutto announced that parliamentary and provincial elections would be held in March. Nine opposition parties responded by forming the Pakistan National Alliance (PNA). This was, in fact, a very broad front including liberals and autonomists, but the three 'Islamic' parties, now supported by what was left of the Muslim League, succeeded in making the demand for Nizam-i-Mustafa appear the dominant element in its programme. Bhutto soon realized that this alliance was more of a threat to him than he had expected, and he tried to take the wind out of its sails by strengthening the Islamic emphasis in his own programme. He dropped the word 'socialism' and contented himself with 'Musawat-i-Muhammadi' — the equality of Muhammad. According to the *Baluchistan Times* of 26 January 1977, 'the major emphasis in the People's Party programme for [the] future is on Islam. This is in sharp contrast to the concept of trinity propounded in the last elections — socialism, Islam and democracy.' Among other things, the PPP manifesto promised to 'ensure that Friday is observed as the weekly holiday instead of Sunday, ... make the teaching of the Holy Quran an integral part of eminence as a centre of community life ... establish a federal Ulema academy and other institutions....'

By polling day the election had become a contest to see which side could be most extravagantly 'Islamic'. Only one local newspaper, the *Baluchistan Times*, remained sufficiently detached to observe: 'What is simply disgusting is an attempt by the contestant parties to drag the name of Islam into the electioneering with each striving to prove that he alone is a bigger Muslim than the others ... FOR GOD'S SAKE LEAVE ISLAM ALONE.'[35]

The election itself did not resolve the situation, because the PNA accused Bhutto of rigging the vote and demanded a re-run. (Ironically, most observers consider that Bhutto would have won even in an honest election, though by a much narrower margin.) The agitation against the government redoubled in intensity and took on an increasingly religious aura: demonstrations would often start from a mosque after a highly political sermon at Friday prayers. Bhutto responded with martial law and curfews, but also with 'Islamic' measures, following up his election promises. In April he announced that Shari'a law would be enforced within six months and declared an immediate and total ban on drinking, gambling and nightclubs. He also looked for help to his Muslim friends abroad. In June Arab diplomats, led by the ambassadors of Saudi Arabia and the United Arab Emirates, succeeded in setting up negotiations between the government and the PNA. (To achieve this, Saudi Arabia is said to have promised to underwrite the full extent of Pakistan's economic losses during the violence of the spring.) A tentative agreement was reached, and Bhutto went on a quick tour of six Middle Eastern capitals to brief his wealthy patrons. On his return, at the beginning of July, he carried out his promise to make Friday the weekly holiday in place of Sunday. But all to no avail. The agreement fell through and on 5 July the Chief of Staff of the armed forces, General Muhammad Zia-ul-Haq, assumed control.

The Order of the Prophet?

Addressing the nation on television that evening, Zia-ul-Haq dispelled rumours that he had intervened at Bhutto's request with a view to suppressing the opposition. He praised the 'spirit of Islam' that had inspired the opposition movement, and concluded: 'It proves that Pakistan, which was created in the name of Islam, will continue to survive only if it sticks to Islam. That is why I consider the introduction of an Islamic system as an essential prerequisite for the country.'

He also announced that new elections would be held in October and power returned to civilian hands. This did not happen. The elections were called off two weeks before they were due, probably because of indications that support for Bhutto and the PPP was still strong in the Punjab as well as in Sind. The switch was justified by the argument that there were criminal charges which should be cleared up by judicial process before the people were asked to make a political judgement. In practice this meant that Bhutto was to be exposed as a criminal, discredited and eliminated from public life. The regime was able to get him convicted on a charge of murder, but the effect was on the whole the opposite of what was wanted. The evidence was dubious and Bhutto was made to look like the victim of a political witch-hunt. His execution on 4 April 1979, in defiance of appeals for clemency from all over the world, amounted to an admission of failure by the new regime; it implied that even as a convicted murderer he was too dangerous an opponent to be left alive. Yet his death made it even harder for the regime, with his blood on its hands, to take the risk of restoring power to the people. Elections were again scheduled, for November 1979, and again cancelled at the last minute when Zia concluded they would not yield 'positive results'. This time political parties were banned, their leaders arrested, and strict censorship imposed on the Press.

Since then, although the objective of restoring democracy has not been formally abandoned and parts of Bhutto's 1973 Constitution remain in force, it has been clear that Zia gives priority to the 'introduction of an Islamic system' and he has from time to time voiced doubts about the extent to which such a system is compatible with 'Western-type elections'.

In October 1979 he appointed a twelve-member committee of 'scholars, jurists, ulema, and prominent persons from other walks of life' to formulate recommendations for the structure of an Islamic governmental system. But no definite conclusions were reached, and in March 1981 Zia promulgated, on his own authority as Chief Martial Law Administrator, a 'Provisional Constitutional Order', which must be an almost unequalled document in world history in the frankness with which it institutionalizes the unfettered arbitrary power of a single man. Article 4, dealing with the 'Federal Council (Majlis-e-Shura)', deserves quoting in full, if only for its brevity:

(1) There shall be a Federal Council (Majlis-e-Shura) consisting of such persons as the President may, by Order, determine.

(2) The Federal Council (Majlis-e-Shura) shall perform such functions as may be specified in an Order made by the President.

Article 9 lays down that the High Court may not in any circumstances prevent the arrest or order the release of any person detained under any law providing for preventive detention, or 'against whom a report or complaint has been made before any court or tribunal, or against whom a case has been registered at any police station, in respect of an offence, or who has been convicted by any court or tribunal including a Military Court or Tribunal established under a Martial Law Order or Martial Law Regulation'; and the same article retroactively nullifies all such habeas corpus orders made by any court since 1977.

Article 14 states that 'when political activity is permitted by the President' only such political parties will be permitted to function as had registered with the Election Commission on 30 September 1979 (which means in practice only the Jamaat-i-Islami). New parties will require the written permission of the Chief Election Commissioner, and the President will have the right to dissolve any party which in his view 'has been formed or is operating in a manner prejudicial to the Islamic ideology or the sovereignty, integrity or security of Pakistan.' Article 15 retroactively overrules all court judgements invalidating earlier Orders issued by Zia, including those which amended the Constitution, and declares that all actions taken under such Orders 'by any authority or any person ... shall notwithstanding any judgement of any court, be deemed to be and always to have been validly made, taken or done and shall not be called in question in any court on any ground whatsoever.' Military courts and cases brought before them are specifically put outside the jurisdiction of all other courts including the Supreme Court.

Finally, under Article 18, 'the Chief Martial Law Administrator may, for the purpose of removing any difficulties, or for bringing the provisions of this Order into effective operation, make such provisions as he may deem to be necessary or expedient.'

All judges were required to take a new oath of office, swearing

223

to abide by this 'Constitution Order', and at least nineteen senior judges, including the Chief Justice of Pakistan appointed by Zia himself and three out of six sitting Supreme Court judges, were dismissed for refusing to do so. (Providentially, Article 5 of the Order empowered the President to appoint *ad hoc* judges to the Supreme Court at will.)

What, it may be asked, has all this to do with Islam? The answer is, very little except that it is done in the name of a supposedly Islamic ideology. To be fair, Zia is not claiming that by this Order he has actually instituted an Islamic system of government in Pakistan. The Order is 'provisional' and its premise, or its excuse, is that 'endeavours will be and are being made to restore as soon as possible democracy and representative institutions in accordance with the principles of Islam wherein the State of Pakistan exercises its power and authority through the chosen representatives of the people and *until then interim measures are necessary*.' (Italics mine – E.M.) But given that the endeavours in question have now (July 1981) been in progress for four years, whereas Zia originally gave himself ninety days, a degree of scepticism about the interim character of the measures seems reasonable. As the French say, *il n'y a que le provisoire qui dure.**

The point is that it is under this unashamedly arbitrary 'interim' regime that 'fundamental and far-reaching measures' are being taken 'to hasten the process of Islamization of the society in Pakistan.'[36] These measures include the following.

Penal measures. Traditional punishments, supposedly prescribed by the Koran, have been officially reintroduced for certain offences. Drinking alcoholic beverages is punishable with eighty lashes, adultery by stoning to death, theft by amputation of the right hand, decoity (highway robbery) by amputation of the right hand and left foot, false accusation of adultery by eighty lashes. The announcement of these measures attracted a great deal of unfavourable publicity for Pakistan in the West, though it may have made

* Provisional arrangements last the longest.

a good impression on some members of the Saudi royal family. It should be pointed out, however, that up to the time of writing (July 1981) no stonings have taken place in Pakistan, and as far as is known no amputations. Floggings and executions have been numerous, but mainly carried out under martial law rather than Islamic law.* This is because the rules of evidence required in Islamic law for a conviction which would make the 'Koranic' punishment applicable are so stringent as to be virtually impossible to meet if they are strictly adhered to. Where they are not met, but there is a strong presumption of guilt, the judge is allowed to use his discretion. By and large Pakistani judges, who were trained in the English common law tradition, have used their discretion to apply English rules of evidence and have given English-style sentences. The few sentences of amputation so far pronounced have been set aside by appeal courts. But the *ulama* are not satisfied with this, and there is pressure to have at least a few amputations carried out as an exemplary deterrent.

Shari'a benches of judges with Islamic qualifications have been set up in each provincial High Court, with a Shari'a Appellate Bench in the Supreme Court. Their function is to declare a law invalid if it is repugnant to the Koran and the Sunna. It is prescribed, however, that their members must be qualified common-law judges as well as being learned in Islam, and this has made the benches difficult to staff. Moreover, a large number of laws are outside their jurisdiction, at least for the time being, including the much-contested Muslim Family Laws Ordinance of 1961 — though there has been talk of repealing this.

Fiscal and economic measures. The most widely publicized of these has been the compulsory levy of *zakāt*, the Islamic poor rate, which began in June 1980. *Zakāt* is a tax on capital, not income, and it has been levied at a rate of 2.5 per cent per annum on savings

---

* Indeed, the death penalty for murder, along with seventeen other sections of the penal code, was pronounced repugnant to Islam by the Federal Shari'a Bench (see below) in September 1980. But its use under martial law has continued.

accounts, various kinds of bank deposits, unit trusts, government securities, shares and debentures of statutory corporations or companies, annuities, life insurance policies and provident funds. Local committees have been set up to distribute the proceeds to the poor. The introduction of *zakat* caused an outcry among Pakistan's substantial Shi'ite minority, because the Shi'a have quite different rules about its collection and distribution, and expect this to be done through their own *ulama* rather than through the state, which (especially when controlled by Sunnis, as in Pakistan) has no Islamic credentials in their eyes. There were furious demonstrations by the Shi'ites in Islamabad and one person was killed when police opened fire. After that the government gave ground, and the Shi'a have been allowed to collect and distribute their own *zakat* in their own way. As for *ushr*, the tithe on agricultural produce that was announced at the same time as *zakat*, the data of its enforcement had still not been announced a year later.

There have also been moves in the direction of interest-free banking. This has not been made the general rule, but experimental schemes have been introduced which allow investors to make zero-interest deposits, which are supposed to be invested in profit-sharing ventures; and the state housing finance agency makes loans that are repaid not with interest but with a share of the house's rental value over a period of years. This apparently works out cheaper for the borrower than a conventional mortgage.

Ideological and educational reforms. Zia has called for a revision of textbooks and curricula, and the production of new textbooks, to promote awareness of Pakistan's national Islamic ideology and of the history of Islam, and he has endorsed demands for separate universities for women. Lists of 'unsuitable' books to be withdrawn from the curriculum have been circulated to university teachers, including the works of George Eliot (because of her atheism). Urdu is being given greater emphasis in schools and the use of English as a language of instruction is being cut, to the chagrin of some middle-class parents. The use of Urdu on the radio and television has also been increased. By contrast, use of the regional languages which most ordinary Pakistanis actually speak — Punjabi, Sindi, Pushtun and Baluch — is regarded as 'divisive' and strongly discouraged.

The promotion of Islam and an 'Islamic' style in public life. All government departments are required to make arrangements for prayers during working hours and heads of department have been instructed to lead the prayers if possible, or at least to participate. Private sector establishments are allowed to conduct business on Fridays, but must close to allow their employees to attend the noon prayer in the mosques. Zia himself makes a point of setting an example of piety and austerity, for instance by using wooden chairs rather than sofas at public functions, wearing 'national' dress (the *kurta* tunic and baggy *shalwar* trousers, a style in fact imported from central India) when not in uniform and urging others to do likewise;* insisting that men and women be segregated at official dinners; and so on. He aspires, apparently, to be a kind of Atatürk in reverse.

A continuation of Bhutto's pan-Islamic foreign policy. Zia has sought to legitimize his regime by playing an active role in the Islamic Conference. He was helped to do this during 1980 by the Afghanistan crisis and by the fact that Pakistan held the presidency of the conference, both of which put him under a more flattering spotlight than the one he had previously attracted through the execution of Bhutto. Two Islamic foreign ministers' conferences were held in Islamabad, in January and May, and in October Zia, as chairman of the Islamic Conference, addressed the United Nations General Assembly on behalf of the Islamic world. In the same capacity he attempted to mediate in the war between Iran and Iraq, but without success. Bilateral relations with other Muslim countries have also been strengthened.

* Judges in particular have been ordered to doff their English robes and wigs in favour of a black *sherwani* — a long, tight-fitting coat buttoned at the neck, which is considered to be more 'Islamic'.

227

One traditional role which has apparently been expanded is the secondment of Pakistani soldiers, sailors and airmen to other countries' armed forces. (Zia himself had taken part, on King Husain's side, in the Jordano-Palestinian civil war of 1970.) In February 1981 it was estimated that some 10,000 Pakistani military personnel were serving in twenty-two foreign countries, mainly in the Arab world, and there were unconfirmed reports of a 20,000-man force being sent to strengthen the Saudi National Guard.[37] At a more prosaic level, Pakistan's economy is increasingly dependent on remittances from civilian workers in the Gulf states, to which as many as a hundred thousand Pakistanis are said to migrate every year.[38]

Whether all this amounts to an approximation to the Order of the Prophet is not, perhaps, for non-Muslims to judge. In Pakistan the *ulama* and the militant Islamic groups seem to be hedging their bets. Clearly many of the measures taken go in the direction they have been advocating, and Zia has flattered them by appointing them to committees and councils and constantly asking their advice. On the other hand they are well aware that his regime is not popular in the country — if only because gross inequalities remain, and the military regime (whatever Zia's personal virtues) is by no means exempt from corruption — and they do not want the idea of Nizam-i-Mustafa to be irrevocably associated with it.

The only political group that seems really close to the military regime is the Jama'at-i-Islami, with which Zia probably had some contact before he came into power, and several of whose members held government posts during the first two years of his regime. Maududi himself (who died in 1979) had given his blessing to Zia's enterprise, but perhaps hardly expected that it would turn into such a prolonged period of arbitrary personal rule. Maududi's successor as Amir or leader of the Jama'at, Mian Tufail Muhammad, who lives in Lahore, is said to be a relative of Zia's and apparently enjoys his confidence, while other Jama'at leaders, in Karachi, have taken to criticizing the dictatorship and calling for elections. In any case there can be little doubt that through Zia's dictatorship the Jama'at's ideas have achieved a greater influence on policy than they would ever have won through the ballot-box; and the Jama'at's student wing, Jamiyat-i-Tuluba, acts as a kind of unofficial auxiliary police, using armed force to prevent even a hint of left-wing activity on the university campuses.

Not all Pakistanis, indeed perhaps not many, believe that this is the authentic Order of the Prophet. To the people of Sind and Baluchistan, and to a lesser extent those of the North-West Frontier, the regime is nothing more than a Punjabi occupation. To many of the peasants and workers in the Punjab, and in Karachi, it is a regime of landlords and exploiters who murdered the only popular leader Pakistan has had since Jinnah's death, and who are using Islam as a transparent veil for their crimes. To many of the middle class the ideological discipline which the *ulama* applaud is in fact a perversion of Islam. They would agree with the late Mr Justice Muhammad Munir:

> The Quran emphasizes the acquisition of knowledge even if you have to go to China for it. 'Seek knowledge from the cradle to the grave' is another great saying of the Prophet. In fact knowledge is a primary religious obligation of a Muslim. The Quran constantly urges Muslims to study nature, to investigate things to find out for themselves the order with which God has created the universe. But knowledge has no limits.... Now if you subordinate the acquisition of knowledge to any ideology, political, economic or religious, you reduce the field of knowledge to what the ideology teaches you because the ideology has to run through a groove or a defined channel and does not let you go out of it.[39]

Perhaps Shah Waliullah and Sir Sayyid Ahmad Khan, if they were alive today, would say much the same.

CHAPTER EIGHT

Arab Nationalism and
Muslim Brotherhood

When the Arabs today look back on the past, they find that the origin of their union and the seed of their amity was the work of the Arab leader Muhammad ...
Qustantin Zuraiq (a Christian Arab nationalist), 1938

Thus we see that the religion of the Arabs allows them to fight in self-defense and to protect the freedom of belief for Muslim and non-Muslim alike....
Abdul-Rahman Azzam Pasha (later First Secretary-General of the League of Arab States), 1943

The notion of nationalism ... melts away and disappears just as snow disappears after strong, sparkling sunlight falls upon it, by contrast with Islamic brotherhood, which the Koran instils in the souls of all those who follow it.
Hasan al-Banna (Founder of the Muslim Brotherhood)

Introduction

We have now examined a case where nationalism replaced Islam as the founding principle of the state (Turkey), a case where Islam has remained the founding principle, to the exclusion of national-ism (Saudi Arabia), and an attempt to build a new nationalism on Islam (Pakistan). These are three clearly different types of Muslim response to the twentieth-century world in which nation-states, governing a defined territory in the name of the 'nation' that inhabits it, are regarded as the norm. Arab nationalism, which will be discussed in this chapter, is not so much a fourth type as a hesitation, or oscillation, between the first three. In some of its moods it follows the Turkish model, and in a sense goes even further. We have seen that Turkey, although a 'secular' state, is inhabited by an exclusively Muslim nation: a Christian, even if he or she speaks Turkish, may be a citizen of the Turkish Republic, but is not considered a Turk. By contrast, the theorists of Arab nationalism consider that anyone is an Arab whose mother tongue is Arabic, be he or she Muslim, Christian or Jewish. In fact several of the most prominent theorists have been Christians themselves, for whom part of the theory's attraction was precisely that it put them on an equal footing with Muslims, releasing them from their inferior status as 'protégés' (*dhimmis*) of the Islamic state.

Yet none of these theorists has attempted to disentangle Arab nationalism completely from Islam. Indeed it is hard to see how that could be done. It was perverse enough of Atatürk in his later years to try and base Turkish nationalism on a spurious connection between the pre-Islamic Turks, who roamed the steppes of Central Asia, and the pre-Islamic cultures of Anatolia, which were not in fact Turkish, while disregarding the achievements of the Muslim Ottoman Empire, which had fashioned the modern Turkish people and their culture. A comparable exercise for the Arabs would involve falling back on the pre-Islamic traditions of the Arabian peninsula and presenting the vast majority of Arabic literature, the spread of the Arabic language to most of the lands where it is now spoken, and the whole of Arab architecture, science and philosophy, as the results of an unfortunate aberration. Indeed, since most Arab nationalists (and all of the non-Muslim ones) lived or live outside the Arabian peninsula, they would have difficulty in explaining, without reference to Islam, how they come to be Arabs at all.

In short, Islam is to all intents and purposes the essence of Arab history and Arab civilization, and anyone who calls himself an Arab nationalist is bound to take pride in Islam and its achievements. Christian Arab nationalists got round this precisely by emphasizing Islam as a civilization and as an Arab national achieve-ment, while playing down its strictly religious content; and many Muslim Arab intellectuals have gone along with this.* This was, and in some cases still is, the dominant outlook of the elites who came to power in the Arab states of Iraq, Syria, Lebanon, Egypt and Sudan as they emerged from European tutelage during and after the Second World War. It can be compared to the outlook of the elite that led the struggle for the establishment of Pakistan and ruled Pakistan for the first thirty years of its history. However, where the Pakistanis tried to turn a religion into a nationality, one is tempted to say that the Arabs turned nationalism into a religion.

One might also say that the idea of an Arab nation is less artificial than the idea of Pakistan. At least the name did not have to be invented. It was the name of a people whose history gave them enduring prestige, even if in recent times their political fortunes had fallen low. For a Muslim to claim descent from the original Arabs who came out of Arabia meant considerably more than for an Englishman to claim that his family came over with the Conqueror, or for an American family to trace its ancestry to the Mayflower. Above all, it was the name of a language, and not just any language but the language of the Koran, a language forever hallowed by God's choice of it for his definitive message to man-kind. A Muslim who spoke Arabic would not necessarily have described himself as an Arab before the present century, but once the idea was put to him that he was a member of 'the Arab nation' he could hardly resist its appeal; and though the spoken dialects which pass for Arabic in different countries are by no means all mutually intelligible, tradition made it easy for people to accept that the language of education, of culture and of public life should be a lingua franca based on classical Arabic, rather than insisting on a literary development of their local demotic. Thus the tension that exists in Pakistan between Urdu and the regional language is not paralleled in the Arab world, except where there are large

---

*Even Faisal, the son of Sharif Husain of Mecca, used to say: 'We are Arabs before being Muslims, and Muhammad is an Arab before being a prophet.'

minorities who speak non-Arabic languages, such as Kurdish or Berber.

Arab nationalism, then, is closely associated with Islam even by its non-Muslim supporters. But whereas they, with many of the Westernized or partly Westernized Muslim Arab elite, have in effect reinterpreted Islam as primarily an Arab national achievement, other Muslim Arabs have done the opposite, interpreting the 'rebirth of the Arab nation' as essentially a comeback by Muslims after a period of Christian ascendancy. The two attitudes are not always easy to distinguish, since both are reflected in a rhetoric that mixes national and religious themes. The nationalist leader is always anxious to enlist religious feeling on his side, and the Islamic revivalist is often eager to offer his leadership to the nation, or at the very least to rebut the charge that he is unpatriotic.

There are thus two strands in Arab nationalism: the secular strand, which emphasizes the brotherhood of all who speak Arabic whatever their beliefs, and the Islamic strand, which sees the Arabs as the natural and rightful leaders of an Islamic revival. Generally speaking the secular strand has been dominant at the level of political theory. But in the response of the Arab masses to nationalist leadership the Islamic strand has always been important. And with time, as the nationalist movement in most parts of the Arab world achieved its immediate goal of political independence from colonial powers and argument began to focus on the *kind* of society the independent Arab nation should be, this Islamic strand began to express itself more forcefully through its own distinctive groups and leaders, separating itself from, and criticizing, the secular-minded politicians and parties who had gained power. Its spokesmen did not, for the most part, condemn nationalism as such. They condemned what they saw as a perversion of nationalism, which glorified the nation at the expense of the brotherhood of all Muslims and put it almost on a par with God Himself, but claimed themselves to represent an authentic, healthy, Islamic nationalism. For them the nation derived its value and its meaning from Islam, not the other way round. Islam was not 'the religion of the Arabs', but the Arabs had a special position, and

233

a special responsibility, in Islam. They quoted the *hadith*: 'The Arab has no superiority over the non-Arab except by virtue of his piety.' Their attitude to Arabism was thus close to that of the Saudis, and indeed they regarded King Abdul-Aziz as 'one of the hopes of the Islamic world for a restoration of its grandeur and a recreation of its unity.'[1] They were not uncritical of the Saudi state, but it was at first an inspiration for them, and later both a place of refuge and a source of support.

Arab nationalism may be a less artificial notion than Pakistan, but that does not mean it has been more successful. Certainly it has not succeeded in bringing all the Arabs together in a single nation-state, any more than Pakistan succeeded in bringing together all the Muslims of the Indian subcontinent. The League of Arab States had, at the last count, twenty-one members, including Somalia and Djibouti (which are not Arab) and the Palestine Liberation Organization (which is not a state), but excluding the most populous Arab country, Egypt, whose membership has been suspended because of its treaty with Israel. Ephemeral 'unions' of two or more Arab states are still announced from time to time, but no one any longer seriously expects to see a single Arab state stretching 'from the Atlantic to the Gulf'.

That is not to say that Arab nationalism is not a serious political force. Anyone who has travelled in the Arab world, or even had contact with Arabs living in foreign capitals, will be aware of the existence of an educated elite that runs across state frontiers, bound together not only by a language but by a culture and a sense of common destiny. The Arab world, like any world composed of human beings, is divided by many conflicts — personal, social, ideological and regional. But these are felt to be conflicts within a family, and any position one takes in them has to be defended as being good for the family as a whole. Arab governments do not always succeed in agreeing on a common policy for dealing with external problems, such as the conflict with Israel, and still less often succeed in carrying out a common policy even when it is agreed in principle. But there is a virtually unanimous feeling that these problems are *national* problems in which all Arabs are concerned, and that therefore a common policy is in principle desirable.

Within this common Arab nationality, state citizenship is almost interchangeable. An Arab who, whether for ideological or purely economic reasons, finds no outlet for his skills and talents in his own country, will frequently find it elsewhere in the Arab world. Thus one is constantly making discoveries, such as that the minister of religious endowments in Jordan and his brother, editor of one of the leading Jordanian newspapers, are actually long-standing political exiles from Egypt; that the Libyan ambassador in such-and-such a capital is Palestinian; that the oil industry in one of the smaller Gulf states is being run by an Iraqi, while the head of the government information services is Sudanese, and so on. Egyptians and Palestinians especially, being the groups which have the greatest difficulty working in their own countries (the former mainly for demographic, the latter for political reasons) but which have a relatively high average level of education, now form an enormous diaspora that provides a very high proportion of the managerial and technical manpower for the newly rich, relatively underpopulated and educationally backward Arab oil-producing states. Only Algeria, where 130 years of French colonization established French rather than Arabic as the main language of educated discourse, is partially excluded from the pan-Arab cultural universe, though great efforts have been made by the government since independence to close the gap by promoting Arabic education. And among Arabic-speakers only the Maronite Christians of Lebanon tend not to share the feeling that they are part of an Arab nation with a common heritage and a common destiny.

But this community of feeling, this idea that 'the Arabs' are not just the people of Arabia or the lineal descendants of the original Arab conquerors, but everyone whose mother tongue is Arabic, and that such people form a single Arab nation, has gained general currency only during this century. At first it was applied only to the Fertile Crescent — Iraq and Greater Syria, including what are now Jordan, Lebanon and Israel. Egypt, which is by far the largest Arabic-speaking country in terms of population, initially looked with interest and some sympathy on the development of Arab nationalism but without feeling herself to be part of it. Egypt had her own nationalism, based on a consciousness of both Islamic and pre-Islamic history, already well developed by the end of the nineteenth century. She tended to look on the surrounding Arab countries as her natural sphere of influence rather than as parts of a wider nation in which her own national identity would be submerged. In Syria too there were those who advocated a specifically Syrian rather than Arab nationalism, and to varying extents the same was true in other Arab countries.

The notions of nationalism and patriotism tend therefore to be somewhat diffuse in the Arab world, focusing at different levels according to circumstances. Different Arabic words, all carrying overtones similar to those of our 'nation' or 'homeland', have come to be used to denote these different levels of loyalty. *Watan* means nation in the sense of 'homeland', and hence one of several or many Arab nations: the nation living in a particular modern state with its 'national' frontiers and 'national' institutions. *Qaum*, 'people', originally in the sense of one's fellow tribesmen or extended family, means the greater Arab nation, stretching from the Atlantic to the Gulf. And *umma*, 'community', means for a Muslim the worldwide community of Muslim believers, which is by far the oldest focus of loyalty and can still, in some circumstances, turn out to be the deepest.

These three claims to loyalty are felt in every Arab country. Political leaders generally try to ensure that all three pull in the same direction, but inevitably they do sometimes compete. Any attempt to trace the interaction of the three in every Arab country would require not a chapter but a substantial book to itself. In this chapter I shall give pride of place to Egypt, which has remained the leading (but not the only) centre of Islamic thought in the Arab world and, partly for that reason, has been the main centre from which what one might call neo-Islamic politics has spread outwards to other Arab countries.

The Theory: Abduh and Ridā

Two Arab thinkers of the late nineteenth and early twentieth century have influenced almost all subsequent Islamic political thought, in the Arab world and beyond: Muhammad Abduh (1849–1905) and Rashīd Ridā (1865–1935). Both were themselves deeply influenced by the ideas of Jamal al-Din 'al-Afghani', and it is largely thanks to them that Afghani's posthumous influence has been stronger in the Arab world than anywhere else. Through Abduh and some of Abduh's followers, the Afghani tradition continued to affect the development of Egyptian nationalism, even in its increasingly secular form. Through Rida and a few others (mainly Syrian Muslims) Afghani's ideas had a great influence on the development of Arab nationalism. Through Abduh, and especially through Rida's interpretation of Abduh, the line of development leads from Afghani's militant reformism, through Islamic modernism, to the defensive and even traditionalist Islamic militancy of the present day.

Muhammad Abduh, an Egyptian, was Afghani's closest disciple until about 1885. In particular he collaborated with him in Paris in editing the short-lived pan-Islamic newspaper *al-Urwa al-wuthqā* ('the firmest bond'). But in 1888 he returned to Egypt and made his peace with its British rulers, and in later life he came to play a role in Egypt not unlike that of Sayyid Ahmad Khan in India, for he realized that agitation, whether nationalist or pan-Islamic, was doomed to failure unless and until the Muslim world had strengthened itself through educational and religious reform, freeing itself from the shackles of scholasticism and absorbing what was valuable and compatible with Islam in the new civilization of the West. He undertook to show that the essence of modern Western thought was perfectly compatible with Islam, hoping thereby to persuade young Muslim intellectuals, who were anxious to participate in modern civilization, that they had no need to forsake Islam in the process. He carried further the process already developed by Afghani, by Khair al-Din in Tunisia and by the

Young Ottomans in Turkey, of 'identifying certain traditional concepts of Islamic thought with the dominant ideas of modern Europe': *maslaha* (the principle of choosing that interpretation or ruling from which the greatest good will flow) became equivalent to utilitarianism; *shura* (consultation) became parliamentary democracy; *ijma* (consensus) became public opinion. 'In this line of thought ... Islam itself becomes identical with civilization and activity, the norms of nineteenth-century social thought.' And thus, while intending to build a wall against secularism, he 'in fact provided an easy bridge by which it could capture one position after another.'[2]

Abduh's main field of practical activity after his return to Egypt was law, where he sought to bring the new Westernized codes and traditional Islamic jurisprudence into harmony. He was appointed a judge in the 'native tribunals' set up after the British occupation to administer new codes of law based on Western models. (The Civil Code was virtually a wholesale adoption of the French Code Napoléon, with only a small minority of provisions derived from the Shari'a.) Later, in 1899, he became Mufti of Egypt — the highest official authority on matters of religious law — and a member of the (consultative) Legislative Council. His approach to Islamic law was determinedly modernist. He extended the traditional principle of *maslaha*, which allowed a jurist confronted with rival interpretations of a passage in the Koran or the *hadith* to choose the one in his opinion most conducive to human welfare. In Abduh's hands this became a rule for deducing specific laws from general principles of social morality: only such general principles, he taught, had been directly revealed by God. Similarly the principle of *talfiq*, by which some classical authorities allowed judges to choose an interpretation from schools of law other than their own if it seemed to fit the particular circumstances of the case, was extended to allow a systematic comparison of all four classical schools of law, and even of the doctrines of independent jurists who accepted none of them, with a view to producing a synthesis that combined the best features of them all: a modern and unified system of Islamic law.

Abduh was only able to take the first steps in this direction in his lifetime. His approach was widely adopted by legislators in Egypt and other Arab countries after his death, but only in matters of personal status — marriage, divorce and testaments — where modern Muslim states (other than Turkey) have allowed the jurisdiction of the Shari'a to continue. For instance Abduh's suggestion, made in a newspaper article in 1898, that a man should not be allowed to take a second wife unless he could satisfy a court that he was in a position to support them both, was enacted into law in Syria as late as 1953. But in other matters the process that Abduh wanted to reverse — that of ignoring Islamic law and enacting by state authority codes derived from European models — has continued. The Shari'a has been reduced to merely one of the sources of inspiration to which the modern legislator may turn.

Abduh held similar views on the reform of political institutions. As reported by his friend Wilfrid Blunt, he opposed the Ottoman Tanzimat not for their content, but because they had been 'instituted not by and through religion, as they should have been, but in defiance of it.... All changes so attempted must fail in Islam because they have in them the inevitable vice of illegality.' What was needed, before temporal governments could proceed with valid reform, was an authoritative restatement of the fundamentals of Islam by a caliph who would claim only spiritual, not temporal authority; he should have the respect of the *umma* but not rule it. There should be 'a chief of our Egyptian nation, acting under the religious sovereignty of the caliphate.'

Abduh's ideal of government was more or less that of the medieval jurists: the just ruler, ruling in accordance with law and in consultation with the leaders of the people. He identified this with limited, constitutional monarchy, but did not believe Egypt was ready for it. She needed gradual training, first in local councils, then in an advisory council, and finally in a representative assembly. What was needed above all was a period of genuine national education, and autocratic or even foreign rule could be tolerated if it would help in this process. His thought on this point is virtually identical with that of Sayyid Ahmad Khan, and contrasts sharply with that of Afghani. Like Sayyid Ahmad, he was prepared to co-operate with the British so far as they were helping in the work of national education, but unlike him he insisted that their stay must be temporary. (The Muslims, of course, were the majority in Egypt, so that there was no danger of independence meaning non-Muslim rule.)

Some followers of Abduh's began working out the principles of a secular society in which Islam would be honoured but would no longer be the guide of law and policy. They were known as 'the Imam's party' and later, after Abduh's death, the 'People's Party' (*hizb al-umma*). Their *umma* was no longer the worldwide community of believers but the Egyptian nation, composed of Christians and Jews as well as Muslims and bound together not by the revealed law, but by the natural link of living in the same country. According to their spokesman, Lutfi al-Sayyid, Islamic nationalism was not true nationalism: 'The idea that the land of Islam is the home-country of every Muslim is an imperialist principle, the adoption of which could be useful to any imperialist nation eager to enlarge its territory and extend its influence.'

This secular line of thought was taken even further in the next generation by Ali Abdul-Raziq, who, in the context of the storm provoked by Mustafa Kemal's abolition of the caliphate in 1924, argued that Islam did not involve *any* particular set of political principles at all. Most Muslim authorities, while accepting that the Ottoman caliphate was at an end, could not accept that this meant the end of the caliphate as such. Nor could they see the self-proclaimed caliphate of Sharif Husain in Mecca as an adequate response. Egypt was now formally an independent country (after being a British protectorate from 1914 to 1922), and Fu'ad, the reigning member of Muhammad Ali's dynasty, had taken the title of king. He felt that Egypt was the natural claimant to the position which Turkey had abdicated as leader of the Muslim world, and rather hoped that a consensus would emerge in favour of his assuming the caliphate himself. With his discreet encouragement the Rector of al-Azhar and other Egyptian *ulama* convened a 'Congress of the Caliphate' to discuss the situation in 1926.

Before the Congress met, Ali Abdul-Raziq produced his book arguing that the whole notion of the caliphate, as generally understood, rested on a misconception. The Prophet could have no successor, for the authority given to him by God had come to an end with his death. Abu Bakr and the other caliphs had been political, not spiritual rulers, and the religion which Muhammad founded could not be held to stand or fall with the particular form of government that they had adopted. 'Islam is innocent of this institution of the caliphate, as Muslims commonly understand it.' Religion had nothing to do with one form of government rather than another, and nothing in Islam prevented Muslims from abolishing their old political system and building a new one on the basis of new and better ideas derived from the experience of nations.

This of course amounted to a flat contradiction of all traditional Muslim teaching about the history, even the nature of Islam, and provoked a violent storm of opposition. The book was formally condemned by a council of the leading *ulama* of al-Azhar, and its author pronounced unfit to hold any public office. Other critics described it as the work of enemies of Islam, and attacked Abdul-Raziq especially for reproducing the views of non-Muslim authors who, one critic suggested, had an obvious interest in denigrating the caliphate, that 'fearful ghost which, if the bravest man in Europe saw it even in his sleep, would cause him to rise in fear and panic.' By reducing Islam to a mere religion, and emptying it of its socio-political content, Abdul-Raziq was said to be importing into the *umma* a distinction between prophecy and political rule, between the kingdom of God and the kingdom of this world — a distinction that belonged to Christianity and not to Islam. Yet even the critic who argued this most forcefully, Muhammad Bakhit, gave an interpretation of Islamic government which amounted to equating it with modern European political institutions: 'The source of the caliph's power is the *umma*, and he derives authority from it. . . . The Islamic government headed by the caliph and universal Imam is a democratic, free, consultative government, of which the constitution is God's Book and the Sunna of God's Prophet.'

As for the Caliphate Congress, it reaffirmed the traditional view that the caliph should have both spiritual and temporal power. But since no Muslim ruler was in a position to exercise temporal power over the whole of the *umma* in present circumstances a valid caliphate could not be restored. (So much for King Fu'ad's hopes.) All that could be done was to hold further meetings to discuss the matter from time to time.

A further campaign was mounted in the late 1930s to secure the caliphate for Fu'ad's son and successor, King Faruq, but this too fizzled out. Today, the idea of a genuinely Islamic government under a just and pious ruler remains very much alive. But the best its advocates seem to hope for is a federation or confederation of such rulers governing a chain of separate Muslim states. The notion of a universal Muslim leader, whether emperor or pope, has been tacitly but unanimously abandoned.

Another Egyptian who belonged to Afghani's circle in the Cairo of the 1870s was Sa'd Zaghlul (1857–1927), who became the leader of Egypt's struggle for independence against the British after the First World War. Zaghlul was also a pupil of Abduh, and sought to apply his utilitarian principles as a judge in the secular courts between 1892 and 1906. Later, as Minister of Justice, he founded a school to give Shari'a judges a modern training. He was essentially a secular politician, 'interested in the Quran mainly as a source of useful quotations', and his great achievement was to build a national movement, the Wafd party,* in which Muslims and Christians fought side by side, on equal terms. He even declared that religion was between man and God, whereas the state was between man and man.† Thus, in essence, his views were the the same as those of Ali Abdul-Raziq, although as it happened

---

*Named after the *wafd* or delegation which he formed to put Egypt's case to the 1919 Peace Conference.

† By 'man' he meant the species, not the sex. Women's emancipation was part of the Wafd's programme, and 'the heroic days of nationalism were also those when educated Muslim women ... threw off the veil and first took part in public life.'

Abdul-Raziq was associated with a dissident splinter-group from Zaghlul's party and therefore Zaghlul gave him no support in the row over his book. Zaghlul and Abdul-Raziq between them represent, in practice and in theory respectively, the end product of one line of development from Afghani's ideas: secular Egyptian nationalism. Rashid Rida, who was both a disciple of Abduh and a vigorous critic of Abdul-Raziq, represents another line of development. He was born near Tripoli, in what is now northern Lebanon but was then considered part of Syria, and educated in Tripoli at a 'National Islamic School', founded by a reformer only twenty years older than himself, which included both Western (French, science) and traditional Islamic subjects in its curriculum. Deeply influenced by the writings of al-Ghazali, Rida at first sought the spiritual life with the Sufi orders, but was soon repelled by their emphasis on exotic rites and ceremonies. Then, in 1892–93, he discovered a set of copies of *al-Urwa al-wuthqa* among his father's papers, and immediately fell under the spell of Afghani's ideas. In 1894 he met Abduh, who was on a visit to Tripoli, and became completely devoted to him, following him to Cairo in 1897 and remaining there for the rest of his life as editor of *al-Manar*, a periodical devoted to advocating the reform of Islam in accordance with Abduh's ideas.

Like Afghani and Abduh, Rida believed that Islam was political and social as well as spiritual, that if properly understood and obeyed it would bring strength and success to the community in this world as well as salvation to the individual in the next. If Muslims were backward and weak, it was because they had lost the truth of their religion. They had allowed the West to monopolize some principles that were really part of true Islam: creative effort (in Rida's view, the underlying meaning of *jihad*), devotion to the welfare of the community, and the search for truth. To revive these qualities, Muslims should return to the true Islam as it was taught by the Prophet and the Elders or Ancestors (*salaf*). This had been the motto of Afghani and Abduh in *al-Urwa al-wuthqa*. Under Rida's leadership it became that of a reform movement, the *salafiya*, whose influence was felt throughout the Muslim world. But whereas Afghani had spoken of the *salaf* mainly to conjure up a vision of the dynamism and militancy of early Islam, and whereas Abduh put the emphasis on the rationalism of early Islam as compared with latter-day superstition, Rida took the slogan more literally.

For him it was important to find out as exactly as possible what the Prophet and his companions had actually said and done and to apply it as precisely as possible to the conditions of the present day. Thus in spite of his devotion to Abduh and his consequent reputation as a modernist, he was in some ways closer in spirit to the puritanical revivalism of the Wahhabis. He was indeed a follower of Ibn Hanbal, became an enthusiastic reader and publisher of the works of Ibn Taimiya, and later welcomed Abdul-Aziz Al Sa'ud's conquest of the holy cities, strongly defending the Wahhabis against the charge of heresy and declaring that theirs was the true religion of the original Muslims.

Once again we must recall that the Hanbali school of legal thought, while intellectually rigorous and often puritanical in its practical effects, is not inflexible. Thus Rida believed in an unchanging and always applicable Islam, that of the *salaf*, but was not bound by the subsequent tradition which had grown up around it. Moreover, where a specific command in the Koran or the *hadith* appeared to be in contradiction of a general principle which had equivalent authority, he argued for the superiority of the general principle; and he followed Abduh in making *maslaha* — the general good, or public interest — the key principle for deciding the law where Koran and *hadith* gave no explicit and unchallengeable guidance. Guided by this principle, in his view, a modern Muslim nation had the right to enact 'a system of just laws appropriate to the situation in which its past history has placed it.'

In other words, Rida allowed a very broad scope to *ijtihad*, in the sense of independent reasoning from first principles. In his writing, *ijtihad* is no longer mere interpretation; it is actual legislation. But this is not a task for just anyone to undertake. It requires a body of specially qualified *ulama* — qualified both by their learning and by their independence of mind. How exactly these *ulama* are to be chosen Rida does not say.

The result, however, should be that new and unified system of Muslim law which Abduh had envisaged, and which should be in accord with 'the spirit of the age'. For instance, Rida favoured abandoning the traditional rule by which a Muslim who abandons Islam is supposed to be put to death. He was prepared on this point to reject the consensus of all the classical jurists, on the grounds that it was in contradiction with the principles of Islam, since there is no text in the Koran saying that all apostates should be killed, whereas there is one that condemns all compulsion in religion. Similarly, he argued that *jihad* — the duty to wage war against non-Muslims — should be interpreted only in a defensive sense, unless it was undertaken against a non-Muslim state where the preaching of Islam was forbidden, or Muslims not allowed to live in accordance with their law. To compel 'people of the Book' (Christians and Jews) to become Muslims by force would contradict the principle of freedom in the faith. He was even prepared to argue, as Abduh had done before him, for the permissibility of interest on loans, which the Koran (as traditionally understood) forbids. 'Can one maintain,' he asked, 'that the law of this religion demands that its adherents should be poor, and that what is essential for their livelihood and for the power of their community and State should be in the hands of covetous men belonging to other peoples?' No, Muslims had to be able to compete with other peoples, and if, in a capitalist world, that obliged them to take interest on loans, that was justified on grounds of necessity. For the Koran said: 'Do not give to fools your property that God has assigned to you to manage.' By contrast, Rida accepted the dominance of men over women, while cautioning that it should be exercised justly and with consultation, and even justified slavery on the grounds that it protected women and gave all of them a chance to bear children.

On the issue of Islamic government and the caliphate, Rida came down firmly against Abdul-Raziq's secularist thesis. Since he envisaged a system of law both modern and Islamic, Rida also looked for a government both modern and Islamic to enforce it.

The specially qualified *ulama* should work with a supremely qualified caliph. Yet it is not clear that Rida saw this caliph as a temporal ruler. He certainly did not think it possible to reunite all Muslims in a single state. His caliph was to be the chief *mujtahid*: the supreme practitioner of *ijtihad* who, with the help of the *ulama*, would deduce from the unchanging principles of Islam laws appropriate to the changing conditions of the world, and would impose — apparently by a purely moral authority, which all Muslim governments would have to respect — their application. This caliph would have been something like a medieval pope. But the doctrine also seems similar to that of *wilayat-al-faqih* (the guardianship of the jurist) later developed by Ayatollah Khomeini. Khomeini, of course, is a Shi'ite, coming from a completely different intellectual tradition. But the attempt to formulate a theory of Islamic government for the modern age has in some ways brought the two traditions closer together. Reformist Sunnis like Rida have re-opened the 'gate of *ijtihad*', which in Shi'ism was never closed', and thereby have exalted the authority of the genuine *ulama*, those qualified to undertake *ijtihad*, to a level similar to that which the Shi'ite *ulama* traditionally enjoy.* At the same time the Shi'ite *ulama*, in order to resist what they see as the corruption of Islam by Western-orientated, despotic governments, have been sucked into the political process and have had to take some responsibility for guiding the state on Islamic lines; and so Khomeini, in his capacity as *faqih* and *mujtahid*, comes to assume a role very similar to that which Rida envisaged for his Sunni caliph.

Rida's caliphate of *ijtihad* was itself a long-term vision. In the short term he would have settled for a 'caliphate of necessity' to co-ordinate the efforts of Muslim countries against the foreign danger, under a dynamic leader such as ... Mustafa Kemal, 'a great man, who unfortunately knew nothing about Islam. If he had known what Islam really was, he would have been just the man who was needed.'

* Indeed Rida, although rather intolerant of Shi'ite 'fairy tales and illegitimate innovations', deplored the fact that Sunni *ulama* generally lacked the prestige and authority of their Shi'ite colleagues.

Rida was convinced that genuine Islamic government would be best not only for the Muslims but also for non-Muslim minorities. He pointed out that an Islamic state would be based on justice and on a law which specifically granted rights and freedom to Christians and Jews, while a secular state as he understood it would be based on a purely natural solidarity rather than a moral system. 'Justice created a link, while solidarity divided: the hatred between those who worshipped their own communities and had nothing else to worship was far worse than between those who had different religions. If there had been persecution in the Near East, it was because of the decline of Islam; a proof of this was the outburst of hatred which followed the revolution of the secularist Young Turks in 1908.'

That may sound like an eloquent condemnation of nationalism. Yet the fact is that Rida himself was one of those who expressed the Arab reaction against the 1908 revolution, and he is regarded by some as the true father of Arab nationalism. He, like Abduh, held the Turks largely responsible for what had gone wrong with Islam, and the Islam of the *salaf*, which he wanted to get back to, was of course an Arab Islam. As early as 1900 Rida wrote:

The Turks are a warlike nation, but they are not of greater moment than the Arabs; how can their conquests be compared to those of the Arabs, although their state lasted longer than all the states of the Arabs together? It is in the countries which were conquered by the Arabs that Islam spread, became firmly established and prospered. Most of the lands which the Turks conquered were a burden on Islam and the Muslims, and are still a warning of clear catastrophe. I am not saying that those conquests are things for which the Turks must be blamed or criticised, but I want to say that the greatest glory in the Muslim conquests goes to the Arabs, and that religion grew, and became great through them; their foundation is the strongest, their light is the brightest, and they are indeed the best *umma* [i.e. people] brought forth to the world. I do not deny that the Turks have virtue, intelligence, and nobility, and I do not like to continue the comparison of the conquests of the Arabs and of the Turks, and the greater import to Islam of the Arab contribution. A little knowledge of past and present history shows that most of the countries where Islam was established were conquered by the Arabs who were the active agents of the propagation of Islam.[3]

In another article, entitled 'The Civilization of the Arabs', he said that 'to care for the history of the Arabs and to strive to revive their glory is the same as to work for the Muslim union which only obtained in past centuries thanks to the Arabs, and will not return in this century except through them, united and in agreement with all the races.'[4] And in his magazine *al-Manar* Rida serialized a book by his fellow-Syrian Abdul-Rahman al-Kawakibi (1849–1902), which denounced the Ottomans and pleaded for the restoration of an Arab caliphate.

After the 1908 revolution, when the Young Turks had deposed Sultan Abdul-Hamid and manifested both their indifference to Islam and their inability to save the Ottoman Empire from defeat in the Balkan Wars, Rida took part in the founding of the Decentralization Party, whose object was to resist the centralizing and Turkifying policies of the Unionist government in Istanbul. He also joined a secret society aimed at reconciling the various rulers of the Arabian peninsula in order to put pressure on the Ottoman government and, if the Empire fell to pieces, to defend the Arabs against foreign encroachment. He was even involved in the negotiations in Cairo which eventually led to the British-backed Arab revolt against the Ottoman Empire during the First World War.

Rida was aware of a potential contradiction between his Arab nationalism and his devotion to Islamic unity. But he resolved it by arguing that the political interests of the Arabs were identical with those of the *umma* as a whole, since an independent Arab state would revive both the language and the law of Islam. Had there been a conflict, he said, he would have given priority to religious duty over national duty, since religious duty concerned the happiness of the next world as well as this.[5] He and his associates stopped short of thoroughgoing secular Arab nationalism, which became fashionable in the 1930s and in which, instead of Arab nationalism being a step towards the revival of Islam, Islam became the cultural heritage of the Arab nation. But unintentionally they had helped to prepare the ground for it.

I have dealt at some length with Rashid Rida partly because he was without doubt the most influential Muslim thinker of his generation (and probably of this century), with disciples as far afield as Morocco and Indonesia, and partly because he illustrates so well the complexity of modern Islamic movements and the difficulty of sticking labels on them. Rida was generally thought of in his time as a leading modernist — rightly so, for he was a sincere follower of Abduh and was prepared to undertake quite a radical reinterpretation of Islam to suit modern conditions, as is shown by his view on the taking of interest on loans. Yet he undertook this reinterpretation in the name of fidelity to the distant past — the *salaf* — and of strict adherence to the basic texts of Islam, the Koran and the *hadith*; and he was an admirer and defender of the militant Wahhabi puritans. Was he then a 'fundamentalist'? I do not think so, although I must admit that the precise meaning of this word when used in the context of Islam eludes me, and for that reason I am trying as far as possible to avoid using it in this book.

Certainly Rida was not a simplistic literalist. He knew that the Koran and the *hadith* required scholarly interpretation and was prepared to set aside particular passages as circumstantial when they appeared to contradict an overriding general principle. But at the same time he was sensitive — more sensitive than Abduh had been — to the danger that by trying too hard to demonstrate the compatibility, or even the identity, of Islam with modern liberal ideals, one would end up draining it of its essence and leaving people perhaps with no reason to reject it, but without any positive reason for adhering to it either. If therefore 'fundamentalism' means an effort to define the fundamentals of one's religion and a refusal to budge from them once defined, then Rida was a fundamentalist indeed. (But surely anybody with serious religious beliefs of any sort must be a fundamentalist in this sense?)

In fact Rida, in common with virtually all the revival movements of modern Islam, was fighting a battle on two fronts. There was the familiar battle against the traditionalism and scholasticism of the *ulama*, who were seen as responsible for the stagnation and weakness of Islam and so for the triumphs of its enemies, and the battle against those enemies themselves. But increasingly, reformists like Rida came to share the view of the *ulama* that the enemy was not only political but also ideological: the penetration of un-Islamic ideas into the Muslim body politic.* Thus the emphasis gradually shifted. The need for reform was not forgotten. It was more than ever important to purify Islam so that all its energizing force could be released and Muslims regain full confidence in their faith. But the emphasis came to be less on cleansing it from medieval Sufi superstitions or scholastic legalism and more on cleansing it from new heresies, Western secular ideas that had crept in under the guise of modernism; less on acquiring (or repossessing) for Islam the sources of Western strength, and more on ridding Islam of the seeds of Western decadence. This change of emphasis was far from complete in Rida's work, but he faces both ways, personifying the transition from the modernist reformism of the late nineteenth century to the tradition-orientated revivalism of today.

The Practice: The Muslim Brotherhood

EGYPT 1928–54

Afghani, Abduh and Rida were all, in one respect at least, typical products of the liberal age; they acted in politics as individuals, not as organization men. Afghani sought to rouse the Muslim world through pamphlets and personal contacts, aimed especially at Muslim rulers; Abduh to strengthen Islam, and especially Egypt, by teaching and by issuing legal rulings; Rida to promulgate a

---

* It is easy for the detached outsider to show that Rida and his associates (and even such a rigorously 'Islamic' thinker as Maududi) were themselves affected by the process they were fighting against. To some extent they were aware of this, but that only made the fight seem more acutely necessary.

coherent body of Islamic social thought through a periodical. All three had great influence on the climate of opinion, but none of them achieved much in the way of political change. Politics in the first half of the twentieth century, in the Muslim world as elsewhere, became increasingly a matter of mass movements and of organization.

'Philosophers have tried to understand the world. Our problem is to change it.' Marx's sentiment might well have been echoed by the founder of the Muslim Brotherhood, Hasan al-Bannā (1906–1949), though he would have been reluctant to acknowledge its source. Banna was born in the small town of Mahmūdīya, in the Nile delta ninety miles north-west of Cairo. His father was a watch-repairer who doubled as prayer-leader and teacher in the local mosque. He had studied under Abduh at al-Azhar, and had written some works on Islamic traditions and jurisprudence, so Hasan grew up in a strongly religious atmosphere tinged with reformism. In his teens he joined a Sufi order, the Hasafiya, and remained active in it for the next twenty years. He was also profoundly influenced by reading the works of al-Ghazali, from whom he imbibed particularly the idea that learning was not something to be pursued for its own sake but only in so far as it helped one to lead a better life.

At the age of sixteen he was sent to Cairo for training as an Arabic teacher in the Dar al-Ulum (House of the Sciences) — a product of nineteenth-century reformism which had now become a repository of Islamic tradition, in opposition to the new secular universities. In Cairo he made frequent visits to the bookshop run by Rashid Rida's Salafiya movement, was an avid reader of *al-Manar*, and got to know Rida himself as well as other former pupils of Abduh. In 1927, at the age of twenty-one, he graduated and was assigned to a post in a primary school at Ismā'īlīya, headquarters of the foreign-controlled Suez Canal Company and capital of the British-occupied Canal Zone.

Fully in sympathy with the ideas of Afghani and Abduh, as conveyed by Rida and *al-Manar*, Banna was deeply distressed to see Egypt moving in what seemed to him the opposite direction:

political turmoil and disunity, increasing moral laxity, decreasing respect for tradition and religion, widespread enthusiasm for Western secular culture among the upper and middle classes, nominal independence made a mockery by continued British occupation and foreign domination of the economy — symbolized in Isma'iliya by the conspicuously luxurious homes of the foreigners overlooking the 'miserable' homes of their workers. The result: Egypt's youth were inheriting a 'corrupted' faith, were overwhelmed by 'doubt and perplexity' and tempted by apostasy. Banna decided it was his mission in life to reverse these trends. He instructed children by day, and their parents by night. He held discussion meetings in the school, in the mosque and in the coffee-houses, and sought to influence the leading members of the community.

One day in 1928 or 1929 a group of six labourers from the British camp came to see him and said (according to his own account):

> We are weary of this life of humiliation and restriction. Lo, we see that the Arabs and the Muslims have no status and no dignity. They are not more than mere hirelings belonging to the foreigners. We possess nothing but this blood ... and these souls ... and these few coins.... We are unable to perceive the road to action as you perceive it, or to know the path to the service of the fatherland (*watan*), the religion, and the nation (*umma*) as you know it. All that we desire now is to present you with all that we possess, to be acquitted by God of the responsibility, and for you to be responsible before Him for us and for what we must do.[6]

So the Muslim Brotherhood was born. By 1932 it had 15 branches, by 1940 500 and by 1949 2,000, corresponding to an estimated 500,000 active members and as many sympathizers. The American historian Richard Mitchell, whose book on the Brotherhood has been justly praised both within the movement and by its critics, describes it as 'the first mass-supported and organized, essentially urban-orientated effort to cope with the plight of Islam in the modern world.' Professor Mitchell, who regularly attended

Brotherhood meetings for a year and a half in 1953–54 and also studied records of trials in which Muslim Brothers were involved, was struck by the high proportion of active members who wore Western suits and belonged to white-collar professions requiring or implying a degree of Western-style education – students, civil servants, teachers, clerks and office-workers, architects, engineers, accountants, journalists. He believes that the initial membership, in the 1930s, was largely rural and working class, and that members of the urban lower classes flocked to the organization in the 1940s, but that the activists who 'shaped the Society's political destiny' were from the educated urban middle class. He sees the movement as part of 'an effort to reinstitutionalize religious life for those whose commitment to the tradition and religion is still great, but who at the same time are already effectively touched by the forces of Westernization'; a movement 'which not only sought to imbue the present with some sense of the past ... but also to redefine the past in terms meaningful for the present.'

The middle-class origins of its activists are also reflected to some extent in the Brotherhood's ideas and programmes: hostility to foreign economic control and to the local minorities (Jewish and Christian) which tended to provide the agents of that control; struggle against the ruling class which had compromised with imperialism, but opposition to class struggle in economic enterprises; a call for harmony between labour and management, landowner and peasant. However, in the 1930s and 1940s, when much of Egyptian industry was foreign-owned, the Brotherhood was an active defender of workers against exploitation and gained great influence in the labour movement, including control of some unions.

Concentrating at first on moral and social reform, the Brotherhood became increasingly a political organization through its hostility to British occupation and also its support for the Palestinian Arabs against Zionism. The Brothers regarded Palestine as 'the heart of the Arab world, the knot of the Muslim peoples' and Jerusalem as 'the third of the holy places'. From the time of the Arab general strike and insurrection in Palestine in 1936–37

253

the Muslim Brothers gave moral and financial support to the Palestinians, and in 1948 they sent volunteers to take part in the *jihad* against the establishment of the Jewish state, before the Egyptian government had officially declared war.

'My Brothers,' Hasan al-Banna told his followers in 1943, 'you are not a benevolent society, nor a political party, nor a local organization having limited purposes. Rather, you are a new soul in the heart of this nation to give it life by means of the Koran...'[7] In fact the Brotherhood was a political organization and officially defined itself as such (among other things) from 1939 onwards. But it was not the old style of political party consisting of a handful of notables — landlords or intellectuals — who got together to plan a conspiracy or put up a slate for elections. It was a mass organization, bearing some characteristic marks of the decade in which it developed — the 1930s. It sought to organize not only the political opinions of its followers but their entire way of life, through a network of clubs and welfare services. It gave its members 'athletics' training, organized them in groups of 'rovers', later in 'battalions', and later still replaced these by a secret 'special section' whose task was to prepare and carry out the *jihad*, in other words armed struggle. It was opposed in principle to political parties, considering that they unnecessarily divided the nation, whose united energies it proposed itself to mobilize in the cause of Islam. It had a charismatic leader who aroused the passionate devotion of the rank and file and exacted unswerving obedience from the cadres. It indoctrinated its members through a network of cells or 'families' each of which had five members.

The Second World War and its aftermath, which plunged the country into an acute crisis, both economic and political, gave the Brotherhood the opportunity to play a major role in Egyptian politics. Egypt suffered both from the disruption of world markets and from the requirements of the British war effort. There were high wages or profits for some, but shortages of consumer goods for almost all. Egypt was officially neutral, but she was the base from which Britain fought a desperate battle to hold the Middle

East against German attack. Egyptian nationalist feeling against Britain was very strong and was ably exploited by Axis propaganda. The British were very anxious to avoid disturbances at their rear, and for this they needed an Egyptian government with genuine popular support. In February 1942 King Faruq found his palace surrounded by British tanks and capitulated to British demands by appointing a government from the nationalist Wafd party.

This had the effect of totally discrediting the monarchy, which had been humiliated, and partially discrediting the Wafd which, though genuinely popular, had accepted power as a present from the British and now had to take responsibility for administering the war economy. The Muslim Brotherhood benefited from this. By 1945 it had emerged as a mass organization competing with the Wafd for the leadership of the nationalist movement.

The King was able to dismiss the Wafd government at the end of 1944 and from then until 1951 he governed Egypt through a series of totally unrepresentative minority governments in an atmosphere of growing violence and chaos. The Muslim Brotherhood's position was ambiguous because it opposed the King's policies on nationalist, religious and social grounds but also opposed the Wafd, especially the leftist and communist tendencies within the latter which emerged strongly at the end of the war, owing partly to the widespread economic discontent and partly to the Soviet Union's soaring prestige and influence. Banna himself seems to have hoped that the King would be forced to come to terms with him and give the Brotherhood a dominant position in the state, while some of the King's advisers thought they could use the Brotherhood as a weapon against the Wafd. But neither side was prepared to make major political concessions and, anyway, the mass following of the Brotherhood was in no mood for compromise.

The government became increasingly alarmed at the Brotherhood's involvement in agitation and violence, especially during 1948 when passions were further inflamed by the Palestine war and Egypt's disappointing performance in it. At the end of that year, reacting to a series of incidents, the government officially dissolved the Brotherhood and arrested most of its prominent members other than Banna himself. Three weeks later the prime minister, Nuqrashi Pasha, was shot and killed by a young member of the Brotherhood. Seven weeks after that, on 12 February 1949, Hasan al-Banna in his turn was assassinated by secret service agents.

The Brotherhood never fully recovered from the death of its founder, but for another five years it remained a significant force in Egyptian politics, and appeared at first to enjoy a privileged relationship with the 'Free Officers', led by Gamal Abdul-Nasser, who seized power and deposed King Faruq in 1952. One member of Nasser's group, Anwar al-Sadat, had been in contact with Banna as early as 1940, at a time when he (Sadat) was plotting an anti-British revolt with the aid of German intelligence. Nasser himself had, it seems, been profoundly affected by a meeting with one of Banna's advisers in 1944, at which he was told: 'Begin to organize in the army groups which have faith in what we believe so that when the time comes, we will be organized in one rank, making it impossible for our enemies to crush us.'[8] He and other officers had much in common with the Brotherhood: anger at the King's capitulation to the British, outrage at the decadence and injustice of Egyptian society, impatience with parliamentary politics, hostility to communism and to any ideology which would divide the nation. Their admiration for the Brotherhood was strengthened during the Palestine war when they saw that Brothers were prepared to fight and die alongside them while the King and the politicians seemed happy to leave the army to its fate.

Before actually carrying out the revolution in 1952, the Free Officers made contact with the Brotherhood and assigned to it various back-up tasks, most of which proved to be unnecessary because the revolution encountered no resistance. The Muslim Brothers felt, with some justification, that they had both inspired and participated in the revolution, and they expected to reap the benefit. In appearance they were vindicated when the new government exempted them from a general ban on political parties and groups in January 1953. But it soon turned out that Nasser and his colleagues had no serious intention either of sharing power with the Brotherhood or of introducing Islamic government as the Brotherhood understood it. Instead, they adopted the slogan: 'Religion is for God and the nation is for all.' In January 1954, after the failure of an attempt to gain control of the Brotherhood from within, the government reversed its decision of the previous year and the organization was once again officially dissolved. This decision was then rescinded two months later when Nasser had to backpedal in the face of popular support for the head of state, General Neguib, whom Nasser had tried to oust and who became, for a short time, the focus of many different kinds of opposition to Nasser's power. But conflict between the regime and the Brotherhood continued to rage throughout 1954, with the Brotherhood rapidly disintegrating for lack of authoritative leadership and clear chains of command, until in October an unsuccessful attempt was made on Nasser's life, giving him an ideal pretext to smash the Brotherhood's organization, execute several of its leaders, and imprison thousands of its cadres.

THE BROTHERHOOD AT LARGE (1948–81)

For years after 1954 the Brotherhood was driven so far underground in Egypt as to be non-existent for all practical purposes. Many of those members who were released or who escaped arrest took refuge abroad, in other Arab countries. They had little difficulty in finding hospitality and moral support, for by this time daughter societies of Muslim Brothers had been founded in most Arab states. Between 1942 and 1945 Banna himself had visited Palestine and Jordan and established branches of the Brotherhood in several towns. In 1948 the Brotherhood was able to raise its own militia in Palestine for the war against the Zionists, in addition to the volunteers sent from Egypt. Its commander was Shaikh Mustafa al-Siba'i, who later became the leader of the Brothers in Damascus. On the east bank of the Jordan there was a separate commando group led by Muhammad Abdul-Rahman al-Khalifa, a young lawyer.

In September 1954, at the height of the conflict between the

Brothers and the new Egyptian regime, a conference was held in Damascus, attended by representatives of Muslim Brothers' societies in Iraq, Jordan and Sudan as well as Syria and Egypt. The five leaders of the Egyptian delegation, including Abdul-Hakim Abidin who had been secretary-general of the Brotherhood under Banna, were stripped of their Egyptian nationality and remained in exile. One of them, Sa'id Ramadan, assumed the leadership of the Brotherhood in exile, travelling through the Muslim world and eventually settling in Geneva where he set up a centre of Islamic studies, with support from Saudi Arabia. (He also arranged for the resumption, in Beirut, of one of the Brotherhood's magazines, *al-Da'wa* — The Call.) Another, Kamil Isma'il al-Sharif, settled in Jordan where he is now Minister of Religious Endowments, while his brother, Mahmud al-Sharif, is editor-in-chief of the pro-government newspaper, *al-Dustur* (The Constitution).

Jordan and the Palestinians. The young King Husain of Jordan, who during the 1950s found himself the target of Nasser's radical propaganda, was happy to give asylum to these Islamic refugees. There was a certain irony in this since in its heyday the Brotherhood had been hostile to the Hashimite family, to which Husain belonged, and especially to his grandfather King Abdullah whom it regarded as a British stooge; and it was precisely the same accusation that Nasser was now bringing against Husain. But after 1954 the Brothers found Nasser a more dangerous enemy than the British, and were glad to reach a *modus vivendi* with a king who, though educated in Britain, was careful always to show respect for Islam. (His claim to legitimacy as a ruler depends in part on his descent from the Prophet.) Today Jordan is one Arab state where the Brotherhood, still represented by the commando leader of 1948 Abdul-Rahman al-Khalifa, enjoys official recognition as a charitable association and is allowed to act as unofficial guardian of the country's moral welfare, applying a discreet censorship to television programmes and school syllabuses. There seems to be a tacit understanding that in return the Brothers will not harass the government, as they do in Egypt, with demands for the application of the 'Koranic' penal code, the prohibition of interest, or the dismissal of Christians from positions of responsibility.[9]

After the 1948 disaster in Palestine some Palestinians, who shared the Brotherhood's general outlook, felt the need for a more radical, or more explicitly political, organization. In 1952 the Party for the Liberation of Islam was founded by Shaikh Taqi al-Din Nabhani, who had been a judge in the Shari'a court of Haifa under the British mandate. In 1948 he had fled to Nablus, in the part of Palestine occupied by the Arab Legion during the fighting and subsequently incorporated into the Kingdom of Jordan.* This party took a much more militant line against the Hashimite regime, and has consequently been banned more or less throughout its history, but it was said to have members all over the Levant, and for a time published its own newspaper in Beirut.

Other Palestinian refugees, who found themselves in the Egyptian-occupied Gaza Strip or studying at Egyptian universities in the years before 1954, were recruited into the Brotherhood proper. One of these was a student at the Cairo University engineering faculty (a noted Brotherhood stronghold) called Yasser Arafat. The ideology of the Fatah movement which Arafat later founded, and which since 1968 has been the dominant group in the Palestine Liberation Organization (PLO), is derived in part from that of the Brotherhood. The name Fatah itself, as well as being a reverse acronym in Arabic for 'Movement for the Liberation of Palestine', is a technical term meaning a conquest for Islam gained in the *jihad*; and Fatah consistently uses Islamic themes and references to rouse the ardour of its members.† Among Arafat's key lieutenants in Fatah today are Khalil al-Wazir (code name 'Abu Jihad' — father of *jihad*), the military commander in Lebanon, who is a former Muslim Brother, and Khalid Muhammad Sa'id al-Sa'id, known in the PLO as Khalid al-Hasan, who was a co-founder of the Party for the Liberation of Islam and still

---

* What is now called 'the West Bank'.

† It is noticeable that Christians are prominent in the PLO as leaders of leftist minority groups, or as independents, rather than in the leadership of Fatah.

favours 'building up an Islamic society which is neither capitalism nor socialism.'* Al-Hasan, who lives in Kuwait, keeps in close touch both with governments and with unofficial Islamic movements in the Persian Gulf region, and tends to be regarded within the PLO as a spokesman for the Saudi Arabian point of view. He is certainly a 'moderate', both in the sense of being anti-Marxist and in the sense of seeking a peaceful solution to the Palestine conflict through the good offices of Europe and the United States.

Some former members of the Party for the Liberation of Islam are now thought to be active within the Muslim Brotherhood in Jordan, where lately a predominantly Palestinian radical wing has emerged to challenge the moderate leadership of Abdul-Rahman al-Khalifa. This group, particularly active in the universities, apparently thinks the Brotherhood should end its collaboration with the Jordanian government. One of its members, Dr Abdullah Azzam of the Shari'a law faculty in the university of Amman, was discharged from the university in summer 1980 after making a speech critical of the government.†

Sudan. One of the demands of the Brotherhood during its bid for leadership of the Egyptian national movement, in the middle and late 1940s, was for 'unity of the Nile Valley', i.e. unity between Egypt and the Sudan, which was then legally an Anglo-Egyptian condominium, but in reality was under British control. In the Sudan itself Muslim opinion was split on the issue as it had been in the nineteenth century, with the Khatmiya Sufi order committed to unity with Egypt while the descendants and followers of the Mahdi stood for independence from both Britain and Egypt. From 1954 onwards the Muslim Brothers in the Sudan naturally became hostile to the idea of unity with Nasser's Egypt, and were therefore able to establish themselves as a religio-political party with Mahdist

---

* He maintains there is no contradiction between this and the PLO's advocacy of a 'democratic state' in Palestine with equal rights for Jews, Christians and Muslims.

† He was discharged not by the university itself but by the military authorities, under a regulation dating back to the war of 1967.

support, calling for the application of an Islamic constitution and the breaking of political ties with Egypt. On the second point their wishes were fulfilled when Sudan became an independent republic on 1 January 1956.

Under the military regime of General Ibrahim Abbud (1958–1964), which dissolved all political parties, the Brothers had to go underground. When civilian rule was restored in 1964 they re-emerged as the Islamic Charter Front — conceived as a broad front for all political movements — with Hasan al-Turabi, dean of the law school of Khartoum University (where the Brotherhood had a strong base) as Secretary-General. Since then they have remained actively involved in Sudanese politics, but they 'seem to draw most of their support from intellectuals and university and higher secondary school students, with little support among the general public. However, they have achieved no small degree of political influence in their newspaper and mosques, creating in this way a climate of opinion that has pushed the more popularly-based parties into adopting some Muslim Brother policies.'[10] In 1965, for instance, they succeeded in getting the Sudanese Communist Party banned, after a period of nationwide rioting and demonstrations against it.

President Ja'far al-Numairi, who has ruled Sudan since he seized power in May 1969, was initially no more sympathetic to the Brotherhood and other Islamic parties than Nasser. But after his showdown with the Communists, who almost succeeded in overthrowing him in 1971, Numairi began to cultivate a more 'Islamic' image. The constitution of 1973 lays down that 'Islamic law and custom shall be the main sources of legislation.' Numairi pursued a policy of rapprochement with Saudi Arabia, which led in 1977 to the inauguration of a 'national reconciliation' policy, aimed especially at the Muslim Brothers and at Sayyid Sadiq al-Mahdi (great grandson of the Mahdi of the 1880s), a potentially dangerous opponent since he combines hereditary charisma, international prestige, Islamic and Western learning and an enlightened, cautiously modernist interpretation of Islam. As part of this policy, Numairi appointed a committee for the 'Revision of Sudanese laws to bring them into conformity with Islamic teaching' and banned from public office any person who took alcoholic drink. Turabi, the Muslim Brotherhood leader, joined this committee in July 1977 and became Attorney-General in 1978.

Thus in the late 1970s Sudan went through a version of the 'Islamization' process that Pakistan was experiencing at the same time, but a milder and more cautious version because the large non-Muslim minority in the south of the country had to be reassured. Turabi has been criticized within the Muslim Brotherhood for making too many compromises, while traditionalist Sufi leaders reject the reformist attitude of the Brotherhood as a whole. (It is, in general, more moderate and gradualist in its approach than its Egyptian counterpart.) Sadiq al-Mahdi, by contrast, regards the Brotherhood as *too* traditional in its interpretation of Islam. He favours a 'new *ijtihad*', transcending all the old sects and schools of law, which would derive from Islam's original sources a philosophy and a set of institutions appropriate to a modern state.

The Persian Gulf. Saudi Arabia and the smaller Gulf states have consistently offered asylum to Muslim Brothers fleeing from persecution in more 'progressive' Arab countries. This is one of a number of factors that have helped to give the Brotherhood a conservative image, though in his lifetime the Brothers alienated King Abdul-Aziz by their firm repudiation of the principle of hereditary kingship, and by their condemnation of the implementation of the law of cutting off hands in Saudi Arabia 'while the rulers swim in the gold stolen from the state treasury and the wealth of the people.'[11] The general view of the Saudi rulers seems to have been that occasional statements of this sort can be overlooked in view of the Brotherhood's good record of anti-communism and its efforts to move Arab countries closer to a traditional Islamic order. In the 1960s, many Egyptian Brothers found employment in agencies and on the publications of the Saudi-sponsored Muslim World League.

The fact that the movement which culminated in the 1979 Mecca uprising had started in the early Seventies at Medina university, which was founded by Muslim Brothers, is hardly a direct enough connection to taint the Brotherhood with guilt in the eyes of the Saudi royal family. It is generally believed that they give financial support to the Brotherhood in several countries, as well as putting pressure on governments to treat it with respect or at least tolerance. In Saudi Arabia itself, of course, no political parties are allowed, but there is an all-but-officially recognized branch of the Brotherhood, led by one of its main theorists, Shaikh Muhammad al-Khattar.

In Kuwait there is a 'Society for Social Reform' led by a Moroccan, Dr Umar Bahair Amiri, who is believed also to be the leader of the Moroccan Society of Muslim Brothers — an active branch credited with a leading part in student demonstrations against the presence of the ex-Shah of Iran in Morocco in early 1979, and in the serious Casablanca food riots of June 1981. Brotherhood activity has also been reported in recent years from Algeria, and especially from Tunisia where it is seen by some observers as a serious threat to the pro-Western regime of the ageing President Habib Bourguiba.

Syria. It is in Syria that the Brotherhood has made its presence felt most spectacularly since 1979, with a campaign of violence against the ruling Ba'th Party, which has responded with a ruthless application of counter-terror. This surprised most observers because the Syrian Brotherhood had scarcely been heard of for twenty years. It was known to have been quite strong in the early Fifties when, in December 1954, after the hanging of the Brotherhood leaders in Cairo, the Syrian leader Mustafa al-Siba'i was able to respond with a mass prayer meeting in Damascus at which the audience pledged 'to revenge the martyrs'. This caused a crisis between Egypt and Syria because the Syrian government either would not or could not take any action against the Brothers. But later in the decade Nasser's prestige soared throughout the Arab world after his nationalization of the Suez Canal and defiance of the Anglo-Franco-Israeli invasion in 1956. Syria especially was engulfed by a wave of Arab nationalism and in 1958 joined Egypt in a United Arab Republic, an immediate consequence of which was that the Muslim Brothers in Syria were outlawed. Siba'i was imprisoned, and died four or five years later. His nominal successor, Issam al-Attar, lived (and in 1982 is still living) in exile in Bonn. Although the union with Egypt lasted only three years, the Brotherhood in Syria had to remain underground.

In 1963 a military coup brought the Arab Ba'th (Renaissance) Socialist Party to power. This party had been founded in Damascus during the Second World War by a Christian, Michel Aflaq, and a Sunni Muslim, Salah Bitar, as a pure Arab nationalist party that would submerge all religious differences in the slogan: 'Unity, Freedom, Socialism'. It had considerable success in attracting support from minorities and underprivileged groups in Syria, including the Nusairis or 'Alawis',* who lived in the backward and mountainous region around the port of Latakia, and who had been recruited into the armed forces in large numbers under the French mandate. The Ba'th government introduced nationalizations and land reforms and won popularity even among the Sunni Muslim peasants, in spite of the '*jihad* against the enemies of God' declared by the clandestine Brotherhood. In 1966 a further coup by the 'left wing' of the Ba'th drove the founders of the party into exile and from then on the regime evolved into a classic military dictatorship dominated by army officers who happened to be Alawis. It incurred the dislike of orthodox Sunni Muslims† on several counts. The Sunni merchants and *ulama* of the big Syrian cities (Damascus, Homs, Hamā and Aleppo) were offended both by its socialist pretensions and by the fact that the men in control were provincial upstarts, many of whom took to feathering their own and their family's nests with little attempt at concealment. Matters were aggravated by the fact that the Ba'th was a secular nationalist party and that the Nusairi sect, because of its alleged worship of Ali, was generally regarded as heathen by Sunni and even by orthodox Shi'ite *ulama*.

* See pp. 48–9.
† See table opposite for percentages of different ethno-religious groups in the Syrian population.

Occasionally a particularly brazen show of secularism by the regime enabled its opponents to bring the faithful out into the streets in anger. In 1967 an article written by a young Ba'thist

Syrian Ethno-Religious Groups*

Language	Religion	Percentage of population	Remarks
Arabic	Sunni	57.4	
Kurdish	Sunni	8.5	On Syrian–Turkish and Syrian–Iraqi borders
Turkish	Sunni	3.0	
	Sunni (sub-total)	68.9	
Arabic	Alawi/Nusairi	11.7	Majority in Latakia area (north-west Syria)
Arabic	Other Shi'a (Isma'ili)	1.5	
Arabic	Druze	3.0	Majority in Jabal al-Druz (Syria–Jordan border)
	Muslim or claiming to be such (sub-total)	85.1	
Arabic	Eastern Orthodox	4.7	Mainly in cities
Armenian	Christian (88.5% Gregorian)	4.0	Mainly in Aleppo city
Arabic	Other Christian (including Roman Catholic)	5.4	
	Christian (sub-total)	14.1	
	Other (Yazidis, Jews)	0.8	

* Figures from *The World Today*, November 1974, based on those in G. Torrey, *Syrian Politics and the Military 1945–58* (Columbus: Ohio State University Press, 1964) p. 419; corrected from Nikolaos van Dam, *The Struggle for Power in Syria*, 2nd edn (London, 1981), p. 15.

officer in the official army magazine, asserting that 'God, religion, feudalism, capitalism, and all the values which prevailed in the pre-existing society were no more than mummies in the museums of history', provoked widespread rioting. The government felt obliged to condemn the article as the result of 'an American-Israeli reactionary conspiracy' and to sentence the author, and the editors of the magazine, to life imprisonment. More mosques were built in Syria in the three years after the incident than in the previous thirty.[12] In 1973 the promulgation of a 'secular' constitution, which made the leading position of the Ba'th party a constitutional principle but omitted any reference to Islam as the state religion, provoked an even more serious crisis. Again the regime compromised, by inserting a clause which required that 'Islam shall be the religion of the head of the state'; but it also imprisoned and tortured religious leaders who were held responsible for the riots.

In 1976 Syria intervened on the 'Christian' side in the Lebanese civil war.* This provoked further rumblings of Muslim discontent in Syria, but it was not until 1979 that resentment of the regime's arbitrary, corrupt and in effect sectarian practices boiled over into something close to a civil war in Syria itself. On 16 June of that year Captain Ibrahim al-Yusuf, a disenchanted Ba'thist political officer who was a Sunni Muslim (and probably believed that for that reason he had been passed over for promotion), assembled a large number of cadets at the Aleppo Artillery School, excused the Sunni Muslims among them, and then signalled to hidden accomplices to open fire with machine guns. Some sixty cadets, apparently all Alawis, were killed.[13] (The opposition has since claimed that 286 out of 300 cadets in the school were Alawis, a fact that 'compelled' Captain Yusuf 'to rebel against that unnatural position.'[14])

* When Lebanon became independent from France in 1943 the Maronite Christians were guaranteed permanent tenure of the most powerful position in the state in return for accepting that Lebanon was an Arab country and should contribute to common Arab causes and struggles. In 1976 an alliance of Muslim and secular Lebanese radicals, supported by the Palestinians, was on the point of upsetting this arrangement. Syria intervened on the side of the status quo.

This spectacular massacre inaugurated a war of terror and counter-terror in which the regime quickly identified its opponents as the Muslim Brotherhood. The Muslim Brothers, it transpired, had been responsible for a series of terrorist attacks on Alawis holding high official positions since early 1977, but until 1979 the regime had concentrated on fighting left-wing and dissident Ba'thist opponents. It seems that, in fact, rather than a single Muslim Brotherhood organization, there were several Islamic groups operating against the regime and claiming to be the heirs of the original Brotherhood.[15]

In the northern cities of Hama and Aleppo the terrorists seemed to benefit from the overwhelming support of the population, and the government was unable to apprehend or identify any significant number of them. In Aleppo ambushes of government officials, informers and sympathizers became an almost daily occurrence. By the spring of 1980 a Western diplomat in Damascus estimated there had been between three and four hundred political killings in the past year.[16] From January 1980 the victims included Soviet military and civilian advisers—a choice that was evidently both tactical and ideological; it both embarrassed the government and expressed the Muslim Brothers' objection to the regime's close relations with an atheist superpower.

In March 1980 Syria seemed close to an Islamic revolution, as shops were closed to express support for the Brotherhood in all the major cities. 'Commercial life in Aleppo was reduced to zero, Hama paralysed and even Damascus threatened with a general strike, not to mention the other northern cities which were practically surrendered to the armed gangs of the Muslim Brothers', a prominent supporter of the government later recalled.[17] The Syrian Bar and other professional associations joined the protest, calling for an end to the State of Emergency, which had been in force ever since the Ba'th party came to power in 1963. In Aleppo young Muslim militants, on Toyota motorcycles and mopeds, forced shopkeepers to ignore government orders to reopen, attacked public buildings and set fire to buses as well as to the offices of the Syrian and Soviet airlines.

After some apparent hesitation Presiden Hafiz al-Asad decided to respond with a ruthless use of force, supervised by his younger brother Rif'at, head of the feared and hated 'Defence Regiments'. An armoured division was sent to surround the two great northern cities. On Easter Sunday, 6 April, the notorious 'Special Units' headed by Ali Haidar (another relative of Asad's) marched into Aleppo and set up their headquarters in the medieval citadel. The town was divided into two sectors which were searched house by house, one of them in six days, the other in three. Thousands of people were marched off to hastily set-up detention centres, where a Western journalist saw some of them whipped with lengths of electric cable. And, to impress the population, 'a military van drove back and forth in front of the best hotel dragging a knot of dusty bodies at the end of a rope.'[18] The inhabitants of Hama received similar treatment.

The same operation was repeated on a smaller scale in May and June, then again with even greater brutality in July, after a new series of attacks during the holy month of Ramadan, including an attempt on President Asad's life. The regime now issued a decree making membership of the Brotherhood a capital offence even for those who played no part in the violence. 'Drumhead courts were held in the streets, and anyone unable to clear himself of connections to the organization faced summary execution.'[19] According to Western diplomats the security forces had killed at least 1,000 people by the end of 1980.

In the short term at least, the repression paid off. According to opposition sources:

The population, and especially the Aleppo bourgeoisie, which up to then had backed the Muslim Brothers, understood that the combat was too unequal and hopeless. The shopkeepers, badly hit by the economic depression resulting from the civil war climate which prevailed since the Artillery School killing, wanted to see things get back to normal. A final massacre, in Aleppo on 11 August, 1980, during which the eighty inhabitants of a house in the old city from which a shot had been fired were dragged from their apartments and executed on the spot, threw the population into total consternation and disarray. After that the rebellion collapsed like a house of cards.[20]

Realizing that their attempt to overthrow the regime by armed struggle had failed, at least for the time being, the various Muslim Brother organizations came together in late 1980 to form a United Islamic Front, which in November published a 'Statement of the Islamic Revolution'. The object of this was apparently to stake the claim of the Islamic movement as a political alternative to the Ba'th regime, and to define its objectives in such a way as to reassure the secular and left-wing opposition, which had been naturally cautious about supporting it. Thus it calls for a multi-party system* in which citizens would be 'equal before the law' and 'freedom of thought and expression' would be guaranteed, as well as the rights of religious minorities. Instead of threatening to 'exterminate' the Alawis (as some Muslim Brothers had done in the past) the Statement calls on the 'enlightened' among them to dissociate themselves from the Ba'thist rulers. In the economic sphere, the Statement takes a centrist line, promising to protect private property and free enterprise, but to 'purge' rather than denationalize the existing public sector and to give shares to the workers in public sector industries.†

In the spring of 1981 the Ba'th regime appeared in full control of the country, yet was still resorting to draconian measures to deal with isolated terrorist incidents. According to opposition sources, between two and three hundred men were summarily executed in Hamah on 25 April 'before the eyes of their families',

---

* Ali Bayanuni, one of the three signatories of the Statement, said in an interview with *Le Monde* (13 May 1981) that this would not, however, extend to Marxist groups, even those which are opposed to the Ba'th regime. Asked whether he would describe the Muslim Brothers as left-wing, right-wing or anti-imperialist, Bayanuni replied: 'The word "imperialism" does not figure in our vocabulary, and Islam is a doctrine situated neither to right nor to left....'

† This programme was not approved by Issam al-Attar, the Bonn-based 'official' leader of the Brotherhood, who is considered by the Brothers in Syria as having lost contact with the realities of his own country. He for his part considers them guilty of 'adventurism' because of their premature and unsuccessful trial of strength with the Ba'th party.

but the Muslim Brothers were able to counterattack, killing some 150 members of the security forces. Even if (which seems likely) these figures are exaggerated, it does seem that the situation is not completely stabilized.* The regime of Hafiz al-Asad probably now (summer 1981) enjoys the least popular support of any in the Arab world — a title for which there is quite strong competition; and Syria is certainly the Arab country where the Brotherhood has been most successful in mobilizing a broad popular movement.

A MUSLIM INTERNATIONAL?

In 1964 Sayyid Qutb, the leading writer and theorist of the Egyptian Brothers after Banna's death — and one who had given their ideology 'an unmistakable socialist flavour'[21] — was released from prison. His devoted young followers 'drafted' him into the leadership of a new conspiracy. Qutb had argued in his widely read book *Malim fi al-Tariq* (Signposts on the Road) that social systems were of two types only. Either there was a Nizam Islami — a true Islamic order — or a Nizam Jahli, i.e. the rule of pre-Islamic ignorance, virtually equivalent to Hobbes's state of nature. Logically this meant that, so long as Egypt was not in the former state it was in the latter, and the duty of true Muslims was to wage *jihad* against the ignorant and despotic government that was oppressing them. Qutb knew that the political conditions were unpromising, but also felt it would be wrong to let the rule of impiety and injustice go unchallenged. Had not the Prophet said: 'Any of you who sees a repugnance ought to remove it with his hands; if unable, then by his tongue; and if unable, then by his heart'?

In 1965 Qutb was arrested and charged with leading a terrorist apparatus which, allegedly, had plotted to assassinate not only President Nasser but also a number of Egypt's most popular film stars and singers of both sexes. At least with respect to the President (and the Chief of Staff and other officials), there seems to have been some truth in the charge. Knowing he was doomed in any

* An even more serious confrontation occurred in Hama in February 1982, when at least two weeks' fighting caused perhaps 2,000 casualties (opposition claims were much higher). See *The Times*, 19 February 1982.

case,* Qutb at his trial did not attempt to deny the substance of the charge but conducted a political defence, seeking to show that revolt against the state was justified. The result was to bring into sharp relief the difference between the Brotherhood's ideology and that of nationalism as conceived by a leader like Nasser. In the eyes of the prosecutor and the court, the profession of loyalty to any entity beyond the state, the acceptance of money from abroad, were in themselves acts of sedition. The official Press repeatedly pointed out that the Brotherhood did not accept the primacy of the *watan* or homeland. Qutb's answers to the prosecutor in effect confirmed this: for him the true *watan* was not a territory on a map but the community of believers:

— I believe that the bonds of ideology and belief are more sturdy than those of patriotism based upon region and that this false distinction among Muslims on a regional basis is but one consequence of crusading and Zionist imperialism which must be eradicated.

The prosecutor: But you have decided that the relation that matters and that matters more than patriotism is to belong to the Muslim Brotherhood and not to Islam!

— In my opinion it is Islam that is the attribute of the Muslim Brotherhood.[22]

(In other words, those who did not share the Brotherhood's ideals could not be considered true adherents of Islam.)

Clearly, then, the Brotherhood is an internationalist rather than a nationalist movement, even though at times — especially in Egypt during the 1940s — it has made itself the champion of nationalist emotions and causes. But is it an international organization, or merely a name, assumed by groups of people in different countries with roughly similar ideas? This has never been entirely clear, but for most of its history the latter seems to have been nearer the truth. Certainly the formation of Muslim Brother groups outside Egypt was often, before 1954, the result of deliberate proselytizing by Banna and associates, and the Egyptian Brotherhood before 1954 had an active international department. But the function of

* He was executed in August 1966.

this department was not, apparently, to exercise control over the foreign branches, but merely to keep in touch with them, exchanging information and propaganda and organizing actions of solidarity when these were called for. As far as is known there was no central decision-making body. Since 1954 the Egyptian Brotherhood has been in no position to provide an organizing centre for the rest of the Arab world, but the travels of Egyptian exiles did help to strengthen informal contacts.

It is apparently only in the last few years, if at all, that anything more formal has been set up. A glimpse of it appeared in the 1978 edition of *Who's Who in the Arab World* where Abdul-Rahman al-Khalifa, leader of the Muslim Brothers in Jordan, describes himself as 'Vice-President of the Executive Council of the Muslim Brothers for the Arab world'. Khalifa also occasionally issues statements as 'world spokesman of the Muslim Brothers' — for instance, to condemn the peace treaty between Egypt and Israel. Hajja Zeinab al-Ghazali, a veteran leader of women's organizations within the Egyptian Brotherhood since Banna's time, said in an interview in 1981: 'There is now, thank God, an international organization of the Muslim Brotherhood which will continue until it creates an Islamic state.' Asked: 'Where is this international organization? When was it formed, who are its members and what is its goal?', she replied: 'All I can say is that this was the dream for which we have been living. We are not supposed to disclose any information about it.'[23]

Islam and Revolution

NASSER

So far we have seen Gamal Abdul-Nasser as an admirer of the Muslim Brotherhood before he came to power and a persecutor of it afterwards. He has also been mentioned as a radical pan-Arabist whose brand of nationalism was quite incompatible with the Islamic world view of King Faisal of Saudi Arabia. He was all those things but he was also himself a Muslim — a sincere believer as far as one can tell, who said his prayers regularly, and who in any case was not disposed to let his opponents monopolize the institutions or the vocabulary of Islam. In 1954, when he came into conflict with the Brotherhood, Nasser not only took measures to control the content of sermons in the mosques (through the Ministry of Religious Endowments, which controlled the incomes of the preachers) but also instructed his propaganda expert, Anwar al-Sadat, to write and publish a series of articles in the new 'revolutionary' newspaper *Al-Gumhuriya* (The Republic) outlining the 'true' and liberal Islam. The shaikhs of al-Azhar, whose fidelity to whatever regime in Cairo currently holds power rivals that of the famous Vicar of Bray,* were instructed to pronounce the Muslim Brothers heretics.

They complied, but Nasser was not satisfied. He saw Islam in general and al-Azhar in particular — a university whose teachers were traditionally respected throughout the Sunni Muslim world — as potential instruments not only for internal security but also for a 'revolutionary' foreign policy. After visiting Saudi Arabia in 1953 to convey Egypt's condolences on the death of King Abdul-Aziz, Nasser evolved his theory of a special role for Egypt in world affairs, based on the fact that it was the point of intersection of three 'circles': the Arab, the African and the Muslim. Contained in this somewhat nebulous theory was an element of political pan-Islam à la Afghani:

> As I stood in front of the Kaaba [the central shrine of Islam, in Mecca] and felt my sentiments wandering with every part of the world where Islam had extended I found myself exclaiming, 'Our idea of the pilgrimage should change. Going to the Kaaba should never be a passport to heaven, after a lengthy life. Neither should it be a simple effort to buy indulgences after an eventful life. The pilgrimage should be a great political power. The press of the world should resort to and follow its news, not as a series of rituals and traditions which are done

---

* Hero of an English popular song, who modified his views on church doctrine at each change of monarch in order to keep his well-endowed living. The *ulama* of al-Azhar even condemned 'sedition' against Bonaparte's occupying troops in 1798.

to amuse and entertain readers, but as a regular political congress wherein the leaders of Muslim states, their public men, their pioneers in every field of knowledge, their writers, their leading industrialists, merchants, and youth draw up in this universal Islamic parliament the main lines of policy for their countries and their co-operation together until they meet again. They should meet reverently, strong, free from greed but active, submissive to the Lord, but powerful against their difficulties and their enemies, dreaming of a new life, firm believers that they have a place under the sun which they should occupy for life.'[24]

The new king, Sa'ud, was at first receptive to this suggestion and in August 1954, on the occasion of the annual pilgrimage, a conference of Muslim leaders was held, which led in November to the establishment of an 'Islamic Congress', with Sadat as its first chairman. This organization soon petered out, as events drove Nasser along a road of confrontation with Western 'imperialist' interests and co-operation with the Soviet Union, where more cautious Muslim leaders were not prepared to follow him. But that only made it more necessary for Nasser to mobilize Islamic ideas and feelings on his side of the argument – that of 'the revolution'. Thus Sadat, in a Friday sermon delivered at al-Azhar in 1959, declared:

We Muslims possess a glorious revolution proclaimed 14 centuries ago, in order to restore to humanity its human sentiment and dignity, and to give man his proper due. He [Muhammad] proclaimed his revolution to destroy despotism and to realize the high principles of God, namely, security and honour. This most grandiose of revolutions included many dimensions: a scientific revolution, a social revolution with which all men become equal before God, distinguished only by piety, and a spiritual revolution in the direct relationship between God and man.... In the face of a world in conflict our answer must be: to return to our Islamic revolution proclaimed by the Prophet in 622, to inspire us by its scientific, moral, and spiritual import.

In 1962 another official propagandist drew a distinction between the true Islam, 'the religion of justice and equality', and the deviationist Islam of 'corruption, reaction, exploitation and tyranny'. This pamphlet refers to Muhammad as 'the first socialist'.

Already in 1954 Nasser's government was pressing for a reform of al-Azhar's curriculum to make it more responsive to the needs of Egyptian society. This pressure culminated in 1961 in a sweeping reform imposed by the government directly in the form of a law. The object was 'to bring al-Azhar closer to the modern age, while retaining its special characteristics and values for the preservation of the faith and the protection of the Islamic heritage'. Al-Azhar would be reorganized as a modern institution of higher learning because 'Islam in its true meaning does not distinguish between religious and secular knowledge. It is a social religion which regulates the conduct of man in life.... Every Muslim must be a man of religion and of the world at one and the same time.' In future, therefore, the *ulama* would be trained in modern professions and techniques as well as traditional learning, so that they would no longer be isolated from their fellow citizens. Thus in addition to the original colleges of Shari'a, Theology and Arabic Studies, there would now be four modern colleges: Government and Public Administration, Industry and Engineering, Agriculture, and Medicine. There would also be an Academy for Islamic Research and a Department of Islamic Education and Missions — both aimed essentially at the Muslim world beyond Egypt's frontiers. The whole would be independent of the state university system and the Ministry of Education; instead it would come directly under the President of the Republic — Nasser himself.

There seems to have been no difficulty in finding a group of *ulama* within al-Azhar willing to apply the reform and to accept enthusiastically the government's new interpretation of their task. One of them, for instance, writing in the university's official magazine, hailed the reorganization as 'one of the greatest revolutionary works', which would have 'a great influence on society and the other Islamic and Arabic nations'. Another wrote that al-Azhar welcomed the revolution because 'revolution is of its nature, and socialism of its spirit'. It accepted the new 'Arab socialist' order because the 'mission of Muhammad cannot deny just socialism, for it was his message which rendered the poor his due of the rich man's wealth.' Nasser's 'Charter for National Action', issued in 1962, was hailed, in what seems a positively blasphemous encomium, as 'words from God, which were not expressed by anyone before him in the old days or today, in the West or the East . . .' and as having recaptured the light of Islam from 'Umar in Medina to the kingship of Mu'awiya in Damascus, from the Empire of Rashid in Baghdad to the Republic of Nasser in Cairo.'* The Rector of al-Azhar himself wrote numerous articles in similar vein. He even congratulated the government on 'aiming at making al-Azhar — as it was 1,000 years ago — the stronghold of the *religion of Arabism*' [sic], which he apparently understood as being synonymous with Islam. These *ulama* may have naively hoped that through an alliance with Nasser they could regain the pre-eminent position in the councils of the state which their forebears had enjoyed up to the time of Muhammad Ali. Certainly they saw Nasser's 'Arab socialism' with its Islamic tinge as preferable to Soviet communism and perhaps a better placed competitor against it than traditional Islam in the climate of the 1960s. They may indeed have convinced themselves that Nasser's great prestige would be the instrument of a worldwide Islamic revival. But it is hard to resist the conclusion that their dominant motive was simple sycophancy towards the man in power. The editor of the *Azhar Journal*, for instance, declared in an open letter to Nasser that the principles of Islam:

> were understood and believed in earlier periods but never applied. In your age government is by consultation, wealth is shared, people are equal, and they are the source of political power.

The same man likened Nasser to the Mahdi, as a leader sent by God to stamp out corruption and tyranny, and even claimed himself to have prophesied his 'coming' back in 1935! With Nasser the Fourth Golden Age of Islam had arrived, in which 'the light

---

* Yet the Charter gave equal status to all religious faiths, and treated Islam merely as a component of Arab nationalism.

of your judicious, balanced and calm Charter will extend to every person and every land, as was extended the word of God, because it [the Charter] is the truth which God has placed in His Shari'a and the programme which He devised for all His creatures.'[25]

It should not be supposed that Nasser took this sort of flattery very seriously. But he certainly found it useful to cultivate an 'Islamic' image; and for instance, in his rivalry with the Ba'thist leaders of Syria and Iraq for the leadership of the Arab nationalist cause during the 1960s he was not above warning the Muslim masses not to follow 'the Christian Michel', in reference to the Ba'th party's founder Michel Aflaq.

QADHAFI

Although Nasser was only 52 when he died in 1970, his charisma and moral ascendancy in most of the Arab world had died three years earlier, on the morning of 5 June 1967, when the Egyptian airforce was destroyed on the ground by Israel's lightning pre-emptive strike. It was therefore something of an anachronism that the revolution in Libya, led by a passionate admirer who set out to model his style of leadership on Nasser's, should have occurred in September 1969. But perhaps this was not surprising, since Libya was by most standards a backward country. Anyway, the 'revolution', which like Nasser's was in fact a coup carried out by a group of 'free officers', adopted Nasser's slogan: 'freedom, socialism, unity'.* The provisional constitution was modelled on that of Egypt. As in Egypt, political parties were banned and a single 'Arab Socialist Union' set up.

Like Nasser the new Libyan leader, Colonel Mu'ammar al-Qadhafi, was a pious Muslim. His piety, however, was that of a young man (he claimed to be only twenty-seven) from a tribal desert background, with a purely military education. It was not softened by the worldly sophistication of the Egyptian middle class. Moreover Qadhafi, having overthrown a monarchy which

---

* The order of the three words, broadcast over Radio Tripoli, told alert listeners at once that this was a Nasserist coup. If Ba'thists had been in control it would have been 'unity, freedom, socialism'.

grew directly out of a Sufi order, the Sanusiya,* and which had been described by qualified observers as 'of all the North African states the one closest to the ancient Muslim ideal',[26] needed to give his new regime a degree of Islamic legitimacy. Strikingly, he did not try to exploit the fact that his tribe was supposed to be descended from the Prophet and had enjoyed political influence based on saintly charisma as recently as the nineteenth century. His appeal was rather to the orthodox, non-Sufi *ulama*, who had been largely excluded from positions of influence under the Sanusi monarchy. His theme (by now an almost tiresomely familiar one to readers of this book) was that whereas the Sanusis had used a mystical perversion of Islam to bamboozle people into accepting an un-Islamic hereditary monarchy, and moreover had tolerated such un-Islamic vices as corruption and drunkenness, now the state would be run on egalitarian lines by simple, pious men who would enforce the Shari'a.

Accordingly, among the first acts of the new government were: the suspension of the maintenance of the king's palaces; a decree making the use of Arabic and the Muslim calendar compulsory in all public communications; the appointment of a senior *alim* as Grand Mufti, i.e. official adviser to the government on interpretation of the Shari'a; the imposition of government control on the Sanusi *zawiyas* and suspension of projects for building new ones; the banning of alcohol consumption; the closure of churches, cathedrals, nightclubs and cafés. Later, in 1972, after consideration by various committees, a law was promulgated imposing the Koranic penalties of amputation for theft and brigandage, though with the 'humanitarian' (but somewhat macabre) proviso that the amputations be carried out 'by a specialist doctor in a surgical operation following suitable medical methods, including anaesthetizing the defendant.' The publication of this law attracted very wide publicity, but no cases have since been reported of the penalties actually being applied.

To the alert observer it soon became clear that the *ulama* were

---

* See Chapter 3, pp. 73–6.

not calling the tune in Libya and, moreover, that the new regime's ideology was more nationalist than Islamic in the traditional sense. In an interview with a Beirut newspaper in the early 1970s, for instance, Qadhafi said: 'You seem to suggest that no religion can exist unless at the expense of nationalism but we are a nation before being anything else.... We were Arab people who received the religion and then believed in it.' And in the conflict between Nasserism and the Muslim Brotherhood Qadhafi made it quite clear where he stood:

The Muslim Brothers in the Arab countries work against Arab Unity, against Socialism, and against Arab nationalism, because they consider all these to be inconsistent with religion. Colonialism allies and associates with them because colonialism is against Arab Unity, against Arab Nationalism, and against Socialism. So the Muslim Brother movement co-operated with colonialism without being aware of this, or perhaps colonialism had to choose one group or another, and thus it chose them.

As the 1970s wore on Qadhafi, often referred to as a 'fundamentalist' in the Western Press, revealed himself to be in fact a modernist of an unusually bold stamp. The more sensitive *ulama* must have guessed that trouble was coming when, still in the early part of the decade, he declared, 'we must not restrict ourselves to one *ijtihad'* — a sure sign that the speaker, particularly if he holds political power, is about to take the task of *ijtihad* upon himself. Sure enough, in 1975 Qadhafi came out with his 'Third International Theory', supposedly an alternative to both Soviet communism and Western liberalism. But surprisingly the first volume of his *Green Book*, which expounded the political aspects of the Third Theory under the title 'The Solution to the Problem of Democracy — People's Power', contained no mention of Islam at all, or indeed of religion, other than oblique references to the potential divisiveness of sectarian organizations and to 'the negative effects on society of tribal and sectarian struggles', and occasional obscure references to 'religious law'. Asked to explain this omission, Qadhafi said:

The Third International Theory is based on religion and nationalism — any religion and any nationalism.... We do not present Islam as a religion in the Third Theory. For if we do so, we will be excluding from the Third Theory all the non-Muslims, something which we evidently do not want. In the Third Theory, we present the applications of Islam from which all mankind may benefit.[27]

The second volume of the *Green Book* — 'The Solution to the Economic Problem — Socialism' — appeared early in 1978. It refers neither to Islam nor to religious law. Its two main ideas are: that the individual should be freed by satisfying his needs and by forbidding him any power over the needs of others (therefore, for instance, no one has the right to charge rent; 'the house belongs to the one who lives in it'); and that wage-labour is the 'modern form of slavery' and should be replaced by a kind of self-management. There was more or less open argument in Libya on the question whether these ideas, whose practical application has meant the abolition of free trade, were compatible with the Koran or not, since the Koran condemns neither wage-labour nor commerce. Some *ulama* accused Qadhafi of moving towards Marxism when he proclaimed that 'land belongs to no one' and 'the house belongs to the one who lives in it'. Qadhafi's reply was disarmingly simple: since the *Green Book* introduces social justice it cannot be in contradiction with Islam.

In fact the ideas in the *Green Book* are clearly drawn not from the Koran but from Rousseau (whom Qadhafi quotes in his speeches) and from prevailing intellectual fashions which in turn derive partly from Marxism. When challenged, Qadhafi will defend himself with quotations from the Koran, but he interprets them in his own fashion,* and since 1978 he has openly rejected the Sunna as a basis for legislation.[28] This announcement was perhaps as much a symptom as a cause of the break between Qadhafi and the *ulama* who originally supported him, and whose opposition to the statement that 'land belongs to no one' stemmed partly from the fact that it was used to justify the virtual abolition of religious

---

* He has even permitted himself some textual emendations.

endowments, through a law of May 1978 limiting the size of landholdings. Qadhafi now declared that the *ulama* had been 'propagating heretical stories elaborated over the course of centuries of decadence' and accused them of 'conducting a reactionary campaign against the progressive, egalitarian and socialist concepts of the regime.' Only after the law on landownership had they 'remembered Islam', he said sarcastically, and on 21 May he instructed the masses 'to seize the mosques'.

An even greater scandal was caused by Qadhafi's statement, in a speech referring to Moses, Jesus and Muhammad, that Libya was 'the kind of society where such messengers were born', with the apparent — or at least possible — implication that he himself might be a new prophet.* The aim of the Third Theory, he went on to say, 'is the realization of divine precepts in spite of the hostility of the ignorant, the spiteful, the bigots and the reactionary enemies of Islam.' And at the celebration of the *id al-adha* (feast of sacrifice) in November 1978 he took it on himself to announce that the Muslim calendar needed revision: it should be dated not from the *hijra* (AD 622) but from Muhammad's death (632), since the latter marked the end of the Revelation of the Koran. The result is that Libya has officially set its calendar ten years behind that of the rest of the Muslim world.

The third volume of the *Green Book*, which came out in mid-1979, purports to give 'The Social Foundations of the Third Universal Theory'. This volume does deal with religion, but in a manner that makes it clearer than ever that for Qadhafi religion is subordinate to nationalism: 'every nation should have a religion,' he says, but the 'national factor' is 'the driving force of human history.' A state established on any non-national basis, including that of a common religion, is a 'temporary structure which will be destroyed.'[29]

---

* One suggested explanation for the disappearance of Imam Musa Sadr, the leader of the Lebanese Shi'ites who has not been seen since he went on an official visit to Libya in August 1978, is that he might have provoked Qadhafi's wrath by reproving him for 'prophetic' pretensions which Qadhafi had asked him to endorse. But this is speculation.

The Qadhafi of 1978–81 must be considered, in his domestic treatment of Islam, as the nearest thing the world has seen to an Arab Atatürk. (Indeed, he was not embarrassed to cite Atatürk as a precedent for his reform of the calendar.) He has in effect made Islam in Libya a private affair, forbidding the *imams* in their sermons to talk about anything but strictly religious (i.e. non-political) questions.[30] In 1980 a further campaign to 'clean up the mosques' turned out to mean simply the arrest of a number of 'reactionaries'.[31] And he has founded a military academy for girls, from which his own bodyguard is drawn![32]

If Qadhafi's image abroad is not exactly that of an Atatürk, that is essentially because his foreign policy is not at all like Atatürk's but like a more extravagant and erratic version of Nasser's. In 1969 he adopted Nasser's strategy of the 'three circles' (Arab, African and Islamic), and like Nasser he has shifted the emphasis from one to another according to circumstances, while being quite prepared when he feels like it to take up 'revolutionary' causes outside all three of them, such as the Irish Republican Army or American Indians. Certainly his policy is not 'Islamic' in the sense of automatically taking the Muslim side in any dispute. (For instance, he has supported the Marxist regime in Ethiopia against the predominantly Muslim Eritrean independence movements.) But he will use Islamic solidarity as an argument when he thinks it can advance the cause of 'revolution', or of Arab unity, or of expanding his own influence in Africa. In 1980 an 'Islamic Legion', trained in Libya, took part in the civil war in Chad, before the decisive and open intervention of Libyan regular troops. Refugees from a long list of African countries were reportedly being trained for service in this Legion, and several Black African governments accused Libya of stirring up Muslim minorities.

But conservative Muslim states do not necessarily find Qadhafi any more friendly. For instance, in October 1980, when Saudi Arabia acquired United States Air Force radar and monitoring aircraft during the Iran–Iraq war, Qadhafi declared, at the high point of the pilgrimage season, that Saudi Arabia and the holy places in it were 'under American occupation'. Claiming that

'American military aircraft were flying over Mecca and Medina', he added that in these circumstances 'the practice of Islamic rituals is an exercise in hypocrisy', and the pilgrimage could not be considered a Muslim duty. This provoked an unusually sharp reply from King Khalid, who accused Qadhafi of being 'a spearhead against Islam and Islamic sanctities.'[33] That view seems to be shared by Hajja Zeinab al-Ghazali of the Muslim Brotherhood, who says:

> Qadhafi, by denying that the Hajj [pilgrimage] is part of Islamic belief, by denying the Sunna and calling for the amendment of the start of some verses in the Koran, is an apostate. He is a madman. It is a religious duty for the Libyan people to fight him as an apostate.[34]

ANATHEMA AND WITHDRAWAL

It is hardly possible to exaggerate the effect of the Arab defeat in the Six-Day War, in 1967, on the morale and psychology of the Arab world. A nation that had convinced itself of its own greatness — indeed of its own existence — through a twenty-year crescendo of nationalist rhetoric found itself suddenly forced to face reality by an extremely brutal shock. In six days the armed forces of three Arab states, which had believed themselves about to 'liberate' Palestine from the Zionist yoke, were completely shattered or (in the case of Syria) withdrew from supposedly impregnable positions virtually without a fight. All three states — Egypt, Jordan and Syria — found large areas of their territory occupied by Israel.

Arab nationalism, in the form represented by Nasser and (with little substantive difference) by the Ba'th party, suffered a blow from which it has by no means yet recovered. The trauma suffered by the Arab educated elite was comparable to that which the corresponding class in West Pakistan was to suffer in 1971, with the defeat by India and the creation of Bangladesh.

Nationalism was not abandoned. It was too deeply ingrained a habit of mind by then. Indeed it was precisely the conviction that there was indeed an Arab nation with a collective destiny which made the disaster so deeply felt, even outside the countries directly affected. But even among the nationalists (except perhaps in Libya) there was a widespread feeling that nationalism by itself was not enough.

Two ideas presented themselves either as alternatives or, more often, as supplements to nationalism which could give it a deeper meaning, make it stronger and more worth fighting for: religion and revolution. Neither was exactly new. As words, indeed, both had already been brandished *ad nauseam* by the nationalist regimes. But that in itself had created a widespread awareness of both as values, and of the extent to which governments had taken their names in vain.

Everyone knew that what were called revolutions in the Arab world were really coups d'état, which left the social structure of the countries where they happened largely unchanged. The only real exceptions were on the fringes of the Middle East: Algeria in the west and South Yemen in the south. These were the only two countries that had had to fight for their independence, against France and Britain respectively, and both had undergone a profound social transformation in the process. The case of South Yemen was particularly striking because victory was finally achieved there six months *after* the Arab–Israel war, and the victors were not the town-based Nasserist movement that had had all the publicity but a little-known Marxist movement that had been working and fighting among the rural masses of the hinterland. The moral drawn by some was that the Arab world needed a true revolution, not a flashy military parade, and that this could be led only by people with clear revolutionary principles, willing to learn in the hard school of prolonged guerrilla warfare against overwhelmingly superior forces. Palestine would be liberated, not by an Egyptian army waltzing across Sinai, but by the revolutionary struggle of the Palestinians, who would lead the Arab masses in confronting not only Israel but also — and perhaps it would have to be first — the corrupt regimes and establishments of the Arab world itself.

Equally, everyone knew that when the nationalist regimes talked about Islam they did so not out of genuine piety but as a way of exploiting the piety of the masses. In the eyes of many the defeat was a just punishment on the regimes, and indeed on the nation as a whole, for the hypocrisy, the neglect of the Shari'a, the whoring after false gods and foreign ideologies, which had characterized the whole of the preceding period. The only road to recovery was also the road to salvation: the road of repentance and reform.

These two ideas, religion and revolution, presented themselves as rivals. Only eleven years later did the Arabs discover that the two could be combined with an extraordinary explosive force, and even then they did not themselves provide the demonstration. They had to learn it from a neighbouring non-Arab country: Iran.

At first, revolution seemed the more serious and politically relevant of the two propositions. 'The outcome of the Six Day War ... was a textbook case of a revolutionary situation ... with all its standard ingredients: military defeat, internal exhaustion, the disaffection of intellectuals, a generation gap that was rapidly turning into an abyss, scathing critiques of the most sacred facets of a culture's life.'[35] A tremor of excitement ran through the Arab world in March 1968 when Palestinian guerrillas stood and fought and inflicted serious casualites on an Israeli raiding party in the Jordanian village of Karameh. Although Jordanian troops also took part in the action, it was the Palestinian performance that caught people's imagination. Inspired by the Vietnamese example, radical Palestinians began to think of installing a revolutionary regime in Amman, the Jordanian capital, and making it their Hanoi. But this dream, too, was shattered in 'Black September' 1970 when the Palestinian guerrillas were crushed by King Husain's army. The Palestinian revolution turned out to be just another version of the nationalist chimera:

> the men who fought for the King were mostly illiterates or barely able to read. They were beyond the reach of the radicals' pamphlets. For them the fight was between the King, their chieftain, their financial provider, a man who claims descent from the Prophet — and atheistic troublemakers, townsmen with alien and offensive ways. Belief was pitted against unbelief. Islam was once again a pillar of political authority.[36]

The religious reaction to the 1967 defeat was deeper and broader. Nasser himself, in his first public speech after the defeat, drew 'an exceptionally enthusiastic roar of applause' when he said that religion should play a more important role in society.[37] A 'religious' explanation for the defeat was widely offered: the Jews had deserved victory by being truer to their religion than the Arabs had been to theirs. To anyone who remembers the strongly secular flavour of Israeli life in the 1960s (and especially before 1967) this explanation may seem laughable. Arabs, of course, were not well informed about Israeli life in those days. But their perception of Israel's 'religious' character was not based on estimates of synagogue attendance or sabbath observance. What they knew was that Israel was a state constructed on religious criteria – a state for Jews. They, the Arabs, had been taught to regard such criteria as discriminatory and reactionary. They had thought themselves progressive because they had tried to build a secular Arab nation, based on a language, with equal rights for people of all faiths. But Arabs had not fought as well as Israelis. Why? Because they knew in their hearts that your religion, not your language, is what you fight and die for. Your language may bind you together in this world, but only your religion offers you salvation if you are killed in battle. The Arabs were back with the problem the Ottoman Empire had faced in the mid-nineteenth century, when the question of recruiting non-Muslim soldiers for the armed forces was raised:

in time of need, how could the Colonel of a mixed battalion stir the zeal of his soldiers? ... If we were to adopt the word 'fatherland' now, and if, in the course of time, it were to establish itself in men's minds and acquire the power that it has in Europe, even then it would not be as potent as religious zeal, nor could it take its place.[38]

Above, or below, the level of rationalizing the defeat, people turned instinctively to their religion for comfort in an hour of deep despair. Muslims and Christians alike flocked, in hundreds of thousands, to the Cairo suburb of Zaitun, where the Virgin

286

Mary had appeared 'in pure light' above the Cathedral, carrying her son in her arms, weeping and hoping. An 'authentic' photograph of the apparition appeared on the front page of the highly serious newspaper *Al-Ahrām* (The Pyramids), edited by Nasser's confidant Muhammad Hasanain Haikal. The Virgin (revered by Muslims as well as Christians) had come to comfort Egyptians because they could no longer visit Jerusalem, now occupied by the Israelis.

Egypt was swept by a 'tidal wave of religiosity'.[39] Much of it took 'retreatist, mystical or sufist forms — individual search for meaning and salvation by turning inward.' But the Muslim Brothers, after thirteen years of persecution by Nasser's regime, felt vindicated at last. The regime had received the divine nemesis which it so richly deserved, and was even showing the first signs of repentance. There was hope of reform. Then in 1970, Nasser died. Anwar al-Sadat became president. He had met Banna in 1940 and had been close to the Brotherhood throughout that turbulent decade. After the revolution, of course, he had taken Nasser's side against the Brotherhood, and had acted as one of the 'Islamic' voices of the regime. In the climate of the early Seventies this Islamic image was well worth preserving, and Sadat knew it.

Moreover, Sadat soon found himself engaged in a power struggle against the 'leftists' within Nasser's entourage who were close to the Soviet Union. He had, it seems, always been hostile to communism and suspicious of Soviet influence; and he knew that even Nasser before his death had realized that the Soviet Union would not help him embark on an offensive war to recover Egypt's lost territory, and he would have to reach some kind of understanding with the United States. Probably quite early in his presidency Sadat decided that this rapprochement with the United States would have to be strategic and total, and accompanied by a complete break with the Soviet Union. In any case, it was vital to reach a close understanding with Saudi Arabia, and to ensure that communist influence within Egypt was reduced to a minimum.

Between religion and revolution, Sadat unhesitatingly chose

religion. Although he recognized that there would have to be peace with Israel (something that Nasser had perhaps never fully faced up to), and even made the first formal offer of peace in March 1971, he also knew that Egypt would have to fight first in order to restore her self-respect and to jolt the complacency of Israel and the United States. The Egyptian soldiers would fight this time with military efficiency, but also with faith.

All these considerations led Sadat to encourage the religious revival in Egypt, and to cultivate an image of himself as 'the Believer President'. They also led him to tolerate a discreet revival of the Muslim Brothers: not the organization as such, but informal groups of former Brothers expressing themselves with due caution in a magazine or two, and encouraging the students and young people with a thirst for commitment to turn to Islam rather than to communism. And such groups did emerge in 1971, the most prominent being that led by Umar al-Tilmisani, a lawyer who had belonged to the leadership of the old Brotherhood and had been sentenced to fifteen years' imprisonment in 1954, but was now elderly, respectable and harmless.

But there were smaller groups of younger people, influenced by the ideas of Banna and Sayyid Qutb, who were not satisfied with this tame version of the Brotherhood; who felt that the 1967 defeat had only demonstrated more conclusively the rottenness of the whole political and social order. Qutb had been right: a true Muslim should not compromise with such a system. He should denounce it for what it is: a pagan (*kafir*) system, and he should withdraw from it, as Muhammad withdrew from pagan Mecca when he undertook the *hijra*, until he has gathered enough like-minded Muslims about him and is strong enough to overcome it. Qutb had been martyred because he was ahead of his time. He had struck bravely at the regime while it was still strong, and had paid the price. But now the regime was weakening: it was time to prepare for a new blow.

Two men in their early thirties, both already veterans of the Brotherhood or like-minded parties and of prison, began separately recruiting followers in Cairo in 1971. One was a Palestinian with a Ph.D. in science education, who had belonged to the Party for the Liberation of Islam in Jordan: Salih Siriya. Like so many others he had flirted with 'revolution' after 1967, joining various Palestinian organizations and trying to co-operate with Arab regimes, such as those of Libya and Iraq, that claimed to be revolutionary. His only reward was to spend brief periods in jail, until in 1971 he settled in Cairo at one of the specialized agencies of the League of Arab States, and began to form secret cells, or 'families', of religious students. The other, Shukri Mustafa, was an Egyptian with a degree in agricultural science who had been jailed for being a member of the Brotherhood at the time of the Sayyid Qutb affair, in 1965. In prison he had become disillusioned with older members of the Brotherhood, some of whom he saw break down under torture and interrogation, while others engaged in petty fighting. He became convinced of the need for a new organization, tougher and tighter, and had formed the first cell of it in prison by the time he was released in 1971. It was not until early 1974 that the two groups became aware of each other's existence.

By then the Egyptian political scene had again been changed radically by the October War of 1973, fought in the holy month Ramadan, with the code name 'Badr' — the name of Muhammad's first decisive victory over the Meccans — and with numerous other evocations of Islamic themes. Although the fighting ended with Egypt in a perilous situation, politically it was an enormous victory for Sadat. The Crossing of the Suez Canal was a brilliantly planned operation and had taken the Israelis completely by surprise. They took two weeks to recover their balance, with the help of a massive airlift of American arms. America was obliged to take an active role in the search for a peace settlement, which had been Sadat's strategic objective. But above all, the morale and self-respect of the Arabs and Egyptians had been restored, and many were convinced that they owed their success to divine providence, vouchsafed to them in recognition of their repentance and at least the beginnings of reform. Soldiers claimed, perhaps inevitably, to have seen angels fighting alongside them.

Sadat was now riding high. The political climate in April 1974 could hardly have been less suitable for an attempt to overthrow his regime by violent insurrection. Yet this is what Siriya's group, the 'Islamic Liberation Organization', tried to do. Siriya himself was against it, arguing that the chances of success at that time were 30 per cent at best. But his followers overruled him. He had taught them to believe that Egyptians were a very religious people, who only needed 'a sincere Muslim leadership' to deliver them from their unscrupulous and 'God-fearless' rulers. Like Qutb nine years earlier, Siriya was dragged into violence against his better judgement by the logic of his own ideas and the zeal of his followers who argued that, whatever the immediate outcome, their action would have an exemplary value as an 'outrage for God'. So the attempt went ahead. They succeeded in taking over the Technical Military Academy in preparation for marching to the headquarters of the Arab Socialist Union where Egypt's ruling elite were scheduled to listen to a speech from Sadat. The plot was foiled only after dozens had been killed or wounded. Siriya and his top lieutenant were executed in 1976 and the rest imprisoned.

Shukri Mustafa's group were less hasty in seeking a confrontation with the regime. They believed that the whole of Egyptian society was deeply corrupt and ignorant. The political system was dedicated to keeping it that way, but was also a product of it. Society would therefore have to be reformed by missionary work. This group particularly insisted on the need for anathema (*takfir*) — the act of denouncing someone or something as *kafir* — and withdrawal (*hijra*) to form a model, uncontaminated Muslim community on the analogy of Muhammad's original *umma* at Medina. For this reason the group was later dubbed *takfir wal-hijra* (anathema and withdrawal), a phrase which has come to be used generically for extremist groups of this type. But it called itself simply *Jama'at al-Muslimin* — the group, or society, of Muslims.

During the mid-1970s, Egypt went through further changes. Sadat dismantled the close relationship that had existed with the Soviet Union and sought to develop much closer relations with Western countries. He liberalized the regulations for foreign investment, and also began to experiment with a multi-party political system. This did not extend to parties like the Muslim Brotherhood, which base their appeal explicitly on religion. But from 1975 Muslim groups were allowed, and at first quietly encouraged, to compete in university students' unions against Nasserist groups that opposed Sadat's new liberal and pro-Western policies: the Muslim groups won landslide victories. At the same time religious publications increased in number and circulation. Two of them — al-Da'wa (The Call) and al-I'tisam (Perseverance) — were run by former members of the Muslim Brotherhood. They first appeared in 1976 and were encouraged by the regime to counterbalance leftist and Nasserist opposition. But while remaining bitterly anti-Nasser they became gradually more critical of Sadat's policies, both foreign and domestic, and their readership steadily increased.

In January 1977 Sadat was badly shaken by serious food riots in Cairo. He chose to blame them on the left and the communists, although Islamic groups were also involved. However the security forces began to clamp down on all kinds of opposition groups and some of Shukri Mustafa's followers were arrested. The group was by no means ready for a confrontation with the regime — it had barely begun to build its model community of believers — but when demands that the arrested members be either tried or set free were ignored, the other members decided to try to force the issue by kidnapping one of the senior *ulama*, whom they despised as pure opportunists at the beck and call of the government: Dr Husain al-Dhahabi, a former minister of Religious Endowments. But the government also ignored the deadline which the group set for the release of its brothers; whereupon the group carried out its threat to kill the former minister. The government then seized all the members of the group it could locate: many resisted arrest. Six people were killed and 57 injured in shootings and explosions. Eventually some 620 members of the group, including all the top leaders, were arrested, and 465 were tried by military courts. Five, including Shukri Mustafa, were executed in March 1978. The rounding-up operations, interrogation and trials revealed that altogether the movement had between three and five thousand members spread through all parts of Egypt and all classes of society.[40]

There were clashes between the authorities and other militant Islamic groups, but nothing on the scale of those with the Shukri Mustafa and Siriya groups. It was clear, however, that these and other groups of similar ideology continued to exist, and that they were only the fringe of a very broad movement of Islamic opposition to Sadat, which shaded off at the other end into non-political manifestations of religious revivalism, such as wearing veils or beards. Islamic societies were very active on university campuses, where they demanded more places set aside for prayer, organized exhibitions of Islamic literature, produced cheap pirate editions of textbooks, broke up musical and other 'un-Islamic' entertainments (mixed parties, for instance), agitated for separate classes for women, objected to the use of human corpses in anatomy lessons and occasionally harassed Christian fellow students as well as secular-minded professors. By 1979 their success in student union elections was so overwhelming as to be an embarrassment to the government, and the unions were dissolved by presidential decree.

What was the relation between such groups and the Muslim Brotherhood, as represented by Umar al-Tilmisani and the magazine al-Da'wa? Until 1981 the general view was that the Brotherhood was a mere shadow of its former self and that the new groups were largely autonomous. But Dr Saad Eddīn Ibrahim, of the American University of Cairo, who made a detailed study of the subject, came to the conclusion that this impression was deliberately maintained by the Brotherhood, whereas in fact it had re-organized itself quite effectively, using a variety of names for better cover.

If there were differences between the mainstream Brotherhood and the militant groups, they were in any case tactical rather than substantive: they might differ in the degree of militancy that they advocated against Sadat's regime, but not about the grounds for opposing it. Even al-Da'wa, whose publication was officially tolerated by the regime until September 1981, had by then become openly hostile to all the four main planks of Sadat's policy. From the start it opposed his peace initiative towards Israel. In 1979, after the Egyptian–Israeli peace treaty had been signed, it came out with a banner headline stating 'It is impossible to live at peace with the Jews' over an article which purported to prove this assertion with many examples from the Koran, the life of the Prophet and Islamic history. (The shaikhs of al-Azhar, by contrast, dutifully endorsed the treaty, citing the precedent of Muhammad's treaty with the Meccans — actually a prelude to his subjugation of Mecca — in AD 628.)

But by 1981 al-Da'wa was attacking Sadat on other issues on which it had once been more sympathetic to him. Whereas initially it had preferred his 'open door' policy of facilitating foreign investment and encouraging free enterprise to Nasser's socialism, now it was bitterly critical of the resulting inequalities in Egyptian society and no longer shied away from words such as 'class', 'contradiction' or 'exploitation', which would formerly have been considered hallmarks of Marxism. In fact, it advocated an interventionist and redistributive economic policy which sounded very much like Nasser's. Similarly, whereas formerly the Brothers had been bitterly opposed to Nasser's involvement with the Soviet Union, now al-Da'wa reserved its venom for Sadat's 'subservience' to the United States and even debunked talk of the 'communist threat' as a manoeuvre of Western imperialism. And, finally, al-Da'wa now denounced as nothing better than a fraud Sadat's attempts to introduce multi-party democracy in Egypt, from which initially the Brotherhood had hoped to benefit. Perhaps the only issue on which the magazine still agreed with the President was in denouncing the Ba'th regime in Syria for its savage repression of the Muslim Brotherhood there. In September 1981, al-Da'wa was banned and its editor, Tilmisani, arrested, as part of a massive crackdown on all Sadat's opponents.

How many Egyptians shared the views expressed in al-Da'wa? It is impossible to judge with any precision. Clearly they did reflect the frustration of at least a section of the middle class which had to live on salaries, most often paid directly or indirectly by the state, rather than on profits and commissions, and which was deriving no benefit from the new freedom of foreign trade. People in this group were often bitterly resentful of the vulgarly ostentatious standard of living affected by other groups who *were* doing well out of the new policy: high officials who took bribes and entrepreneurs who had cornered import franchises. It was quite possible for the same person to belong to both these categories, and such people formed the President's intimate circle. Their public pretence of piety only aggravated their crimes in the eyes of Egypt's often genuinely devout middle and lower middle class. This was the natural constituency of the Islamic groups, but their themes could appeal also to the working class and urban unemployed — as was shown by the outbreak of sectarian violence between Muslims and Christians in one of Cairo's more squalidly overcrowded districts in June 1981.*

At the same time this kind of incident was a liability for the Muslim Brotherhood, in that it reawakened doubts, even among Egyptians who admired the Brothers for their courage and honesty, about the implications of an 'Islamic order' for Egypt's traditions of tolerance towards non-Muslim minorities, and also of participation by women in public life. Doubts existed, too, about the capacity of Islamic militants to cope with Egypt's enormous economic problems; and the record of violence and terrorism associated with the Brotherhood and its offshoots was an argument against them in the eyes of many Egyptians. Finally, the Brotherhood's continued attacks on Nasser a decade after his death, even if understandable in the light of its own experience, reduced its ability to win the sympathy of many who were strongly opposed to the Sadat regime but for whom Nasser's time had come, in retrospect, to seem almost a golden age of national dignity and social justice.

---

* Many Egyptian Christians believed that the regime deliberately turned a blind eye to a certain level of anti-Christian violence as an outlet for Muslim resentment, just as in September 1981 Sadat 'balanced' his crackdown on Islamic militancy by dismissing the Coptic Pope and arresting some Christian leaders.

On 6 October 1981 Sadat was assassinated while watching a parade to celebrate the eighth anniversary of 'Operation Badr'. The attackers were four men taking part in the parade, led by a 24-year-old artillery officer, Lieutenant Khalid Ahmad Shawki al-Islambūli. The authorities alleged that the assassination was the work of the *takfir wal-hijra* group. Whether or not they were actually followers of Shukri Mustafa, the assassins certainly belonged to that milieu. 'I am guilty of killing the unbeliever and I am proud of it,' Islambuli shouted when the charges were read to him in court.[41]

As most of the court hearings were held in secret, it is still not clear how far the assassination was part of a wider conspiracy to overthrow the Egyptian government and introduce Islamic rule, but it does seem to have been taken as a signal for insurrection by other militants. There were three days of fierce fighting in the town of Asyut, in Upper Egypt, which had been the scene of attacks on Christians by Muslim extremists in previous years. Attacks on police stations, and on the home of the interior minister, were also reported in Cairo. According to the authorities, the Asyut uprising was part of a general plan to overthrow the government formed by an extremist organization called Jihad, whose ringleader was said to be a lieutenant-colonel in military intelligence, Abbūd al-Zumūr. He was put on trial with Sadat's killers, and it was suggested that it was thanks to him they had been able to smuggle live ammunition into the parade.

If there was a conspiracy, it was successfully nipped in the bud by fresh waves of arrests. Once the immediate crisis was over, Sadat's successor, Husni Mubarak, began to woo public opinion by releasing those whom Sadat had arrested, and by establishing a dialogue with opposition leaders. Skilfully identifying himself with Nasser, he was able to detach much of the nationalist opposition to Sadat from the hard core of Islamic militants. But the government remained vigilant: in April 1982 another 140 people were arrested and charged with plotting to install an Islamic regime. The militants continued to be fascinated, and the government to be worried, by the successes of the 'Islamic revolution' in Iran.[42]

CHAPTER NINE

Iran — Shi'ism and Revolution

There have been expressed certain ideas concerning a republican form of government which are not to the satisfaction of the masses and inappropriate to the needs of the country. Thus, when His Excellency, the Prime Minister [Reza Khan, later Shah] ... came to Qom ... we requested the elimination of this rubric [of republicanism], the abolition of the above-mentioned expressed ideas and the proclamation of this to the whole country. He has accepted this. May God grant that all people appreciate the extent of this act and give full thanks for this concern.

Telegram from three ayatollahs to the ulama *of Tehran, 1924*

The form of government of Iran is that of an Islamic Republic ...
Iranian Constitution (1979), Article 1

Political Peculiarities of Iranian Shi'ism

But for the 'Islamic' revolution in Iran in 1978–79 it is unlikely that this book would have been written. This was the event which placed 'Islam' on the agenda of innumerable dinner parties, strategic seminars and editorial conferences throughout the non-Muslim world. It made 'Islamic' movements and events in other Muslim countries seem more significant, and caused general reporting on events in Muslim countries to acquire an 'Islamic' slant it would not otherwise have had. For instance, when the revolution occurred in

296

Afghanistan in April 1978, Western reporting and reaction gave little emphasis to the fact that Afghanistan was a Muslim country. But the large-scale Soviet military intervention less than two years later was immediately and repeatedly stigmatized as an aggression against a Muslim country, and the Islamic nature of the Afghan resistance was constantly emphasized. This was undoubtedly due in large part to what had happened in Iran, in between the two events.

The effect was not confined to the West. Muslims too, in many parts of the world, felt a surge of pride in the strength of their culture, and of interest in the political content or implications of their religion. To speak of a revival may be misleading, since Islam had always been a central feature in the lives of ordinary people. But the significance of that fact for the political and intellectual elites was suddenly enhanced.

In a sense, then, Iran was the starting point of this book. Yet I have delayed dealing with it until now, precisely because in this century it was not until 1978 that Iran began to have a major impact on people's thinking about Islam and politics in most other Muslim countries. The main reason for this was that Iran was Shi'ite while most other Muslim countries were predominantly Sunni. The Shi'ites were regarded as heretical and the opinions of their *ulama* would carry no weight with their Sunni counterparts. Although the Koran was common ground between the two sects, the Shi'ites had a completely different set of *hadith* about the sayings and doings of the Prophet and his Companions, and attached almost equal importance to the recorded traditions of their Imams. That is why Jamal al-Din 'al-Afghani', the only Iranian who *did* have a major impact on Sunni Islam in the hundred years before 1978, had to disguise his national origin and intellectual antecedents to do so.

It is not true, as is often asserted, that Shi'ism has been the national religion of Iran since the early years of Islam. Until the sixteenth century AD the great majority of Shi'ites neither spoke Persian* nor

* Persian (Farsi) is the national language of Iran and the mother tongue of the majority of its population. 'Persia' was the name generally used for Iran in English and other foreign languages until 1935.

lived in Iran; and the majority of Iranians were Sunni. It was in AD 1501 that the Safavid dynasty came to power and made 'Twelver' Shi'ism the official religion of the state. We saw in Chapter 2 (pp. 45–6) that in classical times this variant of Shi'ism was politically moderate, providing a way for Shi'ites to reconcile political loyalty to Sunni caliphs with their belief in the rightful Imamate of Ali and his descendants. Unlike the militant Isma'ilis, the 'Twelvers' did not carry on ideological warfare against the Sunni state. In those days, therefore, the line between Sunnism and Twelver Shi'ism was not always clear-cut. Both ideas and people passed fairly easily from one to the other.

In the fourteenth and fifteenth centuries, after the Mongol invasions, very unsettled conditions prevailed in western Asia. Many new Islamic movements sprang up, particularly among the nomadic Turkish tribes, often drawing their ideas from a variety of sources and changing rapidly to suit the personalities of the leaders and the social circumstances of the followers. Safavism was one such: it started as a quietist, Sunni, Sufi order and developed into a warrior dynasty which took up Twelver Shi'ism and gave it a militant twist to justify confrontation with neighbouring Sunni states, particularly the Ottoman Empire. Isma'il, the first Safavid Shah of Iran, was a Turkish-speaker and established his capital at Tabriz in Azerbaijan, but like others before him he relied on Persian-speaking bureaucrats to run his administration. His state was not a national state in any modern sense but a dynastic and ideological state, the ideology being Twelver Shi'ism. He and his successors imported Shi'ite theologians from Arab countries (notably from what is now southern Lebanon, and from Bahrain) to indoctrinate the Iranians; and Isma'il ordered not only that the Friday sermons be given in the name of the Twelve Imams but that the preachers should publicly curse the first three Sunni caliphs (Abu Bakr, Umar and Uthman), who had usurped the rightful place of Ali. For the next two hundred years there was war, sometimes cool but often hot, between the Sunni Ottoman Empire and the Shi'ite Safavid Empire. The frontier moved back and forth with the fortunes of war.

Twelver Shi'ism had developed as a minority religion under Sunni rule. Its doctrine implicitly assumed that Sunni rule, which was not truly Islamic government, would continue until the Return of the Hidden Imam to redeem the world. The establishment of a Shi'ite state in the continued absence of the Imam therefore posed a doctrinal problem of political authority which has never been fully resolved. The Safavid shahs claimed a religious basis for their authority as descendants of Ali through the Seventh Imam, and initially were identified by their tribal followers with the Hidden Imam or even worshipped as incarnations of God. Such claims were of course not accepted by the orthodox Shi'ite *ulama*, who viewed the Safavids as simply temporal rulers who happened to be good Muslims, or at any rate accepted and encouraged a correct interpretation of Islam. But that meant they were expected to enforce the Shari'a, and in the absence of the Imam the qualified interpreters (*mujtahids*) of the Shari'a were the most learned among the *ulama* themselves. The general tendency of the *ulama* was to shy away from temporal power, regarding it as something essentially corrupt so long as the Imam himself did not assume it. The Imam in their teaching became a more and more Christ-like figure — one on whose intercession the individual depended for salvation at the last judgement, one who would come again at the end of time — and less and less a political ruler, even of an ideal and imaginary sort. On the other hand the *ulama*, or some of them, did feel moved from time to time to condemn the impiety or injustice of actual rulers.* In the eighteenth and especially the nineteenth century, when the weak Qajar dynasty was unable either to govern the country effectively or to defend it against foreign encroachments, the *ulama* found themselves drawn increasingly into a political role, though of a rather negative sort — as guardians of the people *against* government, rather than as claimants of the right to govern.

Why were the *ulama* able and willing to play this role in Iran and

---

* A few of them did suggest that leading *ulama* had a better claim to power on religious grounds than the Safavid shahs. But this may have been more an effort to contest the religious basis of Safavid rule than a serious proposal of a theocratic alternative.

not in other Muslim countries, at any rate after the suppression of the Janissaries in the Ottoman Empire in 1826? The classic explanation – that Shi'ite doctrine encourages opposition because it regards all political power as illegitimate – has now been fairly conclusively demolished by Iranian scholars.[1] As mentioned in Chapter 1, Sunni *ulama* had already formulated a sceptical and mistrustful view of political power from an early period in the history of Islam. This attitude tends to promote not active opposition but resignation and detachment; and these qualities were typical of Shi'ite *ulama* too during most of the history of Twelver Shi'ism. On the other hand, it is hard to accept as pure coincidence the fact that the only Shi'ite state is also the only Muslim state in which the *ulama* of modern times played an active opposition role.

It seems to me that the crucial difference between Sunni and Shi'ite doctrine, as far as social relations are concerned, is not in their attitudes to existing political power, which indeed are rather similar, but in their attitude to the organization of religion and religious activities. In Sunni theory religious activities come within the domain of the state, however imperfect, because there is no alternative authority in sight. If the *ulama* take on any organizational role – as judges, for instance, or educators, or *muftis* (sources of authoritative legal opinion) or even preachers and prayer-leaders – they do so under the aegis of the state. If government is bad, one hopes that a good ruler will come along and make it better; one may even (according to some schools of thought) take action to try and replace a bad ruler by a good one. What one does not do – except in the case of some Sufi orders, about which the Sunni *ulama* usually felt rather uneasy – is to organize religion separately from the state on one's own authority. In the case of Twelver Shi'ism, by contrast, the scepticism about political power has a much firmer doctrinal basis. The fact that government tends to be bad or un-Islamic is not just an observable and regrettable fact: it is in the nature of things so long as the rightful Imam has not taken matters in hand, which is now not going to happen until the end of time. Logically this does indeed render any kind of political activism futile, but equally logically it renders a *religious organization*, separate from or at least not dependent on the state, *absolutely necessary.* That organization is provided by the *mujtahids.* They are not in a position to enforce the law, because they do not have power, but it is their job to tell the faithful what the law is, and to adjudicate the disputes that are brought before them. It is their job to see that the faith is correctly taught, that worship is properly conducted, that schools and mosques for these purposes are adequately maintained, that the poor believers — and especially the poor *sayyids,* descendants of the Prophet and therefore members of his household, whose maintenance is the responsibility of the whole community — are succoured. To whom, then, should the dues prescribed by the Koran — the *zakat* for the widows and orphans, and the *khums* or fifth share of booty due to the Prophet — be paid? Not to the state, which lacks any Islamic sanction or significance, but to the *mujtahids,* who have a correct understanding of the faith and act, so to speak, as trustees in the absence of the Imam.

This was not the *ulama*'s only source of support. Like their Sunni counterparts in other countries they frequently benefited from religious endowments (*awqaf*), and they also drew an income from fees for various legal and clerical duties (registration of titles, notarization of affidavits, etc.). But endowments could always be confiscated or nationalized, and legal income could dry up when a modernizing state established secular courts. *Khums* (in the Koran a share of booty, but interpreted by the Shi'a as a general income tax) and *zakat* were much harder for the state to take away so long as the *ulama* retained the people's respect; and their ability to retain the people's respect was strengthened by their independence from the state. Those *ulama* who did accept government-paid posts, and therefore had to toe the government line, such as the chief Friday prayer-leader in each city, were on the whole less respected than those who did not.

Another possible factor is the tradition of *ijtihad* itself. We have seen that almost every reformer of the past two centuries in the Sunni world has asserted the need for *ijtihad,* that is the exertion of independent judgement to apply the teachings of the Koran and the Sunna to one's own circumstances, and that this has usually been resisted by the established Sunni *ulama* who held that the 'gate of *ijtihad* had been closed' with the establishment of the four great schools of legal interpretation in the tenth century AD. The Shi'ites, too, had at first forbidden *ijtihad*, taking it to be synonymous with religious 'innovation' (*bidā*), which in Islam is equivalent to heresy since the revelation in the Koran is final and complete. But the notion of *ijtihad* was rehabilitated by one of the great medieval Shi'ite theologians, Allāma Ibn al-Mutahhar al-Hillī, who died in AD 1325. In the seventeenth and eighteenth centuries a group of theologians known as the Akhbāris again rejected *ijtihad*, arguing that the Koran and the record (*akhbār*) of the acts and deeds of the Prophet and the Imams should be treated as sole and all-sufficient source of law and that no new consensus or reasoning was needed. But they were eventually defeated by their opponents, the Usulis, who insisted that *mujtahids* were needed to interpret the foundations (*usul*) of the faith, and argued moreover that anyone not qualified to undertake *ijtihad* himself must accept the guidance of a *living mujtahid* (since if one takes the interpretation of a dead authority one may in fact misinterpret it, without possibility of correction). Each *mujtahid* himself should accept the guidance of the most learned of his living colleagues as his *marja-i taqlid* or 'source of imitation'. By the mid-nineteenth century it was accepted that there should be one senior living *marja-i taqlīd*, the *marja-yi mutlaq*, by whose interpretation all would be directly or indirectly guided.

In practice it was not always agreed who that individual was at a given moment. But clearly the doctrine gave enormous authority to the *mujtahids* — much more than the Sunni *ulama* enjoyed since they were bound always to follow precedent — as well as enabling them to maintain a degree of unity and mutual coherence in their teachings. Above all, it encouraged them to exercise and rely on their own independent judgement, something which the Sunni *ulama* have left to the radical and the outsider. All those who have studied Shi'a Islam have been struck by the continued liveliness and variety of intellectual activity during the recent centuries when the thought of most Sunni *ulama* had become stodgy and conformist. (This may be attributed in part, perhaps, to the inventive effort required by the process of adapting Twelver Shi'ism to the unexpected situation of a state religion and of making it intelligible to Iranian people who did not speak Arabic and who had their own political and cultural traditions.) Seventeenth-century Iran, for instance, saw a remarkable renaissance of Islamic philosophy; and though the Iranian philosophers, like their classical predecessors (see p. 52), had only a restricted influence and were attacked by the orthodox, philosophy remained a part of the Shi'ite theological curriculum. It should also be noted that Twelver Shi'ite theology in general was based partly on Mu'tazilite rationalism (see pp. 50–1) with its emphasis on the inherent justice of God, the rationality of His creation, and human free will with its corollary, human responsibility for the conditions in which humans live.

In the eighteenth century the Safavid dynasty was overthrown by an invasion of Afghans who tried to reimpose Sunnism on Iran. The leading Shi'ite *ulama* fled to Iraq, then part of the Ottoman Empire, and established themselves in the cities of Najaf and Karbala, built around the tombs of Ali and Husain. Although Afghan rule in Iran lasted only eight years, the tradition of senior Iranian Shi'ite *mujtahids* residing in these cities has continued to the present day and has been an additional factor of independence since it generally puts them beyond the reach of the Iranian state (periods of close entente between the rulers of Iran and Iraq being the exception rather than the rule).

Taken together, these factors may help to explain the *ability* of the Iranian *ulama* to act independently of and in opposition to the monarchy during the nineteenth and twentieth centuries. To suggest that Shi'ite theology *predisposed* them to do so is indeed misleading. On the contrary, in its Twelver form it gave them every encouragement to stand outside politics. But paradoxically that very fact made it easier for them to sustain a distinct corporate identity and thus helped to make them *potentially* an independent political force. Their tradition also gave them the intellectual flexibility to adapt their doctrine to changing political circumstances. Thus, when they saw Iran's Islamic traditions, territorial integrity and economic life threatened by foreign encroachments during the nineteenth century and saw the monarchy in effect capitulating to those encroachments and making itself their accomplice, the *ulama* were able to protest with relative impunity, and were able to justify their protest intellectually. This culminated in their alliance with Western-influenced opposition groups in the great tobacco boycott of 1891 (see p. 113) and in the constitutional revolution of 1906.

The constitution achieved by the revolt of 1906–7, which remained nominally in force until 1979, was based largely on that of Belgium. It should not be supposed, however, that the *ulama* who took part in the constitutional revolution had simply grafted a European liberal political outlook on to their Shi'ite theology. If the Westernizers were able to introduce the Belgian model, it was largely because the *ulama* had no clear positive political project of their own: as we have seen, their Shi'ite tradition did not equip them with a political theory. Their participation in the movement was motivated only by a general desire to curb the absolutism of the Shah and to strengthen Islam politically so that it could better resist European penetration. They thought in terms of 'justice' and the Shari'a rather than constitutionalism as such: the desired assembly (*majlis*) was referred to as *Adalat Khaneh* – 'House of Justice'. Once the Majlis met and began writing the constitution, misgivings and divisions quickly appeared. Many *ulama* were alarmed at the idea of a man-made constitution based on European models, especially as it was entitled 'Fundamental Law'. Was not the God-given Shari'a the fundamental law of society, and if so how could human beings presume to alter it?

The most vigorous exponent of these misgivings was Shaikh Fazlollah Nuri, a learned and highly respected *mujtahid*, who was able, in July 1907, to obtain the passage of the famous Clause 2 of the Supplement to the Fundamental Law, according to which, laws passed by the Majlis would be subject to the veto of a committee of five *ulama*, chosen by their peers, who would verify that proposed legislation was not in contradiction with Islam. In other words the *mujtahids* representing Islam were a higher authority than deputies representing the people. (In point of fact this clause was never implemented, although initially the *ulama* were well represented in the Majlis itself.) Nuri however was not satisfied with this, but moved on to a frontal attack on the whole principle of parliamentary government, arguing that Muslims should not import customs and practices from 'the realms of unbelief'; that the Shari'a was as valid in the twentieth as in the seventh century and should not be tampered with; that freedom of the Press was contrary to the Shari'a; and that Clause 8 of the Supplement to the Constitution ('The citizens of Iran have equal rights before the law of the state') was unacceptable since it ignored the natural and unalterable inequality between the healthy and the sick, the husband and the wife, the learned and the ignorant, the Muslim and the unbeliever. With such arguments Nuri was able to mobilize many hitherto non-political religious dignitaries against the constitution, and to win over or at least silence many of those who had supported it.

Emboldened by this, and helped by the Russian-officered Cossack Brigade, the Shah carried out a coup d'état in 1908, dissolving the Majlis and executing many popular nationalist leaders, including radical preachers (some of whom had connections with the Messianic Babi movement, see p. 110). In Tabriz an armed popular guard fought against the royalist troops and the Russians who were sent to support them (ostensibly to protect European residents). These pro-constitution resistants called themselves *Mujahidin* or *Feda'iyan* — both names implying self-sacrificing fighters for the faith. Soon other parts of the country joined the revolt. The Shah had to abdicate and Shaikh Nuri, sentenced to death by a special tribunal of constitutionalists for his 'reactionary' attitude, was hanged in July 1909.

Clearly people on both sides in this conflict believed they were defending Islam. A group of senior *ulama* in Iraq had supported the constitution, believing, unlike Nuri, that the Majlis would *help* make the Shari'a the effective law of the country. Perfect application of it, they knew, was not possible in the absence of the Imam, but at least it could be taken as a model so as to reduce tyranny and limit the suffering of the believers. According to one of them,

Shaikh Isma'il Mahallati, a limited, constitutional form of government, which would protect the territory of Islam against the unbelievers, was a reasonable half-way house to settle for between the unattainable government of the infallible Imam and the unacceptable tyranny of absolute monarchy. 'If the *ulama* don't take part in the constitutional movement,' he argued, 'the policy of this Islamic country will follow the European model. It is therefore an obligation for them to help the politicians make laws which are in agreement with Islam.'[2]

Another, Mirzā Muhammad Husain Nā'ini, argued that a constitutional regime was preferable to despotism because the latter involved a triple usurpation: of the authority of God, of the function of the Imam, and of the rights of the people. Na'ini strongly defended the notion of equality, which he claimed as one of the original virtues of Islam. Yet he had not fully thought out the implications of equality between Muslims and non-Muslims, for he still argued that apostasy from Islam must be treated as a serious crime. Thus the alliance between him and his colleagues and the Westernizing constitutionalists was based on a partial misunderstanding. The *ulama* saw the Majlis as a means through which they could block, or at least control, some of those 'progressive' reforms which the Westernizers hoped to introduce. For instance, they opposed the new schools which had begun to be founded and in which subjects like mathematics and French were taught as well as religious learning. Only a very few *ulama* or people connected with them at that time were prepared to think in terms of revitalizing Shi'ism by eliminating formalism and obscurantism and obliging it to adapt to social, economic and political change.

The Policies of the Pahlavi Dynasty

I shall not attempt in this chapter to give a comprehensive account of the causes of the 1978–79 revolution, many of which have no specific connection with Islam. I am concerned only to explain why it was an 'Islamic' revolution and what that has turned out to mean. But even that requires an account of some aspects of the policies of the *ancien régime*. Three questions arise, two of which relate specifically to relations between the regime and the *ulama* while the third is more general. First, how did the regime antagonize the *ulama*? Secondly why, having done so, did it — or could it — not act more decisively to destroy their influence? Thirdly, what was it about the regime's policies that caused other political and social forces to accept the leadership, and even dominance, of the *ulama* in the movement that eventually overthrew it?

THE FIRST ASSAULT (1925–41)

During the First World War, despite Iran's declaration of neutrality, British, Russian and Ottoman forces invaded the country. The 1917 revolution in Russia removed the main patron of the ruling Qajar dynasty. By 1919 Iran had no effective central government and separatist movements were in power in the provinces of Khuzistan, Gilan and Khorasan. A treaty signed in that year would have made Iran in effect a British protectorate. But owing to strong Iranian opposition, backed by the Soviet and American governments, the treaty was never ratified. In 1921 Reza Khan, the commander of the Cossack Brigade (the only disciplined Iranian military force) led his troops into the capital, Tehran, installed a new government with himself as war minister and persuaded the reigning Shah Ahmad to leave for Europe.

Although he had been promoted and encouraged to stage his coup by the British General Ironside, Reza Khan soon revealed himself to be no mere British puppet. He was greatly impressed by the success of Mustafa Kemal in defeating foreign intervention in Turkey, and set out to follow his example. He wanted to endow Iran with a government and army modernized on Western lines and therefore strong enough to defend her independence.

Would he emulate Kemal also in proclaiming a republic? He became prime minister in the very same month that Kemal became President of Turkey, and was strongly suspected of intending to lead Iran along the same path. But Kemal by that time had won unchallengeable prestige through his victories over the Greeks, had abolished the Sultanate a year earlier and felt strong enough to defy the *ulama*. Reza Khan was still at the stage of consolidating his power. His military victories had been won only against Iranian separatists, not against foreign invaders. He still needed the *ulama*'s support. In the spring of 1924 he visited the shrine city of Qom, south of Tehran, where a number of senior *mujtahids* had taken up residence since the British occupation of Iraq, and which was therefore being revived as an important centre of Shi'ite learning. There he met with three of the leading *mujtahids* and reassured them that he was not interested in republicanism. On his return to Tehran he issued a proclamation, saying:

> Insofar as I and all the people in the army have, from the very beginning, regarded the preservation and protection of the dignity of Islam to be one of the greatest duties and kept before us the idea that Islam always progress and be exalted and that respect for the standing of the religious institution be fully observed and preserved: thus, when I went to Qom ... I exchanged views with their excellencies regarding the present circumstances. And we ultimately saw it necessary to advise the public to halt the [use of] the term, republic.[3]

Two of these ayatollahs* returned to Iraq soon afterwards, thanks partly to Reza Khan's good offices with the British, protected by an official Iranian military escort. Later in the year they issued a manifesto clearly endorsing Reza Khan's government, and in January 1925 he paid them a further visit in Najaf. Their support was invaluable to him in overcoming opposition from both *ulama* and secular politicians in the Majlis in Tehran. In December 1925 he was crowned Shah.

Once firmly ensconced in power, however, Reza Shah embarked on a series of policies that were deeply offensive to the *ulama*. There was a symbolism, perhaps unconscious, in his choice of the family name Pahlavi—the language of Iran in pre-Islamic times. Both he and his son, who between them ruled Iran under this name for more than fifty years, were to emphasize Iran's national interests, identity and traditions while playing down the Islamic element in them.

---

* *Ayatollah* (sign of God) is an honorific title given to leading *mujtahids*.

In the legal sphere, Reza Shah introduced new civil, penal and commercial codes which, though based in part on the Shari'a, amounted to a secularization of it, since they were administered by state-appointed courts under the control of a justice ministry staffed with European-educated civil servants. The system included a religious court, with a single *mujtahid* as judge, paid by the state. The Tehran appeal court likewise included one *mujtahid*, chosen by lot from a list drawn up by the justice ministry, to deal with religious cases. In 1932 the traditional Shari'a courts controlled by the *ulama* lost the right to register documents such as affidavits, powers of attorney and property titles; this deprived *mujtahids* and *mullahs* (local religious leaders) of a major source of revenue as well as influence.

In education, Reza Shah greatly expanded the secular school system, setting up some thirty teachers' training colleges as well as technical, agricultural and veterinary schools; at the same time he took steps to bring religious education under state control. More spectacularly, he outdid Mustafa Kemal by promulgating a 'uniformity of dress law' that not only required men to wear Western dress including brimmed hats but legally obliged women to renounce the veil. (The *ulama* themselves were exempt from this law, but had to prove their status to the state's satisfaction.) A ban was also imposed on the public holding of the traditional recitations and passion plays based on the martyrdom of the Imam Husain.

In addition, a number of incidents brought the regime into direct physical conflict with the *ulama*: in 1924, even before Reza became Shah, he faced an *ulama*-led insurrection in Isfahan (the former Safavid capital and an important religious centre) against his attempts to restrict poppy cultivation and opium production. (Many *ulama* in the area were also big landowners who benefited from the opium trade.) Later he exiled one of the ayatollahs in Qom, who dared to rebuke the Shah's female relations for entering the shrine of Hazrat Ma'sumah (sister of the Eighth Imam) unveiled. The Shah's chief military aide was said to have violated the sanctuary by marching in with his boots on and dragging the ayatollah out 'by the beard' to the Shah, who kicked him and hit him with his whip.[4] More serious was the disturbance in 1935 at another shrine — that of the Imam Reza* at Mashhad, in north-eastern Iran. Attempts by the local police to enforce the hat law inside the shrine provoked a sit-in by an angry crowd, which was then fired on by the authorities. There were hundreds of casualties in and around the mosque.

By the time of Reza Shah's abdication in 1941 the *ulama* were thoroughly demoralized and debilitated and appeared to be losing their influence; they were virtually unrepresented in the Majlis that met in 1937, whereas they had provided 40 per cent of the deputies in that of 1926–28. The number and size of their theological seminaries had declined sharply owing to competition from government schools, official harassment and declining revenues. Yet in spite of his spectacular move in outlawing the veil, Reza Shah had not gone nearly so far as Atatürk in systematically dissolving all Islamic institutions, or even in formally divorcing religion from the state. And unlike Atatürk's successors, he was unable to keep his country out of the Second World War. In 1941 it was again occupied by British and Russian troops and Reza himself went into exile, having refused an Allied request for the expulsion of all Germans from the country. As a result the state was so much weakened that for the next fourteen years or more the *ulama* were able to regain much of their former influence.

RESPITE (1941–58)

Reza Shah was succeeded by his 22-year-old son, Muhammad Reza, but the latter's authority was no more than nominal so long as the war and the Anglo–Soviet occupation lasted. After that he began to assert himself, with military, economic and political support from the United States. American pressure forced Stalin to withdraw Soviet troops in 1946, leaving the autonomous republics he had sponsored in Kurdistan and Azerbaijan to be crushed by the Shah's troops. But Iran's economy continued to be dominated by the British-owned Anglo-Iranian Oil Company (AIOC). During

* Ridā in Arabic

the late Forties and early Fifties Iran was convulsed with political agitation for the nationalization of AIOC. The situation was somewhat similar to that in Egypt at the same period, the heyday of the Muslim Brotherhood. The National Front, corresponding to the Wafd in Egypt (i.e. liberal and on the whole secular), led the campaign for nationalization. Both the communist party (Tudeh) and Islamic activists joined in the campaign, but sought whenever possible to capture its leadership for themselves. The Shah, like his brother-in-law King Faruq, was caught in the middle, trying to play off the various groups against each other and to mediate between nationalist demands and great-power interests.

The first signs of the *ulama*'s reviving influence were seen immediately after Reza Shah's departure, with the reappearance of the veil in the streets and the resumption of the passion plays and narratives. Later, in 1948, a group of fifteen *mujtahids* went so far as to issue a *fatwa* forbidding women to shop in bazaars and markets without wearing the veil. The government's only response was a polite request to the leading Tehran *mujtahid*, Ayatollah Bihbihānī, to prevent illegal demonstrations and curb attacks on women in public places by religious zealots. By early 1949 the political situation was so confused, and many *ulama* so deeply involved in it, that a large conference was held in Qom to discuss how far such involvement was desirable. Clearly there were a number of issues on which the *ulama* collectively and more or less unanimously held strong views and expected to be listened to. But it was questioned whether the activity of individual *ulama* in the Majlis and in political parties were appropriate or helpful. The conference, convened by the accepted *marja-yi mutlaq* of the time, Ayatollah Borūjerdī, and attended by some 2,000 *ulama*, decided to prohibit all *ulama* from joining parties or trafficking in politics. Anyone who opposed this was to lose his status as an *alim*.

This might have worked if the *ulama* had been what they are often called — a 'clergy' with a clearly defined hierarchy and system of discipline. They are perhaps closer to that in Shi'ite than in Sunni Islam, but still fall well short of it. Even when there is a single generally acknowledged *marja-yi mutlaq*, as Borujerdi was, he lacks the power to 'unfrock' a recalcitrant *alim*. In this instance the decision was spectacularly ignored by the most political *alim* of the time, Ayatollah Kāshānī, who not only remained in the Majlis but became its Speaker in 1952. He also issued a *fatwa* supporting the nationalization of the Anglo-Iranian Oil Company in 1951. Other *mujtahids* then had to follow suit, in response to questions from their followers, although Borujerdi himself, presumably wishing to respect the spirit of the 1949 decision, remained silent. There were no sanctions against Kashani (who remained highly popular with the middle-ranking and junior *ulama* — mosque and itinerant preachers), other than that he found it tactful not to stay the night at Borujerdi's lodgings on his visits to Qom.

Kashani's support for nationalization was motivated by traditional hostility to foreign (i.e. non-Muslim) penetration, rather than by any 'progressive' ideas. Among his supporters, until 1951, was a group called Fidā'iyān-i Islam (those who offer themselves for Islam), which had contacts and ideological affinities with the Muslim Brotherhood in Egypt. Although supported by some other prominent *ulama* (besides Kashani), the leaders and members of this group were themselves either young *ulama* of low status or not *ulama* at all but 'young lower middle-class Islamic radicals'[5] of the Muslim Brother type, who implicitly — and sometimes explicitly — contested the established *ulama*'s monopoly of religious leadership. They aspired to be a mass organization, but in fact relied for their impact on terrorism and assassination.

Their first 'coup' was the murder of Ahmad Kasravi, an outspoken critic of Shi'ite traditions, in 1946. Their attempt to kill the Shah, on 4 February 1949, may have been the event that prompted Borujerdi to call his conference on *ulama* involvement in politics later the same month. The peak of their activity was the assassination of the prime minister, General Ali Rāzmarā, in March 1951, in protest against a highly unpopular agreement between the government and the AIOC, which fell far short of meeting Iran's demands for greater royalties and some control of the oil company's activities. Razmara's death effectively cleared the way for nationalization, which was approved by the Majlis the following day, and for the instalment of the National Front leader, Muhammad Mosaddeq, as prime minister, against the personal wishes of the Shah. But it also led to a split between the Fida'iyan and Kashani who, though he publicly expressed delight at the assassinations, and secured the release of Razmara's killer, rebuffed the Fida'iyan's demands for a share in executive power. Both he and Mosaddeq now became the target of bitter polemics from the Fida'iyan, who attacked the nationalist government for being influenced by Western and leftist ideas.

In March 1953 Kashani broke with Mosaddeq, refusing to support the prime minister's demand that the Majlis grant him extraordinary powers. The other eight *ulama* in the Majlis, however, continued to support Mosaddeq. After this, Kashani's influence declined rapidly, as he was considered politically unreliable. Much more significant was the hostility to the government of the officially non-political *mujtahids*, led by Borujerdi and Bihbihani, who were deeply worried by Mosaddeq's growing reliance on leftist and communist support* in his confrontation with the British and American oil companies, which were backed by their respective governments. Bihbihani is said to have played a major role in mobilizing crowds from south Tehran (the older and poorer end of the city) against the government during the coup of August 1953 which overthrew Mosaddeq and restored power to the Shah.†

During the first years after the coup the Shah (Muhammad Reza Pahlavi) continued to rely heavily on *ulama* support. In this period the leading *mujtahids* were sufficiently scared by the threat of communism to be willing to support the Shah's foreign policy of reconciliation and alliance with the West in return for some more or less token concessions to *ulama* influence in domestic affairs.

---

* There was a very small group of *ulama* willing to co-operate with the left, led by Ayatollah Ali Akbar Burqa'i, who joined the Soviet-backed 'peace movement' and supported votes for women. But it seems to have been completely unrepresentative.

† As is now well known, the US Central Intelligence Agency was also heavily involved in this coup. But the decisive factor was the willingness of the Iranian armed forces to support it.

Religious seminaries flourished, and the student population of Qom was estimated to have risen from about 3,200 in 1952 to 5,000 in 1956. 'Qom became an institution unto itself, a domain where the national government leadership went to pay its respects on a regular basis. In the next few years, it was Qom that was exercising a studied neglect of Tehran and Tehran that seemed in need of wooing Qom.'[6]

In Tehran itself, Bihbihani's views and activities were accorded respectful coverage in the government-controlled Press, and he gave fulsome endorsement to several aspects of government policy (efforts to provide technical education for the peasantry, for instance). The government responded by allowing expanded Islamic instruction in state schools, especially primary ones. It also acquiesced in, and even initially encouraged, an *ulama*-sponsored campaign against the adherents of the Baha'i religion* in 1955. Although the government managed to avoid being tied down to specific legislation which would have forced it to suppress the Baha'i completely, dismiss all Baha'is from public offices and sequestrate their property, the Chief of Staff of the Army and the Military Governor of Tehran did personally take part in the destruction of the dome of the Tehran Baha'i centre. The quid pro quo was *ulama* support for the Baghdad Pact (later CENTO), linking Iran to Britain, Turkey and Iraq in a defensive military alliance — an arrangement which provoked intense nationalist hostility in the Arab world, but was allowed to pass almost without comment in Iran.

THE SECOND ASSAULT (1959–78)

Thus up to 1959 the Iranian *ulama*, although no longer in control of the country's legal and educational systems, remained a prosperous and influential group of people whom the government treated with respect and who, though generally willing to support the government, could certainly not be taken for granted. The conflict

---

* See pp. 110. The episode (including the government's behaviour) bears strong resemblances to the anti-Ahmadi agitations of 1953 and 1975 in Pakistan, referred to in Chapter 7.

between them and Muhammad Reza Shah can be dated only from 1959. The first signs of it came in January of that year, when new proposals to enfranchise women were sharply criticized by Bihbihani and others. But the first issue to bring direct conflict was the government's land reform Bill, submitted to the Majlis in December 1959 and soon condemned as ill-advised and contrary to the Shari'a by Borujerdi. Thanks to religious endowments built up since Safavid times, the *ulama* owned or controlled large areas of land in several parts of the country (notably Azerbaijan and Isfahan) and this was an important element in their economic independence which had been only marginally affected by Reza Shah's reforms. Accordingly they saw the new Bill, which proposed to divide large estates among the peasants, as a threat to their independence, as well as to the principle of private property which they considered to be sanctified by the Shari'a. In particular, they feared that the Bill would break up endowments on which mosques, seminaries and ceremonials depended for their upkeep, and many *ulama* and religious students for their income.

Although the land Bill was ratified in May 1960 it remained inoperative, thanks partly to Borujerdi's opposition and partly to loopholes in the drafting which rendered it all but meaningless. The issue hung fire until 1961, when Borujerdi's death in March left the *ulama* without an undisputed leader, while the Kennedy administration in the United States began pressing the Shah to push ahead with reforms. The Shah appointed a new government headed by Ali Amini, who enjoyed American support, and who persuaded him that the Majlis should be dispensed with for the time being and the necessary reforms introduced by decree. This unconstitutional procedure ensured that the reforms would be opposed by the liberal/secular politicians (what was left of Mosaddeq's National Front) as well as by the landlords and at least some of the *ulama*. There were demonstrations, arrests of National Front leaders, renewed restrictions on political activity and, in January 1962, a major riot by Tehran University students, brutally suppressed by the police and army.

It was in this atmosphere that the new land-reform decree

(formally an amendment to the 1960 law) was approved by the cabinet. Consequently neither the *ulama* nor the secular opposition really considered the proposed reform on its merits. Their hostility to it was bound up with their anger at the growing autocracy of the Shah and the corruption of his regime. Amini, it is true, had had two ex-ministers arrested for corruption and promised a vigorous anti-corruption drive. But in July 1962 he himself resigned, after the Shah had refused to reduce the army budget, and was replaced by Asadollāh Alam, a big landlord who was one of the Shah's oldest cronies and had formed a phony 'opposition' party on the Shah's instructions. The Shah still refused to hold elections. Instead, in January 1963, he held a snap plebiscite on a six-point reform programme grandiosely entitled 'the White Revolution' (later 'the Shah-People Revolution').

Besides land reform, the other points in the programme were: sale of government-owned factories to finance land reform; a new election law including women's suffrage; the nationalization of forests; a national literacy corps, mainly for rural teaching; and a plan to give workers a share of industrial profits. The *ulama*, as we have seen, were almost unanimously hostile to women's rights. They also feared that the literacy corps, by replacing elementary religious schools as the main source of education in remote villages, would further undermine their influence.

On all these points the Shah could with some justice describe his own position as 'progressive' and that of the *ulama* as 'reactionary'. But as the agitation mounted, the reforms as such became less the issue.* The *ulama* denounced the Shah's dictatorship and also his foreign policy, accusing him of subservience towards the United States and condemning his *de facto* alliance with Israel, which they contrasted with his breaking of relations with Nasser's United Arab Republic in 1960. Nasser's claim that the Persian Gulf and the Iranian province of Khuzistan were rightfully Arab had antagonized the Shah, but his use of al-Azhar to project an

---

* The regime was never able to produce a *fatwa* from any *mujtahid* condemning the land reform programme as such.

'Islamic' foreign policy* had favourably impressed the Iranian *ulama*. In 1959 the Rector of al-Azhar had issued a *fatwa* recognizing the Shi'ite Jafari† school of legal thought as a legitimate one, on an equal footing with the four Sunni schools. Borujerdi had been sufficiently impressed to send an ayatollah to al-Azhar to open a dialogue and expound Shi'ite doctrine.‡ So when the Rector later sent a telegram to the Shah questioning Iran's 'pro-Israel' policy it cut some ice with the Iranian *ulama*, though not with the addressee.

These foreign policy issues were especially emphasized in early 1963 by Ayatollah Khomeini, who now emerged for the first time as the regime's most outspoken critic and the leader of a 'radical' faction among the *ulama*. This faction also included Ayatollah Mahmud Tāleqanī of Tehran, who had at least attempted to criticize the land reform constructively, suggesting measures that would be more genuinely helpful to the peasants as well as protecting the religious endowments and the social standing of the landlords. Khomeini too sought to identify himself with the 'oppressed' and 'innocent' masses, demanding an end to exploitation of the poor as well as to corruption in high places. He did not recommend any specific social reforms, but condemned the government for relying too much on urbanization, industrialization and foreign investment. His religious credentials were strong, but not overwhelmingly so: he was regarded as a *marja-i taqlid*, but not the most learned of them. His name, for instance, was not mentioned among those best qualified to assume the mantle of Borujerdi. He had not written a great deal, and he had taught philosophy — always a somewhat suspect subject among the conservative-minded *ulama*, even if less so to Shi'ites than to Sunnis.

It was his political courage that drew attention to Khomeini in 1963, during what turned out to be a kind of dress rehearsal

---

* See Chapter 8, pp. 273–7.

† Founded by the Sixth Imam, Ja'far al-Sadiq.

‡ He returned suggesting that Qom should emulate al-Azhar in including military science in its curriculum, so that the religious students could take their due place in the vanguard of *jihad*!

for the 1978–79 revolution (comparable, perhaps, to the events of 1905 in Russia). His direct criticism of the Shah, in sermons at the main seminary in Qom, led in March 1963 to an attack on the seminary by paratroopers and the secret police (SAVAK) during which several students were killed and Khomeini was arrested. Released after a short time, he resumed his denunciations of the government and its policies. He asserted that Iran was under American control and that America was an enemy of Islam, partly because it supported Israel. He did not, it should be noted, attack the monarchy as such. Indeed he presented himself as a defender of the 1906–7 constitution, which 'has been bought with the blood of our fathers, and we will not permit it to be violated.' But his violent denunciations of the Shah led to a bloody climax in June 1963, which coincided with the month of Muharram (that of Husain's martyrdom) in the Islamic calendar. On the tenth of Muharram, the actual day of the anniversary (4 June 1963), Khomeini was arrested before dawn. When the news became known in Tehran processions of mourning for Husain turned into demonstrations, which spread the next day to the university and to other cities. Over the next few days, amid calls for *jihad* against the regime, hundreds of demonstrators — thousands, by most accounts — were killed by troops. In Qom some of the students were killed by being thrown from the roof of the seminary into the dry riverbed below. Others, it was said, were drowned in the nearby lake.*

Although the revolt was effectively crushed by these methods, opposition continued for a time. The Shah tried to defuse the situation by offering further reforms, by releasing Khomeini in August, and by calling new elections for October. But Khomeini called for a boycott of the elections and was imprisoned again until May 1964. During 1964 opposition focused on a new issue: a $200 million loan from the United States for purchases of military equipment and a Bill to grant diplomatic immunity to the US military personnel who would come with it. (They would be tried, even

---

* In 1979 General Manuchehr Khosrowdad, who commanded this operation, was one of the first four people to be executed by the revolutionary regime.

for crimes against Iranians, by US military courts on Iranian soil.) This was altogether reminiscent, as Khomeini pointed out, of the 'capitulations' which European powers had insisted on for their nationals and protégés in the nineteenth century and which Reza Shah had abolished. It was for his fiery denunciations of this affront to Iranian sovereignty that Khomeini was at last exiled to Turkey in 1964. The following year he took up residence, like so many of his distinguished predecessors, at Najaf in Iraq.

After 1963 the regime did try fairly consistently to reduce the influence of the *ulama*. The Shah continued and extended his father's policy of seeking control of the seminaries through administering the endowments by which they were financed. Inquiries after the revolution revealed that government-appointed administrators of these lands committed embezzlement on a grand scale and also transferred the lands themselves to clubs and individuals — generals and their wives, members of the royal family, entertainers in favour at court — possibly with the intention that they be used for industrial development. Black propaganda was used to smear the reputation of Khomeini and other recalcitrant *ulama* with their colleagues. The state-run Endowments Organization published a journal which sought to convey the impression of Islam as a state religion, glorifying its cultural and mystical aspects, but ignoring its social message and the views of contemporary *mujtahids*.

In 1971 a Religion Corps was created, on the model of the literacy corps. Its members were recruited not from the traditional seminaries but from the modern universities, and included graduates in political science, geography, Arabic, philosophy, social science, Persian literature and archaeology as well as theology. The theory was that these young men were doing 'religious service' in lieu of military service, and so forming a state-controlled substitute for the traditional *ulama*. They were supplemented by a Department of Religious Propaganda, whose functionaries were to work in rural areas, undertaking 'health and development activities', 'social and patriotic activities' and 'administrative duties' (dissemination of pamphlets 'on numerous social issues')

319

as well as religious and educational activities. The two groups together were to be the 'mullahs of modernization'.

There was also, of course, straightforward repression: the arrest and torture of *ulama* who refused to keep quiet. The most notorious case was that of Ayatollah Muhammad Reza Sa'idi of Tehran, tortured to death in 1970 for having objected to a conference exploring further possibilities of American investment in Iran. Some of these activities had a rather amateurish quality to them. The journal of the Endowments Organization, for instance, published only two issues, and by the second year of the Religion Corps 40 per cent of its members were managing to get themselves positions in the capital. Positive state control (as opposed to erratic retroactive censorship) of sermons in the mosques never attained anything like the level achieved in, say, Egypt or Turkey. The *ulama*, though on the defensive, continued to benefit from the special advantages mentioned in the previous section: an awareness of themselves and their function as something separate from, and not dependent on, the state; direct receipt of *khums* and *zakat* from the faithful, particularly the wealthy faithful of the bazaar, whose traditional attachment to Islam was strengthened during the 1960s and 1970s as oil revenues brought into existence a new economy from which they were largely excluded — an economy controlled by foreign investors, by 'self-made' industrialists dependent on state contracts, and above all by the Shah himself, his family and his courtiers; the habit of taking a lead from the *mujtahids*, and in particular from the *maraji*-i taqlid*; willingness to think for themselves, at least within certain limits; and the existence of a relatively secure base beyond the frontiers of Iran, but visited by a constant stream of Iranian pilgrims, in the shrine cities of Iraq.

The Shah and his minions undoubtedly underestimated the danger. Many of the minions, including members of the Shah's family, were clearly more interested in accumulating wealth for themselves and enjoying the luxuries of Western civilization than in mounting a serious attack on the *ulama*'s influence with the

---

* Plural of *marja*.

population at large. The Shah himself scarcely bothered, after 1963, even to pay lip-service to Islam. Instead he promised Iranians the benefits of modern Western civilization, while identifying himself as ostentatiously as possible with a hollow Iranian chauvinism — anti-Arab and in effect anti-Islamic — based on a megalomaniac vision of Iran's pre-Islamic, 'imperial' past. The tasteless jet-set celebrations of '2,500 years of monarchy' at Persepolis in 1971, from which ordinary Iranians were virtually excluded by the security measures, were a provocation not only to the *ulama* but even to secular-minded Iranians who took some pride in their Islamic heritage. (An even more direct provocation was the introduction in 1975 of a new calendar, dating the years not from Muhammad's *hijra*, but from the founding of the Achaemenid Empire in 558 BC.)

Whereas until about 1960 Iranian intellectuals, including and perhaps especially those who opposed the monarchy, were influenced by Western liberal and socialist ideas and regarded the influence of Islam in Iranian life as reactionary and negative, after that date the Iranian intelligentsia split into two camps. On one side was a cosmopolitan group whose members were often critical of the Shah in private on liberal grounds, but which culturally was on the wavelength of the more sophisticated members of the imperial court, particularly the Queen, who emerged as something of a patron of the arts. On the other were intellectuals who, even though they had themselves absorbed liberal or socialist ideas from the West, were bitterly offended by the commercial and philistine brand of Western culture which oil wealth helped to spread through the Iranian middle class. The spokesman of this reaction was Jalal Al-e Ahmad (died 1969), whose essay *Gharbzadegi* ('Westitis') had enormous influence. Himself an ex-communist, Al-e Ahmad set out to rehabilitate Islam as an authentic expression of Iran's identity. He even defended the anti-constitutionalist Shaikh Nuri (see pp. 304–5) as a martyr of the struggle to uphold that identity against Western imperialism. He thus prepared the ground for the influence on the educated classes of Shi'ite thinkers such as Ayatollah Taleqani, Engineer Mehdi Bazargan, Ahmad Reza'i and above all Ali Shari'ati, whose ideas will be described in the next section.

A similar reaction occurred on the popular level. Observers and statistics have attested to the rapid growth of traditional religious activities in Iran in the 1970s: visits and donations to shrines, pilgrimages to Mecca, the building of new mosques, the sale of traditional Shi'ite books, the spread of guild-type 'religious associations' based on humble professions (shoe-makers, tailors, public bath attendants, street-corner fruit-juicers) or on groups of a particular regional origin in the big cities.[7] It seems clear that these activities express the reaction of people disorientated by very rapid urbanization and other socio-economic changes, and also by the swamping of Iran with Western material and cultural products, processes that were accelerated after the oil boom of 1973–74.

Given another generation, for all his amateurishness, the Shah might have succeeded in destroying Iran's traditional culture and the influence of the *ulama* with it. Atatürk did succeed in that in Turkey, and the Shah's policies were in essence the same as Atatürk's, only a little more erratic, considerably more vulgarly bombastic (they included conspicuously wasteful arms purchases and a drive to be the dominant power in the Indian Ocean), and backed by vastly greater economic resources. It was precisely that danger that made the defence of Iranian culture, represented by Islam, seem such a desperately urgent task to so many Iranians, and made them willing to accept leadership even from such an undiluted traditionalist as Ayatollah Khomeini. Iran in the 1970s was experiencing the same 'real impoverishment' of its culture that Turkey suffered in the 1920s and 1930s. That does not explain why there was a revolution. It does perhaps explain why the revolution had to be an Islamic one.

Which Shi'ism? Whose Revolution?

Like any revolution worth the name, the Iranian revolution was a movement that brought together many groups of people with different interests, inspired by a wide variety of ideas. Some of these (Marxism, liberalism, secular nationalism, for example) were not put forward in terms of Islam. Their influence on the revolution was considerable, and it is no part of my purpose to minimize it. But they fall outside the scope of this book. Here I shall only attempt to deal—and that in most summary fashion, for it is a subject on which many books are being and will be written—with interpretations of Islam that figured in the revolution, and with groups and individuals who acted in their name.

KHOMEINI

It is probably best to start with the ideas of Ayatollah Khomeini himself, even though a remarkable number of people seem to have been unaware of his ideas until after they had helped bring him into power. Yet the main lines of his thought had been published as early as the 1940s, when he took advantage of the freer atmosphere following Reza Shah's abdication to voice his strong concern about what was happening to Islam in Iran, and to the *ulama* in particular. He circulated a letter to fellow *ulama*, urging them to unite against the immorality of public life and warning them that the new Shah would probably renew his father's assault on religion if given the chance. He also asked them to react against 'a certain adventurer from Tabriz who is attacking your creed'— a reference to Ahmad Kasravi, the anti-Shi'ite rationalist reformer who was later murdered by the Fida'iyan-i Islam. Khomeini soon followed this up with a work entitled *Secrets Exposed*, which was a reply to *Secrets of a Thousand Years*, a book written by one of Kasravi's disciples. Interestingly, one of the worst labels Khomeini could find to stick on these modernist denigrators of Shi'ite 'superstitions' was ... 'Wahhabi':

> The intellectuals want progress and release from *taqlid* [imitation]. But they are really imitators of the camel-herding savages of Najd.... These arguments have been around since the beginning of Islam.... They think that if we abandon religion, we will advance and catch up with Europe, but they do not realize what Europe has to offer is not civilization but savagery. Nor do they realize that people in Europe are still religious,

that the great men of Europe and America pray every morn-ning. . . .* Nor do our writers realize how little progress there is in the deserts of Najd and the Hijaz: should we seek advice on development from them?

Khomeini saw very clearly that any attempt to reform religion by appealing to the past would ruin the authority of the Shi'ite *ulama* because it invited the believer to interpret the past for himself instead of referring to a living *mujtahid*. This would be a disaster: 'You who want to reduce the power of the *ulama* and eliminate their honour among the people, you are committing the greatest treason to the country.' The result was the penetration of foreign influence and the ruin of the country. Islamic tradition and national interest were inseparable: thus Reza Shah's Westernizing reforms had been a cover for Western appropriation of Iran's economic resources:

> This shameless unveiling, enforced at bayonet point, is materi-ally and spiritually damaging to the country and is forbidden according to the law of God and the Prophet. . . . This pot-like reject [i.e. bowler] hat of the foreigners is the disgrace of the Islamic nation, stains our independence, and is forbidden ac-cording to the law of God. . . . These schools mixing young girls and young passion-ridden boys kill female honour, the root of life and the power of manly valour, are materially and spiritually damaging to the country and are forbidden by God's command-ment. . . . These wine-shops and liquor-producing organizations wear off the brain of the youth of the country and burn away the intellect, the health, the courage and the audacity of the masses; they should be closed by God's commandment. . . . Music rouses the spirit of love-making, of unlawful sexuality and of giving free rein to passion while it removes audacity, courage, and manly valour. It is forbidden by the Shari'a and should not be included in the school programmes.

Khomeini had no doubt of the remedy. 'If the Islamic law of retribution, blood money and punishments is put into practice even

---

* A splendid example of having an argument both ways!

for a single year, the seed of injustice, theft and unchastity will be eliminated from the country. Anybody wanting to extirpate theft from the world must cut off the thief's hands, otherwise such imprisonments [as those imposed by secular courts] would only help the thieves and promote larceny.' The Koran had restricted law to divine law, and 'the calamity of the country is that it possesses such divine laws and yet extends its hand to the countries of the foreigners, and is seeking to execute their artificial laws which have emanated from selfish and poisonous ideas.'

Whose task is it to enforce the law? Who can govern justly? Only a sovereign elected by pious *mujtahids*, knowing divine commands and exercising justice without being prisoner to the pressures and ambitions of this world. Reza Shah, clearly, had not been such. All the legislation passed during this reign had violated the will of God, and must be cancelled. Perhaps the monarchy itself should be suppressed, since 'apart from the royalty of God, all royalty is against the interests of the people and oppressive; apart from the law of God, all laws are null and absurd. A government of Islamic law, controlled by religious jurists (*faqih*) will be superior to all the iniquitous governments of the world.' Yet Khomeini in this work did not go quite so far as to call for the abolition of the Iranian monarchy and its replacement by a government of *mujtahids*. ('No jurist has said, nor is it written in any book, that we are kings or that sovereignty is our right.') Rather he urges the reform of the existing system through greater involvement of the *mujtahids*, particularly by enforcing the defunct Clause 2 of the 1907 Supplement to the Fundamental Law, under which all legislation was supposed to be vetted by a committee of five of them chosen by their peers; and, anticipating objections that the state is by its nature corrupt and good *ulama* should have nothing to do with it, he cites with approval numerous Shi'ite authorities of the past who recommended accepting office from temporal rulers, even unjust ones, in order to reform political systems from within.

It was only on this point that his thinking had significantly changed when, a quarter of a century later during his exile at Najaf, he gave a series of lectures on 'the guardianship of the jurist' (*wilayat al-faqih*), later published from student notes as the book *Islamic Government*. The experience of the early 1960s had by now convinced him that monarchy was an intrinsically anti-Islamic institution, and he declared any form of co-operation with monarchs illegitimate. But this did *not* mean that temporal government had to be given up as a bad job until the return of the Hidden Imam, or that the faithful should be content with knowing the truth in their hearts and applying the Shari'a as best they could in their private lives while dissembling, if necessary, their views on religion and politics to avoid persecution by the corrupt and despotic ruler.

It is *against* these traditional Twelver Shi'ite views that Khomeini musters all his considerable powers of argument and invective. Islam, he insists, is political or it is nothing. 'The Koran contains a hundred times more verses concerning social problems than on devotional subjects. Out of fifty books of Muslim tradition there are perhaps three or four which deal with prayer or with man's duties towards God, a few on morality and all the rest have to do with society, economics, law, politics and the state.... Never say that Islam is composed only of a few precepts concerning relations between God and His creation. The mosque is not the church!' The laws of God 'concern the whole life of the individual from conception to the grave.... Islamic law is progressive, perfectionist, universal.'

Khomeini cites the Imam Husain, not as an example of noble suffering but as a heroic rebel against monarchy and dynastic succession. Then, plunging into contemporary politics, he attacks the 'imperialists' and their puppet governments in Muslim countries for 'obstructing our industrialization and building only assembly-plants'; and to those who reproach him with being a 'political cleric' he replies: 'was not the Prophet, God's prayers be upon him, a politician?'

The absence of the Imam must not be an excuse for leaving the law unenforced. 'Some thousand years have passed since he was hidden, and perhaps a hundred thousand more will pass before he reappears. What would become of the Islamic laws during all that time?' These laws, according to Khomeini, contain the answer to everything, 'from penal codes to commercial, industrial and agricultural law', and also national defence. 'Prepare for them all the force and the horses you can muster so that you may scare away the enemies of God and your enemies,' says the Koran. 'If the Muslim peoples had applied this law,' says Khomeini, 'and if the Islamic government had made serious preparations, proclaiming general mobilization, a handful of Zionists would never have dared to occupy our lands and destroy our al-Aqsa mosque* without the people being able to react at once.' Thus Khomeini's concern is by no means limited to Iran. Indeed to him the division of the *umma* into 'several separate nations' is itself something to be deplored, the work of colonialism and of 'despotic and ambitious rulers'. One of the tasks of Islamic government will be to restore the unity of the *umma*, 'to liberate its lands from the grip of the colonialists and to topple the agent governments of colonialism.'

Islamic government, Khomeini insists, is both possible and necessary. He quotes a saying of the Imam Reza (the Eighth Imam) that 'it would have been quite illogical for God the Most High and Most Wise to leave His people, His creatures, without a guide or a guardian.' God's wisdom cannot be limited to a particular time and place, therefore 'today and until the end of time it will be indispensable that an imam keep order and enforce the Islamic laws.... The reasons that led to the appointment of Ali to the Imamate are still valid: the person has changed but not the function.' The Islamic government of today must be 'the representative of Ali'. It must be constitutional, 'of course not in the usual sense of the term, where laws are approved by people and by majority vote', but in the sense that the rulers must observe a number of 'conditions' defined in the Koran and the Sunna. 'Islamic government is the government of the people by the divine law.' God is the only legislator; so instead of a legislature there will be a 'planning council' to control the work of the various

* The lecture was given in 1969, shortly after the fire in the al-Aqsa mosque in Israeli-occupied Jerusalem (see p. 178).

ministries. But the head of the government, the supreme leader, must be a jurist (*faqih*) – an expert in that divine law which the government exists to enforce. Here Khomeini quotes an adage that 'the jurists are rulers over the sultans', since the pious sultan must ask the jurist to tell him the law before he can carry it out, and deduces from this that real sovereignty belongs to the jurist who gives the ruling rather than to the ignorant sultan who has to follow his instructions.

There is no shortage of jurists qualified to undertake this task, he goes on: 'many jurists of our time have the qualities in question', which are simply fair-mindedness and knowledge of the law. To claim the political powers of the Prophet and of Ali does not imply that one is claiming to be their equal in spiritual virtues, for their virtues did not entitle them to any greater powers than are allotted to all governments by the law of God. The only difference is that whereas the Prophet and each of the Imams in his time had authority over everyone else, including his successor, the jurist cannot have 'absolute custodianship' over other jurists, nor can he appoint or dismiss them. 'There is no hierarchy among them.' The jurists may form the government 'individually or together'. The possibility that they might disagree is apparently not envisaged. 'If a jurist violates the law he commits an act of corruption and will be automatically dismissed. . . .' But who will dismiss him, and by what procedure, Khomeini does not say.

The similarity of Khomeini's *wilayat al-faqih* to Rida's caliphate of the chief *mujtahid* has already been noted (Chapter 8, p. 246), though Khomeini has none of Rida's ambiguity about the involvement of the caliph in executive government. His vision of Islamic government also has points in common with Maududi's (Chapter 7, pp. 201–6), though unlike Maududi he does not attempt to present it as democratic. What is notable, anyway, is that his view of the relation between religion and politics is closer to that of Sunni writers than to any traditional Shi'ite theologian. He revokes the *de facto* legitimacy which Twelver Shi'ism had accorded to non-Islamic, or at least not perfectly Islamic, government; and he asserts that Islamic government can be instituted by a ruler or rulers without any special spiritual qualities, without direct nomination by God or by the Imam of the Age, simply on the basis of their knowledge of the law and sense of justice — the recognition of these qualifications being left, apparently, to the community at large. Moreover he uses the word *'imam'* to refer to such a ruler, which would appear to be a Sunni rather than a Shi'ite use of the term. At about the same time he himself began to be referred to as 'Imam' by his followers.* This enabled him to have the best of both worlds: challenged by the orthodox, he could say that this was merely an expression of respect and affection and that of course there was no question of his claiming to be *the* Imam in the Shi'ite sense. But to the uneducated masses of Iran, by 1979 he was *the* Imam, even if the precise theological implications escaped them.

As a general rule, people get involved in revolutions out of conservatism: they are driven to blame the existing regime for a threatened or actual deterioration in their personal fortunes (or those of a group with which they identify). That is perhaps less often true of revolutionary *leaders*, but it would seem to be true of Khomeini. He developed a revolutionary political doctrine as a response to the political, cultural and economic forces which were destroying the influence of the *ulama* and the traditional Islamic way of life in Iran. Even while leading the revolution he remained a convinced and extreme traditionalist — more so, for instance, than Maududi in Pakistan or the Muslim Brotherhood in Egypt. Both the latter, while attached in principle to the 'Koranic' punishments, believed that they would only be applicable in a truly Islamic society, by which they meant one where there was social justice, where women were treated with respect and men not aroused by indecent displays, and so on. Khomeini by contrast believed — and presumably still believes — that the strict application of such punishments was the means by which a truly Islamic society could be created, or recreated.

* He seems to have been preceded in this by 'Imam' Musa Sadr, the leader of the Twelver Shi'ites in Lebanon (himself of Iranian origin). But Lebanon is an Arab country with Sunni traditions; the title 'Imam' does not carry such strong overtones in Arabic as it does in Persian.

SHARI'ATMADARI

If Khomeini's ideas can fairly be categorized as 'revolutionary traditionalism',[8] those of Ayatollah Sayyid Muhammad Kāzem Sharī'atmadārī could be called 'moderate traditionalism'. Shari'atmadari became a familiar figure to hundreds of Western journalists during the months that preceded Khomeini's return to Iran on 1 February 1979. He was regarded by then as the senior religious leader on Iranian soil — and in terms of learning, senior to Khomeini himself, though not in political charisma.* His views were also, almost certainly, more representative of those of other senior *mujtahids* and *maraji-i taqlid*.

The contrast in style between the two ayatollahs was great. While Khomeini scowled at the world from under his black eyebrows, Shari'atmadari's eyes twinkled owlishly from behind round, metal-rimmed glasses. While Khomeini specialized in categorical, uncompromising statements and usually seemed impatient with questions, Shari'atmadari was willing to answer questions almost endlessly and always managed to soften his answer with touches of ambiguity and compromise. Almost every day he would set aside an hour or more for receiving journalists at his house in Qom, even on days when his frail health obliged him to receive them propped up in bed. There were always a number of his students in attendance, including a young Englishman who had embraced Shi'a Islam, and who acted as interpreter. The atmosphere was that of a tutorial or seminar rather than an interview or press conference. Answering questions about Islamic law and its practical application in given circumstances is after all the essence of the *mujtahid*'s way of life. The only difference when they come from journalists who are totally ignorant of Islam is that one has to be extra-patient ...

Q. Does Islam say that thieves must be punished by amputation of the hand? Will this law be applied in Iran?

A. In principle that is the law. The application of the law will depend on the circumstances.

---

* Or in age; Khomeini was born about 1901 or 1902, Shari'atmadari in 1905.

Q. What about the stoning of women for adultery?
A. That is prescribed by the law. But remember that you need four witnesses *to the act of penetration*. (Twinkle, twinkle.)
Q. Are you in favour of having an 'Islamic Republic'?
A. A republic, yes. I don't think it makes a great difference whether you call it Islamic. If the Iranians are good Muslims it will be Islamic anyway. Even under the existing constitution the laws are supposed to be approved by a committee of five *mujtahids*. It will be good if this is put into practice.

This was when the Shah had already left Iran, and the revolution was about to triumph. Earlier, while protesting against the government's policies, especially the killing of demonstrators, and insisting on the unity of views between himself and Khomeini, Shari'atmadari had been unwilling to condemn the monarchy outright, and contented himself with pointing out that the constitution had not been respected. When asked about differences between his statements and those of Khomeini, he would simply point out that their situations were different, since he was in Iran and Khomeini was abroad. This could be taken as meaning that he could not afford to be as outspoken as Khomeini. Alternatively it could mean that Khomeini's intransigent statements failed to take account of the realities in the country. The ambiguity was typical.

The general assumption was that Shari'atmadari did not in fact share all Khomeini's views, and that he was riled by Khomeini's assumption of political leadership. The above statement, in which he gently debunked the 'Islamic Republic' slogan adopted by Khomeini, was one of the first positive indications that this assumption was correct. In the autumn of 1979 the breach became fully visible when Shari'atmadari refused to support the constitution because it incorporated Khomeini's doctrine of *wilayat al-faqih*. His point of view, in this respect much more traditional than Khomeini's, was that the *ulama* should not involve themselves so directly in the running of the state. He disliked the politicization of the *ulama* and feared that they would bring discredit on themselves and on Islam. He also felt that it was wrong to concentrate so much power in the hands of any one man.

331

Shari'atmadari's opposition was important because of his great following among the Turkish-speaking people of Azerbaijan, of whom he was one. In December 1979 there was an insurrection in Tabriz, the capital of Azerbaijan, led by a party formed to support Shari'atmadari's views, the Muslim Republican People's Party (MRPP). For a day or two the government lost control of the city. But the troops in the area remained loyal, and pro-Khomeini forces, helped by left-wing parties, were able to mobilize many of the poorer people for counter-demonstrations: they adroitly confused and divided Shari'atmadari's supporters by carrying his picture as well as Khomeini's. Shari'atmadari himself, still in Qom, was unwilling to take responsibility for a civil war. He agreed to disavow the insurrection and instructed the MRPP to dissolve itself. Since then he has been prevented from making further contact with the Press, whether Iranian or foreign, and is understood to be under what amounts to house arrest.

It seems there was a class element to the conflict, as well as its ideological and ethnic–regional aspects. Shari'atmadari was regarded, rightly or wrongly, as a spokesman for the wealthier *ulama*, the traditional merchant class of the bazaar, and the middle class generally, whereas Khomeini was seen as the champion of the poor and oppressed — the 'disinherited' of whom he frequently spoke. Shari'atmadari was certainly strongly anti-communist. He had been in Azerbaijan when it was ruled by a Stalinist 'independent' government, backed by Soviet troops, in the aftermath of the Second World War; and in 1979 he was noticeably more outspoken in condemning the Soviet-backed regime in Afghanistan than in attacking 'American imperialism' — again in marked contrast to Khomeini.

TALEQANI AND BAZARGAN

A third ayatollah who played a leading role in the revolution was Mahmud Taleqani, whose attitude to the land reform in the early 1960s has already been mentioned. In fact he had been active politically long before that. Born in 1910, he began teaching theology in Tehran (after studying in Qom) in 1938. In 1939 he was imprisoned for six months for opposing Reza Shah's religious policies, and in the early Fifties he was a strong supporter of Mosaddeq. It was at that time that he formed a friendship with Mehdī Bāzargān, a French-trained engineer whom Mosaddeq made head of the oil-nationalization committee. In 1961 the two of them founded the Freedom Movement of Iran, a new party which was to bridge the gap between the modern and increasingly secular, salaried middle class represented by the National Front on one side, and the traditional propertied middle class with which the *ulama* had close ties on the other.

Bazargan himself, five years older than Taleqani, belonged to both these worlds. He came from a family of Tabriz bazaar merchants and retained strong religious convictions, but was also a Western-trained technocrat who had himself been a member of the National Front. He was strongly opposed to the widening gap between spiritual and temporal, which he felt was a betrayal of the essence of Islam, and sought to show the relevance of Islam to modern life by writing about it with a new vocabulary, taking his examples from contemporary culture and technology. In a much remarked lecture in 1962 he urged the *ulama* to come out of their ivory towers and involve themselves more in the life of the community, including politics. He could hardly foresee that in 1979, as the first prime minister of the Islamic Republic, he would find himself rendered powerless by *ulama* interference!

Both Bazargan and Taleqani suffered imprisonment during the 1960s for their political activities. In prison Taleqani met secular and leftist opponents of the Shah, and impressed them as an unusually liberal and open-minded, even progressive, representative of the *ulama*. Already in 1955 he had shown his liberalism by publishing a new edition of a treatise written in support of the constitution in 1909 by Ayatollah Na'ini. In his introduction, Taleqani argued that dictatorship was a form of idolatry, an offence against the principle of divine unity (*tawhid*), whereas men's efforts to govern themselves through democracy and even socialism could be steps towards *tawhid* provided they were understood as such and not seen as ends in themselves. Later he devoted a work specifically to the problem of 'Islam and Property, in Comparison to the Economic systems of the West', in which he rejected Marxism but endorsed the slogan 'from each according to his abilities, to each according to his needs'.

In his attitude to the role of the *ulama*, Taleqani was somewhat ambivalent. He did feel that only *mujtahids* were qualified to interpret the law correctly, but he was against the *ulama* having special privileges. They should sit in assemblies on the same footing as others, he wrote.

Imprisoned again in 1977 for having supported the leftist Muslim guerrillas, Mujahidin-i Khalq, Taleqani was freed by popular pressure in November 1978, when the revolution was in full swing. From then until his death the following September he was constantly at the centre of events, using all his great prestige and conciliatory powers to try and hold the revolution together. Repeatedly he intervened to soften harsh statements from Khomeini, though without ever directly criticizing him. For instance, when Khomeini offended the women's movement by ordering women to resume the veil, Taleqani explained that 'the Imam was speaking of the veil of human dignity.' He arranged a truce between central government forces and Kurdish autonomists, and staged a kind of one-man strike when two of his sons, members of Mujahidin-i Khalq, were kidnapped by revolutionary guards. In the last weeks of his life he disappointed many of the liberals and leftists who had put their hopes in him by coming out with a strong condemnation of the left and the Kurds (both being then under severe pressure from revolutionary guards acting with Khomeini's blessing). But his last speech before he died was a warning against despotism masquerading as religion and a reminder that true Islam allowed for criticism, protest and the expression of grievances.

Perhaps Taleqani, like the French Socialist leader Jean Jaurès, assassinated on the eve of the First World War, was lucky in the moment of his death. Just as Jaurès would have had to betray either his country or his internationalist principles, so Taleqani would either have had to break with Khomeini – in which case he would probably have been crushed like so many others — or would have had to sacrifice his reputation for liberalism and enlightenment. As it is his memory is still, as of summer 1981, revered both by the regime (one of the main thoroughfares of Tehran is named after him) and by its left-wing and liberal opponents, especially the Mujahidin-i Khalq who refer to him as 'our father Taleqani'.

SHARI'ATI AND THE MUJAHIDIN

The Sazman-i Mujahidin-i Khalq-i Iran (Organization of the Jihad-fighters of the Iranian People), to give it its full name, was formed in the mid-1960s by young members of the Freedom Movement who felt, after the 1963 crisis, that opposing the Shah's regime by non-violent means was hopeless.* They decided to embark on guerrilla warfare, though they realized that this would need long and careful preparation to have any chance of success. Starting with a nucleus of nine people in 1965, they gradually built up a nationwide network, and sent members to Jordan for training with the Palestinian resistance groups. Meanwhile they also developed their ideas, carrying further the discovery of a 'progressive', socially relevant Shi'ism on which Taleqani and Bazargan had embarked. Their chief theorist, Ahmad Reza'i, wrote a book, *The Movement of Husain*, in which he argued that divine unity (*tawhid*) implied not simply the worship of one God but the elimination of class distinctions and interests, the dedication of all to the welfare of all. This was the true nature of the community the Prophet had striven to set up. The order of the first three 'usurping' caliphs and of the Umayyads was, Reza'i argued, essentially a restoration of the power of feudal landlords and merchant capitalists. The Shi'a, in its original form, was a revolt against this class domination, an attempt to carry on the Prophet's egalitarian revolution. The Imam Husain was a revolutionary hero who gave his life in the struggle, not as a purely symbolic gesture but

---

* The Freedom Movement itself never became much more than a private club. Bazargan made no attempt, even after the revolution, to change it into a mass party.

with a real social objective. The duty of Muslims today was to carry on the struggle, to create a classless society and abolish all forms of capitalism, despotism and imperialism. The Mujahidin summed up their attitude in these words:

> After years of extensive study into Islamic history and Shi'ite ideology, our organization has reached the firm conclusion that Islam, especially Shi'ism, will play a major role in inspiring the masses to join the revolution. It will do so because Shi'ism, particularly Husain's historic act of resistance, has both a revolutionary message and a special place in our popular culture.[9]

While such ideas were expounded explicitly, but clandestinely, by the Mujahidin, rather similar ones were put forward in public, but in more cryptic form, by the young sociologist Ali Sharī'atī. Born in 1933, Shari'ati was the son of a well-known preacher in north-eastern Iran and had been educated in the shrine city of Mashhad. After a student career interrupted by imprisonment (for pro-Mosaddeq oppositional activities) he graduated from the Faculty of Letters in Mashhad and, in 1960, got permission to leave the country and pursue his studies further in Paris. There he obtained a doctorate in Persian philology, but also studied religious history and sociology. He was deeply influenced by the great orientalist and Christian mystic, Louis Massignon; by Frantz Fanon, the theorist of Third World liberation, whose *Les Damnés de la Terre** he translated into Persian; and by Jean-Paul Sartre. He was in Paris during the climactic years of the Algerian war, and was an active sympathizer of the Front de Libération Nationale.

After returning to Iran in 1964 (with prolonged detention and interrogation on arrival) he had a brief teaching career in Mashhad which ended with his dismissal from the university because of the political overtones, and consequent popularity, of his courses.

---

*For *damnés* Shari'ati used the Koranic term *mustaz'afin* (the disinherited). This has been picked up by Khomeini during the revolution to express his identification with the oppressed masses. It is also popular with Islamic groups in Egypt and elsewhere who wish to appeal to the exploited without using the vocabulary of Marxism or of class struggle.

Moving to Tehran in the late 1960s, he became a regular lecturer at a new and unofficial religious institution, the Husainīya Irshād (a place for teaching the principles of Husain), founded in 1965 by a group of would-be Islamic reformers with which he was associated.

Shari'ati was a determined modernist and a scathing critic of the traditional *ulama*. His heroes were Jamal al-Din 'al-Afghani', Muhammad Abduh and Muhammad Iqbal. There is no reason to doubt the sincerity of his religious beliefs, but clearly it was of primary importance for him to identify these beliefs with the idea of liberation, particularly in his own time the liberation of the Third World from imperialist domination. Thus for him the Shi'ite doctrine of imamate became identified with the idea of leadership in the liberation struggle — leadership willingly accepted by a people for whom the leader is prepared to sacrifice himself. Similarly he found in Shi'ism a crucial emphasis on the idea of justice: the revolt of Ali and his sons against the Umayyads is a revolt to defend justice against its antithesis, tyranny and oppression.

In Shari'ati's view this central message of Shi'ism had been hidden from the people by the Safavids, who had turned Shi'ism into a state religion and used it as an opiate for the masses. Thus he drew a strong distinction between the authentic 'Alid Shi'ism' and 'Safavid Shi'ism' — the latter being the official Shi'ism as still taught by the *ulama*. For instance the word *isma*, according to Shari'ati, had originally denoted the purity of thought and deed which won the people's respect for the Imams: it implied that people would not and should not follow an 'impure' religious leader connected with the caliphate (the caliphate being, of course, a government that betrays and oppresses the people). But *isma* in 'Safavid' Shi'ism had come to mean a kind of mystic infallibility, reserved only to the 'Sinless Fourteen' — Muhammad, his daughter Fatima, and the Twelve Imams. The people are thus conditioned not to expect *isma* in the absence of the Imam of the age, and therefore to put up with infamous government and the dishonest religious leaders that co-operate with it.

337

Similarly, Shari'ati said that *taqlid* (imitation or following) had been, in 'Alid' Shi'ism, 'a logical, scientific, natural and necessary relationship between non-specialists and specialist theologians, for practical and juridical problems that demand specialization'; but 'Safavid' Shi'ism had perverted it to mean 'blind obedience to the *ulama*, from whom one accepts absolutely, without reserve or logic, belief and orders; quasi-adoration of the *ulama*.' And the principle of divine justice, instead of being the divinely ordained basis of Muslim society, had become a theological problem concerning the after-life and the nature of God, while in this world justice was left to monarchs, according to the un-Islamic principle of 'render to Caesar that which is Caesar's'.

The difference between the two interpretations, as explained by Shari'ati, was systematic and affected all the central concepts of the faith. What the difference boils down to is that Shari'ati interprets Islam as political, and accuses the Safavids and the *ulama* of de-politicizing it. To that extent there is a certain parallelism between his thought and that of Khomeini. Both are particularly anxious to refute the idea that the absence of the Imam of the age and expectation of his return can justify political quietism. On the contrary, says Shari'ati, the fact that the Imam may return at any time means that we must be ready for him at all times, and those he will love best are those who are following the example of Ali and struggling actively on behalf of justice. Indeed for Shari'ati the Imam, though Hidden, is not necessarily absent at all: he lives in the real world, and he has his 'feet on the ground'. We may even meet him without recognizing him: he might be the farmer in that field over there, or that merchant in his shop in the bazaar. (Shari'ati contrasted this with the Christian doctrine of the Messiah who has gone to live in another world: yet the similarity to Christ's saying, 'inasmuch as ye have done it to the least of these my brethren ye have done it unto me', seems striking.)

Where Shari'ati clearly parts company from Khomeini is in his devaluation of the role of the *mujtahid*: for him commitment to the cause is more important than legal learning. An uneducated person can grasp the meaning of Islam if he reads the life of Muhammad, and may even understand Islam better and think and live in a more genuinely Islamic way than a learned jurist or philosopher. (Here too one seems to hear an echo — perhaps co-incidental — of Christianity: the Good Samaritan preferred to the priest and the Levite.) Regarding himself as entitled to propose a reform of Islam without the training of a *mujtahid*, Shari'ati came up with a number of statements which in the eyes of Khomeini and other *ulama* were simply mistaken (for instance that music is an Islamic art) or, perhaps worse, derived from Sunni doctrines and traditions clearly opposed to Shi'ism, e.g. he tried to demonstrate Islam's democratic spirit by referring to the election of the caliphs, and he proposed Saladin, who had suppressed the Shi'ite Fatimid caliphate and persecuted Shi'ism, as a pan-Islamic hero. Moreover, Shari'ati clearly saw the work of the Husainiya Irshad as an alternative to the traditional research and teaching carried on by the *ulama* in their seminaries, and so a way of breaking their monopoly in Islamic thought. He openly poured scorn on the seminaries, declaring that 'the Holy Koran was seized from the hands of students who studied Islam and put away on the shelf; it was replaced by the book of *usul* ['foundations'] and philosophical discussions.' He even, reversing Khomeini's argument, blamed the conservative *ulama* for the success of imperialism, since it was their stubbornness, in his view, that was driving young Iranians to seek refuge in Western culture.

Small wonder that Shari'ati's writings found little favour with the *ulama*, or that he was accused of being an agent of Sunnism, Wahhabism ... and communism. (Khomeini himself, however, does not seem to have attacked him personally; he ignored Shari'ati during his lifetime, and issued an at least implicitly laudatory statement on his death.) Yet since the essence of his criticism of them was that by de-politicizing Islam they had made themselves accomplices of injustice and despotism, he could be interpreted as urging them (like Bazargan and Taleqani, as well as Khomeini) to play a greater role in politics and increase their influence in society. It is true that he emphasized social commitment more than book learning, but he did not discount the importance of learning altogether. The ideal rulers would combine both qualities. The Muslims should

> oblige *one group among them to specialise in the theoretical know-ledge of Islam*, the deducing of Islamic laws, and the resolution of the problems of society and the events of the time. They should confide to this group social and ideological leadership as well as responsibility for people's destiny. *This group can decide the best, most honourable, most conscientious, most enlightened, and purest person for their guidance. And they can elect from among themselves someone in place of the Imam* — which is the place of the Prophet of Islam! And they would invest him. In the execution of his heavy responsibilities — which are those of the Imamate — the people feel a permanent and direct responsibility and build the government of wisdom, of committed wisdom, as Plato wished! That is to say that the one who was chosen by God in the period before the Occultation [i.e. the Prophet and the Imams], during the Occultation is chosen *by the people.* [Italics mine throughout — E.M.][10]

There is a great ambiguity here. The ruler is to be 'chosen by the people' but, it seems, only by a very indirect process. The actual election will be made by the *mujtahids* from among their own number. The *mujtahids* will have been chosen by the people, but presumably quite early in life, since they will have been 'obliged ... to specialize in the theoretical knowledge of Islam.' The comparison with Plato's philosopher-king hardly strengthens the democratic character of the proposal. In fact we are very close here to Khomeini's supreme guardian-jurist, except that he has to be elected by his fellow *mujtahids* and that the latter collectively are endowed with something like legislative power ('the deducing of Islamic laws').

We must remember that Shari'ati was lecturing to audiences which would probably contain at least one member of the Shah's secret police on any given occasion. He could not afford to be too explicit on political matters. In the end he sailed too near the wind. In 1973 the Husainiya Irshad was forcibly closed by government troops. Shari'ati hid, but later gave himself up because the regime was holding his father as a hostage. He was kept for eighteen months in solitary confinement, then for two years under police surveillance at his birthplace, the village of Mazinan, on the edge of the desert, after which he named his autobiography (*Kavir*). In 1977 he was allowed to leave Iran, but died soon after arriving in England, at the age of 44. His sudden and unexpected death was widely assumed to be the work of SAVAK agents, but more probably was caused by a heart attack.

However that may be, Shari'ati did not live to see the revolution or to spell out the political implications of his ideas. But his influence on the revolution was enormous, perhaps second only to that of Khomeini. Westerners who read his works often find them rather disappointing — obscure in places, inconsistent in others, superficial and schematic at times and full of stale *idées reçues* about non-Muslim societies, religions and writers.[11] But the students and young educated Iranians who attended his lectures were evidently spellbound. He must have been a great orator, but he was more than that, for his ideas and charisma carried far beyond the ranks of those who were able to hear him speak. His ideas had an emotional power which derived above all from the fact that they appeared at once authentically Islamic and authentically modern. To young people whose education had disorientated them with half-understood Western ideas he restored confidence in their own culture and their own religion. He, more than anyone, popularized the idea that in fighting for Islam one was not demanding a return to obscurantism but working towards genuine national liberation and enlightenment.*

How enlightened he would have turned out to be in a revolution-

---

* A good example is his 'Islamic' version of women's rights, put forward in lectures on the Prophet's daughter Fatima. He favoured women's participation in public life and strongly opposed their seclusion. But he also opposed what he saw as the Western principle of treating men and women exactly alike, the effect of which was either to turn women into sex-objects or to oblige them to sacrifice their femininity for the sake of a career. The new Muslim woman should model herself on Fatima, taking a full part in the struggles of her menfolk yet retaining her female dignity and her special position in the family.

ary situation it is hard to be sure. There was a totalitarian streak in his thought, as is suggested by the 'Platonic' passage already quoted, and by another in which he advocates 'directed' democracy:

> The government of a group which, on the basis of a revolutionary progressive programme that aims at changing individuals — their view of the world, their language, their social relations, and their level of living — and also at changing social forms in order to perfect them, has, with the above aims, an ideology, a well-defined doctrine, and a precise plan. Its aim is not that everyone by his vote or his acquiescence should be its partisan, but it is to make a society reach the level where, on the basis of this doctrine, it begins to move toward this most elevated goal and to realize its revolutionary objectives. If there are people who do not believe in this path, and whose conduct leads to a stagnation or corruption of society, and if there are some who abuse with their own power, with their own money, this liberty, and if there are social formations and traditions, which keep men in this stagnation, we must suppress these traditions, condemn these ways of thinking, and save society from its own fossilized moulds, by any means possible.[12]

However, it seems reasonable to assume that the 'revolutionary progressive programme' he had in mind would not have coincided exactly with the kind of changes imposed on Iran since the revolution by the *ulama* under Khomeini's leadership. The eclecticism of his thought, indeed his very ability to project Islam in terminology learnt from the West, would have earned him condemnation in the Islamic Republic. He would surely have been a dissenter, and as such would have returned sooner or later to prison or to exile.

The Mujahidin-i Khalq have been seen as a party inspired by Shari'ati's ideas. This is true in the sense that they proclaim their admiration for him and use his name and his portrait in their propaganda, and also that during the 1970s young people influenced by him must have provided one of their most abundant sources of recruitment. But, as we have already noted, the main lines of Mujahidin ideology were worked out by Ahmad Reza'i before Shari'ati began his regular lectures at the Husainiya Irshad; and the Mujahidin programme is much more explicitly socialist. Indeed, after they began military operations against the regime in 1971 the Shah and his propagandists used to refer to the Mujahidin as 'Islamic Marxists'. To this they replied: 'Of course, Marxism and Islam are not identical. Nevertheless, Islam is definitely closer to Marxism than to Pahlavism. Islam and Marxism teach the same lessons for they fight against injustice.'

In the early 1970s the Mujahidin suffered severe losses at the hands of the regime: all their original leaders were either executed or killed in shoot-outs with the police. By 1975 fifty members had been killed and many others were in prison. In spite of this the organization survived and grew, but maintaining contact between the groups in different cities, and between the leaders inside and outside prison, was difficult. There was also considerable ideological disorientation. In 1975 the majority of the leaders in Tehran who were outside jail voted to accept Marxism and declare the organization Marxist-Leninist: they had reached the conclusion that Marxism, not Islam, was the true revolutionary philosophy. Islam appealed mainly to the 'middle class' (to which, in fact, most of the Mujahidin belonged), whereas Marxism was the 'salvation of the working class'. One who accepted this line was one of the sons of Ayatollah Taleqani, who wrote to his father: 'to organize the working class, we must reject Islam, for religion refuses to accept the main dynamic force of history — that of class struggle. Of course, Islam can play a progressive role, especially in mobilizing the intelligentsia against imperialism ...'[13]

But most of the members outside Tehran rejected this change. The organization split into two groups, one Marxist the other Islamic. The Marxist group remained relatively small, because it was competing with an already well established and organized Marxist guerrilla movement, the Feda'iyan-i Khalq (People's Fedayeen). During the revolution it was the Marxist Feda'iyan and the Islamic Mujahidin which emerged as the strongest guerrilla groups and the main left-wing forces. The Feda'iyan had very strong support among the more Westernized intellectuals and salaried middle classes. They also began recruiting industrial workers, as did the pro-Moscow Tudeh party ('party of the masses' – the official communist party), which had no guerrilla forces but still had some veteran supporters left from the 1940s and early 1950s. The Islamic Mujahidin drew their members mainly from the children of the more traditional middle classes who had had a religious upbringing. Initially they seemed less well-organized than the Feda'iyan, but by 1980 they appeared stronger. Their Islamic ideology and vocabulary had a much broader popular appeal than the Feda'iyan's Marxism, and also made it harder for the new regime to attack them. Perhaps because this gave them greater self-confidence they were able to pursue a more coherent and consistent political line. While the Feda'iyan veered from position to position in a desperate effort to align themselves with 'the masses', and eventually split in 1980 on the issue whether to support the Kurdish resistance or adopt the Tudeh tactic of unconditional obedience to Khomeini, the Mujahidin stuck firmly to their line, summarized as 'emphasis upon labour as the basis of value, democratic liberties, and a stress on the full Islamic equality of men and women.'*[14]

The Mujahidin insist that they are not Marxists, but they favour a kind of workers' control socialism. In foreign policy they are not slavishly pro-Soviet, but put the emphasis on the struggle against capitalist imperialism. (For this reason they were reluctant to support the campaign against the Soviet invasion of Afghanistan, which they saw as a diversion.) According to some reports, they were initially represented in the group of students that occupied the US Embassy in November 1979, but were later excluded from it. They have consistently supported the right of Iran's national minorities to complete autonomy (but not to secession), and were the only significant non-Kurdish group to continue supporting the Kurdish resistance after the spring of 1980.

* This means, among other things, that women members of the Mujahidin are required 'to wear Islamic headdress and keep their arms covered', but the Mujahidin do not say this rule should be imposed on women in general.

344

The Mujahidin claim considerable support among the younger *ulama* (and their veneration for Ayatollah Taleqani has already been mentioned). But they are opposed to an institutionalized role for the *ulama* in the state. Thus in the March 1979 referendum they supported the proposal for an Islamic Republic (while opposing its 'class character'), but in that of December 1979 they opposed the constitution which institutionalized Khomeini's *wilayat al-faqih*. Their opposition was then made a pretext for denying their leader Mas'ud Rajavi—a charismatic figure who might have won several million votes—the right to stand in the presidential election of January 1980. None the less, the Mujahidin supported President Bani-Sadr in his struggle with the Islamic Republican Party (IRP), and organized his escape from Iran in July 1981, after which Bani-Sadr named Rajavi prime minister in exile. By then they had again been driven to clandestinity and resistance, and they were blamed by the regime for the explosion in Tehran which caused the deaths of seventy-two members of the IRP leadership, including Ayatollah Beheshti, on 28 June 1981.

Another group which apparently claims to be following Shari'ati's ideas, but about which very little is known, is the terrorist organization Furqān ('Salvation'), which assassinated a number of senior officials and *ulama* after the revolution. It is said to have been established in 1963 and to have had a membership of only fifty people, most of whom the government claimed to have arrested by January 1980. The group apparently rejects the infallibility, esoteric knowledge and purity of the Imams, believing they were merely inspired leaders of their time, and claims to be going back to the original Islam of the Koran and the Prophet. Otherwise, it echoes Shari'ati mainly in its scathing hostility to the *ulama*, whose political role it violently opposes. One of its first victims was the first post-revolution chief of staff of the army, Major General Muhammad Vali Qaranah'ī, who was reported to have had close ties with Shari'ati's particular *bête noire* among the *ulama*, Ayatollah Milani of Mashhad. The reason given by the group for killing him in April 1979 was, however, his role in the destruction of the Kurdish resistance movement in Iraq when the Shah suddenly withdrew his support for it and made a deal with Iraq's Ba'thist regime. Shortly afterwards, on 1 May 1979, Furqan assassinated Ayatollah Mortezā Motahharī, a former pupil of Khomeini's and a prominent member of the Revolutionary Council. Motahhari had been one of the founders of the Husainiya Irshad, but withdrew from it before it was closed down, and criticized Shari'ati for making it too political.[15]

Yet another group influenced by Shari'ati was the 'Movement of Fighting Muslims' led by Dr Habibollah Peyman, who also edited the review *Umma*. This movement started in 1977 and its ideas too have been described (not by the Shah but by a secular left-wing intellectual, speaking after the revolution) as 'tinged with a sort of Islamic Marxism'. The same source described Peyman as 'much more rigid and *fascisant**　than the Mujahidin'. His movement was not well known outside university circles, but it did have a certain influence among students, including some of those who occupied the American embassy.† Dr Peyman himself was a frequent visitor to the embassy (or 'nest of spies', as it was known), at any rate in the early months of the occupation.

BANI-SADR

Like those of Shari'ati, the ideas of Abol-Hasan Bani-Sadr, Iran's first President of the Republic, result from an attempt to synthesize Iranian Shi'ism with post-Marxist Parisian *tiers-mondisme* (third-worldism). Like Shari'ati, Bani-Sadr was born into a religious family in 1933–34: his father and grandfather were ayatollahs from Hamadan, in western Iran. Like Shari'ati he attended a modern university rather than a traditional seminary, and went on to study in Paris after incurring the regime's displeasure by his support of the National Front. Like him too, he was much influenced by

---

*Tending towards fascism.

† According to one of these students, 'Islam is very similar to socialism. But Islam is much more complete.' ('Mary', interviewed by Christos P. Ioannides, *The Washington Quarterly*, summer 1980.)

people he knew and events he witnessed while there. But whereas Shari'ati was a specialist in Persian language and literature who later became a religious sociologist, Bani-Sadr started by studying theology and sociology and later took up economics. He was first exposed to French Marxism in the person of the sociologist Paul Vieille, whom he met at Tehran University, and with whom in France he later published a collection of essays on Iran entitled *Pétrole et Violence*. He did not go to Paris until the mid-1960s, so that it was the 'events' of May 1968 (the student movement and general strike) that affected him directly, rather than the Algerian war; and once in France he stayed there until the revolution, constantly postponing the completion of his doctoral thesis so as to avoid expulsion by the French authorities for his political activity. Among the exiled student leaders opposed to the Shah, Bani-Sadr was known as a passionately earnest Muslim obsessed with a somewhat obscure doctrine of Islamic politics and economics. From 1972 onwards he was in direct contact with Ayatollah Khomeini in Iraq.

The central concept in Bani-Sadr's thought, as in that of Taleqani and of Ahmad Reza'i, is *tawhid*: divine unity, which is reflected in the unity of creation, and should be reflected in human society. 'The principle of unity involves the negation of every sort of economic, political, ideological or other bastion in which power can be concentrated.' This leads him to a radical reinterpretation of the doctrine of imamate. Not only can no one claim any participation in God's unity: no one can be God's representative, because this would set him apart from others and infringe the unity of society. No leader must be adored. All power coming from men is condemned, even if it tries to justify itself by religion. 'Everyone is responsible for all; everyone is imam and guide of all.' Any belief used for domination is an opiate of the people:

> But would not Islam become an opiate if one made of it an instrument of the system? Since Islam is a religion that rests on universal laws and one nature, and which envisages liberation from the traps of these perpetual realities, it is not possible for it to become the opiate of the masses, unless one makes of it

a scourge, as the present regime [1975] has institutionalized it and made it a scourge.

Hence, in an Islamic government, belief must not be an instrument of government, but the government must be an instrument of Islamic belief. And this necessitates guarantees that it be the belief that governs.[16]

Read in 1981, this passage takes on a rather grim irony. Much more than Shari'ati, Bani-Sadr seems to set an intellectual distance between himself and the doctrinal presuppositions of Khomeini's *wilayat al-faqih*. (He also interprets *jihad* as a 'permanent revolution' in which there can be no *marja-i taqlid*, no unchallengeable model or leader: everyone must discover himself the cause for which he is fighting.) Yet in 1979 and 1980 he was frequently to describe himself as Khomeini's spiritual son, and was to accept office under a constitution in which the President and everyone else is clearly subordinate to the *faqih*'s authority. Like many others caught up in the revolution, he was unwilling — until too late — to see the *ulama* as an institution imposing its rule. He saw them, including and perhaps especially Khomeini, simply as spokesmen and executors of the popular will. 'Thanks to the clergy,' he told a French journalist in 1979, 'the people is intervening directly in the revolution. The clergy acts as the people's interpreter.'[17] So saying, he condemned himself in advance to defeat in the battle he was to fight with the *ulama*, or at least their best organized political faction, in 1980–81. His fate was sealed when the *faqih*, predictably even if after much procrastination, came down on the *ulama*'s side.

As Yann Richard, a leading French authority on Iranian Shi'ism, has noted, there is an unresolved contradiction in Bani-Sadr's thought between his Parisian passion for 'organized spontaneity' and his determination to use traditional Shi'ite theological categories even in social and economic analysis. 'But it is also thanks to these tendencies that he attracts numerous partisans, who are trying to reconcile a desire for liberty with the rigours of Islamic law.'[18]

348

TRADITIONALISM TRIUMPHANT

When Khomeini used to address the faithful from his house in Qom, during the spring and summer of 1979, some of them noticed a portrait prominently displayed on the wall behind him: that of Navvab Safavi (1923–56), the founder and leader of the Fida'iyan-i Islam. It is likely that the ayatollah had been connected with this group of Muslim extremists (see pp. 312–13) since the 1940s. Certainly he shared their antipathy to Ahmad Kasravi, the rationalist writer whom they killed in 1946. In fact, though disapproved of by conservatives like Borujerdi who wanted to keep a respectable distance between religion and politics, the Fida'iyan-i Islam seem to have had the secret sympathy of many of the more activist *ulama*, including some who did not share their hostility to Mosaddeq: Taleqani, for instance, was arrested after the 1953 coup for having hidden Safavi at his home.* After that, like their friends the Muslim Brothers in Egypt at the same period, they were hunted down and put out of business for a time by the forces of the regime.

They re-surfaced in 1965 to kill another of the Shah's prime ministers, Ali Mansur, but then were not heard of until June 1979 when Ayatollah Sadeq Khalkhali announced that he was their leader and that they would assassinate members of the Shah's family and other enemies of the revolution who had taken refuge abroad.

Khalkhali, known as 'the cat-strangler' in Iran because he had allegedly once been confined in a mental asylum in that capacity, won worldwide notoriety during the revolution as a kind of Islamic Fouquier-Tinville. As self-appointed head of the Revolutionary Court he boasted, often in a disconcerting high-pitched giggle, of having sent hundreds to their death — drug-peddlers as well as agents of the old régime. Initially the régime appeared embarrassed by this and tried from time to time to deny that he held any official position. But in August 1979, when Khomeini approved a decision

---

* Safavi escaped to Egypt, where he appeared in January 1954 at a rally of the Muslim Brothers (who were just about to be outlawed by Nasser) and announced 'I killed Razmara.' See Richard P. Mitchell, *The Society of the Muslim Brothers* (London, 1969), p. 126.

to seek a military solution of the Kurdish problem, he found it appropriate to send Khalkhali to Kurdistan as special prosecutor. Since then Khalkhali has continued to present himself whenever spectacular revolutionary 'justice' has been called for, and though as a political figure he is not taken seriously, the other ayatollahs have not seen fit to interfere with him. It appears that his notion of 'Islamic justice', in which such decadent Western institutions as defence counsel or cross-examination of witnesses, let alone appeal courts, are regarded as quite superfluous, is also pretty much theirs. Other revolutionary judges have been just as implacably expeditive, if less exhibitionist; and presiding over, if not controlling, the whole judicial machinery was, until his death in June 1981, the most powerful man in the country after Khomeini himself: Ayatollah Sayyid Muhammad Beheshtī.

Of all the Islamic revolutionary leaders, Beheshti was the most enigmatic. Regarded as something of a social reformer in the early 1960s, he was married to the sister of a high official in the Shah's court, and was appointed Friday prayer-leader for the Shi'ite community in Hamburg, West Germany — a position which placed him in close contact both with the Iranian students there (many of whom were actively opposed to the Shah's regime) and with the Iranian officials who kept an eye on them. He was also, secretly, in touch with Khomeini and with the *ulama* opposed to the Shah inside Iran, and when the revolution came he evidently enjoyed Khomeini's full confidence. In the winter of 1978–79 he is believed to have negotiated on Khomeini's behalf with the American and other foreign embassies in Tehran. He spoke Arabic, German and English, and understood French. Interviewers found him invariably cool and polite. But he did not go out of his way to seek publicity, preferring to concentrate on building a political party — the IRP — which the *ulama* would control and which would be dedicated to upholding their principles.

Beheshti had nothing of the fanatic about his outward appearance; if anything, he seemed a 'man of the world'. A secular-minded judge, who had to deal with him in his capacity as Minister of Justice, told me he had doubts whether Beheshti took Islam seriously at all. In this judge's view (which was widely shared in Tehran in 1980), Beheshti was a supreme opportunist, using Islam with Machiavellian cunning to gather power for himself. There were signs of that, certainly, in the way he exploited the issue of the American hostages to undermine the position of President Bani-Sadr, but then allowed his own supporters to negotiate a distinctly inglorious solution (from Iran's point of view) once they were firmly in control of the government; and it appeared likely that at the time of his death he was preparing to do the same with the war against Iraq, having wrested control of the armed forces from Bani-Sadr and finally ousted him from the presidency. One wonders whether some of the excesses of 'Islamic justice' might not also have been modified in time if Beheshti had gained full control of the state, as he seemed to be on his way to doing.

However that may be, the faction of the *ulama* with which he allied himself, and whose policies were therefore adopted by his party, was the one that took Khomeini's revolutionary traditionalism most literally and was most eager to put it into practice. And the instrument by which these *ulama* asserted their control was a kind of organized mob rule. When the army barracks were opened in the days immediately following the revolution, some of the weapons were taken by the already organized left-wing guerrilla groups. But more fell into the hands of an improvised militia, whose members came from poorer homes and had little or no education. For this militia, at first known as the Mujahidin-i Inqilab-i Islam (Mujahidin of the Islamic Revolution, not to be confused with the Mujahidin-i Khalq), the mosques were arms depots and the *mullahs* commanders. The radio in those first days constantly urged people with arms in their possession to turn them in to the mosques. Soon, the militia was reorganized with a clearer command structure under the name of Pasdaran-i Inqilab (Revolutionary Guards). Although its discipline was less than perfect, it benefited from a self-confidence which the regular police and armed forces totally lacked in the revolutionary atmosphere. Its top command structure was closely integrated with that of the Islamic Republican Party. Beyond this semi-regular force were the mobs of uneducated, unemployed people who could be mustered for specific actions such as breaking up a demonstration or smashing the offices of an opposition party or newspaper. These were known as *hizbollahis*, from their slogan *'la hizb ila hizbollah'* — 'no party but God's party'. In practice they acted as auxiliaries of the IRP.

The result was that by 1981 Iran had become a fearsome and depressing place, apparently determined to live up to all the most negative Western stereotypes about Islam. Music is banned. The sexes are rigorously segregated, and women obliged to cover everything but their faces in public. Homosexuals are sent to the firing-squad and adulterers stoned to death. In June 1981 a Bill was submitted for approval to the Majlis by the prime minister — and seemed certain to pass — which would allow the families of murdered or injured people to inflict exactly identical injuries on the criminal by way of vengeance. The family would have to purchase this privilege by paying a blood-wit to a male murderer before executing him, for the benefit of his dependents, but a female murderer, being considered economically a consumer rather than a producer, could be killed for free. In the case of injuries, the width, length and depth of the avenging wound must be identical to those of the original wound, except that the depth of skull wounds need not be measured! And so on.[19] At the same period teenage girls belonging to the Mujahidin-i Khalq were being executed for taking part in demonstrations against the dismissal of President Bani-Sadr. 'By the Islamic canon,' explained the judge who sentenced them, at a press conference, 'a nine-year-old girl is mature.'[20] The Baha'i religion, regarded as a form of collective apostasy from Islam, has been banned and many of its adherents have been killed.

Such, in the summer of 1981, was the outcome of Iran's 'Islamic revolution'. Perhaps not the final outcome, for clearly by now very many Iranians were deeply disillusioned and unwilling to recognize what had happened as an authentic application of Islam. Yet at the same time its popular base should not be underestimated. The uneducated, newly urbanized masses are not particularly interested in liberal or modernist interpretations of Islam. The Shi'ism to which they are attached is essentially a traditional Shi'ism. If there is an aspect of modernism which appeals to them it is the identification of Islam with their grievances as members of a deprived, 'disinherited' social stratum — and it is this aspect which Khomeini and the IRP have recuperated, at least in their rhetoric, astutely combining it with 'anti-imperialism' (alias traditional xenophobia). They can play on a genuine class feeling by portraying Bani-Sadr, the Mujahidin, and other such people, as representatives of privileged classes influenced by foreign ideas — just as Stalinists have often successfully denigrated Trotskyist and new-left ideas as the pipe-dreams of bourgeois intellectuals. In both cases the portrayal is effective because it is largely accurate. Also — and here the parallel with Stalinism is relevant, too — it is not *the whole* of the middle class that has been alienated. Just as the French Communist party, for instance, has always been able to mobilize significant groups of teachers, doctors, engineers, technicians, civil servants and other white-collar workers, often themselves of working-class origin, who accept both the principle of working-class hegemony and the party apparatus as representative of the working class, so the IRP mobilized similar groups who accept Islam as a total philosophy of life and accept the *ulama* as its exclusive interpreters. Such people — engineers, physicians, teachers — formed 'religious societies' during the 1970s in the universities, and even among homesick Iranians working abroad — societies which were not devoted to discussing Shari'ati's ideas but simply to affirming and practising a traditional Shi'ite faith.[21] Muhammad Ali Raja'i, the mathematics teacher who became prime minister in 1980 and president of the Republic in 1981, was a representative of this class. (He was assassinated on 30 August 1981, after only six weeks in office.)

A Revolution for Export?

Like most of the Islamic movements described in this book, the Iranian revolution had an ambivalent relationship to nationalism. It undoubtedly was, for many who took part in it, a nationalist revolution. The Shah, of course, had presented himself as an Iranian nationalist. But the effect of that was not to discredit nationalism with his opponents, because they did not take his nationalist rhetoric seriously. They saw in it, rightly or wrongly, no more than a transparent cover for a policy of total subservience to the West, and specifically to the United States. They knew that the CIA had helped him overthrow Mosaddeq in 1953 and that he had embarked on his 'white revolution' mainly thanks to American pressure in 1962. They saw their country as occupied by thousands of American technicians, military and civilian, who were usually paid much higher salaries than the Iranians working with them. They believed the Shah was expanding oil production to meet Western needs, and then letting the West take back its dollars in return for weapons and other Western goods and services which Iran either did not need or could not absorb. Even the instruments of torture used by SAVAK were imported from the West, and there was known to be co-operation between SAVAK and Western intelligence services. In short, Iran was seen as a colony under American occupation and the Shah as a puppet dictator used by the United States to terrorize Iranians into submission. The revolution was therefore, as much as anything, a nationalist revolt against foreign domination. 'We are Iranian,' was the simple answer I got when I asked a wounded demonstrator how he had the courage to stand unarmed before the bullets of the Shah's troops; and I shall never forget the joy of my Iranian hosts, on the night of the revolution's triumph, when the television closed down with what they considered the authentic national anthem, instead of the 'imperial' hymn which the Shah had imposed in its place.

Yet the Islamic ideology of the revolution was not nationalist. Although Shi'ism has played its part in forging Iran's national identity, the revolution did not attempt to claim Shi'ism as something special to Iran. There was no need to do this because the revolution was not a revolt of Iranians against Arabs, nor of Shi'ites against Sunnis. It was essentially a revolt of Iranian Muslims against non-Muslim foreigners. Its leaders wanted to emphasize their solidarity with other Muslims against non-Muslim domination. One of their strong grievances against the Shah was his ill-disguised alliance with Israel, the oppressor of Muslim Palestinians.

The ideology was, of course, unmistakably Shi'ite. The Shah was 'the new Yazid' and the revolutionaries, facing death in the streets, were re-enacting the martyrdom of Husain. If one asked what would be the policies of the Islamic government, one was offered the text of a letter written by Ali as caliph to one of his provincial governors. Yet the emphasis was not on Shi'ism as against Sunnism, but on 'Islam' as such. (One should remember that Ali is revered by Sunnis too, as one of the four 'orthodox' caliphs, and that Sunni historiography also presents the Umayyads in a bad light, following the tradition established by their victorious rivals, the Abbasids. The names of Hasan and Husain are popular throughout the Sunni world, and the present kings of Morocco and Jordan — who happen to bear those names — both claim descent from Ali, though both are followers of Sunni Islam. The only aspect of Shi'ite hagiography which Sunnis find really offensive is the denigration of the first three caliphs — Abu Bakr, Umar and Uthman. This was not emphasized in the Iranian revolution.) The Arab conquest of Iran in the seventh century AD was not evoked as an invasion, but as the liberation of Iran by Islam from the Sassanian aristocracy. Shi'ism was presented not as 'Iranian Islam' but as true Islam, valid for all believers. Sunnis and Shi'ites alike were called on to join hands against Western domination and rebuild the authentic *umma*.[22]

This message had an enormous impact throughout the Muslim world. For the first time since Nasser in 1956 a Muslim nation successfully defied, humiliated and inflicted material damage on the interests of a major Western power. A civilian and largely unarmed movement, acting in the name of Islam, had mobilized an entire nation and overthrown the best-armed dictatorship in the Third World. Where umpteen bright young army officers spouting nationalist rhetoric had failed, an aged ayatollah, armed only with the Koran, had succeeded. Those — like the Muslim Brothers, or Jama'at-i Islami, or even Necmettin Erbakan — who had always said that Islam was the answer to the political problems of Muslim societies, were triumphant. Those who had hitherto put their faith in revolution, but had been looking either for a national revolution or for a proletarian one, suddenly discovered, or rediscovered, the interest of Islam. Yasser Arafat rushed to Tehran to embrace Khomeini and be illumined by his reflected glory.* The Lebanese cartoonist Mahmud Kahil captured the mood in the Arab world brilliantly with a drawing that showed Arafat leaping from the tip of the (hammer-and-) sickle to the tip of the Crescent, symbol of Islam. Even Muslims who were non-political, or had no definite political affiliation, felt renewed confidence in the political relevance of Islam, in the capacity of the Muslim world to regain its economic and cultural as well as political independence and to assert itself as a force in world affairs. Muslim rulers, too, were conscious of this, and conscious that their peoples expected it. Institutions like the Islamic Conference were taken more seriously, both by Muslims and by non-Muslim observers.

But when Khomeini and his supporters spoke of Islamic solidarity, they were not interested simply in making Muslims around the world feel better, and still less in enabling Muslim rulers to strike grand Islamic postures. 'The conferences which are held in the name of Islam,' Khomeini once said, 'in reality do not have any Islamic objective.' After all the Shah and his ministers used to take part in such conferences, and many of the other Muslim rulers were little better than the Shah in Khomeini's eyes. Which of them was not exploiting and oppressing his subjects? Which was not importing or tolerating foreign ideas and customs contrary to Islam? Which was genuinely enforcing the Shari'a? It must not be thought that the Saudi royal family would be exempt from these strictures. Quite apart from the specific Shi'ite grievances against Wahhabis (the 'camel-herding savages

* The popular welcome he received in Iran was quite genuine. Many Iranians were grateful to the PLO for the training given to Iranian guerrilla fighters in Palestinian resistance camps. The Mujahidin and other organizations used photographs of their leaders with Arafat in their publicity material.

of Najd' who had destroyed the tomb of Husain in 1802), the Saudi regime was guilty of many of the same sins as the Shah. It was the close ally of the United States, pumping oil to suit the West's convenience and squandering the oil revenue on weapons, unnecessary or unrealistic development projects, Western consumer goods and un-Islamic high living in the casinos and nightclubs of Europe and America. It claimed to be the protector of the Arab people and the Muslim holy places, yet did nothing in practice to help the Palestinians or liberate Jerusalem and continued, on the contrary, to help the United States which was the main financier and arms-supplier of Israel. Moreover, was not monarchy itself a form of government contrary to Islam?

Like the French revolution of 1789 and the Russian revolution of 1917, the Iranian revolution was based on principles of universal applicability, and implicitly threatened all the regimes in the neighbourhood, if not in the whole world. Revolutionary France declared war on the crowned heads of Europe, proclaiming *'guerre aux châteaux, paix aux chaumières.'** Bolshevik Russia believed it had broken the imperialist chain at its weakest link and was thus in the vanguard of a world proletarian revolution: the Comintern as originally conceived was a world communist party to provide this world revolution with united and disciplined leadership. Likewise the Islamic revolutionaries of Iran, and their supporters elsewhere, did not see their revolution as confined to Iran. Iran was the vanguard or nucleus around which the Islamic *umma* could be reconstructed as successive Muslim countries threw off their chains and restored authentic Islamic government. As Mr Kalim Siddiqui of the Muslim Institute in London wrote, in a preface to a translation of the Iranian draft constitution: 'Iran is no longer a nation-State but merely a geographical area of the *Ummah*. It would appear that all the prerequisites for the creation of a model society of Islam now exist in Iran. The borders of Iran now are in fact the borders of the nation-States that surround it. Islam itself has no borders.'

* War to the château, peace to the cottage.

357

So interpreted, the Iranian revolution was a boost not for just any Islam but for a specific, revolutionary interpretation of Islam, and therefore a threat to the status quo in the rest of the Muslim world and the regimes in power. The Muslim Brotherhood in Egypt or Syria might draw encouragement from it but only at the price of putting a certain distance between themselves and the regimes to which they had previously looked for inspiration and support, especially of course that of Saudi Arabia.

The rulers of Muslim countries, and especially of those in Iran's neighbourhood, were thus put on the defensive. Essentially there were two ways they could react. Either they could reject the Iranian model as a distortion of Islam, or they could try to deflect Iranian criticism by expressing support for the revolution and cultivating good relations with the new regime. In either case they were liable to feel that a greater emphasis on Islam (however interpreted) in their own policies would be a useful prophylactic. No one would want to repeat the Shah's mistake of underrating Islam as a political factor.

The second alternative—minimize trouble by having good relations with the new regime—was most rulers' instinctive first preference. The only one who unhesitatingly chose the other was President Sadat of Egypt. He played host to the Shah on the first stage of his exiled wandering, braving demonstrations from leftists, Nasserists and Islamic militants. Soon thereafter he took to denouncing Khomeini in the most robust fashion, proclaiming him a madman and asserting that the revolution had nothing to do with Islam. In March 1980 the Shah, by then *persona non grata* in Mexico, the United States and Panama, returned to Egypt where Sadat declared him and his family welcome to stay as long as they liked. (In fact the Shah died in Egypt four months later.)

Sadat's motives can be sought on several levels. No doubt he felt genuine friendship, or at least compassion, for the Shah. (The thought 'there but for the grace of God go I' must surely have crossed his mind!) Certainly he was anxious to impress Western, and especially American public opinion, and to offer a more attractive image of Islam than the one Iran was currently giving.

But he may also have felt he had little to lose. The Iranian revolution, with its uncompromising pro-Palestinian fervour, occurred between the Camp David agreement and the Egyptian–Israeli peace treaty. Sadat had committed himself to a unilateral peace with Israel and knew that he could expect nothing but brickbats from revolutionary Iran and her sympathizers in Egypt and the Arab world. He had no chance of posing as a friend of Islam, Iranian style. Better to meet the challenge head on and throw it back at his Egyptian opponents: was the Iranian model one they seriously wanted Egypt to follow?

The Saudi rulers, although they had always been irritated by the Shah's pretensions to act as policeman and protector of the Persian Gulf and Arabian peninsula (and in 1973–77 also by his hawkishness on oil prices), were profoundly upset by the revolution and made little attempt to conceal it. They complained especially about what they saw as American failure to support an important ally in a crisis. Unlike Sadat, however, they did not go out of their way to provoke the new regime. That is not their style. In spite of this they found themselves on the receiving end of a constant barrage of hostile propaganda on Radio Tehran's Arabic service, and from time to time they have been moved to reply. But in general their official response has been to ignore Iran while improving their relations with other countries in the region, particularly Iraq. When Iraq went to war with Iran in September 1980 it was generally assumed that Saudi Arabia had given her the green light, but the Saudis officially declared their neutrality. The other Arab Gulf states have on the whole followed the same line.

The problem presented by the revolution for most of these states is not simply one of Islamic radicalism. In the case of Bahrain there is a potential threat of actual annexation. Bahrain, which is an island-state on the Arab side of the Persian Gulf, has a substantial Persian-speaking population and used to be claimed by Iran as rightfully part of its territory. The Shah's decision to recognize its independence in 1971 was contested by some Iranian nationalists, and revolutionary leaders have hinted from time to time that this decision might not be regarded as valid. But the more immediate problem, for Bahrain as for the neighbouring states, is the effect of the revolution on the attitudes of the local Shi'ite population. Shi'ites are to be found in significant numbers in the United Arab Emirates, Qatar, Bahrain, eastern Saudi Arabia, Kuwait and above all in Iraq where they are the majority of the population. The rulers of these states are all Sunni. The Iranian revolution is not against them *qua* Sunnis, but it is against them *qua* rulers, and it is a Shi'ite revolution; and the Shi'ites in these Arab states do on the whole feel themselves to be an underdog community. The dangers are obvious, and there were in fact Shi'ite disturbances in several Gulf states during 1979 and 1980, the most serious being those in Qatif and other towns of Saudi Arabia's oil-producing eastern province in the month of Muharram, AH 1400 (November-December 1979), which happened to coincide with the seizure of the Holy Mosque in Mecca by a quite different group of Islamic radicals. (See Chapter 6.)

It was, however, the Ba'thist regime in Iraq which very quickly emerged as the real enemy of the new Iranian regime. The Shi'ites of Iraq, although a majority of the population,* were traditionally an underdog community and a recruiting ground for opposition parties. In the 1940s and 1950s they provided a high proportion of the members and supporters of the Iraqi Communist Party, which emerged as a powerful force during the revolution of 1958. But in 1963 army officers belonging to the Ba'th party, themselves mainly Sunni, seized power and instigated a massacre of Communist Party cadres. The ensuing military regime of General Abdul-Salām Ārif (1963–66) had a pronounced Sunni character. After Arif's death in an air-crash, followed by two years of drift under his brother Abdul-Rahman, the Ba'thists again seized power, this time determined to establish full and permanent control of the state and to stamp the country indelibly with their secular brand of Arab

---

* According to most estimates. They are certainly a majority of the Arabs. The Sunni community includes Kurds and Turkish-speakers as well as Arabs.

nationalism. For help in doing this they looked initially to the Soviet Union, with which they signed a friendship treaty in 1972. Anxious to maintain their influence in this strategically located oil-producing state, especially at a time when they were losing influence elsewhere in the Arab world (Egypt, Sudan), the Soviet leaders instructed the Iraqi Communist Party, or what was left of it, to accept the Ba'th party's leading role and to join the government in a token capacity where it had to support policies over whose formulation it had no real influence. In spite of this, apparently suspecting the communists were secretly infiltrating the armed forces, and feeling strong enough by then to dispense with Soviet support, the Ba'th broke with the communists in 1978–79 and again began to arrest and execute their members, no less than three thousand of whom fled into exile in 1979.

Many of the Shi'ite *ulama* therefore felt the need to involve themselves in politics to contest the spread both of secular ideas promoted by the Communist Party and of secular institutions promoted by the state, especially under the Ba'th regime from 1968 onwards; while the impoverished Shi'ite masses, especially in the slums of the capital, Baghdad, found themselves deprived of the Communist Party as an effective spokesman for their grievances and were therefore ready to follow the *ulama*'s lead. The result has been the growth during the 1970s of militant opposition movements with a specifically Shi'ite religious ideology and leadership, which of course received a boost from the success of the Iranian revolution in 1979.

The main movement of this type, at least until 1979, was *al-Da'wa al-Islāmiya* ('the Islamic Call'), founded in 1968–69 and said to have had the blessing of Ayatollah Muhsin al-Hakīm, who was regarded by Iraqis as the senior *marja-i taqlid* of the Shi'ite world — and had indeed been the Shah's candidate to succeed Borujerdi as *marja-yi mutlaq*, or sole source of imitation, though this had not been accepted by most of the Iranian *ulama*.* Certainly Hakim protested in 1969 about the treatment of the Shi'ite *ulama*

* The Shah presumably thought that Hakim, as an Iraqi Arab, was less likely to interfere in Iranian politics than any of the Iranian candidates for the succession.

in the shrine cities by the Ba'thist regime, and condemned the government officials involved as 'infidels'. He himself was harassed, or at least kept under close surveillance, by the regime during that year, and his son Sayyid Mahdi al-Hakim, who was accused by the government of 'spying on behalf of the CIA' and 'conspiring to overthrow the existing régime', was associated with the Da'wa movement from the start. The Da'wa's initial support, however, came mainly from younger and lower-ranking *ulama* in the shrine cities. None of the three *maraji-i taqlid* remaining in Iraq after Muhsin al-Hakim's death in 1970 — Khomeini, his fellow-Iranian Abūl-Qāsim al-Khū'ī (regarded as Hakim's successor, but non-political) and the Iraqi Muhammad Bāqir al-Sadr — was associated with it.*

In the mid-1970s the lower Euphrates Valley, where much of Iraq's Shi'ite population lives, was badly affected by drought after the Syrian Ba'thist regime, in the course of a bitter quarrel with its Iraqi rival,† reduced the flow of the river Euphrates through the newly built Syrian dam at Tabqa. Hundreds of thousands of peasants were ruined by the loss of their fruit orchards and rice crops. Many of them expressed their misery in the annual processions from Najaf to Karbala, commemorating the Imam Husain's martyrdom, which the Da'wa used as opportunities to spread its ideas and gain recruits. In 1974 the processions broke into angry political protest, and in 1977 there were much worse riots when the police attempted to interfere with the processions halfway between the two holy cities. On both occasions the Ba'thist leader, Saddām Husain, reacted with his customary firmness and vigour: five members of Da'wa were executed in 1974, and eight other Shi'ites in 1977.‡ His regime had no difficulty in suppressing the disturbances, but clearly it could not fail to be alarmed by the

* To begin with, in fact, it had some support from the Shah, who at that time was anxious to get rid of the Iraqi Ba'th regime.

† The Iraqi wing of the Ba'th party has never accepted the Syrian coup d'état of 1966. It continued to support the founder of the party, Michel Aflaq, who took up residence in Baghdad after the party returned to power there in 1968.

‡ These were executions officially announced. Opposition sources reported a much more extensive repression.

implications of the Iranian revolution and the role which the Shi'ite *ulama* played in it.

The revolution caught the Iraqi regime on the wrong foot. Having been bitterly hostile to the Shah and actively fomented opposition to him throughout the early 1970s, in 1975 Saddam Husain had done a deal with him under which the Shah withdrew his support for the Kurdish resistance to Ba'thist rule in northern Iraq, while Iraq recognized Iranian sovereignty over the eastern half of the Shatt al-Arab waterway (hitherto in dispute) and undertook to give no further support to 'subversion' (i.e. opposition movements) in Iran. This live-and-let-live arrangement worked well except that Khomeini, still resident in Najaf, was able to use the constant flow of pilgrims and other visitors to communicate with his followers in Iran, to whom he sent fiery denunciations of the Shah recorded on cassettes. At the beginning of October 1978, when events in Iran were already beyond the Shah's control, the Iraqi government, acceding to a request from the Iranian government that it respect the terms of the 1975 agreement, expelled Khomeini from its territory. This proved a disastrous mistake for the Shah, and a serious one for Saddam Husain. Khomeini went to France, where his access to world news media, and thereby to the Iranian public, was very much easier than it had been in Iraq. Four months later the Iraqi government, like all others that had had close relations with the Shah, faced a revolutionary regime in Iran that had every reason to regard it as hostile.

Without pretending to any enthusiasm about the revolution, Iraq at first took the line that it was an internal Iranian affair and that it wished to maintain good-neighbourly relations based on mutual non-interference. But it quickly became apparent that the nature of the revolutionary regime would not permit that. Iranian expressions of solidarity with suffering Muslims in other countries, and calls for the overthrow of other corrupt and un-Islamic regimes, were more and more obviously directed at Iraq. In Iraq itself, many of the Shi'ites were excited and encouraged by Iran's example. Attention turned to Iraq's most learned native ayatollah, Sayyid Muhammad Baqir al-Sadr, who although not until then connected with any political organization, was known to be in broad agreement with Khomeini on the political relevance of Islam and the political responsibilities of the *mujtahids*. He had written books on philosophy, on Islamic economics and on non-usurious banking, and was well known and loved by the common people. His Iraqi admirers, indeed, regarded him as superior to Khomeini both intellectually and in his personality: he was said to be less emotional and impulsive, and more enlightened.

Baqir al-Sadr wrote that in an Islamic state incomes should be closely related to effort and need. No one should be able to make money simply by hoarding goods or specie. Money should not feed on itself: it should revert to its 'natural' role as a medium of exchange. Banks, instead of being places for individuals to accumulate capital, should be instruments for enriching the community as a whole. Monopolies, whether of labour (trade unions) or of commodities (big business), must be fought in every area of economic life because they resulted in artificially high prices. The state should intervene in the economy to break up concentrations of capital, to prevent waste and extravagance, and to ensure that everyone received a reasonable minimum of material comfort. There should be free education and health services for all, and one fifth of the country's oil income should be devoted to social security and low-cost housing.

Inspired by these ideas, a new organization emerged in Baghdad in 1979, composed of graduates from modern schools and colleges and committed to bold and violent action against the Ba'thist regime. These were the Mujahidin — apparently unconnected with the Iranian Mujahidin-i Khalq, and less socialistic than them. They have been described as close 'in temper' to Abol-Hasan Bani-Sadr. Despite their reverence for Ayatollah Baqir al-Sadr they do not favour an institutional role for the *ulama* in politics and have blamed the Iranian *ulama* for the difficulties which the Iranian revolution has encountered.

In June 1979 Saddam Husain ordered the arrest of Ayatollah Baqir al-Sadr, now dubbed by Radio Tehran's Arabic service 'the Khomeini of Iraq'. Protest demonstrations in the Shi'ite township of al-Thawra ('Revolution'), which contains Baghdad's worst slums and one quarter of its total population, were violently suppressed, though Ayatollah Sadr remained under house arrest at his home in Najaf. In July Saddam, who was formally only Vice-President, although well known to be the 'strongman' of the regime, used the crisis to persuade President Hasan al-Bakr, who had long been in poor health, to step down and let him gather all the reins of power in his own hands. This was followed in August by a ruthless purge of all his opponents or potential opponents in the party and the armed forces. Twenty-one high-ranking Ba'thists, including four members of the top policy-making body, the Revolutionary Command Council, were executed for participation in an alleged pro-Syrian conspiracy. Although relations with Syria were the main issue in this split, it is said to have been precipitated by disagreements about the anti-Shi'ite repression.

In Europe a press release attacking Saddam's dictatorship was issued by an 'Islamic Liberation Movement of Iraq' which claimed to have been formed earlier in the year by the fusion of three un-named groups and to have Ayatollah Sadr as its leader. In Iraq itself both Da'wa and Mujahidin now took to guerrilla tactics against the regime. A series of grenade attacks on police posts and Ba'th party offices in and around Baghdad culminated, in April 1980, in an attempt on the life of Tariq Aziz, one of Saddam Husain's closest associates. Saddam responded with a wave of terror against the Shi'ite opposition, even harsher than that which had struck the communists a year earlier. Ayatollah Baqir Sadr and his sister were seized and summarily hanged. A law was passed making anyone suspected of Da'wa membership liable to the same fate. More than 15,000 Shi'ites, most of them from families which had lived in Iraq for generations, were pronounced to be Iranians, driven to the frontier and hustled across, without even being given the chance to collect their belongings. By the end of 1980 Da'wa claimed that since 1974 'no fewer than five hundred of the best men of Iraq' had been put to death.

These events coincided with the imposition of sanctions on Iran by the United States for the continued detention of the American hostages, and were soon followed by the abortive American rescue raid. In sermons in the mosques of Iran, in posters on the walls of Tehran, and in radio programmes beamed at the Iraqi population, Saddam Husain was depicted as a butcher, his hands dripping with Muslim blood, manipulated by the United States, Britain and — however improbably — Israel. Iraq by now was giving as good as it got in this vein, with daily broadcasts in Persian calling Khomeini a child-rapist (because he had declared girls of nine and over marriageable according to Islamic law) and other choice names, to the delight of Iran's Westernized upper middle class.

Iraq, much more than Iran, matched deeds to words. General Oveysi, the Shah's military governor of Tehran, and Shahpur Bakhtiar, his last prime minister, were invited to Iraq and given radio time, and were rumoured also to be training military forces. Iraq supplied weapons and material to Kurdish guerrillas who were fighting the Tehran government. The grievances of the Arab minority in Iran's oil-producing Khuzistan province were intensively canvassed by Baghdad, and a series of assassinations and sabotage operations occurred in the oilfields. When a group of Iranian Arabs seized the Iranian embassy in London and held its staff hostage, Iraq made no attempt to conceal its support for them. On the frontier, exchanges of artillery fire became increasingly frequent.

As Iran's revolutionary turmoil continued through the summer of 1980, with executions almost daily, with the government paralysed by the conflict between President Bani-Sadr and the IRP-dominated Majlis, and with oil production and living standards both falling, Saddam Husain must have decided that a military solution to the conflict was easily attainable. Intelligence reports suggested Iran's armed forces were utterly demoralized and because of sanctions they would be unable to get spare parts for their Western-made military equipment. There was a good chance, he probably thought, that a decisive military thrust would actually bring down Khomeini's regime. Failing that, it should at least destroy his prestige among the peoples of Iraq and the Gulf, while establishing Saddam Husain as the dominant figure in the region and a desirable leader for the Arab world as a whole; and with Khuzistan and the Iranian oilfields in his hands, he would be able to dictate the terms of peace. The Saudis must have been consulted and have given their approval; and it is likely that Saddam received some assurance, perhaps indirectly, of America's benevolent neutrality.*

On 17 September Saddam Husain formally abrogated his 1975 treaty with Iran. 'The ruling clique in Iran,' he declared, 'persists in using the face of religion to foment sedition and division among the ranks of the Arab nation despite the difficult circumstances through which the Arab nation is passing. The face of religion is only a mask to cover Persian racism and a buried resentment for the Arabs. The clique in Iran is trying to instigate fanaticism, resentment and division among the peoples of this area.' Iran predictably refused Iraqi demands for the restoration of Arab sovereignty in the Shatt al-Arab and in three small islands in the Persian Gulf which the Shah had seized in 1971. On 22 September Iraqi forces invaded Iranian territory.

The ensuing war was clearly more ideological than territorial. It was a war between nationalism and revolutionary Islam. While Iraq invoked the rights of the Arab nation against Persian racism in a religious mask, Iran presented its struggle as that of all true Muslims against corruption, tyranny and unbelief. 'It is the duty of all Muslims,' declared Khomeini, 'to struggle against the Baghdad regime and to help the Iraqi people free themselves from Ba'thist oppression.' Saddam Husain was a 'megalomaniac' and an 'agent of American imperialism' just like the Shah. Indeed, Khomeini issued a *fatwa* formally declaring him a *kafir*, or unbeliever. Ayatollah Sayyid Muhammad Baqir al-Hakim, one of the sons of Muhsin al-Hakim, was presented to the Press in Tehran in October 1980 as the person capable of 'gathering round him all the opposition forces in Iraq'.

---

* As it turned out, the war delayed negotiations for the release of the US hostages, but American policy-makers are unlikely to have foreseen this. Indications that Iran was willing to negotiate seriously emerged only days before the war began.

He has been trying to do that under an umbrella organization, Jama'at al-Ulama (the Community of Ulama), but the task is not easy, for he lacks the authority of the late Ayatollah Sadr. The Shi'ite opposition is fragmented. Besides the division between Da'wa and Mujahidin, a third group split off from Da'wa after the execution of Ayatollah Sadr: the Organization for Islamic Action, which argues for a longer-term policy of training, recruitment and organization on a pan-Islamic basis rather than an immediate and apparently suicidal confrontation with the Iraqi regime. Even within the Da'wa there is a conflict between a Khomeini school of thought and a Shari'atmadari school of thought. Beyond that, although Muhammad al-Hakim presents himself as the spokesman of 'all Iraqis' rather than Shi'ites only, the Shi'ite opposition had not, as of summer 1981, succeeded in forming a united front with other Iraqi opposition forces, except for the Kurdistan Democratic Party led by the sons of Mullah Mustafa Barzani (leader of the Kurdish nationalist movement in Iraq up to 1975) who had accepted support from the Iranian revolutionary regime even at the price of fighting against their fellow-Kurds in Iran. The other secular opposition forces, supported by Syria — the Patriotic Union of Kurdistan led by Jalal Talabani, the Nasserists, 'left-Ba'thists', and communists — have formed a united front but are not willing to let it be taken over by an 'Islamic' leadership, while the Da'wa refuses to work with it so long as it includes the Communist Party.

Nor should it be supposed that all Iraqi Shi'ites — or for that matter all Iranians — necessarily view the conflict in the light of Islamic revolutionary ideology. Although Iraq's attack on Iran was, in the main, a response to this ideology, the Iranian response to the attack was, in part at least, a reflex of national defence against a foreign aggressor. We have already noticed that the revolution in Iran mobilized nationalist feelings behind an internationalist Islamic ideology. The same has been true of the defence of revolution against Iraqi attack. Like Stalin during the Second World War, the revolutionary leaders even appealed explicitly to national sentiments, including those of their opponents, in order to maximize participation in the war effort.* A number of pilots and officers were even released from prison when they volunteered to rejoin their units. It was, once again, the combination of nationalist and religious fervour that made the Iranian resistance so much more effective than the rest of the world expected.

But Iraqi Shi'ites too are capable of having nationalist feelings — in their case Arab nationalist ones. While many of them were inspired by Iran's revolutionary example, it is perhaps another matter actually to take the enemy side in a war between Iran and one's own country, especially now that Ayatollah Baqir al-Sadr, who was the only living Arab *marja-i taqlid*, is no longer there to give the lead. There has always been an undercurrent of feeling among Iraqi Shi'ites, including Shi'ite *ulama*, that Iranians should not be allowed to get away with behaving as if Shi'ism was their property and all Shi'ites must automatically follow their lead. Such nationalist feelings are bound to have been exacerbated, at least in some cases, by the outbreak of war; and Iraqi Shi'ites must also have been aware that the position of Arabs in Iran — most of whom are Shi'ites too — did not improve noticeably after the revolution.†

The Iraqi regime, of course, does everything possible to appeal to these nationalist feelings among Shi'ites, if only because they form the bulk of the Iraqi army. 'We take pride,' says the official banner at the entrance of the Imam Ali mosque in Najaf, 'in the presence here of our great father Ali, because he is a leader of Islam, because he is the son-in-law of the Prophet, and because he is an Arab.' After the war broke out, posters appeared throughout southern Iraq (the main Shi'ite region) showing the Iraqi flag with the words

---

* They resembled Stalin in another respect, too, it seems. They were given advance warning of the invasion from intelligence sources, and ignored it. Ironically the warning came from the Soviet Union, via the Iranian Communist Party (Tudeh). Even more ironically, Iranian armoured units were concentrated on the Soviet frontier, expecting an invasion from that quarter! See *Le Monde*, 6 January 1981.

† The expected mass uprising of Iranian Arabs to welcome the invaders did not occur, however. In fact, many Arabs, in common with members of other ethnic minorities in Iran, fought loyally against the invaders.

Allahu akbar ('God is the greatest') – the rallying cry of the Iranian revolution.

It should be stressed that neither Ba'thist ideology nor Saddam Husain personally are against Shi'ites as such. They are simply, as secular nationalists, against the politicizing of religion; and as Arab nationalists they accept Islam as a part of Arab national sentiment. 'Our party,' Saddam Husain said in 1977, 'is not neutral between belief and unbelief; it is on the side of belief always but it is not a religious party and should not be so.' He made considerable efforts, from the mid-1970s onwards, to recruit Shi'ites into the party and otherwise associate them with the regime.

Since 1979, faced with the competing claim of the Iranian revolution on Shi'ites' loyalty, he has made positive efforts to show his sympathy for Shi'ism and to win over Shi'ite *ulama* to his side, for instance by donating money impartially to both Sunni and Shi'ite mosques and other religious causes. (He himself is a Sunni by origin.) He declared the birthday of Ali a national holiday, paid visits to the holy places, and toured Shi'ite districts promising reforms and new services. He even promised an audience in Najaf that he would 'fight injustice with the swords of the Imams', and on another occasion, recalling that his own family claimed descent from the Prophet, declared: 'We have the right to say today – and we will not be fabricating history – that we are the descendants of Imam Husain.'

This combination of the carrot with the stick has given him a certain self-confidence, so that in 1980, not long after the execution of Ayatollah Baqir al-Sadr, he was able to go and make speeches in the most solidly Shi'ite districts of Baghdad. After the war broke out he went to Karbala and called on the people 'to fight with the spirit of Ali.'

Some second-rank Shi'ite religious dignitaries – regarded, of course, as collaborators by the militant opposition – have given the government public support; and though the studiously non-political Iranian *marja-i taqlid*, Ayatollah Khu'i (regarded by many as the senior living *marja* since Muhsin al-Hakim's death), has not been persuaded to make any statement for or against the government, he was filmed by Iraqi television in October 1980, at a service in the mosque of Najaf where prayers were said for the victory of Iraq's Arab army 'over the Persian aggressors'.

To conclude, in July 1981 Saddam Husain seemed still firmly in control of the Iraqi population, including the Shi'ites and no doubt for many Iraqis the attraction of revolutionary Iran as a model would by then have dulled considerably. But the danger was not necessarily past. The Da'wa was reported to be carrying out hit-and-run attacks on Iraqi anti-aircraft batteries in and around Baghdad, as well as assassinations, a month or so after the war began,[23] and it is said to have some followers among Iraqi rank and file soldiers. Its military arm, the Revolutionary Army for the Liberation of Iraq, has training camps in Iran not far from the Iraqi border. In the words of Professor Hanna Batatu of the American University of Beirut — the greatest living authority on Iraqi politics and the source of much of the above information — the Shi'ite opposition 'is poised to benefit greatly if Saddam Husain would fail to extricate himself from the morass of the Iraq–Iran war or would be forced to withdraw his troops from Iran under humiliating terms.'[24] By April 1982 that seemed more and more likely.

Iraq, by drawing most of revolutionary Iran's proselytizing zeal upon itself, has relieved the pressure on some other Muslim countries which might have expected to feel it. Iran could not afford to antagonize all her neighbours at once. Thus secular, pro-Western Turkey and reactionary pro-Western Pakistan have made polite noises about the revolution and have been able to maintain more or less normal relations with the new regime. There was a moment in November 1979 when Khomeini urged a delegation of Pakistani naval officers, who visited him on their way home from the *haj*, to undertake an Islamic revolution. But there was no follow-up to this, and it seems to have been more an expression of the general excitement of that month (the hostage seizure, the seizure of the mosque in Mecca — attributed by Khomeini to an American-Zionist conspiracy — etc.) than a premeditated attack on Zia ul-Haq's regime. Zia had no success in autumn 1980 when he tried to mediate, as chairman of the Islamic Conference, in the Iran–Iraq war, but that was because Iran was not ready to negotiate, rather than because he was personally unacceptable.

Those countries that were prepared to take Iran's side against Iraq and/or the United States were able to establish quite good relations with her even when on other grounds they might have expected hostility. Colonel Qadhafi did have some problems to start with because many Iranian *ulama* were anxious to know what had happened to Imam Musa Sadr, the leader of the Lebanese Shi'ites, who had disappeared mysteriously while on a visit to Libya in August 1978. (The Libyans claimed they had put him on a flight to Rome, but no one had seen him either on the flight or on arrival, so this explanation met with general scepticism. Several Iranian fact-finding missions were sent to investigate the matter and returned without satisfactory answers.) But in November 1979 it was decided that Libya's support in the battle with 'Great Satan' (the United States) was too valuable to be ignored, and diplomatic relations were established.

To Lebanon itself a number of Iranian 'volunteers' were sent soon after the revolution, ostensibly to fight for the Palestinian cause. It turned out, however, that their real purpose was to obtain military training so as to play a more effective part in Iranian revolutionary politics. The sponsors of this operation were the defence minister, Mustafa Chamran, who had previously served in Musa Sadr's militia, the Amal ('Action'), and Muhammad Munta-zerī, son of a senior ayatollah, who sponsored the organization of a similar militia in Iran: in due course it became part of the corps of *pasdaran* (revolutionary guards), a key instrument, with the IRP, of the consolidation of the traditionalist *ulama*'s power.* The Lebanese Amal did, however, receive a boost from the revolution, which helped it in its main task of winning away Lebanese Shi'ites from the Communist Party. The general effect was an accentuation of the confessional aspect of Lebanese politics, at the expense of secular ideologies. The mainly Sunni 'Murabitun', who had

*Both Chamran and Muntazeri were killed in June 1981 – the former at the front, the latter in the holocaust of the IRP leadership.

figured as 'Nasserists' in the civil war of 1975–76, now took on a more positively Islamic aspect. Later the Iran–Iraq war was fought by proxy in Beirut between the Amal and pro-Iraqi Palestinian groups (with attacks on the Iranian and Iraqi embassies as well). The PLO, being unwilling to quarrel publicly with a major Arab state, tried to offer itself as neutral mediator in the war. This, following an earlier unsuccessful attempt to gain brownie points with the United States by mediating on behalf of the US hostages, cost the PLO much of its revolutionary glamour in Iran.

Syria was one state which managed to maintain good relations with revolutionary Iran even while drowning in blood an attempted Islamic revolution of its own. Some observers attributed this to the fact that Syria's rulers were Shi'ites of a sort (Alawites), whereas their opponents were Sunni. But this was a misunderstanding. The Syrian Ba'thists had no desire at all to draw attention to their confessional origin, nor—if possible—to politicization of Islam in any form. Their initial motive for coming out strongly in support of the Iranian revolution may have been, in part, anxiety to pre-empt Iranian support for the Muslim Brothers in Syria. (If so, it seems to have succeeded.) But geopolitical considerations also played an important part. Syria by 1979 was bitterly opposed to American policy in the Middle East (the Camp David agreement) and welcomed the Iranian revolution as a blow to American influence. After the summer of 1979 Syria also returned to her usual state of cold war with Iraq. Therefore she welcomed the deterioration of Iran–Iraq relations and in 1980, along with Libya, took the Iranian side in the war. Relations with Iran were not entirely smooth, however, since Syria and Iran were backing rival fronts of Iraqi opposition groups—respectively secular and Islamic. In autumn 1980 Iran intercepted a consignment of arms from Syria intended for the Iraqi Kurdish group which Syria supported. President Asad of Syria responded by holding up a delivery of light weapons which Iran had requested for her own armed forces. 'We don't see why Imam Khomeini has to go through us to get Soviet weapons,' a Syrian diplomat remarked. 'Why doesn't he ask Moscow himself?'[25]

373

The other neighbour of Iran which did *not* succeed in establishing good relations with her after the revolution, besides Iraq, was Afghanistan. At first sight this was paradoxical, since the Iranian revolution came less than a year after a 'revolution' (or coup) in Afghanistan, that of April 1978, which was also directed partly against the Shah of Iran and American influence. But the new rulers of Afghanistan were, or were trying to be, communists. Their bungled attempt to impose social reforms on their own country, of whose rural structure and traditions they seem to have had no understanding at all, had provoked a strong traditionalist resistance which was conducted, inevitably, in the name of Islam. It was not hard to guess which side Ayatollah Khomeini would take (although other Iranians, such as the Mujahidin-i Khalq, were more hesitant). Anti-Afghan prejudice is anyway endemic in Iran, and one of the first acts of the new Iranian regime was to round up a number of Afghans (allegedly criminal elements, in fact mainly migrant workers) and push them across the border. Little more than a month later Radio Kabul claimed that Muslim rebels fighting the government in Herat, the main city of western Afghanistan, were in fact Iranian soldiers masquerading as Afghan citizens expelled from Iran.

The charge could hardly have been less plausible, and simply reflected the desperation of the Afghan regime at its inability to control its own country. But it was true that the Afghan rebels enjoyed a good deal of sympathy from the Iranian *ulama* (Ayatollah Shari'atmadari was particularly vocal on the subject) and that Iranian support for them in some form was on the cards. Relations between the two countries remained extremely bad until, in December 1979, Soviet forces were sent into Afghanistan to get rid of the embarrassing do-it-yourself Communist Hafizullah Amin and put in the carefully groomed, Moscow-approved Communist Babrak Karmal. Babrak's instructions were to pursue a conciliatory line towards Islam (for instance he restored the green national flag — colour of Islam — which Hafizullah and his front man, Nur Muhammad Tarakki, had thoughtlessly replaced with a red one). Part of this *offensive de charme* was directed at Iran. Babrak addressed a moving letter to Khomeini, as one revolutionary leader to another, blaming all previous problems on Amin, who 'can be considered on a par with the Pahlavis and other murderers throughout history' and pleading for 'consolidation of the fraternal and friendly Islamic relations between the Afghan and the Iranian people' with a view to 'administering an ultimate rebuke to world-craving Imperialism and Zionism.' This cut no ice. Khomeini condemned the Soviet invasion in terms almost as strong as he habitually used for American activities. He allowed the Iranian foreign minister, Sadeq Qotbzadeh, to attend a conference of Islamic foreign ministers in Islamabad in May 1980 where he sponsored the admission of Afghan resistance groups and insisted on them being given maximum support. Qotbzadeh also agreed to serve on a three-man commission (with the Pakistan foreign minister and the secretary-general of the conference) to seek a negotiated solution based on Soviet withdrawal, but this got nowhere for lack of Soviet interest. It is not clear how much practical help Iran has given to the Afghan resistance in the confused circumstances since then, but certainly Tehran has refused to have anything to do with the Babrak Karmal government.

In spite of this, and of a number of direct Iranian provocations such as abrupt increases in the price of gas supplied to Soviet Azerbaijan, the Soviet Union was careful to refrain from public criticism of the new Iranian regime. In its confrontation with the United States Iran has had every kind of Soviet moral support short of actually approving the seizure of diplomats as hostages. In the Iran–Iraq war, the Soviet Union proclaimed official neutrality but cut off arms supplies to Iraq while offering them to Iran. (They were contemptuously rejected.) Arab states close to the Soviet Union, such as Syria and Libya, supported Iran. And inside Iran the Tudeh party, unfailingly loyal to Moscow, consistently and slavishly proclaimed its support for Khomeini at every twist and turn.

Undoubtedly there is an element of opportunism here. Although the Soviet Union maintained quite good commercial relations with the Shah it could not but be pleased to see one of the pillars of US influence in the Middle East removed, and is naturally anxious to maximize its own influence in the new Iran. Supporting 'anti-imperialist' regimes even under 'bourgeois' or 'petty-bourgeois' leadership has been a consistent theme of Soviet policy for many years, and the present regime in Iran seems to fit that bill.* On the other hand, one should not forget that the Soviet leaders are ruling over some 45 to 50 million Muslims (or people of Muslim origin) and that Radio Tehran's revolutionary propaganda is addressed to them too. Should the Soviet Union then be put in the category of Muslim countries maintaining good relations with Iran for defensive reasons? Is the 'Islamic revolution' likely to spread northwards? That question will be considered in the next chapter.

---

* Up to mid-1981 Iran proved very disappointing in its response to Soviet overtures, while Western powers took advantage of the conflict to improve their relations with Iraq. Presumably because of this, the Soviet Union was reported to have agreed to resume arms supplies to Iraq in the spring of 1981. (See *The Nation*, 8–15 August 1981.)

CHAPTER TEN

Russia's Colonial Reckoning —
Islam and Nationality
in the Soviet Union

... Muslims of Russia, Tatars of the Volga and the Crimea, Kirgizes and Sarts of Siberia and Turkestan, Turks and Tatars of Transcaucasia, Chechens and Mountaineers of the Caucasus, all you whose mosques and houses of prayer have been destroyed, whose beliefs and customs have been flouted by the Tsars and the oppressors of Russia!

From now on your beliefs and customs, your national and cultural institutions are free and inviolable.

Organize your national life freely and without impediment. Such is your right. Know that your rights, like those of all the peoples of Russia, are protected by all the power of the Revolution and its instruments, the Soviets of deputies, of workers, of soldiers and of peasants.

Support this Revolution ...!

Appeal 'to all the Muslim
workers of Russia and the Orient', 24 November 1917

That appeal, published less than three weeks after the October Revolution, was signed by Lenin, Chairman of the Council of People's Commissars, and Stalin, Commissar for the Nationalities. Atheists both, theorists of a workers' revolution which was to abolish national frontiers, they appealed without blushing to the national and religious feelings of Russia's subject peoples.

Opportunism? Yes, but the real contradiction was not this one. Lenin, needing the support of Muslim and other non-Russian nationalities to secure the yet-precarious success of his revolution,

377

was consistent with his own proclaimed principles in seeking to dismantle the colonial empire of the Tsars and promising self-determination to its component peoples. The real contradiction was between this promise and his equally firm determination to hold the former empire together, albeit under a new social system and a new state, as the nucleus of the new world proletarian order. Self-determination was offered, but only one choice was possible because only one could be in the interest of the 'toiling masses': union with the Russian workers, soldiers and peasants against the reactionary local elites and their masters, the capitalist imperial powers.

Thus the true paradox is not that in 1917 internationalist revolutionaries condemned imperialism and threw open 'the prison of peoples'. The paradox is rather that sixty-four years later the Russian empire, which had seen itself and been seen by its subjects as one of the great European colonial empires, is still largely intact while those of Britain, France, Holland and Portugal have vanished from the map.

The Asiatic frontier of the Soviet Union is today identical with that of the Russian empire in 1914, with one single exception: an area of Armenia, taken from the Ottoman Empire by Russia in 1878, was re-conquered by the Turks in 1920 and remains part of Turkey. This was not a case of a subject people making good its claim to independence but of a rival imperial power reasserting its sovereignty before the new rulers of Russia had had a chance to pull the empire together again.

One is tempted to conclude that the Soviet Union is simply a sham — nothing more than a cloak for Russian rule, successfully re-imposed on the subject peoples by the Red Army after the brief interlude of disintegration caused by the Revolution and the Civil War. But if that is all there is to it, why have the Russians got away with it for so long? Everywhere else the colonized peoples have revolted — sometimes peacefully, sometimes with violence — and asserted their independence. The world of Islam especially seems now to be seething with anti-imperialist ferment — and it is to the world of Islam that Russia's most populous Asiatic colonies

378

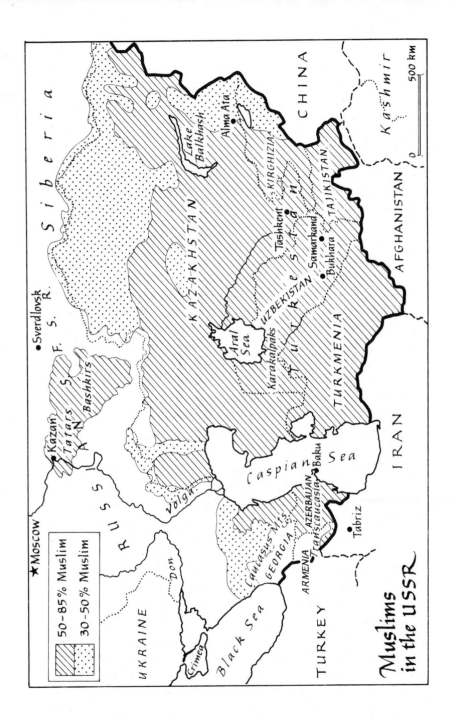

Muslims in the USSR

Legend:
- 50–85% Muslim
- 30–50% Muslim

historically belong. The southern frontier of the Soviet Union cuts across religious, ethnic and geographical boundaries. It is hard to see any historical inevitability about the separation of the Soviet Socialist Republic of Azerbaijan, for instance, from the neighbouring province of Iran which bears the same name. The inhabitants of both speak the same Azeri Turkish dialect and, by tradition at least, belong to the same branch of Islam — Twelver Shi'ism. Is the rule of atheist Russians more tolerable to the citizens of Baku than was the presence of American military advisers to those of Tabriz? Where are the ayatollahs of Soviet Azerbaijan? Why are no crowds thronging the streets with shouts of 'God is Great! Death to Brezhnev!'?

Several answers have been suggested to this question. The first is, in essence, 'They are, but we're not told.' Is there more 'Muslim' opposition in the Soviet Union than we hear about? Almost certainly, yes, but not necessarily as much as the more enthusiastic students of the subject like to imagine. Of course it is true that the Soviet system is a closed system, in which any form of opposition will usually go unreported. It is also true that some evidence of opposition can be found from an attentive reading of Soviet official sources. The richest vein here is the writings of specialists employed to study religion in order to struggle more effectively against it. It is a vein that has been heavily mined by the leading French authority on Islam in the Soviet Union, Alexandre Bennigsen, who claims to have detected 'an unexpected and multiform religious revival'. The institutional framework for this revival, he says, is provided not by the 'official' religious leaders, who enjoy government recognition in return for total political loyalism, but by clandestine Sufi brotherhoods which are resolutely hostile to communism. He cites references to this kind of activity going back over the last fifteen years or so. But it is noticeable that the great majority of these references relate to the northern Caucasus — the most mountainous and backward of the regions inhabited by Soviet Muslims. They amount to impressive evidence for the survival of militant Sufism in that region, but rather weak evidence for a revival affecting Soviet Muslims in general.

There are other intriguing glimpses of something stirring beneath the surface. On 4 December 1980 the prime minister of the Kirgiz Soviet Socialist Republic in Central Asia was murdered. A month later the Supreme Soviet in Moscow devoted a session to discussing ways of 'strengthening the legal order and the fight against crime' in this small, mountainous republic which borders on China and is not far from Afghanistan, while official sources revealed that the murder had been politically motivated. But who killed him, and what was the political motive? Was it an isolated act, part of a clan feud, or is there some kind of Muslim nationalist insurgency going on? At the same time the regional party leader and the chief of police in Azerbaijan, a thousand miles or so to the west, were issuing public calls for vigilance against any attempt to spread subversion from neighbouring Muslim states. Was this simply a reaction to Western interest in such a possibility, or did they have a specific reason to be worried? We don't know, but it should be noted that Bennigsen himself is the first to admit that Islam is not an imminent danger for the regime, and that 'we are very far from Algeria in the 1950s.'

A second answer to the question goes something like this: 'They don't dare to, because they know that Brezhnev is no namby-pamby liberal like Carter or the Shah and that Russia is still a world power in its prime, not a clapped-out has-been like Britain or Portugal.' It can hardly be doubted that a crucial element in Russia's success as a colonial power is her overwhelming military strength and the confidence of her subjects in her willingness to use it. The right of secession accorded to individual republics in the Soviet constitution is purely theoretical, since all fifteen republics are firmly controlled by the same Communist Party, whose central leadership is overwhelmingly Russian and whose decision-making processes are highly centralized. Any challenge to communist rule in any part of the Union would certainly be repressed with the full force of the Soviet state.

A subtle reminder of this appeared during 1980 in the media of the Central Asian Soviet republics, with a spate of articles, memoirs, television shows, short stories and novels about the 'Basmachi' — the Muslim rebel movement against Bolshevik rule in the years after the revolution. This subject had been taboo for the previous forty years. Now, two themes were stressed. The first was the alleged links between the Basmachi and foreign imperialists, reactionary clerics and Sufi brotherhoods. The second was the heroic efficiency of the Cheka (ancestor of the KGB) in outwitting and crushing the rebels. The message seemed to be: 'We have beaten you once before; if need be we will beat you again.' It is none the less interesting that the authorities should feel such a reminder is needed.

A third answer is: 'They no longer want to because they're brainwashed by two generations of Soviet indoctrination which has destroyed their traditional culture and their identity more deliberately and systematically than has been attempted by any other colonial power.' Are we wrong to think of these people as Muslims at all? Two generations have now grown up under communist rule, and communism has made a most determined effort to ensure that they grow up as communists rather than as Muslims. In the 1920s the Soviet authorities followed the example of Mustafa Kemal in Turkey: by 1928 religious courts had been completely outlawed and religious schools abolished; by 1930 the system of *awqaf* — lands whose revenues were assigned in perpetuity for religious purposes — which had been the economic basis of both mosques and schools, had also been practically abolished throughout the Soviet Union. Thereafter Stalin went well beyond Atatürk in suppressing Islam, even as a religion. The payment of *zakat* was forbidden, as was pilgrimage to Mecca. Fasting during Ramadan was rigorously discouraged. Mosques were closed and converted into clubs or cinemas.

Since then the fluctuations of Soviet policy towards Islam have been parallel to those affecting other religions, notably Christianity and Judaism. Although an 'official' religious leadership was allowed to re-emerge during the Second World War, when Stalin sought to rally Muslims to the war effort, the anti-Islamic campaign was resumed under Khrushchev. It is only since the 1960s that the regime has taken to making a show of its tolerance of Islam in order to impress Muslims in other countries. But there are still not more than a few hundred mosques, compared to nearly 30,000 in 1917, while the 'Muslim' population has grown from 18 million to 45 million. It seems clear that the great majority of this population has to live its life in an institutional framework formed by Communist party and state organizations, rather than by Islamic ones.

Moreover, the Soviet system has provided the people in question not merely with a communist, class-based ideology, but also with new national identities and loyalties which cut across the old pan-Islamic or pan-Turkist links. It did this in two stages. In the first stage, the Bolsheviks enlisted the support of reformers and nationalists from within Muslim society who saw the revolution as a chance to do away both with Russian colonialism and with the conservative Muslim establishment, which to a large extent had collaborated with it. Many of these reformers joined the Communist Party. The ones with the most advanced and ambitious political ideas were Tatars from the area round Kazan, on the Volga, who saw themselves as the natural leaders of a national revival among the Muslims of the Russian empire, three quarters of whom spoke one or other variety of Turkish. This group, the most famous of whom was Sultan Galiev, tried to develop a Muslim 'national communism' (Muslim in the cultural rather than strictly religious sense) which they hoped would inspire other Muslim peoples to liberate themselves from colonial rule. They emphasized national liberation while playing down or postponing class struggle and favoured a conciliatory policy towards Islam as a religion. This soon brought them into conflict with the Russian communists.

In the second stage, the Soviet leadership gradually eliminated all these nationalist leaders, while systematically building up the different ethnic groups as separate nationalities. Many of these, initially at least, were quite artificial. The Bashkirs, for instance, close relatives and neighbours of the Tatars on the Volga and virtually assimilated by them, were given an autonomous republic of their own even though they made up only 26 per cent of its population and most of its officials were either Russian or Tatar. Bashkir, hitherto only a spoken dialect, was deliberately transformed into a literary language as distinct from Tatar as possible. And both Tatars and Bashkirs were given only limited autonomy within the Russian Federation (RSFSR). The same policy was adopted in the North Caucasus, where a whole series of small groups, which were little more than tribes, suddenly found themselves endowed with 'national languages', constructed by Soviet philologists, while their territories became 'autonomous' republics or regions within the RSFSR.

Further south, the Muslims of Azerbaijan and of Central Asia were allowed to join the Union as separate Soviet Socialist Republics, but not as Muslims nor yet as Turks. The steppes of northern Central Asia became the SSR of Kazakhstan, while the neighbouring mountains became the SSR of Kirgizia — although the Kirgizes spoke and wrote a dialect of Kazakh and the Kazakhs until 1924 were generally known as Kirgizes. The Kirgizes had no separate historic or cultural traditions of their own, and 'Kirgiz' did not become a separate written language until 1923.

The historic region of Turkestan, stretching from the Caspian Sea to China, was now found to contain five separate 'nations', one of which (the Tajiks) spoke an Iranian language while the other four — Turkmens, Uzbeks, Kirgizes and Karakalpaks — spoke closely related Turkic languages. Each was given its own SSR, except the Karakalpaks ('Black caps'), a tenuous grouping related to both Uzbeks and Kazakhs, who had to make do with an 'autonomous republic' within the SSR of Uzbekistan. (A Karakalpak literary language was invented in 1930, but in 1939 only 37 per cent of Karakalpaks answered 'Karakalpak' when asked to name their mother tongue.) All these languages were at first written in Latin script, so as to minimize contact between those who spoke them and the rest of the Muslim world. But when the Turkish Republic adopted Latin script, Stalin made Soviet Muslims switch to the Russian Cyrillic alphabet, which is still in use today.

The carve-up of Turkestan provoked a great deal of argument

between the national groups concerned about the delimitation of their respective territories, but no outright opposition. Only a small elite of reformist intellectuals, mostly educated in Tatar schools, defended the idea of a united Turkestan. The Soviet leaders seem to have acted in time to prevent this elite from gaining a decisive influence and to prevent the old lingua franca of Turkestan, known as Chagatai, from being revived as the nucleus of a new 'pan-Turkestani' national consciousness. Instead, the separate Turkic languages of the new nations gradually grew further apart and these nations themselves, 'so fragile and artificial to start with, acquired ... a sense of their own identity and a local patriotism.' Such, at least, was Bennigsen's conclusion in 1968, in his book *L'Islam en Union Soviétique* (written with Chantal Lemercier-Quelquejay). Today he says that 'the relationship between ethnicity and religion is constantly changing' and that in the last five years the emphasis has been less on the ethnic or national identity and more on the religious or supranational identity. But there is no consensus on this point, and it seems that at least an important percentage of the people concerned think of themselves not primarily as Muslims but as Uzbeks, Turkmens, Tatars, etc. — members of particular Soviet nationalities with particular problems to resolve *within the Soviet system* rather than as members of a wider Islamic culture.

At this point we have to consider a fourth answer: Could it be that Soviet 'Muslims' are actually not all that dissatisfied with their lot? Could it even be that the Soviet system really is different from classic European colonialism in that the colonies have not been exploited and a really serious effort has been made to enable them to catch up with the metropole materially and culturally while preserving and promoting their own cultural heritage? Unpalatable as it may be to those for whom communism is not merely an evil but an unmitigated evil, there is a good deal of evidence to support this view. In 1957 the UN Economic Commission published a report entitled *Regional Economic Policy in the Soviet Union: The Case of Central Asia* which, while discounting the extravagant claims of Soviet propaganda, showed that there had been great improvement in the economy and that average living standards in Central Asia were now on much higher levels than in the neighbouring Asian countries. Today, according to the leading British expert on the subject, Colonel Geoffrey Wheeler, 'it is generally conceded that the economy of Soviet Central Asia has been completely transformed, that in respect of their standard of living and internal security the Soviet Moslems have little to complain of and that the Soviet government has some reason to be satisfied with their contribution to the Soviet economy as a whole.' Colonel Wheeler also considers the claim of over 90 per cent literacy for the Muslims of Soviet Central Asia as probably accurate, and compares it both with the 4 per cent figure for the same region in 1917 and with the 45 per cent achieved in Turkey by 1972.

Living standards in Soviet Central Asia not only compare well with those of other Muslim countries but also compare not unfavourably with those of European Russia, especially if such factors as climate, price and availability of goods and 'the quality of life' are taken into account. If per capita incomes are lower, that is mainly because Soviet 'Muslims' have larger families. Family incomes, especially in the agricultural sector, are good, and Central Asia has not seen the rapid unplanned urban growth, high unemployment and squalid housing conditions which characterize so many Third World countries. Soviet 'Muslims', in fact, show a marked reluctance to move into towns and this leads demographers to doubt that they will be easily persuaded to move into more northerly areas of the Soviet Union to provide a work force for expanding industry.

It should be added that the Soviet nationalities policy, with its remarkable effort in promoting national languages and cultures, finds no obvious parallel in the history of other empires. And although the reality of ultimate Russian control persists — symbolized by the second secretary of the Communist Party in each non-Russian republic, who is invariably Russian and discreetly fulfills the true functions of a colonial governor — the fact remains that an increasing proportion of jobs at all levels is occupied by nationals of the republic concerned; and though they are careful not to question the Soviet system in any respect they are also less and less inhibited in insisting that their compatriots get a full share of the cake within that system. There is no political freedom, but there is a degree of self-government and participation.

All those answers have in common that they seek an explanation in the particular character of the colonizing power and its political system. A fifth type ignores this and points simply to the geography of the area. While it is true that the southern frontier of the Russian empire is geographically arbitrary, it is equally true that there is no obvious natural frontier separating the colonies from the motherland. It is not an overseas empire. On this view, overland expansion has a legitimacy, a 'natural' quality, which overseas expansion lacks, and the situation of the natives in Central Asia or the Caucasus would be comparable, say, to that of the Hispano-Indian inhabitants of the south-western United States — condemned to absorption in the 'manifest destiny' of a more dynamic continental culture. Some would even argue that the Russian empire was not a case of European colonial expansion at all, and that Russia has always been, in reality, an Asiatic nation, which deluded itself into thinking it had become European in the eighteenth and nineteenth centuries much as Turkey has done in the twentieth.

Have the Muslims, then, simply been irreversibly absorbed by the 'natural' expansion of Russia into its continental hinterland? In the case of the Crimean Tatars they have not been absorbed but displaced — deported en masse by Stalin in 1944 to Central Asia, the Urals and Siberia, and not allowed to return. Gradual absorption may perhaps be the fate of some of the smaller Muslim groups incorporated in the RSFSR: and even for some groups who have resisted absorption — such as the Volga Tatars and Bashkirs, surrounded by Russians on all sides, or the Kazakhs, who are outnumbered by Russian settlers within their own republic — it may be utopian to think in terms of national independence. By contrast the republics of the 'Southern Tier', whether 'Muslim' (Tajikistan, Uzbekistan, Turkmenia, Azerbaijan) or 'Christian' (Armenia,

Georgia) remain overwhelmingly non-Russian and indisputably outside Russia. It is hard to see that any law of geography predestines them to perpetual Russian rule, which, whether considered as 'European' or 'Asiatic', remains for the inhabitants of these regions indisputably foreign.

In demographic terms Russian expansion has in fact spent itself and gone into reverse. The crude birth-rates in the Central Asian republics are now more than twice as high as those in European Russia. The Soviet Union is increasingly dependent on Asians to man both its industry and its armed forces; and there is evidence that Russians have begun to migrate back to Russia, out of the 'Muslim' republics where they find themselves increasingly discriminated against in employment and promotion.

Thus while the evidence for a revival of Islam as a religion in the Soviet Union remains patchy and uncertain, the evidence for a persistent, probably growing, sense of separate identity among the Muslim nationalities is strong. This shows itself through adherence to certain Muslim rites, such as circumcision, marriage and burial. A striking example is the riot which occurred in March 1980 in Alma-Ata, capital of Kazakhstan. A number of Kazakh soldiers had been killed fighting in Afghanistan, and their bodies had been brought home for a heroes' funeral. The population protested, not against the fact that its sons had been drafted into the Soviet army, nor even against the fact that they had been sent to their deaths in an unjust and unnecessary war, but against the proposal to bury them in a Russian communist cemetery without religious rites. They were Muslims, and therefore should be buried in a Muslim cemetery. Confronted with violent demonstrations, the Soviet authorities gave way and the young heroes of an atheist state, who had died in the attempt to subjugate a neighbouring Muslim nation, were given a proper Muslim burial.

The persistence of Muslim culture also shows itself in certain behaviour patterns, such as the high birth-rate and the refusal to intermarry with non-Muslim nationalities; and the Muslim elites show increasing self-confidence. Even the 'official' religious leaders — the members of the four state-approved 'spiritual director-ates', who are publicly loyal to the Soviet government, and never protest against anti-religious pressure — are not mere agents of the regime as is, for instance, the Russian Orthodox patriarch. In return for their support they are able to obtain some concessions, such as the opening of new mosques, because Soviet foreign policy requires that visiting Muslims from abroad be shown that 'Islam is alive and well in the Soviet Union.' Moreover, these official religious leaders, according to Bennigsen, are authentic *ulama*, 'whose intellectual and professional standards may be compared to those of the best Islamic scholars of the Muslim world.' Indeed, some students from the Muslim seminary in Tashkent have been able to complete their education in Muslim universities abroad, such as al-Azhar in Cairo and those of Fez (Morocco), Libya and Damascus.

The official *ulama* have shown independence, according to Bennigsen, in refusing to denounce Sufism as heretical or un-orthodox, contenting themselves with a few vague *fatwas* against particular Sufi practices such as pilgrimage to shrines, collection of *zakat* and performance of ecstatic rituals. At the same time they have been quietly trying to expand their role in guiding the lives of the faithful. In 1976, for instance, an article in their official journal, *Muslims of the Soviet East*, called on Muslim preachers to answer all the questions of those who came to the mosque, and to consider the mosque as a 'religious-cultural centre where believers obtain spiritual food.' Never attacking communism, they seek instead to portray it as a kind of by-product of Islam. 'By the will of God,' wrote the chairman of the Muslim Spiritual Directorate of Transcaucasia on the occasion of the fiftieth anniversary of the USSR, 'Soviet science has assumed advanced positions in the development of human thought. Liberty, equality, fraternity and friendship among nations and nationalities have triumphed. All this is in accord with the Holy Koran and is being achieved with the blessing of God.' Indeed a communist writer, specializing in atheist propaganda, complains that Muslim preach-ers are giving credit to Islam and its principles for the union and friendship of the peoples of North Caucasus, Central Asia, Kazakhstan and so on with 'all the peoples of the country' under the Soviet government; and that 'heads of religious centres candidly propose to preachers to address themselves to socialist ideas that are popular among believers, recommending that they "relate" them to the teachings of Islam.'

The building of communism was a great earthly 'ideal of the Prophet Muhammad', according to a statement adopted by a congress of *ulama* of the North Caucasus in 1975. Muslim preachers are quoted as saying that the Koran contains 'the principles of socialism'. 'The aim of their talks is to convince their hearers that Islam is "progressive", that the ideas of communism are borrowed from the Koran and the Sunna.' Even the articles of the new Soviet constitution were pronounced, by a Turkmen preacher in 1977, to be 'in complete accord with the teaching of the Holy Koran and the pronouncements of the Prophet Muhammad.'[1] As for the official atheism of the Soviet Union, that is portrayed not as *kufr* (unbelief) or *shirk* (idolatry), but as *jahiliya* — the state of pre-Islamic ignorance. The implication is that it will in time wither away, just as the communists expect religion to do. Each side is convinced of the superior rationality of its own beliefs, and therefore of their eventual triumph.

A similar confidence is displayed in a different sphere by the local communist leaders of the 'Muslim' republics, who present themselves less and less as representatives of the Soviet Communist Party in the provinces (that role being assumed by the 'Russian' second secretary of each non-Russian Communist Party) and more and more as representatives of their own nationalities bargaining with Moscow for more power, more perks, more exclusive control of their own affairs. Thus the religious and the political elites of the Muslim nationalities, while ideologically on opposite sides, can be seen as adopting, each in their own way, the same attitude towards the Soviet system: they let it roll over them, yet remain unassimilated by it. For even the communist leaders of Muslim nationalities remain Muslims in the sense that they circumcise their sons, are buried in Muslim cemeteries, have larger families than their Russian counterparts, are reluctant to let their daughters marry non-Muslims, and show great respect for the older generation within their own families.[2]

In short, one may conclude that each of the different answers I have suggested to explain the longevity of Russian domination over the Muslims of the Volga, the Caucasus and Central Asia contains elements of truth. Russian colonialism, in its Soviet form, has been more single-minded and consequently more thorough than the West European variety. Soviet leaders, while proclaiming the right of self-determination in theory, have been in practice far more seriously committed than any West European government to the idea of integrating the peoples of their empire into a single political culture: that of Marxist-Leninist socialism, in the particularly authoritarian interpretation which Russian state power has put on it. On the one hand they have not tolerated even token political opposition. On the other hand they have made efforts unparalleled by those of any other colonial power to improve both the material and the cultural standards of the colonized peoples. These peculiarities may partly be explained by the class and ideological nature of the state, and partly by the nature of the Russian empire as a continuous land mass, which can more plausibly be seen as a single country than the far-flung maritime empires of France or Portugal (let alone Britain, which was never assimilationist even in theory). Yet the declared objective of forging a single Soviet nation is still far from being realized, and in the republics of the Southern Tier the movement now seems to be if anything the other way: Russian and non-Russian alike are more and more conscious of belonging to different nationalities with different cultures and even different interests. An 'Islamic revolution' in the southern Soviet Union is hardly the most probable outcome. But the development of a collective dissidence based on nationality, and on national cultures of which Islam is the essential ingredient, is something that can easily be imagined; perhaps a Muslim equivalent to what has been happening in Catholic Poland.

Soviet Muslims and the Invasion of Afghanistan

How might such considerations affect Soviet policy towards Islam beyond the frontiers of the Soviet Union? Were they, in particular, a factor in the Soviet decision to invade Afghanistan? In the summer of 1979, when I began planning this book, it looked (from London at least) as though the newly established Communist regime in Afghanistan might be swept away by an 'Islamic' re-action. This naturally prompted me and others to wonder whether the same could happen in the Soviet Union itself. The 'others' may have included some of the policy-makers in the Kremlin, and it could be for this reason that some 80,000 Soviet troops were sent into Afghanistan at the end of 1979. This is by no means certain, however. Selig S. Harrison, perhaps the most authoritative American commentator on South Asian affairs, who was in Afghanistan during 1979 and interviewed Hafizullah Amin at length, came to the conclusion that the Afghan rebel *mujahidin*, while undoubtedly of great nuisance value, were nowhere near being in a position to overthrow the Amin-Tarakki regime. In his view the Soviet intervention was directed not primarily against the *mujahidin* but against Amin himself, who although a communist was showing a Tito-like independence from Moscow in his attitudes and policies.

The comparison with Tito is an interesting one. It should not be forgotten that the background to Tito's rift with Stalin in 1948 was Tito's insistence on carrying out a thoroughgoing communist revolution in Yugoslavia at a time (during and immediately after the Second World War) when Stalin was prepared to concede hegemony to the Western allies in southern as well as western Europe and therefore favoured conciliatory policies including even the preservation of the monarchies in Yugoslavia and Italy. Brezhnev's problem with Amin seems to have been similar. Amin was going too far and too fast. Even if he was not in danger of provoking a successful counter-revolution in Afghanistan — a de-batable point — he was, by symbolic decisions such as the replace-ment of the green flag with a red one and by his ruthless suppression of Islamic resistance to his ill-thought-out 'reforms', giving a very bad impression of communism to Muslims elsewhere, at a time when the Soviet Union had hopes of exploiting the strong anti-Western feeling in the Muslim world and of developing close relations with the new Islamic regime in Iran. It seems unlikely that concern about the implications for Muslims in the Soviet Union was at that stage a major consideration, since 40 per cent of the initial invasion force sent into Afghanistan in December 1979 was actually made up of Muslims from Soviet Central Asia. If the decision to invade had been motivated even partly by fears about the loyalty of Soviet Muslims, it would surely have been tempting fate to send some of those very Muslims to do the job.

But at the end of February 1980 these Soviet Muslim contingents were recalled. This was not in itself surprising, since they were composed mainly of reservists on short-term call-up. However, the units that replaced them were almost entirely Russian. It seems, therefore, that at *this* stage the Soviet leadership did have second thoughts about the suitability of Muslim units for the task in hand.

Probably it had been under some illusions about the nature of the task itself. The Soviet leaders must have hoped that the over-throw of the brutal Amin regime would win the gratitude of the Afghan population and that the task of the invading force would be as much political as military. Soviet Muslim troops, many of them belonging to ethno-linguistic groups which are found also in Afghanistan, would have been well placed to fraternize with the locals and convince them of the benefits, economic and cultural, which sixty years of communism had brought to Central Asia. (The disparity in living standards, literacy, etc., between Afghanistan and Soviet Central Asia is certainly very much in the latter's favour.)

But by the end of February 1980 it was clear that the Afghans were more or less unanimously hostile to the invasion and that the occupying force would be directly and heavily involved in operations against resistance forces fighting in the name of Islam. Had they anticipated this, the Soviet leaders might have hesitated to send in Muslim troops in the first place. According to Murray

393

Feshbach, a leading American expert on Soviet demography, the tasks to which soldiers from Muslim backgrounds are allocated in the Soviet armed forces indicate that the military command does not have full confidence in them as fighting troops. They tend to be relegated to service in rear battalions, construction divisions, and farm troops. Anxiety is also expressed in Soviet military journals about the number of recruits coming into the armed forces insufficiently prepared, both educationally and socially, for military service, and in particular lacking adequate knowledge of the Russian language. It is clear that such anxieties relate primarily to 'Muslim' recruits, who for demographic reasons form an increasing percentage of the total: by the year 2000 one-third of the total intake will come from the Southern Tier.

We do not know for certain whether Soviet commanders are also anxious about the political reliability of their Muslim troops, but in actions against a Muslim enemy it seems reasonable to suppose a degree of anxiety would be felt, and reports from Afghanistan suggest that it would not be misplaced. Some fraternization between Soviet Muslim troops and the locals did occur, and the results were the opposite of what Soviet leaders would have wanted. The Soviet Muslims were influenced by the Afghans rather than the other way round. There is said to have been an active black market in copies of the Koran, for clandestine importation into the Soviet Union, and some Soviet Muslim soldiers even went so far as to desert and join up with the Afghan resistance. (Some of these later reached Pakistan and were interviewed there.)

Even if concern about Soviet Muslim loyalties was not a primary motive for the Soviet invasion of Afghanistan, it must surely be a factor in Soviet Afghan policy from here on. The British defeat in Afghanistan in 1842 destroyed the myth of British invincibility in India, and so planted the seeds of the Mutiny of 1857.[3] A Soviet defeat in Afghanistan, or a negotiated withdrawal on humiliating terms, could sow the seeds of a Central Asian Mutiny in the 1990s — something Soviet leaders will certainly not risk if they can possibly avoid it. The war in Afghanistan is undoubtedly an embarrassment to them, and for the moment (August 1981) their policy seems to be to avoid escalating it so long as they control the main cities and roads, even if that means leaving large parts of the country in the hands of the *mujahidin* (usually local tribal leaders with only loose connections to the various 'Islamic' parties that claim to be leading the resistance from Peshawar in Pakistan). But a settlement which meant replacing the communist government in Kabul with an anti-communist 'Islamic' one would be a far greater embarrassment than the war at its present level. To avoid that, the Soviet leaders will be willing, if necessary, to pay a very high price.

CONCLUSION

What is Islam?

> Myself when young did eagerly frequent
> Doctor and Saint, and heard great argument
> About it and about: but evermore
> Came out by the same door where in I went.
> *The Rubaiyat of Omar Khayyam,*
> trans. by Edward Fitzgerald

The reader may think that this question should have been asked, and answered, in the preface rather than the conclusion. But if he (or she) has been patient with me this far, he will perhaps have found an implicit answer in the way the book is constructed. I am not a Muslim. I suppose that if I were I should have to be prepared to make a statement of my own beliefs and say that that, for me, was Islam. As it is, I can only define Islam as 'the religion of the Muslims', and a Muslim, for me, is simply one who calls himself that. For me, in my condition of *jahiliya*, there is no Islam, in the sense of an abstract, unchangeable entity, existing independently of the men and women who profess it. There is only what I hear Muslims say, and see them do.

What do they say? That there is no God but God, and that Muhammad is his Messenger. All agree, therefore, that the Koran, which Muhammad brought, is in some sense a message from God, and that Muhammad was a special human being whose life and teachings are a guide to right conduct. Consequently all acknowledge the authority of the Koran, and most also that of the

396

Sunna* — the tradition of the Prophet, as recorded in the *hadith*. (There are a few, known as *ahl al-Qur'an*, or people of the Koran, who argue that the text of the *hadith* is so corrupt that nothing is really known of the Prophet's words or actions beyond what the Koran itself states or implies; but even these in practice have to rely on the *hadith* to make certain passages in the Koran intelligible.)

The text, or rather texts, of the *hadith* have been subjected to an enormous amount of critical scholarship over the centuries, with a view to sifting the authentic record of the Prophet's words and deeds from later inventions and misconstructions. In the third century after Muhammad (ninth century AD), six compilations were made which 'came to be accepted as the authoritative second source of the content of Islam' besides the Koran.[1] But they were compilations of traditions which had first existed in oral form, authenticated essentially by a list of their successive transmitters: A says he heard it from B on the authority of C who said this on the authority of D that the Prophet of God said.... A text in this form can never really be definitive, and to the present day we find Muslim scholars quoting different *hadiths* to refute each other, with each asserting that the *hadith* on which his opponent's argument rests is 'weak'.

The text of the Koran, by contrast, was definitively established within a generation of Muhammad's death, in the reign of the Caliph Uthman. Only the most daring modernists, such as Colonel Qadhafi, will today propose actual emendations of the text. But interpretation is quite another matter. The Koran consists of statements and injunctions addressed by God to Muhammad, for him to pass on — at first to his fellow-citizens in Mecca, and later to his followers in Medina. Evidently the meaning was crystal clear at the time to Muhammad and to his immediate hearers. This is because the revelations alluded directly to problems that the early Muslims were confronting in their spiritual, social and

* This has nothing to do with the distinction between Sunni and Shi'ite Islam. The Shi'ites too accept the authority of the Sunna, but they give a different account of the Sunna's content.

political lives; and because they were couched in a language that these early Muslims used and understood: 'Behold, We have made it an Arabic Koran; haply you will understand.'² But of course, as society develops, the problems it confronts will change, and language too will evolve. The very success of Islam accelerated this process. Even in Muhammad's lifetime his community had developed from a small embattled sect to a major Arabian power; within a generation after that it had become a vast Arab empire; and another two or three generations turned it into a cosmopolitan civilization stretching across three continents, absorbing the heritage of many different cultures, with Arabic still its lingua franca, spoken by the ruling and intellectual elites, but comprising peoples of different language and ethnic character and breaking down gradually into separate states. In the political sphere especially, this community had to deal with problems entirely different from those of Muhammad's time. The Arabic language also developed, to deal with these new problems and to absorb new concepts from other cultures. The precise meaning of the Koran for its first hearers thus soon became hard to recapture. Its interpretation became a matter of scholarship and tradition, closely dependent upon the *hadith*, which provided the indispensable context; and so uncertainty about the meaning of the Koran corresponds to uncertainty about the text of the *hadith*.

The result is that if one takes Islam to be what Muslims say and do, one is bound to conclude that there is not one Islam but many Islams, because one finds such an enormous variety of Islamic thought and practice. There is argument about what precisely the Koran meant, in many passages, to its original hearers; and even where that is agreed, there is argument about the lesson to be drawn from it for later generations. Take, for instance, the famous passage on polygamy (Sura IV, verse 3):

> If you fear that you will not act justly towards the orphans, marry such women as seem good to you, two, three, four; but if you fear you will not be equitable, then only one, or what your right hands own; so it is likelier you will not be partial.

It is fairly clear that this injunction presupposes a society in which polygamy, slavery, and concubinage with female slaves were normal institutions. Does that mean that it *prescribes* such norms for all Muslim societies? Few Muslims would go so far as to argue that. Indeed, slavery has now been legally abolished in all Muslim countries (though there are undoubtedly several where it continues to exist in practice). Traditionally, the verse has been taken simply as authorizing polygamy up to four wives. Some modernists have emphasized the limitation to four, suggesting that this was a 'progressive' step away from the unrestricted polygamy of pre-Islamic Arabia. Others have suggested that the passage really enjoins monogamy, since a later verse states: 'You will not be able to be equitable between your wives, be you ever so eager.' Both interpretations seem a little forced. A more radical one, but perhaps more plausible (at least to the Western mind) is to point out that the reason given for polygamy is to ensure just treatment for orphans, and to suggest that a modern society may find more systematic and equitable ways of providing that; or, more restrictively, that a second (or third, or fourth) marriage should be permitted only when the new wife is a widow with at least one dependent child.

My point is not that one of these interpretations is right and the others wrong, but merely that *any* interpretation depends first on reconstructing the original context and then on deciding how much of that context is transferable to one's own situation. That being the case, one should not be surprised to find a variety of marriage laws in force in different Muslim countries, most of which are said to have been framed in accordance with the Koran and the Sunna.

The same goes for more or less all of the social problems which combine to give 'Islam' a negative image in the minds of Western liberals: the subordinate status of women, the enforcement of drastic physical punishments such as amputation, flogging or stoning,* the treatment of non-Muslim minorities, the doctrine

---

*The stoning of adulterers is not in fact mentioned in the Koran at all, as it stands; the penalty prescribed is scourging. But a very early tradition, attributed

of *jihad* (usually translated as 'holy war'), the prohibition of interest
on loans, alcohol and pork. On all these subjects there are passages
in the Koran, and episodes in the life of Muhammad, which reflect
the prevailing norms of seventh-century Arabian society. In many
cases it can be argued with a fair degree of plausibility that the
practice introduced by the Koran or by Muhammad was an
improvement, in the sense that it implied broader notions of
common humanity and a stronger sense of responsibility for the
welfare of one's fellow creatures than what had gone before. Often
the text contains qualifications which suggest that the harshest
measures would be applied only in very exceptional circumstances,
while many other passages can be quoted to show that the general
spirit of the Koran is one of tolerance and compassion. In the
case of prohibitions, there is great scope for argument about the
exact meaning of the words used for things which are prohibited:
is it really interest in any form, or only excessive interest amount-
ing to usury and exploitation? Is it alcohol in any form, or only
excessive drinking, or a particularly potent liquor derived from
date-palms? And if it is alcohol in any form, should that be taken
to include other 'drugs' not known in seventh-century Arabia, such
as caffeine and nicotine?

On all these points the interpretation, and even more so the
enforcement (or non-enforcement), of Islamic law is really a matter
of tradition — a tradition which varies with time and place and in
which the words of the Koran are mingled with a great variety
of customs of tribal or pre-Islamic origin. A classic case in point
is the use of the veil. The Koran in several places enjoins modesty
on women, 'that they cast down their eyes and guard their private
parts ... and let them cast their veils over their breast.' It says
nothing about veiling the face and head. This custom was known
in many Mediterranean countries before Islam, but apparently not
in pre-Islamic Arabia. In later Islamic societies it became common
especially among the urban middle classes; the fact that you could

---

to the Caliph Umar, insists that there was a passage on stoning which somehow
got lost. (According to one version a domestic animal ate part of the page on
which it was written!)

afford to seclude your wife rather than make her work was a sign of social status. Among countrywomen it seldom became a general rule. Yet this did not prevent the *ulama* of almost every Muslim country from condemning, as a gross affront to Islam, the abandonment of the veil by upper and middle class women under Western influence.

To identify religion with the status quo and to condemn change as irreligious is hardly peculiar to Muslims. It can be argued, indeed, that Islam is more adaptable than other religions to many kinds of change. The Koran appeals constantly to man's rational faculties. It urges him to seek knowledge. It contains no dogmatic account of the creation of the world or the nature of the universe which later scientific discoveries would have to challenge. Even in the political sphere, its insistence on righteous government and social justice and its sanctification of activism generally give more comfort to the revolutionary than to the conservative.

What distinguishes Islam, politically, from Christianity, is not that one is more progressive or more reactionary than the other, but that Islam makes larger claims. As we saw in Chapter 1, Christianity can accommodate the separation of church and state within its doctrine very easily, since Christians have never completely lost the sense that their true vocation in this world is to be a non-political, or even anti-political minority, preparing only for salvation in the next. In practice things are not so simple, since Christianity also teaches the individual to feel responsible for the earthly welfare of his fellow-men — a concern that can hardly be kept separate from politics. But Islam's involvement with politics is much more fundamental and all-encompassing. The Muslim's duty is not merely to help the needy, but to build a good society in which God's law will prevail. The Koran tells the Muslims: 'You are the best community ever brought forth to men, bidding to good and forbidding evil*, and believing in God.' With such a divine mandate, political responsibility is difficult to shun.

* The words for 'good' and 'evil' can also be translated as 'honour' and 'dishonour'.

Once again, that does not predetermine the content of political action or the direction it will take. Islam can be, and has frequently been, identified with revolution, with progress, with tolerance and freedom, and Muslims will fight for those causes with much stronger conviction when they identify them with Islam. But where Islam is identified with tradition — and in societies which have been Muslim for a long time it is only natural that that should happen — it will also give extra intensity and conviction to the struggle to defend tradition. And the identification of Islam with tradition has been strengthened in the last century and a half by the fact that the threats to tradition have been perceived as coming not from within Muslim societies but from the outside, from the non-Muslim 'West'. The Muslims who have advocated change, even when they have done so as Muslims using a purely Islamic vocabulary, have been perceived — usually with some degree of justice — as advocates of Westernization.

Perhaps this is the moment, since I have all along been comparing Islam to Christianity, to point out the much greater similarities there are between Islam and Judaism.[3] Both are uncompromisingly monotheist, eschewing the Christian doctrine of the Trinity as a form of disguised polytheism. Both derive historically from a community that was political as well as religious. Both set great store by the observance of divine law, and consequently both, while rejecting the notion of a priestly caste intervening between man and God, accord great authority to a class of scholars specialized in the study of law. Both are faced, in the present day, with the problem of maintaining or rebuilding a society based on their authentic tradition while absorbing what is valuable in the post-enlightenment culture that has developed out of Western Christianity. The modern Jewish state, like most of the modern Muslim states, was founded by people of secular Western culture, motivated by nationalism rather than by religious feeling. But like their Muslim counterparts, these people have found themselves ideologically on the defensive against the argument that in the last resort a Jewish state is meaningless unless defined in religious terms; and in Jewish politics too — although many individual Jews derive liberal and progressive values from their religion — collective religious activism has been mainly associated with the defence of tradition. 'Orthodox' Judaism prevails, just as traditionalist Islam prevails, because in both cases the peoples sense that only the stubborn identification of religion with tradition through the centuries has preserved their identity and culture. The Jews resisted assimilation into the societies where they were dispersed, and the Muslims resisted assimilation into the culture of the colonizing powers, by clinging firmly and instinctively to their religious traditions. (The same, incidentally, goes for Christian groups under Muslim rule, such as Greeks and Armenians.)

Religious traditionalism, then, is not something peculiar to the Muslim world. It is, so to speak, a 'natural' defence mechanism, triggered by cultural insecurity. In the Jewish case, the phenomenon of insecurity and its causes are well understood in the West. But the Muslim world, with its population variously estimated at six to eight hundred million people and its billions of petrodollars, feels no less insecure. It is aware of its potential strength, but that only makes more frustrating the knowledge of its actual weakness and vulnerability. To the great majority of Muslims the petrodollars might as well be token paper money in a giant game of monopoly devised by Western powers for their own amusement, so little effect do they seem to have on the standard of living and of education of ordinary Muslim people.

In all the Muslim societies studied in this book we have glimpsed an upsurge of Islamic traditionalism in the last ten years or so, although its origins can always be traced much further back. It encompasses quite a wide variety of social groups, but in general they are groups whose lives are in one way or other disorientated by rapid change: merchants and manufacturers being edged out by foreign competition or by the growth of a new capitalist class; students and graduates in technical professions who have come from a traditional, religious home background to a formal education derived largely from the West; former peasants or their children trying to make sense of life in a new urban environment, which

403

may or may not provide them with employment, seldom provides them with adequate housing, and almost never with a set of effective social and cultural institutions to give a framework to their lives.

Whether the result is a revival of Islam as such can be debated. But what has been observed and reported from almost every Muslim country — not only those covered in this book — is a visible clutching at the traditional *forms* of Islam, or what are taken to be such. Thousands of new mosques are built every year. Women students in universities from Dakar to Dacca adopt veils more all-enveloping than their grandmothers ever wore. Young men grow beards and refuse to attend mixed parties. Some of them go further, banding together to break up mixed parties or to attack nightclubs. At that point they cross the frontier into politics. Consciously or unconsciously they adopt a model of what they consider Islamic society, and set themselves the task of imposing it on their fellow citizens.

In this book I have examined some of the theoretical models available, and have described some of the problems which those who sought to impose them have encountered. I have drawn attention, from time to time, to similarities between the problems encountered in different countries, and between the ideas put forward by different Muslim thinkers, as well as the influence that thinkers in one country can have on movements in another. (Rida, for instance, was read all over the Muslim world, while some of the student activists in Egypt today acknowledge Maududi as a principal source of their ideas.) But I have given more emphasis to the national and regional contexts in which the various movements operate, and that is quite deliberate. I have tried to show that the differences in history, geography, social and economic structure and so on between different Muslim countries have the effect of giving Islam a different colouring, a different resonance in each of them; so that even groups with ostensibly similar programmes find themselves playing a different political role. An Islamic state in Pakistan will never mean precisely the same thing as it does in Iran, and neither could reproduce the kind of Islamic society there is in Saudi Arabia. The Iranian revolution may perhaps succeed in exporting itself, in the sense that it could help to inspire revolutionary change in some other Muslim countries. But it is impossible to imagine other Muslim countries adopting precisely the same laws and institutions as revolutionary Iran, for these reflect a specifically Iranian Islam, which is a product of Iranian history. Shi'ism of course plays a part in this, but it is not a simple matter of sectarian differences. Shi'ism exists outside Iran, after all, but its role in Iranian history and society is unique.

Secondly, I have tried to show that in any given Muslim society at any given time there is always more than one political interpretation of Islam being put forward. Even if, in many places, traditionalist interpretations are now dominant, they are certainly not unchallenged. Nor is there in any country an effective consensus on what the authentic Islamic tradition consists of, or how much of it can be restored in practice, or how fast, or in what order. (For instance, are the traditional Islamic punishments a means of recreating a genuine Islamic society, or are they only applicable once it has been recreated?)

Although many Muslims assert that Islam is a complete system, not only ethical and religious but political, social and economic, clearly distinct from both socialism and capitalism, they are by no means in agreement on its political, social and economic content. Some see it as essentially democratic, while others argue that democracy is a Western notion that has nothing to do with Islam. Some emphasize the sanctity of private property and condemn nationalization, while others emphasize social justice and the need for state intervention to curb the excesses of the rich, protect the needy and ensure responsible stewardship of communal resources. Some say that all forms of interest should be banned immediately, others that this is an ideal which presupposes many prior reforms, including the abolition of inflation! Some present Islam as a kind of economic *via media* which sounds remarkably like Keynesian social democracy: free enterprise would be encouraged but hoarding and exploitation forbidden; social security would be guaranteed for all through a wealth tax (*zakat*), which would also encourage spending rather than saving, and thereby stimulate production.*

In practice it is not too difficult to adopt whatever social, political or economic system one fancies and label it 'Islamic'. Appropriate quotations from the Koran and the *hadith* (albeit usually of a very general nature, since words like 'capitalism' and 'socialism' were not part of the seventh-century Arabic vocabulary) can always be found. But, as the great French Marxist orientalist, Maxime Rodinson, has put it, 'One should always look behind the words and ask the real questions: how is the social product redistributed? Who takes the investment decisions?'[4] Any serious inquiry would find different answers to such questions in different Muslim societies, or in the same society at different periods. It is hard to say with confidence that any one set of answers represents 'Islam'.

My conclusion, therefore, is sceptical — not about the validity of Islam as a system of belief, nor about the sincerity with which many Muslims devote themselves to organizing society in accordance with their belief, but about the possibility of definitively identifying Islam with any social blueprint more specific than motherhood and apple pie. Consequently I think that Western notions about 'Islam' as a geopolitical force — whether a menace to the 'free world' or a potential ally against Soviet communism — are fundamentally misplaced. I believe it is more useful, in politics at any rate, to think about Muslims than to think about Islam. It is true that most Muslim scholars (though not all) believe that Islam is radically incompatible with communism. It is also true

---

* The most original feature of such proposals is the abolition of interest in favour of a banking system where all lenders share both the risks and the profits of the venture which their capital is used to finance. This can work quite well as an option alongside the conventional banking system — but then capitalist countries do usually have stock exchanges and unit trusts as well as banks. It has yet to be tried as the sole system of raising capital in any country, and most economists (perhaps because they are Western-trained) are highly sceptical about that possibility. Certainly the need for interest has been felt in Muslim societies since the Middle Ages, when Muslim merchants devised many ingenious ways of evading its prohibition by the Shari'a. (See Maxime Rodinson, *Islam and Capitalism*, London, 1977.)

that many Muslims — but again, not all — believe that 'the West', whatever its professed doctrines, has been and continues to be guided in its dealings with the Muslim world entirely by self-interest and greed. In practice, Muslim attitudes towards non-Muslim powers are guided by experience — personal and collective, immediate and historical. Most Afghans at the moment are anti-Soviet. Most Palestinians are in some degree anti-American. Resentment against the West is probably more widespread in the Muslim world as a whole than anti-Sovietism, because up to now more Muslim countries have had direct experience of Western imperialism than of the Soviet variety — and Russia has done a more thorough job in her Muslim colonies than any of the Western powers in theirs (see Chapter 10). But that has little to do with Islam as such. Islam is a political culture: it often provides the form and the vocabulary of political action. It can greatly strengthen personal commitment to a cause. But it is not in itself a sufficient explanation for the commitment, or a sufficient content for the cause.

References

Preface: Western Approaches

1 Edward W. Said, *Orientalism* (New York and London, 1978); *Covering Islam* (New York, 1981).

PART ONE

Chapter 1: Traditional Muslim Attitudes to Political Power

1 In this, as for all other quotations from the Koran, I have used Arthur J. Arberry (trans.), *The Koran Interpreted* (Oxford University Press, 1964).
2 Albert Hourani, *Arabic Thought in the Liberal Age, 1798–1939* (London, New York and Toronto, 1963), p. 6, quoting al-Ghazali, *Ihya' 'ulum al-din*, ii/4, chapters 5–6, pp. 124ff.
3 Maxime Rodinson, *Marxism and the Muslim World* (London, 1980), p. 147.

Chapter 2: The Historic Divisions of Islam

1 Fazlur Rahman, *Islam*, 2nd edn. (Chicago and London, 1979), pp. 87–93.
2 ibid., pp. 117–27.
3 J. Spencer Trimingham, *The Sufi Orders in Islam* (Oxford, 1971), *passim*; Rahman, *Islam*, pp. 128–66.

Chapter 3: Decline and Revival

1 Quoted in Peter Gran, *Islamic Roots of Capitalism* (University of Texas at Austin, 1979), p. 161.
2 Aziz Ahmad, *Studies in Islamic Culture in the Indian Environment* (Oxford University Press, 1964), p. 189.
3 ibid., p. 198.
4 H. St John Philby, *Sa'udi Arabia* (New York, 1955), pp. 39–40.

408

REFERENCES

5 Muhammad Iqbāl, *Reconstruction of Religious Thought in Islam* (London, 1934), p. 162.
6 For this summary of Shah Waliullah's economic and political ideas I am indebted to Professor Ahmad Ali of Karachi.
7 Fazlur Rahman, *Islam*, 2nd edn. (Chicago and London, 1979), p. 204.
8 Jamil M. Abun-Nasr, *The Tijaniyya* (Oxford University Press, 1965), p. 20.
9 Quoted in J. Spencer Trimingham, *The Sufi Orders in Islam* (Oxford, 1971), p. 115.
10 Quoted in N. A. Ziadeh, *Sanūsīyah* (Leiden, 1958), p. 38fn.
11 ibid., pp. 41–4.
12 Quoted in P. M. Holt, *The Mahdist State in the Sudan* (Oxford, 1958), p. 51.
13 ibid., p. 112.
14 ibid., p. 115.

Chapter 4: Western Impact and Muslim Responses

1 Quoted in Hafeez Malik, *Sir Sayyid Ahmad Khan and Muslim Modernisation in India and Pakistan* (New York, 1980), p. 99.
2 I. H. Qureshi, 'Islam and the West: Past, Present and Future' in Altaf Gauhar (ed.), *The Challenge of Islam* (London, 1978), p. 241.
3 ibid., p. 242.
4 Albert Hourani, *Arabic Thought in the Liberal Age, 1798–1939* (London, New York and Toronto, 1962), pp. 41–2.
5 ibid., pp. 51–2.
6 Quoted ibid., p. 52.
7 Niyazi Berkes, *The Development of Secularism in Turkey* (Montreal, 1964), p. 92.
8 Quoted ibid., p. 113.
9 ibid., pp. 115–16.
10 ibid., pp. 98–9.
11 Hourani, *Arabic Thought in the Liberal Age*, p. 46.
12 ibid., pp. 203–4.
13 H. A. R. Gibb, *Modern Trends in Islam* (Chicago, 1947), p. 11.
14 Malik, *Sir Sayyid Ahmad Khan and Muslim Modernisation in India and Pakistan*, p. 245.
15 This section is based on 'Le Mouvement réformiste', in A. Bennigsen and C. Lemercier-Quelquejay, *L'Islam en Union Soviétique* (Paris, 1968), pp. 38–57.
16 R. R. Palmer and Joel Colton, *A History of the Modern World*, 3rd edn. (New York, 1965), p. 630.
17 ibid., p. 630.
18 Berkes, *The Development of Secularism in Turkey*, p. 257.
19 ibid., p. 268.
20 ibid., pp. 287, 290.
21 ibid., p. 271.

REFERENCES

22 Wilfred Cantwell Smith, *Islam in Modern History* (Princeton, 1957), p. 49.
23 Nikki R. Keddie, *Sayyid Jamāl ad-Dīn 'al-Afghānī'* (Berkeley, Los Angeles and London, 1972), p. 21.
24 Malik, *Sir Sayyid Ahmad Khan*, p. 6.
25 Keddie, *Sayyid Jamāl ad-Dīn 'al-Afghānī'*, pp. 353–4.

PART TWO

Chapter 5: Turkey – Muslim Nation, 'Secular' State

1 As reported by the British acting Consul in Monastir, and quoted in Bernard Lewis, *The Emergence of Modern Turkey* (Oxford University Press, 1961), p. 214.
2 Christopher J. Walker, *Armenia: The Survival of a Nation* (London, 1980), p. 230.
3 Niyazi Berkes, *The Development of Secularism in Turkey* (Montreal, 1964), p. 483.
4 Quoted in Lewis, *The Emergence of Modern Turkey*, pp. 253–4.
5 M. M. van Bruinessen, *Agha, Shaikh and State* (Utrecht, 1978), pp. 367–8.
6 Quoted in Lewis, *The Emergence of Modern Turkey*, p. 263.
7 ibid., pp. 404–5.
8 Quoted in Wilfred Cantwell Smith, *Islam in Modern History* (Princeton, 1957), p. 193.
9 Dankwart A. Rustow, 'Politics and Islam in Turkey 1920–1955' in R. N. Frye (ed.), *Islam and the West* (Cambridge, Mass., 1957), p. 84.
10 Quoted in Berkes, *The Development of Secularism in Turkey*, p. 502.
11 Şerif Mardin, 'Religion in modern Turkey', in *International Social Science Journal*, XXIX, no. 2 (1977), p. 279.
12 Lewis, *The Emergence of Modern Turkey*, p. 413.
13 Rustow, 'Politics and Islam in Turkey 1920–1955', p. 95.
14 Quoted by Feroz Ahmad in *The Islamic Assertion in Turkey: Pressures and State Response* (paper prepared for the First International Seminar, Institute of Arab Studies Inc., 5–6 June 1981).
15 van Bruinessen, *Agha, Shaikh and State*, pp. 338–9.
16 Uriel Heyd, *Revival of Islam in Modern Turkey* (Jerusalem, 1968), p. 19.
17 Şerif Mardin, 'Religion and Politics in Modern Turkey' in James P. Piscatori (ed.), *'Islam in the Political Process'* (London, 1982).
18 Mardin, 'Religion in modern Turkey', p. 290.
19 *Le Monde*, 5–6 October 1980.
20 *New York Times*, 16 October and 14 November 1980.

Chapter 6: Saudi Arabia – the Koran as Constitution

1 David Howarth, *The Desert King* (London, 1964), p. 142.
2 Christine Moss Helms, *The Cohesion of Saudi Arabia* (Johns Hopkins Univer-

REFERENCES

sity Press, 1980), pp. 120–1, quoting Ameen Rihani, *Ibn Sa'oud of Arabia: His People and His Land* (London, 1928), pp. 39–40.

3 James P. Piscatori, *Islamic Law in a Changing World: The Sa'ūdī Experience* (paper presented at the International Conference on Saudi Arabian Development at Duke University, 27 September–1 October 1979), p. 20.

4 Moss Helms quoting Rihani, *The Cohesion of Saudi Arabia*, p. 212.

5 H. St John Philby, *Sa'ūdī Arabia* (New York, 1955), p. 3.

6 ibid., p. xiii.

7 Ministry of Justice of the Kingdom of Sa'ūdī Arabia, *The Saudi Report on the Legal System in the Kingdom of Saudi Arabia* (mimeo, n.d.), p. 2.

8 Piscatori, *Islamic Law in a Changing World*, p. 18. I am very grateful to Dr Piscatori for letting me see this paper, on which I have drawn heavily for this section.

9 Helen Lackner, *A House Built on Sand* (London, 1978), p. 64, quoting *The Times*, 19 October 1962.

10 Speech in Riyadh, 21 January 1963. Quoted by David E. Long, 'King Faisal's World View' in Willard Beling (ed.), *King Faisal and the Modernisation of Saudi Arabia* (Boulder, Colorado, 1980), pp. 177–8.

11 Adeed I. Dawisha, *Saudi Arabia in the Eighties: The Mecca Siege and After* (paper presented to the International Security Studies Program Core Seminar on 'The Security of the Middle East and Persian Gulf Region in the 1980s' at the Wilson Center, Smithsonian Institution, Washington DC, 6 November 1980), p. 9.

12 James Buchan in the *Financial Times*, 28 April 1980.

13 Quoted by Eric Rouleau in *Le Monde*, 4 May 1981.

14 ibid., 29 April 1981.

15 See *The Nation*, 4 April 1981, p. 403.

16 *Financial Times*, 28 April 1980.

Chapter 7: Pakistan — Islam as Nationality

1 Objectives Resolution adopted by the Constituent Assembly of Pakistan, Karachi, 12 March 1949.

2 *Pakistan: An Ideological State* (pamphlet published by Pakistan Publications, Islamabad; undated, but distributed at the time of President Zia ul-Haq's visit to the United Nations in October 1980).

3 Aziz Ahmad, *Studies in Islamic Culture in the Indian Environment* (Oxford University Press, 1964), p. 64.

4 Quoted in Khalid bin Sayeed, *Pakistan: The Formative Phase 1857–1948*, 2nd edn. (Oxford University Press, 1968), p. 43.

5 Maulana Hasrat Mohani, quoted in Sayeed, *Pakistan: The Formative Phase*, pp. 55–6.

6 ibid., p. 59.

7 Aziz Ahmad and G. E. Grunebaum (eds.), *Muslim Self-Statement in India and Pakistan 1857–1968* (Wiesbaden, 1970), p. 13.

8 Sayeed, *Pakistan: The Formative Phase*, p. 179.
9 Quoted ibid., p. 105.
10 Both quotations from Hamid S. Rajput, Jinnah and the Ideology of Pakistan (typescript in my possession).
11 Wilfred Cantwell Smith, *Islam in Modern History* (Princeton, 1957), p. 234.
12 *Pakistan Times*, 20 September 1977.
13 Charles J. Adams, 'The Ideology of Mawlana Maududi', in D. E. Smith (ed.), *South Asian Politics and Religion* (Princeton, 1966), pp. 375, 381–90.
14 S. Abul A'la Maududi, *The Islamic Law and Constitution*, 6th edn. (Lahore, 1977), pp. 211–32.
15 ibid., p. 308.
16 ibid., p. 237.
17 ibid., pp. 236, 282, 288–97.
18 ibid., p. 308.
19 *Pakistan Times*, 20 September 1977.
20 Quoted in Muhammad Munir, *From Jinnah to Zia* (Lahore, n.d.), p. 30.
21 Maulana Shabbir Ahmad Usmani, quoted by Khalid bin Sayeed, 'Islam and National Integration in Pakistan', in D. E. Smith (ed.), *South Asian Politics and Religion*, pp. 402–3.
22 Maududi in *Pakistan Times*, 20 September 1977.
23 See 'Selections from the Munir Report' in Ahmad and von Grunebaum (eds.), *Muslim Self-Statement in India and Pakistan*, pp. 190–4.
24 Quoted by John L. Esposito. 'Pakistan: Quest for Islamic Identity' in *Islam and Development* (Syracuse, 1980), p. 145.
25 Quoted in Munir, *From Jinnah to Zia*, p. 82.
26 Quoted in Esposito, 'Pakistan: Quest for Islamic Identity', p. 150.
27 Waheed-uz-Zaman, 'Editor's Note', in *The Quest for Identity* (proceedings of the First Congress on the History and Culture of Pakistan, held at the University of Islamabad, April 1973), p. i.
28 Munir, *From Jinnah to Zia*, p. 96.
29 William L. Richter, 'The Political Dynamics of Islamic Resurgence in Pakistan', *Asian Survey*, June 1979, p. 549.
30 See Selig S. Harrison, *In Afghanistan's Shadow: Baluch Nationalism and Soviet Temptations* (New York and Washington, 1981), pp. 34–6.
31 Abdul Wali Khan, Affidavit to the Supreme Court of Pakistan, 1975 (typescript kindly lent by Selig Harrison), p. 133.
32 Waheed-uz-Zaman, 'Editor's Note' in *The Quest for Identity*, p. 4.
33 *Dawn*, 16 April 1972, quoted in Richter, *The Political Dynamics of Islamic Resurgence in Pakistan*, p. 550.
34 Local political leader interviewed by William Richter in Bahawalpur, 1 August 1977, *The Political Dynamics of Islamic Resurgence in Pakistan*, p. 553.
35 Quoted by Richter, ibid., p. 552.
36 *Pakistan: An Ideological State*, p. 11.
37 *New York Times*, 6 February 1981.
38 *Le Monde Diplomatique*, March 1981.
39 Munir, *From Jinnah to Zia*, pp. 26–7.

Chapter 8: Arab Nationalism and Muslim Brotherhood

1 Hasan al-Banna, 'To What Do We Summon Mankind?' in Charles Wendell (ed.), *Five Tracts of Hasan Al-Bannā* (*1906–1949*) (University of California Press, 1978), p. 97.

2 Albert Hourani, *Arabic Thought in the Liberal Age 1798–1939* (Oxford University Press, 1964), p. 144. The remainder of this section is based almost entirely on Chapters 6, 7, 8 and 9 of Hourani's admirable book.

3 Sylvia G. Haim (ed.), *Arab Nationalism: An Anthology* (University of California Press, 1962), pp. 22–3.

4 ibid., p. 23.

5 Hourani, *Arabic Thought in the Liberal Age*, p. 306.

6 Richard P. Mitchell, *The Society of the Muslim Brothers* (London, 1969), p. 8.

7 ibid., p. 30.

8 ibid., p. 97.

9 *Le Monde*, 21–22 June 1981.

10 *Sudanow*, November 1979.

11 Mitchell, *The Society of the Muslim Brothers*, pp. 241, 247.

12 B. Lewis, 'The Return of Islam', *Commentary*, January 1976, p. 48.

13 Stanley Reed III, 'Dateline Syria: Fin de Régime?' in *Foreign Policy*, Summer 1980, pp. 176–7.

14 Memorandum prepared by the Higher Command of the Islamic Revolution in Syria, 20 December 1979 (typescript in my possession), p. 7.

15 *Le Monde*, 12–13 April and 13 May 1981.

16 Reed, 'Dateline Syria: Fin de Régime?' p. 177.

17 *Le Monde*, 11 April 1981.

18 Stanley Reed III, 'Little Brother and the Brotherhood', *The Nation*, 16 May 1981, p. 592.

19 ibid., pp. 592–3.

20 Reported by Jean Gueyras in *Le Monde*, 11 April 1981.

21 Nazih N. M. Ayubi, 'The Political Revival of Islam' in *International Journal of Middle East Studies*, December 1980, p. 489.

22 Quoted by Fouad Ajami, 'In the Pharaoh's Shadow: Religion and Authority in Egypt' in James P. Piscatori (ed.), *Islam in the Political Process* (London, 1982).

23 *The Middle East*, May 1981.

24 Gamal Abdul Nasser, 'The Philosophy of the Revolution', in Haim (ed.), *Arab Nationalism*, pp. 231–2.

25 For quotations on pp. 274–7, see P. J. Vatikiotis, 'Islam and the Foreign Policy of Egypt', in J. Harris Proctor (ed.), *Islam and International Relations* (New York, 1965), pp. 120–57.

26 Flory and Mantran, *Les Régimes politiques dans le monde arabe*, quoted by Hervé Bleuchot and Taoufik Monastiri in *Pouvoirs*, December 1979, p. 131.

27 Lisa S. Anderson, Religion and Politics in Libya (typescript kindly lent by the author), pp. 15–21.

28 Bleuchot and Monastiri, *Pouvoirs*, pp. 133–4.

29 Anderson, Religion and Politics in Libya, pp. 21–3.

413

30 Bleuchot and Monastiri, *Pouvoirs*, p. 134.
31 *Le Monde*, 27 December 1980.
32 ibid., 28–29 December 1980.
33 *The Times*, 24 October 1980.
34 *The Middle East*, May 1981.
35 Fouad Ajami, 'The Revolution That Failed', in *The Nation*, 9 May 1981, p. 569.
36 ibid., p. 570.
37 Ayubi, 'The Political Revival of Islam', p. 489.
38 Jevdet Pasha, quoted in Bernard Lewis, *The Emergence of Modern Turkey* (Oxford University Press), p. 332.
39 Saad Eddin Ibrahim, 'Anatomy of Egypt's Militant Islamic Groups', *International Journal of Middle East Studies*, December 1980, p. 435.
40 ibid., pp. 423–53.
41 *The Times*, 1 December 1981.
42 *Middle East International*, 9 April 1982.

Chapter 9: Iran – Shi'ism and Revolution

1 See especially Said Amir Arjomand, 'Religion, Political Action and Legitimate Domination in Shi'ite Iran: Fourteenth to Eighteenth Centuries AD' in *European Journal of Sociology*, XX, 1979, pp. 59–109.
2 Quoted in Yann Richard, *Le Shi'isme en Iran* (Paris, 1980), pp. 54–5.
3 Quoted in Shahrough Akhavi, *Religion and Politics in Contemporary Iran* (Albany, 1980), p. 30. In the whole of this section I have inevitably relied on Professor Akhavi's book, supplemented by Richard, *Le Shi'isme en Iran*; Michael Fischer, *Iran From Religious Dispute to Revolution* (Harvard University Press, 1980); Nikki R. Keddie, *Roots of Revolution* (Yale University Press, 1981); and a paper entitled 'Traditionalism in Twentieth Century Iran', kindly lent by its author, Dr Said Amir Arjomand.
4 See Akhavi, *Religion and Politics in Contemporary Iran*, p. 42, and Fischer, *Iran From Religious Dispute to Revolution*, p. 129, for three different accounts of this incident, with different dates.
5 Arjomand, 'Traditionalism in Twentieth Century Iran'.
6 Akhavi, *Religion and Politics in Contemporary Iran*, p. 73.
7 Arjomand, 'Traditionalism in Twentieth Century Iran'.
8 ibid., p. 44.
9 Quoted by Ervand Abrahamian in *MERIP Reports*, March/April 1980, 'The Guerrilla Movement in Iran 1963–77', pp. 9–10.
10 Quoted in Keddie, *Roots of Revolution*, p. 224.
11 See Fischer, *Iran From Religious Dispute to Revolution*, p. 167, for several examples.
12 Keddie, *Roots of Revolution*, pp. 221–2.
13 Abrahamian, *MERIP Reports*, pp. 10–11.
14 Interviewed by Fred Halliday in *MERIP Reports*, March/April 1980.
15 Akhavi, *Religion and Politics in Contemporary Iran*, pp. 144, 177–8.

16 From 'The Fundamental Principles of Islamic Government', quoted in Keddie, *Roots of Revolution*, p. 228.

17 Gilles Anquetil, *La Terre a Bougé en Iran* (Paris 1979), p. 134.

18 Yann Richard in Keddie, *Roots of Revolution*, p. 228.

19 *New York Times*, 15 June 1981.

20 *Time*, 6 July 1981.

21 Arjomand, 'Traditionalism in Twentieth Century Iran', pp. 32–3.

22 See Richard, *Le Shi'isme en Iran*, pp. 112–13.

23 *Le Monde*, 29 October 1980.

24 Hanna Batatu, 'Iraq's Underground Shi'a Movements: Characteristics, Causes and Prospects', *Middle East Journal*, autumn 1981, p. 594.

25 *Le Monde*, 22 October 1980.

Chapter 10: Russia's Colonial Reckoning — Islam and Nationality in the Soviet Union

1 N. Ashirov, 'Muslim Preaching Today', in *Nauka i Religiya*, no. 12, 1978, (JPRS: 073279.), pp. 30–3.

2 See Rasma Karklins, 'Islam: How Strong is it in the Soviet Union? Inquiry Based on Oral Interviews With Soviet Germans Repatriated from Central Asia in 1979', *Cahiers du monde russe et soviétique*, XXI (1), January–March 1980, pp. 65–81.

3 See Tom Ricks, 'The Afghan Resistance' in *New Republic*, 20 June 1981.

Conclusion: What is Islam?

1 Fazlur Rahman, *Islam*, 2nd edn. (Chicago and London, 1979), p. 43.

2 The Koran, Sura XLIII, verse 2, Arthur J. Arberry (trans.), *The Koran Interpreted* (Oxford University Press, 1964).

3 See Uriel Heyd, *Revival of Islam in Modern Turkey* (Jerusalem, 1968), pp. 7 et seq.

4 Maxime Rodinson, *Marxism and the Muslim World* (London, 1980, p. 213.

Index

Abbās, 44

Abbāsid caliphs, 36–7, 42, 56, 355; adopt Mu'tazilite view of the Koran, 51; Kemal Atatürk and, 134, 136; opposition to, 47–48; and Shi'ism, 44; Western influences, 89

Abbud, General Ibrahim, 261

Abduh, Muhammad, 247, 250; and al-Afghani, 116, 237; influence of, 249, 251, 337; and reform of Muslim law, 237–40, 242, 244–5

Abdul-Aziz, Shah, 69n., 101

Abdul-Aziz, Sultan, 106

Abdul-Aziz ibn Abdul-Rahman Al Sa'ud (Ibn Sa'ud), King of Saudi Arabia, 162–171, 173, 184n., 234, 244, 262, 273

Abdul-Hamid II, Sultan, 106, 107–9, 113, 125, 126–8, 152, 193, 248

Abdul-Majid, Sultan, 93, 95–6

Abdul-Raziq, Ali, 240–1, 242–3, 245

Abdullah, King of Jordan, 162, 258

Abidin, Abdul-Hakim, 258

Abu Bakr, 34–5, 241, 298, 355

Achaemenid Empire, 321

Aden, British in, 84

Administration of the Ottoman Public Debt, 108

Advisory Council on Islamic Ideology (Pakistan), 211, 212

al-Afghānī, Sayyid Jamāl al-Dīn (Sage of the East), 109–17, 160, 240, 250, 297; background, 110–14; importance of, 109, 114–117, 121; influence, 194, 237, 243, 244, 251, 273, 337

Afghanistan, 303, 381; Britain and, 69, 84, 86, 110–11, 394; defeats Marathas, 68;

Indian Muslims migrate to, 195; 1978 revolution, 296–7, 374–5; resistance movement, 375; Saudi foreign aid to the *mujahidin*, 180; Soviet invasion, 17, 227, 297, 332, 344, 374–5, 388, 392–5

Aflaq, Michel, 264, 277, 362n.

Africa: European colonialism, 84–5; Ibadiya, 42; Libyan activities in, 282; and the Ottoman Empire, 93; reform movements, 70–1, 72; Sanusiya, 75–6; Saudi foreign aid, 180; Sufism in, 56, 71–2; Wahhabism, 64; *see also* North Africa

Aga Khan, 48, 137

ahl al-Qur'an, 397

Ahmad, Shah of Iran, 307

Ahmadis, 209–11, 218n.

Al-Ahrām, 287

Ahrar, 209

Ahsa'i, Shaikh Ahmad, 110

Akbar, Emperor, 58

Akhbāris, 302

Âkif, Mehmet, 134, 144–5

Āl Shaikh, 63, 172

Al-e Ahmad, Jalal, 321

Alam, Asadollāh, 316

Alamut, 48

Alawis (Nusairis), 48–9, 264, 266–7, 269, 373

Albania, 85, 128–9

Aleppo, 264, 266–9

Alevis, 156

Algeria, 130, 284; and Arab nationalism, 235; French occupation, 84, 85; and the Muslim Brotherhood, 263; Tijaniya, 72

Algerian war, 126–7, 336, 347

417

INDEX